THE LOST WORLD OF CHAM

THE TRANSPACIFIC VOYAGES OF THE CHAMPA

David Hatcher Childress

Adventures Unlimited Press

Other Books by David Hatcher Childress:

VIMANA
ARK OF GOD
ANCIENT TECHNOLOGY IN PERU & BOLIVIA
THE MYSTERY OF THE OLMECS
PIRATES AND THE LOST TEMPLAR FLEET
TECHNOLOGY OF THE GODS
A HITCHHIKER'S GUIDE TO ARMAGEDDON
LOST CONTINENTS & THE HOLLOW EARTH
ATLANTIS & THE POWER SYSTEM OF THE GODS
THE FANTASTIC INVENTIONS OF NIKOLA TESLA
LOST CITIES OF NORTH & CENTRAL AMERICA
LOST CITIES OF CHINA, CENTRAL ASIA & INDIA
LOST CITIES & ANCIENT MYSTERIES OF AFRICA & ARABIA
LOST CITIES & ANCIENT MYSTERIES OF SOUTH AMERICA
LOST CITIES OF ANCIENT LEMURIA & THE PACIFIC
LOST CITIES OF ATLANTIS, ANCIENT EUROPE & THE MEDITERRANEAN
LOST CITIES & ANCIENT MYSTERIES OF THE SOUTHWEST
YETIS, SASQUATCH AND HAIRY GIANTS

With Brien Foerster
THE ENIGMA OF CRANIAL DEFORMATION

With Steven Mehler
THE CRYSTAL SKULLS

THE LOST WORLD OF CHAM

THE TRANSPACIFIC VOYAGES OF THE CHAMPA

Adventures Unlimited Press

The Lost World of Cham

ISBN 13: 978-1-939149-72-5

Published by:
Adventures Unlimited Press
One Adventure Place
Kempton, Illinois 60946 USA
auphq@frontiernet.net

AdventuresUnlimitedPress.com

10 9 8 7 6 5 4 3 2 1

A bust of the Hindu god Shiva from My Son in Vietnam.
Note third eye and top knot of long hair, mustache and long earlobes.

A Champa statue of the consort of Shiva, Parvati.

THE LOST WORLD OF CHAM

David Hatcher Childress

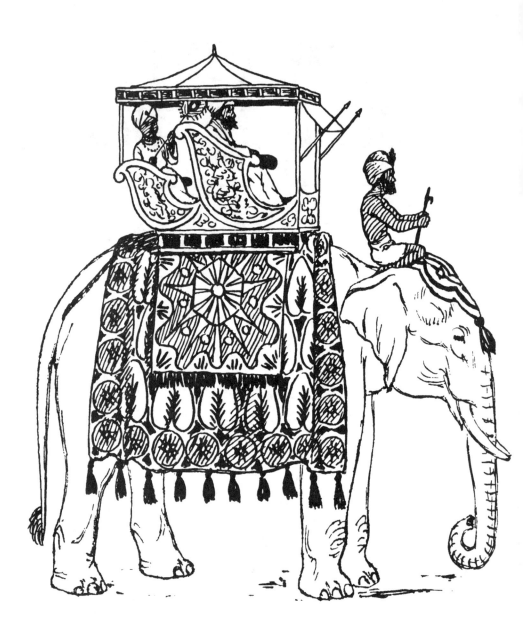

TABLE OF CONTENTS

A ship depicted at Borobudur.

Chapter One

WHO WERE THE CHAMPA AND CHAM?

*By reason of the constant and repeated destructions by water
and fire, the later generations did not receive from the former the
memory of the order and sequence of events.*
—Philo of Alexandria

My journeys in search of lost cities and ancient mysteries have
taken me around the world, from the mountain peaks of the Andes to
beneath the waters of the oceans. My search for the answers to such
enduring mysteries as the building of megalithic walls in prehistory
and evidence for ancient transoceanic contact has taken me from
Mexico and Peru to Easter Island, Tahiti, Tonga, Micronesia,
Indonesia and Vietnam. In fact, it was when I was in Vietnam in
2007 that I took an interest in the Champa civilization.

What I learned while in Vietnam surprised me—historians
were unaware of any civilization in southern Vietnam or Cambodia
prior to circa 192 AD. Not only that, but other areas of Southeast
Asia also do not seem to have any history prior to about 600 AD.
While countries like China, India, Persia and Mesopotamia have
chronicles of history going back to 1000 BC or more, history is silent
on Malaysia, Cambodia, Thailand (before the Thais), Sumatra, Java
and other Indonesian islands.

Surely, the great ships of India and China had been sailing these
waters by 900 BC or earlier. Were there any known port-cities that
were visited? What rulers reigned over these islands and rivers? What
was their religion and what did these seafarers and kings know of
the geography of their area—a vast area of thousands of islands and
jungle rivers. On many of these islands are the remains of baffling
megalithic structures and the evidence of ancient mining operations.
Who were the people sailing these island seas and what did they call
themselves? What my studies have shown me is that these people

were a confederation of seafarers and farmers that were Hindus who called themselves the Cham and the general region Champa.

In central Vietnam, a few miles south of the famous DMZ of the Vietnam War (called in Vietnam the "American War") was the mysterious capital of the Cham civilization, the impressive megalithic city of My Son. The Cham, or Champa, were a Hindu maritime people, apparently related to the Hindus of ancient Indonesia, whose influence can still be seen on the island of Bali, the last bastion of Hinduism in a predominantly Muslim country. They were also in direct contact with the Chinese.

The Cham (pronounced "Kom") peoples inhabited much of central Vietnam and a group of islands off the coast called the Cu Lao Cham, or Cham Islands. I think that this island base, as well as cities up several rivers in the area, were once the center of an accomplished maritime trading empire—an empire that not only traded with China to the north and Indonesia to the south, but also with nations across the vast Pacific!

Eventually the Cham lost their island territories and there were wars with Cambodia and Sumatra. The Chinese also sacked the Champa cities in Vietnam and the Dai Viet tribes centered around Hanoi annexed all the remaining Champa territories by 1832 as they took over all of southern Vietnam. This migration south of the Dai Viet tribes drove the last of the Cham in Vietnam westward into the mountains that separate Laos from Vietnam today. At this time only a small number of Cham villages remain in the mountains of central Vietnam and northern Cambodia. Some of these Cham became Muslims toward the end of the 17th century, while other Cham retained their original Hindu faith.

The Lost World of the Cham

Having apparently arrived from India via Malaysia and Indonesia, the Champa kingdom was a federation of several smaller states called Mandala and comprised several ethnic groups. According to Ivan Van Sertima and Runoko Rashidi in their book *African Presence in Early Asia,*[15] Chinese records from as early as 192 AD reference a kingdom in what is now central Vietnam

12

known as Lin-yi, which meant "land of black men." Its inhabitants possessed "black skin, eyes deep in the orbit, nose turned up, hair frizzy." The kingdom of Lin-yi was known in Sanskrit documents as Champa, a substantially Indianized kingdom (Buddhist and Brahmin) with close contacts with India and China. Other states had names such as Huang-Wang and Chang-Chen.

The Cham territories of Vietnam included the coastal plains, highlands and mountain ranges. This area of Vietnam is very mountainous, with cliffs often coming right up to the coast. Occasional rivers and hidden bays are found along the coast, making it a rugged area best traversed by boat. An army marching through this region would not get very far, so the Cham harbors were something of a naturally protected territory. The Cham Islands off the coast were even more protected, and these islands were probably the central base for what is assumed to be a very large navy of the Cham.

The Cham were seafarers and rivermen, going deep into Cambodia (named after the Cham— Khmer in Sanskrit). In fact the larger area of southern Vietnam and Cambodia, including parts of Laos, was certainly controlled by the Cham from an early time, though many historians only acknowledge the Cham or Champa as being in southern Vietnam. The online encyclopedia Wikipedia says (with minor typos corrected):

> The term Champa refers to a collection of independent Cham polities that extended across the coast of what is today central and southern Vietnam from approximately the 2nd century through 19th century (1832), before being absorbed and annexed by the Vietnamese state. The kingdom was known variously as nagara Campa (Sanskrit; Khmer) in the Chamic and Cambodian inscriptions, Chăm Pa in Vietnamese (Chiêm Thành in Sino-Vietnamese vocabulary) and Zhànchéng in Chinese records.
>
> The Chams of modern Vietnam and Cambodia are the remnants of this former kingdom. They speak Chamic languages, a subfamily of Malayo-Polynesian closely

13

related to the Malayic and Bali–Sasak languages.

Champa was preceded in the region by a kingdom called Linyi or Lam Ap (Vietnamese) that was in existence from 192 AD; the historical relationship between Linyi and Champa is not clear. Champa reached its apogee in the 9th and 10th centuries. Thereafter, it began a gradual decline under pressure from Dai Viet, the Vietnamese polity centered in the region of modern Hanoi. In 1832, the Vietnamese emperor Minh Mạng annexed the remaining Cham territories.

Hinduism, adopted from India since early in its history, has shaped the art and culture of [the] Champa kingdom for centuries, as testified with numbers of exquisite Cham Hindu statues, and red brick temples dotted the landscapes in Cham lands. My Son, a former religious centre, and Hoi An, one of Champa's main port cities, are now World Heritage Sites. Today, some Cham people adhere to Islamic faith, a conversion which was started in [the] 15th century, and they are called Bani Cham. There are however, Balamon Cham (from Sanskrit: Brahman) people that still retain and preserve their Hindu faith, rituals and festivals. Balamon Cham people are one of only two surviving non-Indic indigenous Hindu peoples in the world, with a culture dating back thousands of years. The other one is the Hindu Balinese of Indonesia.

So, Wikipedia is saying the word Champa or Cham is "Khmer" in Sanskrit. It seems that the words "Cham" or "Khem" are interchangeable with the word "Khmer" as we witness in the modern name for Cambodia. It is not spelled Khembodia, but more simply Cambodia, showing that there is really no difference between the terms Cham and Khem (er).

The original Cham-Khmer were an ancient Hindu group, according to Wikipedia, that still survive as an ethnic group in central Vietnam and Cambodia; the dictionary compares them to the Hindus of Bali. I surmise that Bali may have originally been part of Greater Champa, a Hindu kingdom that encompassed much

14

QUẢNG TRỊ

HUẾ

ĐÀ NẴNG
2 1 My Sơn
3 4 Cham
5 Islands
6
QUẢNG NGÃI

7
10 9 8
11
12 13 QUI NHƠN

TUY HOÀ
14

DAK LAK 15 NHA TRANG

16 17
18
19 PHAN RANG

HỒ CHÍ MINH CITY
20 PHAN THIẾT

**Cham Sites
in Vietnam**

of Southeast Asia and Indonesia. Some historians say that another Chinese word, Funan, refers to a different culture than the Cham, this one up the Mekong River in Cambodia. As will be discussed later, Funan and Champa are certainly one and the same. Cambodians, like the Champa, are a dark-skinned race with wide noses and thick lips and distinct from the lighter-skinned Thai, Dai Viet and Chinese peoples. The temples at Angkor Wat and Angkor Thom in central Cambodia depict men with thick lips and wide noses.

In fact, as I will show in this book, the Cham were not just all over the coasts of the Malayan Peninsula and at upriver sites in Cambodia, reached by the Mekong River, but they were present all over the islands of Indonesia. They went beyond the islands of Indonesia to New Guinea and the Philippines out into the Pacific and voyaged to Mexico, Colombia and Peru. Nearly any civilization in Indonesia or elsewhere in Southeast Asia that showed some Hindu influence was probably part of the Cham Empire. Says Wikipedia of the far-flung influence of the Cham that is only now being understood:

> Evidence gathered from linguistic studies around Aceh confirms that a very strong Champan cultural influence existed in Indonesia; this is indicated by the use of the Chamic language Acehnese as the main language in the coastal regions of Pidie, Aceh Besar, Aceh Jaya, North Aceh, East Aceh, West Aceh and Southwest Aceh Regencies and the cities of Lhokseumawe and Bireuën.
>
> While today the Balamon Cham are the only surviving Hindus in Vietnam, the region once hosted some of the most exquisite and vibrant Hindu cultures in the world. The entire region of Southeast Asia, in fact, was home to numerous sophisticated Hindu kingdoms. From Angkor in neighboring Cambodia, to Java and Bali in Indonesia.

So we have linguistic studies showing that northern Sumatra (Aceh) once apparently spoke a dialect of the Cham. If Sumatra and Vietnam were speaking the Champa dialect then it seems likely that other Indonesian islands such as Java and Bali were part of this

Hindu maritime empire that spoke the Cham language. Wikipedia had noted that the Cham languages were closely related to the Bali-Sasak languages. This is further evidence that Champa really extended throughout Southeast Asia and included Sumatra, Java and Bali plus all the islands in their vicinity. Northern Sumatra is important because it is the gateway to Indonesia and the Gulf of Siam from India. As Hindu traders left ports on the east coast of India they would land in northern Sumatra and they were now in the land known as Champa or Suvarnabhumi (Land of Gold). The Chinese called this area Funan, as we will discuss a bit later.

Today the wealthy island-state of Singapore sits in this general area, at the southern tip of the Malay Peninsula opposite Sumatra. Singapore was not a desirable Champa site, however, because it was a huge swampy area in antiquity. The British drained these swamps and built Singapore. Champa ports were typically in sandy bays where a major river met the ocean. The Cham never had any major cities in the Mekong Delta area because of the unpredictable river, with its flooding and changing of course from time to time.

It would seem that the Cham had many cities in Vietnam, Cambodia, Sumatra, Java and elsewhere, but it seems that their

Cham brick and stone towers Po Sa Nu near Phan Thiet.

An old photo of one of the temples at My Son.

most important city was the basalt, granite and brick city called My Son (pronounced Mee Sun).

The Megalithic City of My Son

In December of 2007, my wife Jennifer and I visited the most important of the Cham cities, the site known as My Son. My Son is situated in Quang Nam Province about 60 kilometers from the historic cities of Danang and Hue. It was an all day bus and boat ride, highlighted by a tour of the main group of monumental complexes scattered over an area of about 10 hectares.

My Son is the impressive remains of the holy city built over the centuries around the sanctuary of Bhadresvara (Shiva), which was thought to be founded in the early 4th century AD. Known as Amaravati in ancient times, it is situated in the center of a mountain chain and accessible only through a narrow gorge. Today, there are some seventy brick buildings still visible, constructed by the Cham kings to commemorate the great events of their reigns and to perpetuate the memory of the kings.

One of the temples at My Son has a curious inscription mentioning the Nagas, serpent gods in the *Mahabharata*, and a

18

spear taken from Drona's son, a priest named Asvatthaman. Drona is a king in the Hindu epic the *Mahabharata*, and takes part in the great wars of antiquity. The founder of the Cham civilization is said to be a man named Kaundinya, who has this legendary spear from Drona. This is clearly thousands of years ago, as Drona would have lived circa 700 to 1500 BC. Some historians think that the *Mahabharata* was written as far back as 3000 BC. Says Wikipedia of the inscription about Kaundinya:

> The story of Kaundinya is also set forth briefly in the Sanskrit inscription C. 96 of the Cham king Prakasadharma found at My Son. It is dated Sunday, 18 February 658 AD and states in relevant part (stanzas XVI-XVIII): "It was there [at the city of Bhavapura] that Kauṇḍinya, the foremost among brahmins, planted the spear which he had obtained from Drona's son Asvatthaman, the best of brahmins. There was a daughter of a king of serpents [nagas], called "Soma," who founded a family in this world. Having attained, through love, to a radically different element, she lived in the abode of man. She was taken as wife by the excellent Brahmin Kaundinya for the sake of (accomplishing) a certain task..."

So, according to the My Son inscription, the Champa civilization goes back thousands of years to the wars of the *Mahabharata* and was created by the union of a Hindu priest with a Naga goddess from the river waters—probably the Mekong River. An identical legend involving the daughter of a naga king exists in Cambodia.

According to Wikipedia the name Kaundinya is actually from southern India:

> The name "Kaundinya" is well-known from Tamil inscriptions of the 1st millennium AD, and it seems that Funan was ruled in the 6th century AD by a clan of the same name. According to the Nán Qí shū (Book of Southern Qi) of Xiāo Zīxiǎn (485–537) the Funan king Qiáochénrú Shéyébámó (Kaundinya Jayavarman) "sent in the year 484

19

the Buddhist monk Nàqiéxiān (Nāgasena) to offer presents to the Chinese emperor and to ask the emperor at the same time for help in conquering Línyì (north of Campā)... The emperor of China thanked Shéyébámó for his presents, but sent no troops against Línyì."

So we see from this inscription that the kings of Funan and the founder of Champa bear the same name: Kaundinya. Many historians make the mistake of thinking that Champa and Funan were different places, but since both Funan and Champa are ruled by a clan called Kaundinya, they are likely to be the same place.

My Son was a ritual center and had a nearby port at Hoi An on the Cau Do River. Opposite My Son, Hoi An and modern day Da Nang, off the coast of Vietnam, is the important Cham Islands sanctuary where thousands of Champa ships would converge from time to time. My Son was a religious center by the time of a Hindu king named Bhadravarman, towards the end of the 4th century AD. For centuries My Son was the main intellectual and religious center of Cham civilization and was the place where kings were cremated. Brick towers were built to commemorate each king's great deeds of conquests. Even though the capital was moved to Tra Kieu (Quang Nam) and then to Tra Ban (Binh Ding) in about the year 1000 AD, construction at My Son continued until the 13th century. Scholars say that this gave rise to the longest religious occupation in Southeast Asia.[2]

Scholars at the museum in Da Nang say that the majority of the temples at My Son were dedicated to the Cham kings who, after their death, were associated with divinities of the Hindu pantheon, particularly Shiva. According to them, Shiva, with his third eye, long hair and trident was considered the founder of the Champa Dynasty. This, like the Kaundinya inscription referencing a king from the *Mahabharata*, means that the Cham kings considered their lineage to be very old—much older than the dates that historians right now give to the Cham, like 192 AD or 400 AD. The Champa obviously considered their lineage as going back thousands of years—was the realm of the Champa something going back to 1500 BC or before?

20

A brick and stone tower at My Son. Note the cut basalt door frame.

Monumental Cham architecture is basically identical to that found in Cambodia, and often features high shrine towers, with a door to the inside of the tower facing the east. There are false doors on the other sides. The doorways have elaborate designs carved into sandstone lintels and door jams. The shrine tower, generally referred to by its Cham name 'kalan,' is decorated with double pillars and arches in relief in its lower parts—a very complicated decoration of skillful stonework. The shrine tower is crowned with four stories of stone, each decreasing in size.[1]

Cut and shaped basalt blocks at the ruins of My Son.

The temples and towers themselves are considered to be sculptural artifacts. They are decorated on the exterior of their brick walls with bas-relief columns, flowers, leaves and worshipping figures between brick pillars. The tympana, lintels and the ornamental corner pieces are of sandstone carved with figures of gods, the holy animals of the Hindus and more flowers and leaves. The greatest piece of architecture at My Son was an enormous, 70-foot-high tower that was destroyed by United States Army commandos in August of 1969. Unfortunately, the temple site is just a few miles to the south of the Demilitarized Zone and hence was considered "fair game."

It is said that great treasure in the form of gold statues and jewels were kept in each shrine tower. But starting with the rise of Srivijaya in 645 AD the Champa were fighting wars with breakaway factions of the greater Champa Empire. They fought wars with the Khmer, a sort of civil war among the Cham, and then had Chinese and Dai Viet tribes attacking them. In fact, the Champa port of Qusu, located above the Kien Giang River, was a fortified city with a high wall and a surrounding moat as were other cities in Cambodia and the

Champa parts of Vietnam. When Qusu was sacked by the Chinese in 446 AD, Chinese records says that "all inhabitants over the age of 15 were put to the sword" and as much as 48,000 kg of gold was taken from the city as loot. Indeed, Champa was the Land of Gold in Hindu geography.[4] Where did it all come from?

The treasure kept in the shrine towers at My Son is said to have been entrusted to the Cham hill tribes, known as the Degar or Montagnard peoples.[5] All of this valuable jewelry and precious metal objects became known as the treasure hoard of the Cham kings. These tribes still faithfully guard the treasures today, or so the story goes.

The Keystone Cuts of Cham

We were quite impressed by the stone and brick structures, and the fine decorations. I pointed out to our guide the use of keystone cuts, and metal clamps that were evident on some stone walls that had been partially demolished. He had never seen or heard of keystone cuts and clamps before, and was genuinely amazed at the discovery of these unusual construction techniques at the site. For that moment, I became the guide and he the tourist.

A photo of the T-shaped keystone cuts on granite blocks at My Son.

Who Are the Champa and Cham?

Many parts of My Son are constructed of large slabs of basalt that has been expertly cut and articulated. In some cases hourglass or T-shaped keystone cuts have been made into the basalt blocks. Basalt is a very hard rock and it is difficult to cut. Diamond drills and power tools are needed today to cut and articulate basalt slabs such as those at My Son. Did the Champa use power tools when building My Son? It would seem that they did. Also, the use of keystone cuts is a distinctive building style used almost exclusively on megalithic structures.

A basalt block at My Son with T-shaped keystone cuts on it.

Keystone cuts are an unusual and sophisticated method of fastening two stone blocks together. A cut is made on each block and then a molten metal clamp is poured into the cuts. When the metal (usually an alloy such as bronze) hardens, it then spans both blocks of stone and holds them together. Most megalithic blocks of basalt or granite are so heavy that they hardly seem to need metal clamps holding them together, yet the clamps were used anyway.

That this construction technique is used at certain unusual megalithic sites around the world is very curious, as this is not the

Hourglass-shaped keystone cuts on basalt slabs at My Son.

A photo of the T-shaped keystone cuts on granite blocks at My Son.

sort of thing that would be independently developed on different continents. Keystone cuts identical to those found at My Son can be found in Peru at Ollantaytambo and Cuzco and at Tiwanaku and Puma Punku in Bolivia. These T-shaped and hourglass-shaped cuts are also found at Angkor Wat, Angkor Thom and Preah Vihear in Cambodia and at Borobadur in Java. They are found at the megalithic structures at Axum in Ethiopia and at temples in Egypt. They are also found at megalithic structures in Greece and Turkey as well as in India. In Mexico are found the 20-ton basalt heads of the Olmecs, worked in a similar fashion as the basalt slabs at My Son.

How is it that structures from various continents, and seemingly different time periods, are constructed in this unusual fashion? Many of the structures, such as those at Puma Punku, Tiwanaku and Ollantaytambo, are not easily explained and engineers are unsure how these huge structures, now mostly destroyed, were actually built. In some cases it would seem that the locals lacked the technology to quarry, articulate and lift some of the largest of the stones, often weighing many hundreds of tons. Obelisks, huge as they are, generally weigh around 400 to 500 tons.

If we assume that My Son was built by the Cham, then can we assume that the same engineers and stonecutters also built Angkor Wat, Angkor Thom and Preah Vihear? It would seem so, and it is likely that all of these structures were built around the same time. The structures in Cambodia are probably older than archeologists are now considering. This would be the same for those structures in Peru and Boliva that also contain keystone cuts. They are probably older than archeologists are currently saying. Are the builders of My Son and Tiwanaku, Puma Punku and Ollantaytambo one and the same? Megalith building and the use of keystone cuts in both Vietnam-Cambodia and South America is strong evidence for the transpacific voyages of the Cham.

The Advanced Construction Abilities of the Cham

The Cham built mostly out of stone and kiln-fired brick. Some of their work is in very hard basalt or nearly as hard granite—but high quality bricks were also used—something also seen in Peru and Bolivia.

While many of their early buildings were quasi-megalithic with keystone cuts and clamps used to hold large blocks together, the most important legacy of the Cham are the brick temples and towers that are scattered over the coastal lowlands and highlands. In these coastal lowlands is also found an ancient network of Champa wells that were used to provide fresh water to Cham ships or other vessels. Cham wells are recognizable by their square shape and many are still in use, providing fresh water even during times of drought.

The earliest towers are presumed to have been built around the year 192 AD, but many Cham sites and structures may be much earlier, including parts of My Son. These shrine towers were still being built during the 7th and 8th centuries and are concentrated in Quang Nam, Da Nang, Binh Dinh, Khanh Hoa, Ninh Thuan and Binh Thuan. The famous Po Nagar Tower can be found at Nha Trang, a city known as Kauthara under the Champa. Nha Trang is famous for its sandy bay that could hold thousands of ships. Today it is a major beach-oriented tourist area.

The brickwork in Cham temples is so incredibly sophisticated

Cham brick and stone structures known as the Po Nagar Tower.

and durable that a number of legends have sprung up about them. Ngo Van Doahn says in his book, *Champa: Ancient Towers—Reality & Legend*,[1] that the construction method of these buildings remains a mystery to modern architects and archeologists. He mentions an old Vietnamese legend that says that the Cham people built their towers from air-dried bricks, then shaped them, and finally heated the whole structure in a gigantic furnace. He mentions that at the beginning of the 20th century the French archeologist H. Parmentier commented on the "foolish" idea of this legend. Parmentier could not figure out how air-dried brick could withstand the tremendous weight of a structure that was 20 or 30 meters high before baking.

Since this seemed impossible, Parmentier surmised that the bricks must have been fired separately and were very hard. Yet, the structures were so finely built with the bricks so perfectly fitted together that it appeared that the structure had been fired all at once in a huge kiln. Fieldwork on the structures showed that mortar was used between the bricks, but that in the outermost layers of bricks, the mortar was "so thin that the bricks look stuck together." [1]

The other mystery of the Cham brick construction is the elegant

28

carvings found on the brick faces of many of the temples. The later Vietnamese wondered how it was possible to carve out bricks like stones, as they would normally crumble. This was one of the reasons for the legend of the towers being fired as a whole, rather than being built one brick at a time. Modern archeologists surmise that the motifs may have been carved on each brick as part of a larger pattern while still soft, and then the bricks were fired individually and each brick placed in its artistically appointed spot.[1]

The Po Nagar Tower is in honor of a Chinese connection to the Cham. Says the Vietnamese website Asiatouradvisor.com of a

Detail of some of the excellant brickwork at temples in My Son.

tradition of a magical princess from Champa named Po Nagar:

> Po Nagar is an old Cham temple that was founded back in the 7th century and it is one of the oldest remnants of Cham civilization. It was built for the worship of the goddess of the country; Yan Po Nagar. She is reputed to have founded the nation of Vietnam. Legend has it that she once sailed all the way to China on a piece of wood. In China she met a handsome young prince and married him and bore him two sons. Then one day when she wished to return to the Kingdom of Champa to visit relatives; things went sour. The prince had a royal hissy fit and forbade her to leave. However, she grabbed her original piece of wood and snatched her children and disobeyed her husband to return home. The Chinese prince was not amused. He decided to punish his disobedient wife and brought a fleet to conquer her homeland and enslave her people. Unfortunately for him— she was also capable of great magic and she turned him and his crew into stone. Today she's better associated with the Hindu goddesses of Bhagavati and Mahishuramardini and much of the lore associated with Yan Po Nagar has become theirs and vice-versa.

The Cham were thusly connected to the imperial lords of various regions of China, but also to the islands of Southeast Asia and the Malay Strait, where Singapore now lies, which led to the ports in India and Sri Lanka. The culture of the Cham was very distinctly Indo-Buddhist and they were thought to be largely dark skinned, but apparently were of every racial type.

The Chinese actually called the many lands of the Champa "Funan," which meant "Pacified South," referring to the high quality of civilization to be found there. Other outsiders were typically referred to as barbarians by Chinese scholars.

The Mystery of the Land of Funan
The Land of Funan was certainly the same land as Champa, but

how extensive was this territory? Certainly it was a network of ports well beyond southern Vietnam and the Mekong River.

Says Wikipedia about Funan:

Based on the testimony of the Chinese historians, the polity Funan is believed to have been established in the 1st century CE in the Mekong Delta, but archaeological research has shown that extensive human settlement in the region may have gone back as far as the 4th century BCE. Though regarded by Chinese authors as a single unified polity, some modern scholars suspect that Funan may have been a collection of city-states that were sometimes at war with one another and at other times constituted a political unity.

From archaeological evidence, which includes Roman, Chinese, and Indian goods excavated at the ancient mercantile center of Oc Eo (from the Khmer Ou Kaeo, meaning "glass canal") in southern Vietnam, we know that Funan must have been a powerful trading state. Excavations at Angkor Borei in southern Cambodia have likewise delivered evidence of an important settlement. Since Oc Eo was linked to a port on the coast and to Angkor Borei by a system of canals, it is possible that all of these locations together constituted the heartland of Funan.

This Wikipedia article is clearly describing the vast realm of the Champa, called by the Chinese Funan, the "Pacified South." Writers on Funan seem to think it is different from Champa, yet the Chinese sources do not mention Champa at all. Rather than the land of Champa being separate from Funan, it would seem that they are the same country—and that Champa was far more extensive than originally believed. Indeed, until about 650 AD, it is my contention that all Hindu-Buddhist areas of Southeast Asia, including Indonesia, were the land of the Cham.

It seems that for the Chinese, the land of Funan starts in central Vietnam, the exact site of My Son and the Cham Islands and includes the Mekong Delta of Southern Vietnam and Cambodia, the interior waterways of Cambodia all the way to Angkor Wat and Angkor Thom, plus the Malayan Peninsula to Singapore and the islands of Sumatra and Java to the south. The lands of the Cham and the land of Funan are the same territory. What other culture was there? Until the rise of Srivijaya in Sumatra, circa 650 AD, it seems that the Champa ruled the Indonesian seas and their ports.

The Legendary Origins of Funan

The Chinese have a curious story about the origin of Funan. Chinese scholars say that an ancient text called *The Book of Liang* (compiled in 635 AD) records the story of the foundation of Funan by a foreigner named Huntian who came from a southern country called Jiao. This unknown country would seem to be India, Sri Lanka or possibly Sumatra.

The story goes that this Huntian fellow had a dream that his personal genie had directed him to embark on a large merchant ship and to take a magical bow with him on the journey. Huntian, with his dream fresh in his mind, proceeded to the temple in the morning where he found a marvelous bow (complete with magical arrows) at the foot of the genie's special tree.

Huntian then set sail in his great ship, presumably going north to southern Vietnam. The genie caused the great ship to land in the Mekong Delta area—a core Champa district. Huntian met with the locals, who did not wear clothes, and discovered that the queen of the country, named Liuye (Willow Leaf), wanted to seize his ship. Huntian then shot a magical arrow from his divine bow at Liuye's ship. The magical arrow pierced through Liuye's ship and almost sank it. The frightened warrior queen surrendered to Huntian, and the man from the south founded the highly civilized society known by the Chinese as Funan.

The text also mentions that Huntian was unhappy to see his wife run around without any clothes, so he folded a piece of material to make a garment through which he made her pass her head. Finally, the origin of Funan concludes with: "Then he governed the country and passed power on to his son, who was the founder of seven

32

cities."

So now we have the familiar tale of seven cities applied to Funan and therefore to Champa. The Spanish searched for the Seven Gold Cities of Cibola, so should we be looking for the Seven Gold Cities of the Cham? These great cities, if My Son and Angkor Wat are good examples (which they are), may be far-flung indeed. The Seven Cities of the Champa might include My Son, Po Nagar, Angkor Wat, Preah Vehear, Borobadur, and others.

Says Wikipedia about Huntian and the establishment of Funan:

According to modern scholars drawing primarily on Chinese literary sources, a foreigner named "Huntian" established the Kingdom of Funan around the 1st century CE in the Mekong Delta of southern Vietnam. Archeological evidence shows that extensive human settlement in the region may go back as far as the 4th century BCE. Though treated by Chinese historians as a single unified empire, according to some modern scholars Funan may have been a collection of city-states that sometimes warred with one another and at other times constituted a political unity.

The ethnic and linguistic origins of the Funanese people have been subject to scholarly debate, and no firm conclusions can be drawn based on the evidence available. The Funanese may have been Cham or from another Austronesian group, or they may have been Khmer or from another Austroasiatic group. It is possible that they are the ancestors of those indigenous people dwelling in the southern part of Vietnam today who refer themselves as "Khmer" or "Khmer Krom." (The Khmer term "krom" means "below" or "lower part of" and is used to refer to territory that was later colonized by Vietnamese immigrants and taken up into the modern state of Vietnam.) It is also possible that Funan was a multicultural society, including various ethnic and linguistic groups. In the late 4th and 5th centuries, Indianization advanced more rapidly, in part through renewed impulses from the south Indian Pallava dynasty and the north Indian Gupta Empire.

The only extant local writings from the period of Funan are paleographic Pallava Grantha inscriptions in Sanskrit of the Pallava dynasty, a scholarly language used by learned and ruling elites throughout South and Southeast Asia. These inscriptions give no information about the ethnicity or vernacular tongue of the Funanese.

Funan may have been the Suvarnabhumi referred to in ancient Indian texts. Among the Khmer Krom of the lower Mekong region the belief is held that they are the descendants of ancient Funan, the core of Suvarnabhumi/Suvarnadvipa, which covered a vast extent of Southeast Asia including present day Cambodia, southern Vietnam, Thailand, Laos, Burma, Malaya, Sumatra and other parts of Indonesia.

So, this Hindu-Buddhist land of Funan/Suvarnabhumi/Suvarnadvipa is essentially the same territory that is associated with Champa.

Wikipedia says that nearly the same story appeared in another book called the *Jìn shū* (*Book of Jin*), compiled by Fáng Xuánlíng in AD 648.

Wikipedia has this interesting thing to say about the Huntian-Kaundinya correlation and the curious Emperor Mu of Jin:

> Even if the Chinese "Huntian" is not the proper transcription of the Sanskrit "Kaundinya," the name "Kaundinya" is nevertheless an important one in the history of Funan as written by the Chinese historians, however, they transcribed it not as "Huntian," but as "Qiaochenrú." A person of that name is mentioned in the *Book of Liang* in a story that appears somewhat after the story of Huntian. According to this source, Qiaochenru was one of the successors of the king Tianzhu Zhantan ("Candana from India"), a ruler of Funan who in the year 357 AD sent tamed elephants as tribute to the Emperor Mu of Jin: "He [Qiaochenru] was originally a Brahmin from India. There a voice told him: 'you must go reign over Funan,' and he

rejoiced in his heart. In the south, he arrived at Panpan. The people of Funan appeared to him; the whole kingdom rose up with joy, went before him, and chose him king. He changed all the laws to conform to the system of India.

So, it seems that Funan, like Champa, was a Hindu-Buddhist culture whose origins were in India. One of the features of this land was the use of elephants, including war elephants. As we shall see, the gifting of war elephants to other kings was a common tribute in the ancient world of the Cham. It would also seem that the country of Suvarnabhumi/Suvarnadvipa was also the same land as greater Champa which included Cambodia, Vietnam, the Malay Penninsula, Sumatra, Java and other islands.

Suvarnabhumi: the Land of Gold

Suvarnabhumi is the Sanskrit name for the Southeast Asia and the islands of Indonesia. Some historians think that the island of Sumatra was Suvarnabhumi but it is likely that Suvarnabhumi was a very large area and included the coastal areas of many islands. The very modern international airport in Bangkok is named Suvarnabhumi Airport after this legendary land. Scholars argue as to where and how large Suvarnabhumi was. Apparently Suvarnabhumi is the same as Champa—a vast Hindu-Buddhist land of ports and islands. Says Wikipedia:

> Suvarnabhumi means "Golden Land" or "Land of Gold" and might be a region named Aurea Regio in "India beyond the Ganges" of Ptolemy, also referred to as the Golden Chersonese. The *Periplus of the Erythraean Sea* refers to the Land of Gold, Chryse, and describes it as "an island in the ocean, the furthest extremity towards the east of the inhabited world, lying under the rising sun itself, called Chryse… Beyond this country… there lies a very great inland city called Thina." Dionysius Periegetes mentioned: "The island of Chryse (Gold), situated at the very rising of the Sun." Avienus referred to the Insula Aurea (Golden Isle)

located where "the Scythian seas give rise to the Dawn." Josephus speaks of the "Aurea Chersonesus," which he equates with the Biblical Ophir, whence the ships of Tyre and Israel brought back gold for the Temple of Jerusalem. The city of Thina was described by Ptolemy's Geography as the capital city of the country on the eastern shores of the Magnus Sinus (Gulf of Thailand). Some have speculated that this country refers to the Kingdom of Funan. The main port of Funan was Cattigara Sinarum statio (Kattigara the port of the Sinae).

If the land of the Champa stretched from Sumatra to Java, Borneo and other islands, then it would naturally be this "Island of Gold" which was more than one island. In my book *Ark of God* I discuss the Biblical land of Ophir—a land of gold—and suggest that it was Indonesia or beyond. It was a three-year journey from the Red Sea to Ophir and back.

Wikipedia mentions that the 3rd century BC Indian emperor Asoka sent Buddhist missionaries to Suvarnabhumi as mentioned in Asoka's edicts and the Sanskrit text known as the "Mahavamsa." The site also says:

> The term Suvarnabhumi ("Land of Gold"), is commonly thought to refer to the Southeast Asian Peninsula, including lower Burma and the Malay Peninsula. However there is another gold-referring term Suvarnadvipa ("Islands of Gold"), which may correspond to the Indonesian Archipelago, especially Sumatra. Both terms might refer to a powerful coastal or island kingdom in present-day Indonesia and Malaysia, possibly centered on Sumatra or Java. This corresponds to the gold production areas traditionally known in Minangkabau highlands in Barisan Mountains, Sumatra, and interior Borneo. An eighth century Indian text known as the "Samaraiccakaha" describes a sea voyage to Suvarnadvipa and the making of bricks from the gold rich sands which they inscribed with the name dharana

and then baked. These pointing out to the direction of western part of insular Southeast Asia, especially Sumatra, Malay Peninsula, Borneo and Java.

Benefited from its strategic location on narrow Strait of Malacca, the insular theory argued that other than actually producing gold, it might also based on such kingdom's potential for power and wealth (hence, "Land of Gold") as a hub for sea-trade and on vague descriptions provided by contemporary Chinese pilgrims to India. The kingdom referred as the center of maritime trade between China and India was Srivijaya. Due to the Chinese writing system, however, the interpretations of Chinese historical sources are based on supposed correspondences of ideograms—and their possible phonetic equivalents—with known toponyms in the ancient Southeast Asian civilizations. Hendrik Kern concluded that Sumatra was the Suvarnadvipa mentioned in ancient Hindu texts and the island of Chryse mentioned in the *Periplus of the Erythraean Sea* and by Rufius Festus Avienus.

The interpretation of early travel records is not always easy. The Javanese embassies to China in 860 and 873 CE refer to Java as rich in gold, although it was in fact devoid of any deposits. Javanese would have had to import gold possibly from neighboring Malaya, Sumatra or Borneo, where gold was still being mined into the 19th century and where ancient mining sites are located. Even though Java did not have its own gold deposits, the texts make frequent references to the existence of goldsmiths, and it is clear from the archaeological evidence such as Wonoboyo Hoard, that this culture had developed a sophisticated gold working technology, which relied on the importing of substantial quantities of the metal.

The Padang Roco Inscription of 1286 CE, states that an image of Buddha Amoghapasa Lokeshvara was brought to Dharmasraya on the Upper Batang Hari—the river of Jambi, transported from Bhumi Java (Java) to Suvarnabhumi

(Sumatra), and erected by order of the Javanese ruler Kertanegara: the inscription clearly identifies Sumatra as Suvarnabhumi.

So, here we learn that a late inscription, from 1286 AD, identifies Sumatra as Suvarnabhumi. We also learn that Sumatra is a source of gold and is mentioned in the Greek sailing manual *Periplus of the Erythraean Sea*. It would seem that, at the very least, Suvarnabhumi began at Sumatra and may have included the many islands to the east. It was these islands, especially the small Spice Islands such as Ambon, that were sought for an even more valuable commodity than gold—that being the spices of nutmeg, cinnamon, cloves and allspice. So, it seems that the Hindus in India may have called Sumatra "Suvarnabhumi," while the area of the Malay Penninsula, Thailand, Cambodia and Vietnam they called themselves Cham or Champa. The Chinese called the area Funan.

But the larger island world spanned further east into the Pacific—a vast chain of islands through Indonesia, New Guinea, the Philippines, Micronesia, Melanesia, Tonga and beyond. What great fleet was going to these far-flung areas of the western Pacific and leaving megalithic remains behind? The evidence, in my view, is pointing to the Cham and, even earlier Indo-Sumerians, from the Indus Valley, circa 2000 BC.

The search for the "Islands of Gold" and the Spice Islands was the world-changing quest of Portuguese, Spanish, Dutch and English expeditions during the Age of Exploration. This important time of naval expeditions and the charting of the Seven Seas culminated in the discovery of the Spice Islands in eastern Indonesia, near the mini-continent of New Guinea.

Says Wikipedia:

The thirst for gold formed the most powerful incentive to explorers at the beginning of modern times; but although more and more extensive regions were brought to light by them, they sought in vain in the East Indian Archipelago for the Gold and Silver Islands where, according to the legends, the precious metals were to be gathered from the ground and did not need to be laboriously extracted from the interior of the earth. In spite of their failure, they found it difficult to give up the alluring picture. When they did not find what they sought in the regions which were indicated by the old legends and by the maps based thereon, they hoped for better success in still unexplored regions, and clutched with avidity at every hint that they were here to attain their object. The history of geography thus shows us how the Gold and Silver Islands were constantly, so to speak, wandering towards the East. Marco Polo spoke, in the most exaggerated language, of the wealth of gold in Zipangu, situated at the extremity of this part of the world, and had thus pointed out where the precious metals should preferably be sought. Martin Behaim, on his globe of 1492, revived the Argyre and Chryse of antiquity in these regions. In 1519, Cristóvão de Mendonça, was given instructions to search for the legendary Isles of Gold, said to lie "beyond Sumatra," which he was unable to do, and in 1587 an expedition under the command of Pedro de Unamunu was sent to find them in the vicinity of Zipangu (Japan). According to Antonio de Herrera y Tordesillas, in 1528 Alvaro de Saavedra in the ship *Florida* on a voyage from the Moluccas to Mexico reached a large island which he took for the Isla del Oro. This island has not been identified although it seems likely that it is Biak, Manus or one of the Schouten Islands on the north coast of New Guinea.

Funan, Cambodia and Champa

Funan, what little is written about it, is typically said to be the forerunner of the Khmer Civilization in Cambodia. Says the Encyclopedia Britannica about Funan, giving an alternative explanation for the origin of the name "Funan":

> Funan, ancient state in Cambodia that arose in the 1st century AD and was incorporated into the state of Chenla

in the 6th century. Funan (perhaps a Chinese transcription of pnom, "mountain") was the first important Hinduized kingdom in southeast Asia. It covered portions of what are now Vietnam, Thailand, and Cambodia. Funan had trade relations with India as well as China, to whose emperor the people of Funan sent tribute between the 3rd and 6th centuries. Archaeological evidence shows that Funan was influenced markedly by Indian cultures.

The civilization that they are describing is clearly that of the Champa. The online Encyclopedia Britannica continues to say in its article about the early history of Cambodia that Funan is essentially Cambodia and southern Vietnam, yet does not mention the Cham, from which Cambodia and the Khmer get their name:

It is not known for certain how long people have lived in what is now Cambodia, where they came from, or what languages they spoke before writing was introduced (based on a Sanskrit-style alphabet) about the 3rd century CE. Carbon-14 dating indicates that people who made and used pottery inhabited Cambodia as early as 4000 BCE. Those and subsequent findings suggest that those early people, like Cambodians today, were of slight to medium build, constructed their houses on wooden piles, consumed a considerable quantity of fish, and raised pigs and water buffalo.

Whether the early inhabitants of Cambodia came originally or primarily from the north, west, or south is still debated, as are theories about waves of different peoples moving through the region in prehistoric times. Archaeological finds since 1950 suggest that prehistoric mainland Southeast Asia, including Cambodia, had a comparatively sophisticated culture. Those finds include artificial circular earthworks thought to be from the 1st millennium BCE. Some scholars have even traced the first cultivation of rice and the first casting of bronze to the region.

This article is essentially saying that civilization came to Cambodia, in the form of writing, around 300 AD. It does stipulate, however, that the prehistoric culture of Southeast Asia appears to have been "comparatively sophisticated." Early megalithic remains in the area, such as the Plain of Jars in Laos, are many thousands of years old. Megalithic civilization in Cambodia easily goes back to 1000 BC. Any river or large lake in Southeast Asia, including all

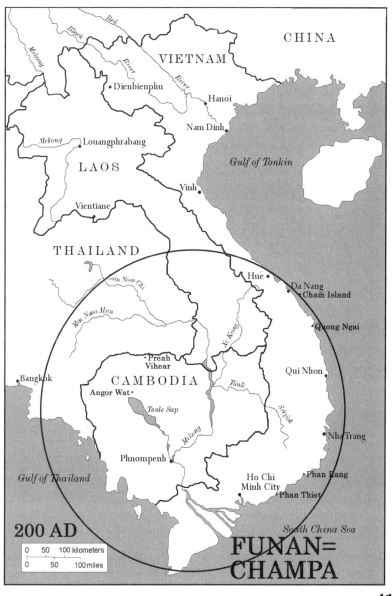

200 AD

FUNAN=CHAMPA

of those in Cambodia, would have been visited by the vast fleet of trading ships that were controlled by the Cham. They apparently had many fleets of ships and each of these fleets was at least a thousand vessels—large ocean-going trading ships.

The online Encyclopedia Britannica goes on to say that the area of Funan-Cambodia was known in later Chinese historical texts as Chenla:

> Indian influences were the most important in Cambodia's early history during the first centuries CE, when Chinese and Indian pilgrims and traders stopped along the coasts of present-day Cambodia and Vietnam and exchanged silks and metals for spices, aromatic wood, ivory, and gold. Written sources dating from that period are almost entirely in Chinese and describe a kingdom or group of kingdoms flourishing in southern Cambodia, known to Chinese writers as "Funan." Over a period of 300 years, between the 3rd and 6th centuries CE, its rulers offered gifts from time to time to Chinese emperors. Chinese writers testified to the extent of Indian influence in the kingdom and accounted for it by citing a local story, dating from the 6th century, of an Indian Brahman named Kaundinya who went to the area and "changed its institutions to follow Indian models." One consequence of that early contact with Indian civilization was the introduction of large-scale irrigation, which allowed people to produce three or more crops of rice per year in some districts and brought previously unproductive areas under cultivation. Another was the worship of the Hindu god Shiva, who was conceptualized as a tutelary ancestor or spirit of the soil and was often represented by a stone lingam, or phallus. A third was the relatively peaceful coexistence in Cambodia of Hinduism and Buddhism, which endured for more than a thousand years.

The capital city of Funan was probably located at the site of the village of Phumi Phnum Angkor Borei in Takeo (Takev) province, where systematic archaeological digs have been conducted since the mid-1990s. The most important legacy of Funan, though it may have been exaggerated by Chinese writers, was a centralized state apparatus. At the pinnacle of that structure was a theoretically absolute ruler who relied on an agricultural workforce and off-season labor to generate agricultural surpluses to sustain his lifestyle, support a priestly caste, and build fortresses, palaces, and temples. In a general way, those social arrangements resemble those found in medieval Europe, but it would be imprecise to use a term such as feudalism to characterize Funan and its successor states. Instead, it is probably more fruitful to seek links between ancient and present-day Cambodia than between ancient Cambodia and countries far to the west about which the Khmer would have known nothing.

The appearance of Sanskrit inscriptions in the 6th century—the earliest-known Khmer inscription dates from the early 7th century—has made it possible to use indigenous sources to supplement Chinese ones, but they all fail to clarify the confusing political developments that occurred in the Cambodian region between the decline of Funan in the 6th century and the founding of a centralized state in northwestern Cambodia about three centuries later. It has been common practice for modern writers to use "Chenla," the contemporary Chinese term for the region, when referring to Cambodia during that time. Chinese sources suggest that there were at least two kingdoms in Cambodia, known as "Water Chenla" and "Land Chenla," that vied for recognition from China in that period. Whereas the geographic centre for both Funan and Water Chenla lay in the Mekong River delta south and east of present-day Phnom Penh and extended into what is now Vietnam, the heartland of Land Chenla appears to have been farther north along the Mekong, with an important cult site called Wat Phu located in present-day southern Laos. It seems likely that Water Chenla looked outward and welcomed foreign trade, while Land Chenla was more inward-looking and based its economy on intensive agriculture. Surviving inscriptions in Sanskrit and Khmer testify to a multitude of small kingdoms on Cambodian soil between the 7th and 9th centuries. Remarkable sculptures and architectural remains also have survived from that period, displaying a mixture of Indian influence and local inspiration. The appearance of local styles reflected, in part, declining Indian commercial interest in the region beginning in the 7th century.

This capital, Phumĭ Phnum Ângkôr Borei in Takeo (Takêv) province was no doubt an early Hindu-Cham port on the Mekong River, founded by 500 BC. Since the Encyclopedia Britannica is describing pre-Khmer Cambodia as some mysterious culture with clear cultural links to ancient India—yet fails to mention the Cham as an important culture in the exact same vicinity (the Mekong River and surrounding areas)—we have to wonder what they must say about Champa. The online Encyclopedia Britannica says that Champa was created as the Han dynasty of China was breaking up in 192 AD:

Champa, (Chinese Lin-yi), ancient Indochinese kingdom lasting from the 2nd to the 17th century AD and extending over the central and southern coastal region of Vietnam from roughly the 18th parallel in the north to Point Ke Ga (Cape Varella) in the south. Established by the Cham, a people of Malayo-Polynesian stock and Indianized culture, Champa was finally absorbed by the Vietnamese, who in turn were strongly influenced by Cham culture.

Champa was formed in AD 192, during the breakup of the Han dynasty of China, when the Han official in charge of the region established his own kingdom around the area of the present city of Hue. Although the territory was at first inhabited mainly by wild tribes involved in incessant struggles with the Chinese colonies in Tonkin, it gradually came under Indian cultural influence, evolving into a

44

decentralized country composed of four small states, named after regions of India—Amaravati (Quang Nam); Vijaya (Binh Dinh); Kauthara (Nha Trang); and Panduranga (Phan Rang)—whose populations remained concentrated in small coastal enclaves. It had a powerful fleet that was used for commerce and for piracy.

In about AD 400 Champa was united under the rule of King Bhadravarman. In retaliation for Cham raids on their coast, the Chinese invaded Champa in 446, bringing the region under their suzerainty once again. Finally, under a new dynasty in the 6th century, Champa threw off its allegiance to China and entered into an era of great independent prosperity and artistic achievements. The centre of the nation began to shift from north to south; around the middle of the 8th century Chinese sources cease to mention Lin-yi and begin to refer to the kingdom as Huan-wang, a Sinicization of the name of the northernmost province, Panduranga (Phan Rang). In the late 8th century the Chams were distracted by attacks from Java, but in the 9th century they renewed their pressure on the Chinese provinces to the north and the growing Khmer (Cambodian) Empire to the west. Under Indravarman II, who established the Indrapura dynasty (the sixth in Champan history) in 875, the capital of the country was moved back to the northern province of Amaravati (Quang Nam), near present Hue, and elaborate palaces and temples were constructed.

In the 10th century the Vietnamese kingdom of Dai Viet began to exert pressure on Champa, forcing it to relinquish Amaravati in 1000 and Vijaya in 1069. Harivarman IV, who in 1074 founded the ninth Cham dynasty, was able to stave off further Vietnamese and Cambodian attacks, but in 1145 the Khmers, under the aggressive leadership of Suryavarman II, invaded and conquered Champa. Two years later a new Cham king, Jaya Harivarman I, arose and threw off Khmer rule, and his successor, in 1177, sacked the Cambodian capital at Angkor. Between 1190 and 1220 the Chams again came under Cambodian suzerainty, and later in the 13th century they were attacked by the Tran kings of Vietnam, as well as by the Mongols in 1284. By the late 15th century, incessant wars of aggression and defense had for all practical purposes wiped out the Champa kingdom; one by one their provinces were annexed until Champa was entirely absorbed in the 17th century.

While the online Encyclopedia Britannica mentions that the Cham had a "powerful fleet that was used for commerce and piracy" it fails to mention where this fleet would be going. Clearly to China and India—where its culture and religion were originating from—and clearly to Java and other Indonesian islands as referenced by the war between Java and the Champa areas of Vietnam in the 8th century. This war was essentially the Indonesian principalities of the Cham exercising their independence from the core Champa areas of southern Vietnam. Finally, the last Cham states were absorbed by the northern Vietnamese kingdom of Dai Viet and the Tran kings.

Also, the Encyclopedia Britannica does not explain how Champa is a culture from Han China and strongly linked to Chinese culture and history, but is a dark-skinned Hindu-Buddhist maritime culture with obvious cultural links to ancient India—just like the mythical neighboring kingdom of Funan. Funan is obviously the same as Champa, yet scholars refuse to recognize this.

Furthermore, what the online Encyclopedia Britannica and Wikipedia entries for the Champa fail to mention is that the lost world of Cham or Champa was inherently a seafaring empire, one known as a thalassocratic empire. Archeologists are now confirming that some sort of thalassocratic empire existed in Southeast Asia by at least 1000 BC. Stone jars and monuments at Bada Valley on the island of Sulawesi are dated to 2000 BC or older.

We might give a different timeline for the Cham or Champa: starting by 1500 BC (or earlier) Hindu seafarers began to move through Southeast Asia and Indonesia and into the Pacific. By 500 BC the trade networks of mini port states of the Champa were well formed. Voyages across the Pacific were made. Around 250 BC Asoka began to spread Buddhism east and west. By 200 AD megalithic structures such as My Son, Preah Vihear, Angkor Wat and Borobadur were being built. By 700 AD the Cham Empire had shrunk to central Vietnam. This was a thalassocratic empire that existed for over a thousand years across the entire Pacific Ocean.

But first, what is a thalassocratic empire?

The Thalassocratic Empire of Cham-Kam-Khem 1000 BC

A thalassocratic empire is essentially a maritime empire that maintains naval supremacy through the use of a huge fleet (or fleets) of ships. A country that is a thalassocracy is a maritime trading empire with many port cities in far-flung islands and coastlines. The Phoenicians (who later became the Carthaginians) are a well-known thalassocratic empire that spanned the Mediterranean, North Africa and beyond.

The Merriam-Webster dictionary gives the rather terse definition of thalassocracy as simply "Maritime supremacy." (http://www.merriam-webster.com/dictionary/thalassocracy)

But Wikipedia gives us a much fuller definition:

A thalassocracy (from Greek language (thalassa), meaning "sea," and (kratein), meaning "to rule," giving (thalassokratia), "rule of the sea") is a state with primarily maritime realms—an empire at sea (such as the Phoenician network of merchant cities) or a sea-borne empire. Traditional thalassocracies seldom dominate interiors, even in their home territories (for example: Phoenician Tyre, Sidon and Carthage or Srivijaya and Majapahit in Southeast Asia). One can distinguish this traditional sense of thalassocracy from an "empire," where the state's territories, though possibly linked principally or solely by the sea lanes, generally extend into mainland interiors (for example: the Bruneian Empire (1368–1888) in Asia). Compare to tellurocracy— land-based hegemony.

The term thalassocracy can also simply refer to naval supremacy, in either military or commercial senses of the word supremacy. The Greeks first used the word thalassocracy to describe the government of the Minoan civilization, whose power depended on its navy. Herodotus also spoke of the need to counter the Phoenician thalassocracy by developing a Greek "empire of the sea."

So, economic powers and their corresponding city-states are divided into two groups: those based on inland cities and control of the roads and rivers (a tellurocracy) and those trading empires based on a vast fleet of ships goings from port to port and visiting different continents and far-flung island archipelagos. Some nations may be a combination of the two.

What concerns us in this book is the amazing thalassocracy of the Cham, or Champa. In this book, I hope to show that the Indo-Egyptian Cham of Vietnam and Indonesia had a thalassocratic empire that spanned eastward through Indonesia and out into the Pacific. The Cham thalassocracy may have been the largest ever known in the ancient world. In modern times it could be argued that the British thalassocratic empire, on which "the sun never set," was the largest in all of history. It is an amazing accomplishment that a small island archipelago in the North Sea would have a maritime empire spanning all the oceans of the earth, to remote areas such

A Cham tower made of fine brick mixed with cut stone blocks at My Son, Vietnam.

Top: A photo of the megalithic city of My Son in central Vietnam. *Left and Above*: The stone blocks with their unusual and complicated articulation and keystone cuts are very similar to those found at Tiwanaku and Puma Punku.

T-shaped keystone cuts on granite blocks at My Son.

Finely-cut granite pillars at My Son. Were these pillars cut with power tools?

A Cham tower made of fine brick and cut basalt at My Son.

A Champa bust of Shiva made
of the gold-silver-copper alloy
of electrum. Note the third eye
and topknot.

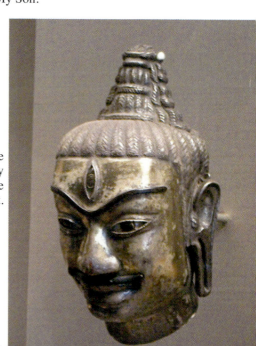

The amazing brick and basalt temple known as the Po Nagar Tower.

A general look at the central ruins of stone and brick at My Son.

A Cham tower made of fine brick and cut basalt at My Son.

The Mayan-looking statue at the Museum of Cham Culture in Da Nang.

The Cham brick and stone towers at Po Klong.

Right: A granite statue of a bearded Shiva wearing a crown and holding a trident now at the Museum of Cham Culture in Da Nang.

Above: The Cham brick and stone towers at Po Sa Nu near Phan Thiet. *Right and Below*: The Cham Islands off the coast of central Vietnam where fleets of Cham ships would meet from time to time.

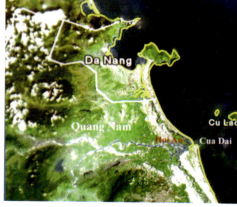

Above: War elephants were
the tanks of the ancient world
and were transported on ships
all throughout Southeast Asia.
Below: A war elephant used by
the Carthaginians in North Africa.

Right: The famous Kon Tiki statue
at Tiwanaku with its mustache and
beard. It holds its arms across its
chest with its hands on its heart
and stomach in the classic Pacific
Island tiki pose.

The wall of three windows at Preah Vihear.

A T-shaped keystone cut at Preah Vihear.

Above: An aerial view of Preah Vihear. *Right*: A granite boulder carved into a tiki face in a rice paddy in Besoa Valley. *Below*: A stone jar and lid in Besoa Valley.

Left: A stone vat in Bada Valley. *Below*: The large tiki statue in Bada Valley.

Two photos of the mysterious megalithic site of Gunung Padang in western Java.

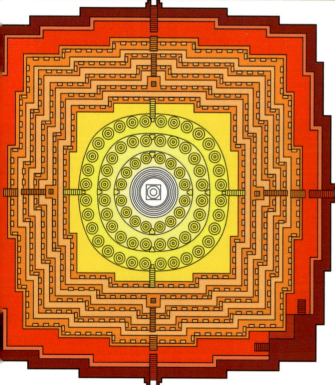

Above: The amazing and mysterious Buddhist stupa known as Borobudur. *Left*: Borobudur is built as a gigantic mandala that is to be walked in a certain pattern to the top. Did the Cham build Borobudur?

Above Left: The mysterious precision-cut monument on Sumba Island called Kampung Paronabaroro. *Above Right*: Huge slab dolmens on Sumba Island. *Left*: More slab dolmens on Sumba Island. *Below Left*: Two stone tiki faces from northern Sumatra. *Below Right*: The Toraja megaliths on the island of Sulawesi

The Fuente Magna Bowl at the Museum of Precious Metals in La Paz.

A series of keystone cuts on the sandstone platforms at Puma Punku, near Tiwanaku, Bolivia.

as New Zealand, the Falkland Islands and much of North America, Africa and the Middle East. It was the large British navy and other cargo ships that linked this vast network that continues to this day as the British Commonwealth.

It was the Cham who built a gigantic naval base out of millions of tons of basalt on the volcanic Micronesian island of Pohnpei, today the capital of the Federated States of Micronesia. From here they moved out into the central Pacific, to Fiji, Tonga, Tahiti and Marquesas Islands. Easter Island was also colonized by them.

They arrived at the west coast of Mexico where they created ports and began the Olmec civilization in Mexico, Guatemala and other areas of Central America. Later some of these areas became dominated by the Maya. Others became dominated by the Zapotec or Toltec. The Aztecs came at a much later period.

A map of the Cham voyages out into the Pacific.

The Cham continued to the Pacific Coast of Colombia, Ecuador and Peru and interacted with cultures here. In all these places they were after metals of all kinds, including iron, gold, copper, tin and silver. They had iron tools and advanced technology. They set up mining camps in areas that the locals had helped them discover and washed and smelted ores. They worked hard stone such as basalt and granite with relative ease and assembled stone walls that still amaze visitors today at places like Cuzco, Tiwanaku, Ollantaytambo, Machu Picchu and Chavin.

They left stone crucibles that baffle archeologists today as well as stone towers that were used for smelting the ore into the liquid metals. Archeologists today believe them to be burial towers. Despite the fact that archeologists know that bronze metals were poured into granite or sandstone molds at Tiwanaku and Puma Punku, they do not explain where the metallurgical complex is located. As I explain in my book *Ancient Technology in Peru and Bolivia*,[38] the purpose of the megalithic site of Tiwanaku and Puma Punku was the washing and smelting of ores. Ultimately the liquid metals of gold, silver, copper and even iron were created and mixed into their alloys. The Cham were fond of using electrum—a mix of gold and silver—for many of their metal statues and the area around Tiwanaku was a major source of both metals.

The return across the Pacific may have involved Easter Island on many of the trips. This isolated island has a good source of fresh water and has similar stone walls as those seen in Peru and Bolivia. This island and the fact that the gigantic statues there wore a special style of Hindu hairstyle known as the topknot will be discussed in a later chapter.

Does an empire that extends from Southeast Asia to Central and South America seem like too far a distance for ships to make steady continuous trips? The thalassocratic empires of the Phoenicians and later the Romans spanned huge distances. They probably included transatlantic and trans-Indian Ocean voyages as well. The Phoenician thalassocratic empire was the main trading partner on the Atlantic coast of Mexico.

Remember, the crossing of the Pacific by Ferdinand Magellan in

1521, on a mission to find the Spice Islands of Indonesia, set sail from Peru and did not spot another island until he had completely crossed the Pacific to the Mariana Islands and the southern Philippines.

Later the Acapulco, Mexico trade to Manila in the Philippines was a keystone of the Spanish Empire, allowing them to import the spices, silks and other luxuries from the Far East to Mexico and then to Spain after being moved overland to Mexico City and then to Veracruz where they would go by ship to Seville in Spain.

The Sulu Islands, the southernmost island group of the Philippines, was part of the Cham thalassocratic empire and later embraced Islam just as the Cham did in Vietnam and Cambodia. The Sulu Islands were also the furthest into the Pacific that the Cham war elephants were known to be distributed, as we will discuss in the next chapter. Certain small islands such as Bali, Pohnpei, Kosrae and Tonga would have been completely controlled by the Cham since they are relatively small territories. Starting by 1000 BC or before, all of these areas would have essentially been Hindu, as archeologists have shown that Gobekli Tepe and areas of central Turkey were.

Statues from Gobekli Tepe and Nevali Cori show men with the distinctive Hindu ponytail—a small shock of hair known as a sikha. Hindu brahmins and various devotees, such as Hari Krishnas, are known to shave their heads and leave this bit of hair at the back. In ancient times, every male Hindu was to wear a sikha, and it was one of the few symbols of Hindusism that transcended caste, language and regional barriers.

A different hairstyle is worn by Hindu ascetics, known as sadhus (and as Shaivites—worshippers of Shiva), who typically wear their hair unshaven and very long—never getting a haircut in most cases. This long hair is sometimes worn hanging down, like a woman with long hair, or it is tied up in a large bun, or topknot, on the top of the head. This is the

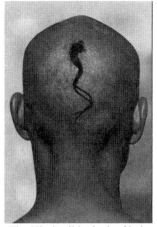

The Hindu sikha lock of hair.

51

way that the Hindu god Shiva wears his hair and it was a popular hairstyle among the Cham, as witnessed by the many statues at the Museum of Cham Culture in Da Nang. This topknot of hair—along with long earlobes—is also seen on the Easter Island statues, to be discussed later. Sometimes this topknot was beneath a turban,

A stone head of the Shiva from My Son. Note third eye, topknot and long ears.

popular in Fiji and Indonesia.

The Cham Empire was largely confined to the coastal and river areas of Southeast Asia. It is important to note that mountainous inland areas of Southeast Asia, including the many islands, were never really part of the Cham Empire, even when this empire spanned the Pacific as I propose in this book. Inland areas of Cambodia and the Mekong Delta were part of the Champa realm, but generally—with some exceptions—the Champa influence was limited to the coast and along navigable inland rivers. Inner mountainous areas of islands such as Borneo, Sumatra, Sulawesi and New Guinea have always held indigenous natives who were often headhunters and fiercely protective of their inland territories.

Some of the exceptions to the coastal rule of the Cham civilization would be Gunung Padang, which is far inland in the mountains of western Java; Bada Valley in the mountains of central Sulawesi; and Preah Vihear, which is on top of a mountain in the very north of Cambodia.

The African—Cham—Mesoamerican Connection

A further mystery of the Cham is that many of them were dark-skinned with wide noses and thick lips, as seen in their art, and in many cases would seem to be African. Is it possible that the Cham people were seafarers out of Egypt and Nubia, voyaging across the Indian Ocean to Sri Lanka and India and on to Sumatra, Vietnam and Cambodia?

Curiously, the ancient name that the Egyptians gave their own country was Khem or Kham. In his book *Esoteric Egypt: The Sacred Science of the Land of the Khem*,[25] Egyptologist J.S. Gordon claims that ancient Egypt—Khem—was descended from early civilizations that had been destroyed in cataclysms. Similarly, Egyptologist Stephen Mehler says in his book *The Land of Osiris*[30] that ancient Egypt was called Khem or Khemit and was the remnant of an earlier civilization. In both books the authors argue that the advanced civilizations that preceded Khem were seafaring nations with power tools, electricity and flight.

So, are the Cham named after "Khem"—essentially calling

themselves "Egyptians" by saying that they are the Champa? Khem and Cham seem to be the same word, but one describes Egypt while the other denotes a territory in Southeast Asia.

Oxford historian W.J. Perry wrote of the Egyptian and Hindu presence in the Pacific Ocean in his 1923 book *The Children of the Sun*.[24] He called the co-exploration of the Pacific by Egypt and India a "dual system" that colonized all the Pacific Islands and was an important influence on the civilizations in Mexico ad Peru.

The British historian and physician Stephen Oppenheimer proposed a drowned land in Indonesia that was flooded with the rise of sea levels at the end of the last ice age in his 1998 book *Eden in the East*.[40] Oppenheimer thinks that civilization started in Indonesia and went to Egypt and the Middle East from there. Did Egypt-Khem begin in Indonesia and Southeast Asia? Perhaps the name Cham-Champa began in Southeast Asia and was then transferred to Egypt—a fascinating thought!

That the Cham were coming from Egypt and East Africa would explain why many of the Cham seemed to be blacks. The Hindu Tamils of southern India and Sri Lanka are also very dark-skinned. The black populations of the Solomon Islands, Vanuatu and Fiji might also be explained by Egyptian-African seafarers voyaging out into the Pacific. This was one of the points made by historian and language expert Barry Fell in his books such as *Saga America*.[27]

Anthropologist Runoko Rahshidi, coauthor of *The African Presence in Early Asia*[15] with Ivan Van Sertima of Rutgers University, maintains that the Cham were, in fact, Africans who had come to Vietnam from the Indian subcontinent.

Rahshidi visited Vietnam in 2001 and says on his website about the Museum of Cham Culture in Da Nang:

> The Cham Museum has many of the finest objects of Cham art in the world and is just magnificent. It is an open air museum holding about three-hundred artifacts. Many of the objects, superb sandstone Buddhist and Hindu works, I had previously only seen in books, and so in many ways the visit was a dream come true. Many of the pieces are as

Africoid (dark skin, full lips, broad noses) as any art that you will ever see. The Cham Museum has to be one of the finest museums in all of Southeast Asia and is a must see for any African who goes to Vietnam.

My initial interest in the African presence in Southeast Asia started almost thirty years ago, stimulated by the reports that I received from numerous friends, acquaintances and family members who had served in the United States military during the Vietnamese War. I remember, beginning even back then around the age of sixteen, how fascinated I was when I heard their descriptions of the different Black people that they had encountered. They referred to these Black folks as *Montagnards*. I was later to find out that these so-called *Montagnards* were not recent arrivals to Vietnam. Nor were they the offspring of African-American soldiers and Vietnamese women, but, rather, these were people who had been in Vietnam for a very long time.

...The Cham seem to have possessed what appears to have been a strong Melanesian element and are believed to have settled along the coastal plains of mid-southern Vietnam more than two millennia ago. Another view is that the Cham were actually Black colonists from south-central India. Either way, it is clear that the Cham dominated the region for centuries.

According to one account the kingdom of Champa was born of a victory by the Blacks "over the Chinese province of Je-Nan... later, it frequently demonstrated its unruliness and the spirit of conquest, including against China." Early records further note that, "For the complexion of men, they consider black the most beautiful. In all the kingdoms of the southern region, it is the same." Chinese scribes added that the people of Champa adorned themselves "in a single piece of cotton or silk wrapped about the body... They are very clean; they wash themselves several times each day, wear perfume, and rub their bodies with a lotion compounded with camphor and musk."

55

H. Otley Beyer believed that between 900 and 1200 C.E. a group of seafarers made their exodus from central Vietnam and found their way to the Philippines. These seafarers, noted Beyer, were called the "*Orang Dampuans* or Men of Champa." During this same period Cham ships, known to the Chinese by the appellation *kun-lun-bo* (the "vessels of Black men") were navigating the currents of the Indian Ocean ranging from Southeast Asia to Madagascar.

According to Leonard Cottrell, "The term *k'un-lun* found in Chinese texts relating to south-east Asia, is an ethnic term which seems to apply to a number of peoples who are characterized by black skin and frizzy hair... Their geographical location and their maritime skills made them important contributors to the cultural history of Southeast Asia and south China. There are also pointers to a connection with the Kao-li of Korea. By association, and as a conventional Chinese transcription, the term k'un-lun is also applied to the Khmer. Later, by extension, because of physical resemblances, the term was used by Chinese writers for African Negroes. The connection with the Khmer was justified because of the parallel between the mythical K'un-lun Mountain of Chinese cosmology and the mountain cult, assimilated with the Indian Meru, of the Khmer kingdoms."
(http://www.cwo.com/~lucumi/vietnam.html)

Both Rashidi and Van Sertima advocate that Egyptian-African seafarers were voyaging across all of the oceans, the Atlantic and the Pacific, not to mention the Indian Ocean and Java Sea. They see evidence for this in the obviously African nature that is seen in the statues of the Olmecs in Mexico and the Champa statues found at the museum in Da Nang.

So, we start to get the idea that the Cham were a mixture of races, much like the Olmecs and the Egyptians, with some blacks and whites mixed in with oriental races. Seafarers on large ships are often a mix of races, and sailors are a group who tend to treat each other equally. It does not matter about one's racial makeup on a ship, what matters is the sailor's ability to do his job and keep the ship moving. It is the kind of comraderie that only a crew can really know.

I have come to the conclusion that these Hindu-Buddhist-Egyptians had several large fleets that roamed the Indian Ocean to India, Sri Lanka and Sumatra and other fleets that that roamed the Java Sea and Gulf of Siam. Other fleets went up the Mekong and other rivers deep into Cambodia, Laos and Thailand (at a time before the Thai people migrated from the north). Still another fleet went north from My Son and the Cham Islands to China, Taiwan and the Philippines. Was there a time when the Cham fleet amassed at the Cham Islands and then went directly eastward through the Sulu Sea and out into the Pacific? It is my contention that they did.

The Mystery of the Cham Islands

I have tried to establish that the Cham were amazing Hindu-Buddhist seafarers who were ranging from Madagascar to Indonesia, Vietnam and beyond. They were well situated in central Vietnam, and especially the Cham Islands, to voyage out into the Pacific—to the Philippines and even further afield. By passing between Borneo and the Philippines, they could have sailed along the north coast of New Guinea and into the Melanesian islands of the Western Pacific, possibly even populating them! The people of Melanesia are black while the Polynesians of the central Pacific Island groups are considered to be Caucasian. Some anthropologists believe they came from northern India, but no one is sure where the Polynesians originated. Some believe it was Egypt.

From Melanesia it would have been an easy trip to Tonga, Samoa, the Marquesas Islands and the Americas. This is essentially one of the transpacific routes that I suggest in my book *The Mystery of the Olmecs*.[22] In that book I show that Shang Chinese were in contact with the Olmecs as early as 1300 BC. The Cham are from a later period, but they may have been making transpacific contact during the period of around 200 BC to 800 AD. Perhaps they had inherited from the Shang Chinese the long distance sea routes that went beyond the Philippines and New Guinea to even New Zealand

and Australia.

From a balcony on the second story of the Da Nang museum I looked out to the Pacific Ocean in the distance. Only 25 kilometers off shore were the Cu Lao Cham, or Cham Islands, that must have been the Cham's main naval base. Lao, the main island of seven, has a deep and protected cove on the western side that is a very good shelter for ships during storms and even typhoons. It would seem that the sizable Cham fleet of presumably gigantic ships must have been based here. It is known that a huge fleet of ships would gather among the sandy islands and take on provisions, including fresh water. Then the fleet would leave the islands, but no historian is sure where it went.

Some historians have postulated that the Cham went out on huge looting expeditions to surrounding lands while others maintain—rightly I would say—that they were massive trading expeditions. This fleet, or various fleets, assembled several times a year, could have been traveling east across the Pacific while other fleets may have been bound for China or India. The Cham Islands were a perfect starting spot for a transpacific voyage that would take them to the southern Philippines (the Sulu Islands) and then out into the Pacific for the long voyage to the Americas. They could stop in Pohnpei or Kosrae in Micronesia for fresh water or continue straight to the Hawaiian Islands and then land along the southern California coast.

Or they could go the southern way across the Pacific: by sailing south to Java, Bali and Sumba Island and then through the Torres Straits between New Guinea and Australia eastward into the Pacific. From there they could head for Rotuma Island in the very north of Fiji or to the Fiji Islands themselves. From here they would continue eastward to Tonga, Tahiti and the Marquesas Islands to finally reach a sandy bay in Mexico such as Acapulco.

The sandy beaches of the Cham Islands are reached from the mainland in a day by boat. These islands were first settled some 3,000 years ago according to archeologists. If the Cham were the first settlers, then we could extend the reign of the Cham people

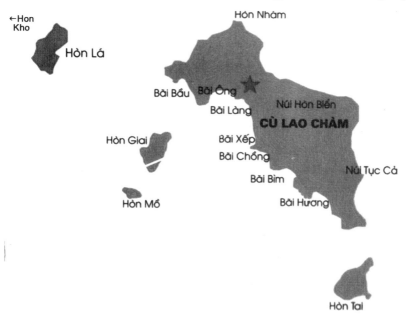

CHAM ISLANDS

Hòn Ông

back to 1000 BC, which puts them within the time frame of the early Olmecs.

Today there are about 3,000 people living on the Cham Islands in small fishing villages. Some curious features on Lao include a rock-cut, square well that, amazingly, provides clear fresh water all year round, while most wells have salty, brackish water. There are many good beaches that are ideal for dragging ships up onto, plus cliffs with millions of swallows and several ancient temples including the Ong temple where a "giant fish" is buried and "worshipped." Could this possibly be one of the giant Cham ships, now buried on the island?

In 2007, races were held at the Cham Islands to swim the channel between the islands and the mainland. It was won by Rudy van Bork, a Dutch swimmer, who did the 25 km stretch in just six hours and seven minutes. Van Bork is actually the second person to accomplish the channel swim, as Akkiko Izawa, a female swimmer from Japan, performed the feat in 2002. The Dutch swimmer competed with ten Japanese and two Vietnamese rivals. About 20 volunteers on boats, kayaks and speedboats accompanied the swimmers to ensure safety.

"It was a great race," said van Bork in the local tourist publication. "It is strange to swim in a direction with only seawater on the horizon. After several hours I start seeing some land and structures. Then I knew I could finish the adventure."

As the moon began to rise over the ocean, I thought of the adventurous Cham and their far-flung journeys. Where did they originate? Well, Cham, or Kam, is a familiar name in many places, including Kampuchea and Cambodia. Also, Kam is the name of ancient Egypt. The ancient Egyptians called their land Khemit, or "Kam-et," or "Kem-it." Were the Cham of Vietnam the same as the Kam of Egypt? Egypt-Kam is located in northeast Africa, and many Egyptians were Black Africans, including a number of the Pharaohs. The famous Giza Sphinx is thought to depict a Black African with thick lips and a wide nose.

Egypt-Kam had the advantage of having ports on both the Mediterranean Sea and the Red Sea. From the Red Sea ports, the Kam seafarers could journey to the Maldives, Sri Lanka, India,

60

Indonesia, Vietnam and beyond. The ancient Kam seafarers could continue across the Pacific to the coasts of North and South America. Easter Island would have been used as a stopover on return voyages from South America.

Yet, Egypt-Kam could also send out ships to reach the Atlantic coasts of Mesoamerica by leaving from their Mediterranean ports. It is now thought that the ancient Spanish port of Tartessos, near Cadiz, was originally an Egyptian-Kam port, which was later taken over by the Phoenicians.

Had Egypt circumnavigated the world in 1400-1000 BC and established ports in the Olmec areas of Mesoamerica, the Tiwanaku areas of Peru, and on such Pacific Islands as Tonga, Pohnpei (with the city of Nan Madol), Samoa, Tahiti, Hawaii, Easter Island and others? Apparently, their main port in Southeast Asia was the Cham Islands and the trading ports on the mainland opposite, where the bustling modern cities of Da Nang and Hue stand today.

I took one last look at a statue of Shiva, his third eye distinct on his forehead. He was no doubt content on his mountaintop home in the Himalayas. Yet his calm and reassuring smile reached the world over, to Cham and the Pacific Islands beyond.

The Mysterious Kingdom of Zabaj

One name, it would seem, for a Champa territory was Zabaj or Zabag, thought to have been an ancient kingdom located south of China somewhere on the oceans around Borneo. It may have been a far-flung Cham outpost in the Sulu Archipelago—the southern most islands of the Philippines.

A number of historians associated this kingdom with the Cham offshoot of Srivijaya, established circa 650 AD, which was located somewhere in southern Sumatra. The exact location is debatable. Historians have proposed other possible locations such as northern Borneo, Sulawesi and the Philippines. Likely it refers to a collection of seaborne city-states that was part of the vast Champa realm. As this vast empire broke up starting around the time of Srivijaya, the Champa realm began to shrink.

The naval force of a Maharaja of Zabaj played a major role in a legend recorded by an Arabic merchant name Sulaimaan in 851, and published by the historian Masoudi in his 947 book *Meadows of Gold and Mines of Gems*. Masoudi includes a chapter in the book about the Legend of the Maharaja of Zabaj.

The story is about a young Khmer ruler in Cambodia who one day made a remark to a faithful councilor in a fit of jealousy while holding court. "I have one desire that I would like to satisfy," said the young ruler.

"What is that desire, O King?" inquired his councilor.

"I wish to see before me on a plate," said the monarch, "the head of the King of Zabaj."

"I do not wish, O King, that my sovereign should express such a desire," the minister answered. "The Khmer and Zabaj have never manifested hatred towards each other, either in words or in acts. Zabaj has never done us any harm. What the King has said should not be repeated."

The Khmer ruler was angered by this good advice, raised his voice and repeated his desire in a loud voice so that he was heard by all of the generals and nobles who were present at court. Word of the young ruler's impetuous outburst passed from mouth to mouth until it finally arrived at the court of the Maharaja of Zabaj.

Upon hearing the words of the Khmer ruler, the Maharaja ordered his councilor to prepare a thousand ships for departure. When the fleet was ready, the Maharaja himself went aboard and announced to the crowd on shore that he would be making a pleasure trip amongst his islands. Once at sea, however, the Maharaja ordered the armada to proceed to the capital of the Khmer ruler, where his troops took the Khmers by surprise, seized the city, and surrounded the palace. After the Khmer ruler had been captured, he was brought before the Maharaja of Zabaj.

"What caused you to form a desire which was not in your power to satisfy, which would not have given you happiness if you had realized it, and would not even have been justified if it had been easily realizable?" inquired the Maharaja of Zabaj.

Since the Khmer king had nothing to say in return, the Maharaja of Zabaj continued. "You have manifested the desire to see before you my head on a plate. If you also had wished to seize my country and my kingdom or even only to ravage a part of it, I would have done the same to you. But since you have only expressed the first of these desires, I am going to apply to you the treatment you wished to apply to me, and I will then return to my country without taking anything belonging to the Khmer, either of great or small value." When the Maharaja returned to his own palace back home, he seated himself on the throne. Set before him was a plate upon which rested the head of the former Khmer king.

The King of Zabaj was able to magically have the head of the Khmer ruler sent to his capital in Zabaj. This story of karma, magic, and right thinking illustrates how one of the Champa outlying islands, such as Java, Bali, Sumba, Sulawesi—or even the Sulu Islands of the Philippines—were thought of as having a magical naval force that could project their power to formerly friendly cities that were now enemies. The kind of powers that are attributed to the Maharaja of Zabaj are those generally reserved for the Hindu

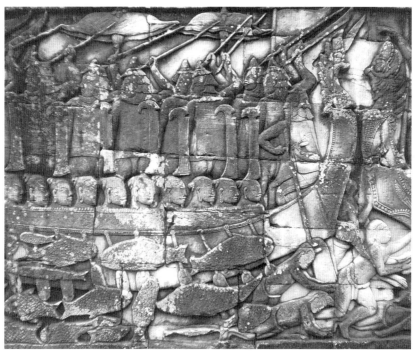

The back of a ship of Cham-Khmer sailors from the Bayon Temple, Angkor Wat.

gods themselves: Rama, Hanuman, Krishna and many others who flew through the air in their vimanas and fought their foes psychic powers as well as deadly mechanical weapons.

Did the King of Zabaj also have the power to levitate millions of tons of basalt logs in such places as Gunung Padang in Java or Nan Madol on Pohnpei Island in Micronesia? Indeed, the vast ruins of artificial islands and canals at Nan Madol (to be discussed in a later chapter) could have held the fleet of a thousand ships that the King of Zabaj was said to have. Was faraway Zabaj the island of Pohnpei?

A document with similar tales of flight and remote Cham kingdoms is the Hindu Indian text *Harscha Charita of Bana*, from about 600 AD, translated by E.B. Cowell and F.H. Thomas (1897, Oriental Translation Fund, London[20]). This book was quoted by the British ancient astronaut theorist W. Raymond Drake in his 1968 book *Gods and Spacemen of the Ancient East*.[19] Drake used the rare text largely because it mentions ancient aircraft, but it also mentions Champa.

The *Harscha Charita of Bana*, is a Sanskrit text, the oldest known copy is from 600 AD. It tells the story of Harscha, a young prince who becomes a king after many trials and tribulations. As king he now wants to attack and seek vengeance against the King of Ganda. He calls in the commander of his war elephants, a knowledgeable general named Shandagupta. Shandagupta gives the young king a long speech, shortened here, about the disasters which befell other kings and princes due to mistaken carelessness. His tale includes a flying machine and mentions the Champa kingdom of Southeast Asia. Says Shandagupta:

> Dismiss therefore this universal confidingness, so agreeable to the habits of your own land and springing from innate frankness of spirit. Of disasters due to mistaken carelessness frequent reports come daily to your Majesty's hearing...
>
> The fate of the Yavanna King was encompassed by the holder of his golden chariot, who read the letters of a

document reflected in his crest jewel.

By slashes of drawn swords Viduratha's army minced the avaricious Mathura King Brihadratha while he was digging treasure at dead of night.

Vatsapati who was wont to take his pleasure in elephant forests was imprisoned by Prahasena's soldiers issuing from the belly of a sham elephant [Trojan Horse?]…

Kakavarna, being curious of marvels, was carried away, no one knows whither, on an artificial aerial car made by a Yavanna condemned to death.

…The life of the chaste-loving Pushnava, King of Cammidi, was sipped [absorbed, such as by quicksand], while he was extirpating [eliminating] rhinoceroses of the Lord of Champa's soldiers ensconced in a grove of tall-stemmed reeds.[20]

Raymond Drake explains that Yavanna was the general term for any light-skinned Westerners who were generally thought to all be "Greeks" from the Eastern Mediterranean. Drake further likens the term Yavanna to the Arab notion that all Europeans during the Crusades were "Franks."[19]

So, this curious section from the *Harscha Charita of Bana*, mentions a number of apparently famous historical incidents including a king being carried away—never to be seen again—on an aerial vehicle constructed by some western visitor, who was a prisoner. Perhaps it was a simple balloon-type vehicle capable of a long voyage with a good wind and a knowledgeable meteorologist. Or perhaps it was an even more complicated winged and powered craft.

This tantalizing bit of information, a mere teaser to a bigger story, is very intriguing to me. It is not unusual to have a valued captive from a foreign power, such as this unnamed Yavanna-person, as a hostage who can provide valuable scientific knowledge. This knowledge is often of an alchemical nature in that it involves minerals and chemistry, the making of explosives and metals, and even such arcane trades as making flying machines.

Who Are the Champa and Cham?

In this fascinating tidbit of a story we might imagine the prisoner extolling his vast knowledge of many subjects to the king, Kakavarna, who was curious of marvels. Then one day, after much preparation, the king, the imprisoned inventor, and presumably a small staff for the king, making a total of five or six, began their journey—westward?—never to be seen again.

The next paragraph is about a man named Pushnava, King of Cammidi, who was apparently famously known to have been devoured by a swamp while hunting down rhinoceroses in the land of the Champa. To be sipped by a swamp was to be trampled into mud by the rhinos he and his companions were hunting, or swallowed into the quicksand of a mud hole in a watery swamp of tall reeds.

The Javan rhinoceros, slightly smaller than the Indian rhinoceros, once roamed southern China and Vietnam and until recently roamed Sumatra and Java. So this story may be referencing the Champa lands in Sumatra, Java or Vietnam. The distribution of elephants—an animal very important to the Champa—was wider, as we shall see in the next chapter. It seems that rhinos were largely hunted for sport and for their food and medicinal value and have virtually been hunted to extinction. Today the Javan rhinoceros is critically endangered and the last Vietnamese rhinoceros reportedly died in 2011.

Much of the charm of the *Harscha Charita of Bana* is the way it mentions a wide variety of tales as if they are common knowledge, yet we know nothing about them today except for this tantalizing reference. This book illustrated how books and knowledge, have been destroyed throughout history. An entire library seems to be missing about the Cham.

In another interesting passage in Drake's book, he says:

> The Buddhist monk, Gunavarman, in the fourth century
> AD claimed to have flown from Ceylon to Java in order to
> convert its King to the Wisdom of the 'Way of the eight paths.'
> The day before his landing, the King's mother dreamed that
> a great Master had descended from the sky in a flying ship.

As the dawn sun illumined the earth, Gunavarman arrived; believed to be a messenger from the Gods he was treated with immense respect. All the beholders marveled to see a glittering vessel glide and land without the slightest sound.[19]

Drake continues:

Another Jataka [tale of Buddha and early Buddhism] told of a King in Benares who owned a vehicle decked with jewels which flew in the air; the dramatist Bhavahuti in the fifth century AD wrote about a flying vehicle used for general work in the community by local council officials. In his remarkable *War in Ancient India*[21] Ramachandra Dikshitar recalls that the Vikramarvastya (Drona, p 176) King Puruvrasvas rode in an aerial car to rescue Urvasi in pursuit of the Danava, who was carrying her away.

The story of the Buddhist monk Gunavarman is a well-known one. He is known for bringing Buddhism to Java circa 400 AD. After being born in Kashmir, he is said to have gone to China, although originally planning to go to Java. His aerial voyage takes him from Sri Lanka to China and back to Sri Lanka, where he finally flies to Java, fulfilling the prophecy of the dream of the King's mother, with a glowing craft, possibly disk-shaped, landing silently on the temple grounds.

Drake's mention of the classic 1944 book by Indian-Oxford professor Ramachandra Dikshitar is important. *War in Ancient India*[21] is a scholarly treatise on how wars were waged in ancient India—according to ancient Sanskrit texts. No other book, published up to this time, could authoritatively say that these old Hindu (and Buddhist or Jain) texts were describing actual aerial vehicles that were armed and could be shot down.

The professor was criticized at the time for including a chapter on aerial warfare which assumed that the ancients had flying machines and other weapons. He responded that he was only a student of the texts and this is what they described. His book does not include the many later Buddhist texts, such as those referenced by Drake, since they do not usually have anything to do with warfare.

Vishnampet R. Ramachandra Dikshitar was born in 1896 in the southern Indian state of Tamil Nadu, and was a historian, Indologist and Dravidologist. He was a professor of history and archaeology at the University of Madras and authored a number of standard textbooks on Indian history. In 1928, he was appointed as a lecturer at the University of Madras. He was promoted to reader in 1946 and made Professor in 1947. Dikshitar specialized in Indian history in general, and Tamil history in particular. He was a renowned Sanskrit scholar of his time.

He published a number of scholarly books, including *Some Pandya Kings of the Thirteenth Century* (1930); *The Śilappadikāram* (1939); *War in Ancient India* (1944); *Origin and Spread of the Tamils* (1947); *Pre-historic South India* (1951); and others.

We can find an updated biography for him on his Wikipedia page:

> Ramachandra Dikshitar introduced a new methodology in the study of ancient Indian history. His book *Warfare in Ancient India* speaks of the usage of vimanas in wars in ancient India and claims that the boomerang was invented in South India. As a result, this book is widely referenced by the historians of the Sangh Parivar for its notes on vimanas and by Dravidologists for its theory on the origin of boomerangs.
>
> He believed that... *vimanas* were quite real as evidenced by his writings in *Warfare in Ancient India*.
>
> ...In his *Origin and Spread of the Tamils*, Dikshitar includes Australia and Polynesia among the regions known to the ancient South Indians thereby suggesting that South Indian traders might have at least had a general idea of existence of the Australian continent even before it was discovered by Portuguese and Dutch sea-farers of the 16th and 17th centuries.

So, we can see that Dr. Dikshitar was someone who did not follow the official dogma of his time and instead pursued the ancient texts—wherever they led him. Let us now look at what he concluded from the ancient texts in his book *War in Ancient India*.

The Contribution of Ancient India to the Science of Aeronautics

Dr. Dikshitar begins his chapter called "Aerial Warfare in Ancient India" in his 1944 book with several paragraphs on how interesting it is that India was an early contributor to the then newly emerging science of aeronautics, including airplanes, zeppelins, blimps and other aircraft:

> No question can be more interesting in the present circumstance of the world than India's contribution to the science of aeronautics. There are numerous illustrations in our vast Puranic and epic literature to show how well and wonderfully the ancient Indians conquered the air. To glibly characterize everything found in this literature as imaginary and summarily dismiss it as unreal has been the practice of both Western and Eastern scholars until very recently. The very idea indeed was ridiculed and people went so far as to assert that it was physically impossible for man to use flying machines. But today what with balloons, aeroplanes and other flying machines a great change has come over our ideas on the subject.
>
> The use and value of air forces is not hard to assess. Their chief use lay until recently in the rapidity and skill with which the men flying did the scouting and reported to headquarters. They located the position of the enemy, which enabled them to direct the attack. We know from modern history that the French were the first to use balloons for this purpose. The discovery of aeroplanes has revolutionised the realm of strategy and tactics. The present World War has demonstrated that before the air army everything else pales into insignificance.
>
> Turning to Vedic literature, in one of the *Brahmanas*

occurs the concept of a ship that sails heavenwards. The ship is the Agnihotra of which the Ahavaniya and Garhapatya fires represent the two sides bound heavenward, and the steersman is the Agnihotrin who offers milk to the three Agnis. Again in the still earlier *Rg Veda Samhita* we read that the Asvins conveyed the rescued Bhujya safely by means of winged ships. The latter may refer to the aerial navigation in the earliest times.

In the recently published *Samarangana Sutradhara* of Bhoja, a whole chapter of about 230 stanzas is devoted to the principles of construction underlying the various flying machines and other engines used for military and other purposes. The various advantages of using machines, especially flying ones, are given elaborately. Special mention is made of their attacking visible as well a invisible objects, of their use at one's will and pleasure, of their uninterrupted movements, of their strength and durability, in short of their capability to do in the air all that is done on earth. After enumerating and explaining a number of other advantages, the author concludes that even impossible things could be affected through them. Three movements are usually ascribed to these machines—ascending, cruising thousands of miles in different directions in the atmosphere and lastly descending. It is said that in an aerial car one can mount up to the Suryamandala 'solar region' and the Naksatra mandala (stellar region) and also travel throughout the regions of air above the sea and the earth. These cars are said to move so fast as to make a noise that could be heard faintly from the ground. Still some writers have expressed a doubt and asked 'Was that true?' But the evidence in its favour is overwhelming.

The make of machines for offence and defense to be used on the ground and in the air is described. ...Considering briefly some of the flying machines alone that find distinct mention in this work, we find that they were of different shapes like those of elephants, horses, monkeys, different kinds of birds, and chariots. Such vehicles were made usually of wood. We quote in this connection the following stanzas so as to give an idea of the materials and size, especially as we are in the days of rigid airships navigating the air for a very long time and at a long distance as well. [21]

The professor goes on to give some direct quotes, with sanksrit text and then his English translation beneath them. He then provides us with the famous text from the *Samarangana Sutradhara* of Bhoja describing a craft that is obviously a winged airplane:

An aerial car is made of light wood looking like a great bird with a durable and well-formed body having mercury inside and fire at the bottom. It has two resplendent wings, and is propelled by air. It flies in the atmospheric regions for a great distance and carries several persons along with it. The inside construction resembles heaven created by Brahma himself. Iron, copper, lead and other metals are also used for these machines. [21]

Dr. Dikshitar is absolutely certain that there was flight in ancient times and goes on to defend himself in the face of the considerable criticism that was leveled at him when he first wrote about the sophistication and glory of ancient India, including aerial warfare:

All these show how far art was developed in ancient India in this direction. Such elaborate descriptions ought to meet the criticism that the vimanas and similar aerial vehicles mentioned in ancient Indian literature should be relegated to the region of myth.

The ancient writers could certainly make a distinction between the mythical which they designated *daiva* and the actual aerial wars designated *manusa*. [21]

Dr. Dikshitar tells the tale of King Satrujit who is presented with a magic horse that can convey him anywhere on earth as he wishes and then discusses other "magical" conveyances including references in the *Ramayana*:

> King Satrujit was presented by a Brahman Galava with a horse named Kuvalaya which had the power of conveying him to any place on the earth. If this had any basis in fact it must have been a flying horse. There are numerous references both in the *Visnupurana* and the *Mahabharata* where Krsna is said to have navigated the air on the Garuda. Either the accounts are imaginary or they are a reference to an eagle-shaped machine flying in the air. Subrahmanya used a peacock as his vehicle and Brahma a swan. Further, the Asura, Maya by name, is said to have owned an animated golden car with four strong wheels and having a circumference of 12,000 cubits, which possessed the wonderful power of flying at will to any place. It was equipped with various weapons and bore huge standards. And in the battle between the Devas and the Asuras in which Maya took a leading part, several warriors are represented as riding birds.
>
> In the *Ramayana* when Ravana was flying with Sita in his aerial car to Lanka, Jatayu, a giant bird, charged him and his car and this led to a duel between the bird and the Raksasa king. Golikere draws attention to a number of instances where fierce duels have been fought between man and bird of prey resulting in the damage of the aeroplane and its inmates, in some cases leading to a forced landing. Again, the Raksasa Dronamukha offers his services to Ravana in his encounter with the vanara hosts to fight them either on the sea or in the sky or in subterranean regions. After the great victory of Rama over Lanka, Vibhisana presented him with the Pushpaka vimana which was furnished with windows, apartments, and excellent seats. It was capable of accommodating all the vanaras besides Rama, Sita and Laksmana. Rama flew to his capital Ayodhya pointing [out] to Sita from above the places of encampment, the town of Kiskindha and others on the way. Again Valmiki beautifully compares the city of Ayodhya to an aerial car.

Finally, he goes on to why the knowledge and science of these flying machines was a dying art in ancient times, but was real nonetheless, with winged planes and tubular airships that were built in numbers (100 or 200? More?) and were used by royalty and military commanders in ancient times. Clearly, if such flights were being made in the Hindu-Buddhist world of 1000 BC to 500 AD, many of them would have been made to Cham areas in Cambodia and Vietnam plus the many islands which took months to reach by boat (of which there were many). These island ports and airports would have included Java, Bali, Sulawesi, Sumba, and beyond.

Indeed, it is interesting here to look at the revolution that swept India and Southeast Asia—including Cham—which is the reign of Asoka.

Asoka and Nine Unknown Men

The story of the Nine Unknown Men was apparently a common one among Buddhists and Hindus in India and was mentioned by the French researcher Louis Jacolliot in the 1860s. According to Jacolliot, the society of the Nine Unknown Men was formed around 320 BC by the Mauryan Emperor Asoka. Asoka campaigned in the regions to his south, between Calcutta and Madras, a region known as the Kalingan Kingdom. The Kalingans resisted Asoka and the emperor's overwhelming forces are said to have killed over 100,000 Kalinga warriors and deported over 150,000 villagers to other areas of India. However, Asoka thought deeply about the violence that his victory entailed and from that time became a Buddhist and renounced military campaigns.

He was still the ruler of a powerful and prosperous kingdom that spanned across northern India all the way to Afghanistan in the west and as far south as the border of the Tamil-Nadu area. His empire also stretched eastward into Burma and Southeast Asia. Asoka is well known for his efforts to spread Buddhism throughout India, Sri Lanka, Malaya, the Cham areas, and Indonesia. Asoka's efforts contributed to Buddhism's rise in a later period when missionaries spread over the Himalayas into Nepal, Tibet, China and Mongolia.

Asoka became a vegetarian but did not force others to be, and was tolerant of other religious sects of the time. He did, however, prohibit the consumption of alcohol. He wanted to bring together the most important knowledge in the world and so assembled the Nine Unknown Men.

The Nine Unknown Men are mentioned in the 1960 book *The Morning of the Magicians* by Louis Pauwels and Jacques Bergier.[11] They said that the Nine Unknown Men had been founded by the Indian Emperor Asoka and that Pope Silvester II had met these men at one point. Much of their material, they said, came from Louis Jacolliot, a nineteenth century French colonial administrator and writer who insisted on the reality of the Nine Unknown Men. Say Pauwels and Bergier:

> ...[Asoka] renounced the idea of trying to integrate the rebellious people, declaring that the only true conquest was to win men's hearts by observance of the laws of duty and piety, because the Sacred Majesty desired that all living creatures should enjoy security, peace and happiness and be free to live as they pleased. ...he sought to prevent his fellow man from putting their intelligence towards perpetrating evil, particularly the evil involved with warfare. The task of collecting, preserving, and containing all knowledge was too great for one emperor to do alone, not the least because of the other duties required by ruling an empire. So Asoka summoned nine of the most brilliant minds in India at the time. For security purposes, the identity of these men was never made public. Together, these geniuses formed a secret society that came to be known as the Nine Unknown Men.[11]

This organization began accumulating all of the scientific knowledge possible, from natural science to psychology to the composition of matter. Asoka feared that if ordinary men were given too much scientific and technical knowledge it would be used for destruction, so only the Nine Men were allowed to study and develop scientific technology that was to be definitive. Each of the nine was charged with a specific science and was to write a book that he was to update and revise as the knowledge was expanded. When one of the nine could no longer complete the task—whether from the wish to retire, fading health, or death—the obligation was passed to a chosen successor. The number of members in the society was always to be nine. And in this way the secret society of the Nine Unknown Men has allegedly lived on for more than 2,000 years.

In 1923 the British (and later American) pulp writer Talbot Mundy serialized his novel *The Nine Unknown* in *Adventure* magazine. It has since been published in various hardback and paperback editions. His book was a fictionalized version of the Nine Unknown Men and contained a list of the nine books. Mundy's book starts with the project commissioned by Asoka to gather and guard advanced knowledge from around the world over the years and turn it into nine books. Mundy's story focuses only on Book Four, a book on metallurgy that reveals the secret process of producing gold and silver in colossal amounts, to be used as an economic weapon. Mundy's list of the nine books has come to be generally accepted by researchers and seems to have come from Jacolliot and the Theosophical Society:

> 1. *Propaganda*: The first book dealt with techniques of propaganda and psychological warfare. "The most dangerous of all sciences is that of molding mass opinion, because it would enable anyone to govern the whole world," according to Mundy. 2. *Physiology*: The second book discussed physiology and explained how to kill a person simply by touching him or her; known as the 'the touch of death,' it involved the reversal of a nerve impulse. It is said that the martial art of Judo is a result of 'leakages' from the second book. 3. *Microbiology*: The third book

focused on microbiology and biotechnology. 4. *Alchemy*: The fourth book dealt with alchemy and transmutation of metals. Mundy says that according to legend, in times of severe drought, temples and religious relief organizations received large quantities of gold from "a secret source." 5. *Communication*: The fifth book contained a study of all means of communication, terrestrial and extraterrestrial, alluding that the Nine Unknown Men were aware of extraterrestrials. 6. *Gravity*: The sixth book focused on the secrets of gravitation and contained instructions on how to make a flying machine known as a vimana. 7. *Cosmogony*: The seventh book contained cosmogony and all matters of the universe. 8. *Light*: The eighth book dealt with the properties of light such as the speed of light and how to use it as a weapon. 9. *Sociology*: The ninth book was about sociology. It included rules for the evolution of human societies and a means of foretelling their eventual decline.

This fascinating list of books, allegedly from the time of Asoka, is an advanced look at the important sciences that should be studied by any society seeking knowledge and technology. The fact that alchemy (metallurgy in general) and gravity are being studied—as well as uses for light—is an indication of the seriousness of these books and that at least some knowledge in these various areas was accumulated. Although it is not explicitly spoken of here, the nine books hint at the knowledge of electricity and power tools used for cutting and dressing rock. Is it possible that Asoka and the Nine Unknown Men had accumulated a wide assortment of flying machines, weapons and power tools?

Pauwels and Bergier get most of their information from the French colonial judge, author and lecturer Louis Jacolliot (1837-1890). Jacolliot was a lawyer who lived several years in Tahiti as a colonial judge and later in India during the period 1865-1869. He wrote several pamphlets, and his important *Occult Science in India* was published in 1875 (the English translation was published in 1884). Jacolliot was searching for the 'Indian roots of western occultism' and was apparently a prolific writer for his time. He was fascinated by India and during his time there he collected Hindu and Buddhist myths, which he popularized starting with his 1874 book *Histoire des Vierges: Les Peuples et les continents disparus* which combined a lost continent in the Pacific with ancient Hindu myths. Jacolliot claimed that 'Sanskrit tablets' told the story of a sunken land called Rutas in the Indian Ocean. Having been in Tahiti and Tonga and seen the megaliths there, he relocated this lost continent to the Pacific Ocean. He believed that Rutas was connected to the Atlantis myth. Jacolliot's story is very similar to the tale told by the British Colonel James Churchward in his 1924 book *The Lost Continet of Mu*.[12] It would seem that Churchward took some of his ideas from Jacolliot, as did Helena Blavatsky and Talbot Mundy.

Helena Blavatsky in her 1877 book *Isis Unveiled* quoted from Jacolliot and touted his belief in a lost Pacific continent which she also argued for—and called Lemuria, a name proposed in 1864 by a German geologist named Philip Sclater. Like Blavatsky and her mysterious sources, Jacolliot makes reference to an otherwise unknown Sanskrit text called the *Agrouchada-Parikchai,* which was apparently his personal invention, a mixture of Sanskrit texts and a bit of Freemasonry.

The claim of Pope Sylvester II meeting the Nine Unknown Men is a curious one. Pope Sylvester II—originally known as Gerbert of Aurillac—was the first French Pope and only reigned for five years, from 999 to his death in 1003. Pope Sylvester II was a prolific scholar and teacher. He endorsed and promoted study of Arab and Greco-Roman arithmetic, mathematics, and astronomy, reintroducing to Europe the abacus and armillary sphere, which had been lost to Latin (though not Byzantine) Europe since the end of the Greco-Roman era. He is said to have been the first person to introduce the decimal system using Arabic numerals to Europe.

Pope Sylvester II/Gerbert was supposed to possess a bronze head that was a computer of some kind and was capable of speech and answering yes and no questions. This bronze head was called Meridiana and was said to have a female voice that spoke to Gerbert, the new Pope Sylvester II.

A statue of Shiva's consort Parvati at the Museum of Cham Culture in Da Nang.

This talking object, according to popular legend, told Gerbert that if he should ever read a mass in Jerusalem, the Devil would come for him. The Pope then cancelled a scheduled pilgrimage to Jerusalem; however, while still in Rome he read mass in the church Santa Croce in Gerusalemme ('Holy Cross of Jerusalem'). He became sick very shortly afterward and on his deathbed he asked his cardinals to cut up his body and scatter it across the city.

This man is probably the most mysterious of all the Catholic Popes—could he have actually met with the ongoing secret society of the Nine Unknown Men? Clearly Gerbert is suspected of having a magical device that sounds a lot like a modern radio or wireless Internet device. A tract from the time accused him of being involved with demons, largely because of the time he had spent in Spain, but also because he had the magical talking bronze head. Had the group known as the Nine Unknown Men given this device to Gerbert before he became Pope? Pauwels and Bergier believed this to be the case, as did apparently Jacolliot. It is an amazing thought!

What concerns us here is that Asoka was the man who convened the Nine Unknown Men and this spread of science, social justice, technology and the icons and memes of Buddhism and Hinduism grew not only from India to the west but also from India to the east. Because of the many large islands and archipelagos of small islands in Southeast Asia (reaching northward in a great arch to Japan and then far eastward into the Pacific) the spread of Asoka's philosophy and his quest for knowledge would require the use of ships.

Indeed, he had his own fleet of ships by which to spread his social message, but there were many other fleets of ships that were plying the waters of India, Sri Lanka, Malagasy, Sumatra and

A statue of Shiva with Cham features at the Museum of Cham Culture in Da Nang.

Java. The king of all these ancient navies was that of the Cham, which matched or surpassed the naval power of Egypt and India, but operating in the vast archipelago of islands in Southeast Asia. Some of their cities were on the mainland—on a river and close to the coast, such as My Son in Vietnam—and mountain tribes would freely come down to these coastal ports and trade. The Phoenicians in North Africa, Cyprus and the eastern Mediterranean did much the same with the mountain and desert tribes who came in caravans to their port cities full of many ships. Though the Phoenicians or the Cham did not rule these interior areas of Morocco or Vietnam, they

A Cham king with the wide nose and lips at the Museum of Cham Culture.

were nominally within their control, mainly in an economic sense. There was no need to try to conquer nearby mountain areas—or any areas—as their superior way of building, trading and socializing was conducive to locals wanting to be part of their society. These locals and country village people could benefit tremendously from the port facilities and shipping of cargo offered by such seagoing civilizations with a large trading network.

Similarly, Asoka and his missionaries, including specialists working for the Nine Unknown Men, were voyaging to these far-flung ports in Southeast Asia in search of knowledge, including the source of metals, gems, jade, obsidian and quartz crystal. They were also searching for "soma," the elixir of immortality. This search included all kinds of psychotropic mushrooms, cacti, and other plants. Herbs and medicinal plants of all kinds were part of this worldwide search for knowledge.

It would seem that Champa was already a part of Asoka's world in 250 BC. That power tools and other machines were part of that world is obvious from the stonework at My Son and the Cham Museum in Da Nang. Work on the basalt and granite slabs and statues could only have been done with diamond saws and power tools. Metal forges and other high-tech mining skills must have been used. Not only did they have huge fleets of ships, apparently a limited few had access to airplanes or some other form of flight. Just as we have flight today, and even spaceships, we still rely on ships for most of our transport, and the ancient world of India and Cham would have been similar. While certain high-tech devices such as diamond tipped power tools and flying machines might have existed, the every day world was quite normal, with most people engaged in typical fishing and farming activities that have existed for many thousands of years. In this regard, it is thought that some rice paddies in Vietnam, the Philippines and Indonesia have been continuously used for over 4,000 years.

A Mayan Statue at the Cham Museum in Da Nang?

On the day Jennifer and I visited the Cham Museum, our taxi driver let us off at the gate to the museum. Upon entering, I was immediately impressed by the quality of the statuary. Although the art in most cases was distinctively Hindu much of it looked like Mayan or Olmec art from Mexico.

Built in 1915, the museum displays an intensive and diverse collection of Champa sculpture dating from the 7th to the 15th centuries. The museum was established by the Ecole Francaise d'Extreme Orient with a collection of artifacts gathered in central Vietnam, from Quang Binh to Binh Dinh. Today, the museum displays a trove of altars, statues and decorative works collected from Hindu and Buddhist Cham temples and towers.

Cham sculpture displays various styles, and the museum divides the statues and other art into two categories, those made before the year 1000 AD and those made thereafter. Little, if any, statuary has survived from the earliest periods of Cham art (thought to have originated sometime BC, though the earliest records are from 192 AD) and most of earliest art discovered is from 600 AD to 800 AD.

Among the masterpieces of this period on display at the museum is the Tra Kieu Altar. The altar was used for the worship of Shiva,

The Maya-looking Cham decoration stone at the Museum of Cham Culture.

the creator and destroyer of the universe, and the symbols of his creative ability, the Lingam and Yoni, are present on it. The four scenes carved around the base of the altar tell part of the story of Prince Rama, the subject of the famous *Ramayana*. In that epic, he went to the citadel of Videha to try to break the sacred bow of Rudra so that he could marry Princess Sita. Prince Rama broke the bow, a task that had been tried by many before him, and he and the princess were wed in the beginning of the epic. Later Sita runs off with—or is kidnapped by—the Prince of Lanka. After some years of penance

A Cham statue showing the wide nose and lips at the Museum of Cham Culture.

83

A Cham statue of Shiva with a round head, third eye and long ears.

and meditation, Rama goes to get her in his flying machine. Museum literature says:

> Artifacts in the Dong Duong room (the 9th and 10th centuries) create a deep impression with their vigorous, lively and exaggerated style and represent the climax of the development of Champa art. These statues of the first Champa kings, with the characteristic big eyes and noses and thick lips of the native people, show their vitality and imposing appearance. These carvings show the absolute belief that a supernatural force was supporting the rule of the Champa kings during the

period when Buddhism was the dominant force.

The second period lasted from the 11th to the 15th centuries. The devastating wars from the end of the 10th century onwards took the Champa kingdom into decline, and the relocation of the capital from Tra Kieu (Quang Nam) to Tra Ban (Binh Ding) in about the year 1000 brought about a new direction in their art. Artifacts discovered at Thap Mam (style of the 12th-14th centuries) are monumental sculptures of large animals such as elephants, makara (sea monsters) and garudas (the birds of the gods, much like the American Thunderbird) that served as protectors of the temples and towers.

After the Thap Mam period Champa art declined. The Shiva statue displayed in the Kontum room has an exhausted appearance. This was one of the last artifacts of the Champa sculptors. By the end of the 17th century the Cham dynasties came to an end.

By this time, like many Malaysians and Indonesians, the Cham had become Muslims, and embraced the religion of Islam.

Several pieces of art caught my eye as unusual and significant. One was a stone plaque that looked amazingly Mayan and Olmec to me. The Cham were said to appear African in some of their features, which is also an important factor in Olmec art. The sign with the statue said that it was "Nam Tham," a "forest spirit." I showed the statue to Jennifer, who agreed that it looked remarkably Mayan and Olmec.

Was there a connection between the Cham and the Olmecs? The Olmecs are now known to have been the predecessors of the Maya in Mesoamerica, and many of their statues depict people with the African features of thick lips and wide noses, distinctly non-American Indian traits. We do not think of the Vietnamese or Chinese as looking African, but it is admitted that the Cham had these features.

In later chapters I will show how the Cham went out through Indonesia and into the Pacific in search of gold and other metals.

A statue of the Hindu deity Dvarapala at the Museum of Cham Culture.

Chapter Two

WAR ELEPHANTS ACROSS THE PACIFIC

The stumbling way in which even the ablest of
scientists in every generation have had to fight
through thickets of erroneous observations,
misleading generalizations, inadequate
formulations and unconscious prejudice is rarely
appreciated by those who obtain their scientific
knowledge from textbooks.
—James Bryant Conant

In order to establish the kind of far-reaching empire that the Cham apparently had, it was necessary for them to master the very high technology that included casting large metal cauldrons and drilling and cutting very hard stone objects that became balls, tubes or megalithic statues. They had metal mining tools and metal weapons. They had fleets of hundreds and hundreds of large ships. These ships all had metal fittings, large sails, cabins and men to man the many oars. They also carried animals. Along with hogs and chickens they carried elephants. Elephants were important to the Champa and others in Southeast Asia and India. They were often carried in ships and exported, mainly to Persia and the Middle East where they were highly valued. War elephants from Sri Lanka were said to the be the largest and best trained of all the war elephants available in the Middle Ages. They were brought by ship from Sri Lanka (and also Kerala in India) to ports in Persia or Iraq.

Elephants were extremely important to all the civilizations of

Southeast Asia from India to Vietnam and were an essential part of any army of the time, more than horses, cows or oxen. So, while it may seem astonishing that the Champa brought elephants with them to Central America, Mexico and the American Southwest, when we see the amazing ability and obvious advantage that war elephants could bring to the battlefield I expect to show that this transpacific voyaging of elephants to the Americas probably happened on many occasions. War elephants were an important part of the ancient world, but are poorly understood.

Elephants and Ships

Some historians have suggested that the Asiatic elephant once resided in the marshes of southern Persia and Iraq, giving rise to the name 'Syrian' elephant. This elephant was extinct by 100 BC or earlier. Other researchers have considered these elephants extinct much earlier, and there has been some confusion as to how many species of elephants there are in the world. For a long time it was thought that there were just two species of elephant: the African elephant (*Loxodonta africana*) and the Asian elephant (*Elephas maximus*). The Asian elephant is Asia's largest land animal and is distributed from India and Sri Lanka to Southeast Asia and Indonesia as far to the east as the island of Borneo. How elephants came to exist in northern Borneo (they are not in the southern part of the island) is a mystery. It is possible that the Champa brought them to Borneo from the Vietnam-Cambodia area. The Asian elephant is said to have three subspecies: *E. m. maximus* from Sri Lanka, the *E. m. indicus* from mainland Asia, and *E. m. sumatranus* from the island of Sumatra.

The controversial Borneo elephant is smaller than the normal Asian elephant and is also known as the Borneo pygmy elephant. A definitive subspecific classification of *Elephas maximus borneensis* has not yet been given, awaiting genetic testing. Interestingly, Wikipedia has this to say about the Borneo elephant (note that it mentions elephants being sent as gifts and traveling by ship):

Elephants were appropriate gifts from one ruler to another, or to a person of high standing, and it was customary to transport them by sea. In about 1395, the Raja of Java gave two elephants to the ruler Raja Baginda of Sulu. These animals were reputedly the founders of a feral population at the western end of Borneo. When in 1521 the remnants of Ferdinand Magellan's circumnavigation of the Earth reached Brunei [in northern Borneo], the chronicler of the voyage recounted that the delegation from the flagship Victoria was conveyed to and from the ruler's palace on elephants caparisoned in silk. This custom had been discontinued by the time later visitors arrived in Brunei in the 1770s, who reported wild-living elephant herds that were hunted by local people after harvest. Despite the early records of royal elephants in Brunei and Banjarmasin, there was no tradition of capturing and taming local wild elephants in Borneo.

The Asian elephant is considered to be the best elephant for training and warfare. African bush elephants, which are the largest of these amazing creatures, are considered to be virtually untamable. One probably very important difference between the two species is that African elephants have larger ears and concave backs while Asian elephants have smaller ears and level backs. This makes it easier for a howdah (wooden riding platform) to be mounted on the back of the elephant. Except for some possibly taken from Ethiopia by the Ptolmaic Greek Egyptian rulers, no African bush elephants were ever used as trained elephants for warfare. However, it is now recognized that there is a third species of elephant—sometimes said to be extinct—called the African forest elephant (*L. cyclotis*).

It would seem that Hannibal and the Carthaginians of modern-day Tunisia were mostly using African forest elephants, which are smaller than the huge bush elephant, standing as high as 13 feet (four meters). However, it has been proposed that there is a fourth subspecies called the North African elephant. Says Wikipedia about the mysterious North African elephant:

> The North African elephant (*Loxodonta africana pharaoensis*) was the subspecies of the African bush elephant (*Loxodonta africana*), or possibly a separate elephant species, that existed in North Africa north of the Sahara until becoming extinct in Ancient Roman times. These were the famous war elephants used by Carthage in the Punic Wars, their conflict with the Roman Republic. Although the subspecies has been formally described, it has not been widely recognized by taxonomists. Other names for this animal include the North African forest elephant, Carthaginian elephant, and Atlas elephant. Originally, its natural range probably extended across North Africa and down to the present Sudanese and Eritrean coasts.
>
> Carthaginian frescoes and coins minted by whoever controlled North Africa at various times show very small elephants, perhaps 2.5 meters (8 ft, 2 in) at the shoulder, with the large ears and concave back typical of modern African elephants. The North African elephant was smaller than the modern African bush elephant (*L. a. africana*), probably similar in size to the modern African forest elephant (*L. cyclotis*). It is also possible that it was more docile and plainer than the African bush elephant, which is generally untamable, allowing the Punics to tame it as a war elephant by a method now lost to history.
>
> After they conquered Sicily in 242 BCE, the Romans wanted to capture some specimens that had been left behind in the middle of the island by the Carthaginians, but failed in the endeavor. The elephants with which Hannibal crossed the Pyrenees and the Alps in order to invade Italy during the Second Punic War (218-201 BCE) belonged to this group, with the exception of Hannibal's personal animal, Surus (meaning 'the Syrian,' or possibly 'One-Tusker'). This individual, according to his documented name and large size, may have been a Syrian elephant (*Elephas maximus*

asurus), a subspecies of the extant Asian elephant, which became extinct shortly after Hannibal invaded Italy but before the extinction of the North African elephant.

The North African elephant was also trained and used by the Ptolemaic dynasty of Egypt. Writing in the 2nd century BCE, Polybius (*The Histories*; 5.84) described their inferiority in battle against the larger Indian elephants used by the Seleucid kings. A surviving Ptolemaic inscription enumerates three types of war elephant, the 'Troglodytic' (probably Libyan), the 'Ethiopian,' and the 'Indian.' The Ptolemaic king prides himself with being the first to tame the Ethiopian elephants, a stock which could be identical to one of the two extant African species.

During the reign of Augustus, Roman circus games resulted in the killing of 3500 elephants.

Hannibal and the Carthaginians were said to be on smaller elephants with a less elaborate howdah on the back of the elephant. Asian elephants controlled by Indian mahouts (elephant drivers) were often in very elaborate, multi-storied howdahs, often filled

An old print of the ceremonial elephants of the Raja of Travancore, India.

with archers and other soldiers. The local king also rode on such an elaborate howdah, with bodyguards and servants around him.

It is unlikely that any of the elephants arriving in Carthage came overland. Desert dwelling elephants do live in Namibia and Mali (around rivers and large water holes) and elephants did live in Morocco in antiquity but are extinct now. Although it is not spoken of much by ancient historians, we must assume that most war elephants were delivered by ship to Carthage, Egypt, Greece, Spain, Italy or any other Mediterranean port. As reported by Wikipedia above, at least 3,500 elephants were killed in various circus games, including those at Rome. The vast majority of these elephants would have been transported at some time by ship. This was just as common in eastern Asia.

A ceremonial elephant with a mahout (driver) and howdah (carriage).

Although we do not know all of the details, elephants and other animals were commonly transported by merchant ships in the ancient world. We know that they were transported by ship to Borneo. Were they transported across the Pacific?

The Origins of the War Elephant

It is largely assumed that the war elephant originated in India or somewhere in Southeast Asia, such as Malaysia, Thailand or Vietnam, but China is another area where the training of elephants may have occurred at a very early time. This early history is not really known. It seems that elephants were domesticated thousands of years before the horse. Its origin goes back to the early mists of history and the ancient Indian text the *Rigveda* mentions elephants used for transport, but not necessarily for war. The *Mahabharata* and the *Ramayana* both mention war elephants, as well as vimanas and various types of extremely destructive weapons that could be likened to the exploding missiles of today. It is interesting to note here that in these and other old Sanskrit tales, flying machines are mentioned along with war elephants. Shall we say: it was a different world back then. Let us explore the fascinating world of the war elephant, the tank of the ancient world.

The war elephant was used for thousands of years in India and Southeast Asia, including on the Indonesian islands of Sumatra and Java, before the war elephant was brought to the Mediterranean region from Persia. There is much confusion as to where all the war elephants originated in the Mediterranean and exactly how many species of elephants actually exist. As we have seen, the African elephant, the largest of the species, lives mainly in East and Central Africa and is largely thought to be very difficult to train and therefore was probably never used as a war elephant. Rather, smaller elephants from India, Sri Lanka and Southeast Asia were used and, as noted above, were early on exported to Persia and the Middle East.

Elephants as trained war animals were already a well-honed military asset by the time Europeans first encountered them during Alexander the Great's invasion of Persia and India (started in 333

BC) at the Battle of Gaugamela (331 BC), where the Persians deployed 15 war elephants. These war elephants were placed at the center of the Persian line and made a deep impression on the Macedonian troops when they first spied the army from afar. Alexander was amazed at the sight of the war elephants and decided to make a sacrifice to the God of Fear the night before the battle. However, the elephants were apparently not deployed in the final battle because of their long march the day before. Alexander won the battle at Gaugamela, and his greatest prize was the 15 enemy elephants that he now integrated into his own army. Alexander was able to add more war elephants to his army as he captured the rest of Persia. War elephants all came with an Indian mahout or two—elephant drivers—who alone were capable of controlling the animals. These mahouts were essentially mercenaries who readily switch sides when they were captured.

Alexander continued his campaign to the east, travelling through Afghanistan with his war elephants and huge army, conquering the lands as he went. He reached the Indus River, today in modern Pakistan, in 326 BC and discovered the Hindu King Porus of the Punjab and his forces amassed on the other side of the very wide and swift-flowing waterway. King Porus had between 85 and 100 war elephants spaced out in intervals among his troops. Porus kept the war elephants facing the enemy across the river and for weeks the opposing armies eyed each other warily. Porus hoped that his war elephants would scare away Alexander's army and the invader would eventually leave and go back to Persia rather than try the risky crossing of the river to do battle.

However, Alexander's scouts had found a bend in the river some 18 miles south of the encampment that was heavily wooded and would be a good place to cross the river in a surprise move. So, leaving a double dressed as Alexander to stay behind with a large force at the main encampment, (to give spies the idea that the great general was still in the camp) Alexander and a large force crossed the river during the night.

They attacked the Hindu army of King Porus and ultimately turned the war elephants against their own soldiers. In what is now

An old print of war elephants charging at the Battle of Zama in 202 BC.

known as the Battle of the Hydaspes River, Porus' war elephants initially charged Alexander's Macedonian cavalry and created much damage with tusks fitted with iron spikes. The war elephants grabbed enemy soldiers with their trunks and threw them in the air. The hapless soldiers would then be gored by the iron-spiked tusks or trampled under the elephants' feet.

Says the Greek Historian Arrian describing the war elephants in the Battle of the Hydaspes River:

> …whenever the beasts could wheel around, they rushed forth against the ranks of infantry and demolished the phalanx of the Macedonians, dense as it was.

Alexander's Macedonian army adopted the standard tactic of fighting elephants—loosening their ranks to allow the elephants to pass through and then attacking the unarmored legs from all sides with spears and javelins while the elephants struggled to wheel around. Once the elephants had a few spears in their legs they might panic, and a wounded elephant might turn around and begin trampling its own army as it seeks to escape the pain. Because of the danger of war elephants running amok among their own troops, it has been reported that the Indian mahouts had poisoned rods to kill the beasts if they were out of control. Later, the Carthaginians had a different 'stop button' on their war elephants: a hammer and chisel were carried by the mahout who would put the chisel to the base of the elephant's skull where the neck came in and strike it with one powerful blow, bringing the giant creature to the ground almost instantly.

Alexander's men fought the war elephants by thrusting javelins and spears into their legs, and the elephants panicked in the predicable manner. Alexander's archers were able to slay the mahouts on top of the beasts and soon King Porus' army was defeated. King Porus had been on a special platform on a large war elephant in the center of his massive army. Now the defeated King was confronted by the victorious Alexander, who asked him how he would like to be treated. King Porus answered him, "Like a king."

Alexander rewarded him by giving him his kingdom back, plus several other nearby lands that Alexander had conquered, and making him a vassal of the Greek Empire that Alexander was building. However, the Battle of the Hydaspes River was to be Alexander the Great's last big victory. He learned that the kings further to the east in the Nanda Empire could deploy as many as 6,000 war elephants and such a force was too massive for even Alexander to contemplate. According to the Greek historian Plutarch, the size of the Nanda army was 200,000 infantry, 80,000 cavalry, 8,000 war chariots, and 6,000 war elephants.

Essentially, the terrific power of the Nanda Empire's war elephants discouraged Alexander's army and effectively halted its advance into India. His army turned south, and, after a few minor battles along the river, Alexander's generals informed him that they would not support any further expansion of his empire into India and wanted to return to Babylon and the Mediterranean.

Alexander reluctantly agreed and the army continued south to the Arabian Sea where some would build boats and return to Babylon by ship while others would make the long march back through Persia. On his return to Babylon, Alexander established a force of elephants to guard his palace, and created the post of elephantarch to lead his elephant units. He died shortly after this, apparently from being poisoned. He had, however, brought the war elephant into the Greek army and these tanks of the ancient world would become ever more popular as history rolled on.

War Elephants in the Mediterranean

The use of war elephants continued after Alexander's death. Alexander's huge empire was being violently carved up by various generals and relatives in campaigns known as the Wars of the Diadochi or Wars of Alexander's Successor. These wars occurred between 322 and 275 BC and it was at this time that war elephants were used in Egypt, Greece, Turkey and Israel. Says Wikipedia:

> The successors to Alexander's empire, the Diadochi, used hundreds of Indian elephants in their wars, with the Seleucid empire being particularly notable for their use of the animals, still being largely brought from India. Indeed, the Seleucid–Mauryan war of 305-303 BC [to be described later] ended with the Seleucids ceding vast eastern territories in exchange for 500 war elephants—a small part of the Maurya forces, which included up to 9,000 elephants by some accounts. The Seleucids put their new elephants to good use at the battle of Ipsus four years later, where they blocked the return of the victorious Antigonid cavalry, allowing the latter's phalanx to be isolated and defeated. Later in its history, the Seleucid Empire used elephants in its efforts to crush the Maccabean Revolt in Judea. The elephants were terrifying to the lighter-armed Jewish warriors, and the youngest of the Hasmonean brothers, Eleazar Maccabeus, famously defeated one of the creatures in the Battle of Beth Zechariah, sticking a spear under the belly of an elephant he mistakenly believed to be carrying Seleucid king Antiochus V, killing the elephant at the cost of Eleazar's own life.
>
> The first use of war elephants in Europe was made

in 318 BC by Polyperchon, one of Alexander's generals, when he besieged Megalopolis (Peloponnesus) during the wars of the Diadochi. He used 60 elephants brought from Asia with their mahouts. A veteran of Alexander's army, named Damis, helped the besieged Megalopolitans to defend themselves against the elephants and eventually Polyperchon was defeated. Those elephants were subsequently taken by Cassander and transported, partly by sea, to other battlefields in Greece.

Around this same period of 300 BC the Carthaginians began using war elephants that were presumably taken from the African forest elephant populations that roamed Morocco and areas of Mauretania in antiquity. These now-extinct elephants did not need an Indian mahout but were controlled by Phoenician-Carthaginian elephant drivers. The African forest elephant was actually smaller, harder to tame and could not swim deep rivers as compared to the Asian elephants used by the Seleucids in the eastern Mediterranean

An old print of war elephants at the Battle of Zama between Rome and Carthage.

region, particularly those from Syria, which stood 2.5 to 3.5 meters (8–10 ft) at the shoulder. These Syrian elephants were really Asian elephants from India and Sri Lanka, and they had probably been brought to Iraq by ship and then marched overland from Babylon to Syria. Other war elephants, though historians have yet to recognize this, were probably brought by ship from Kerala in southern India or nearby Sri Lanka to Egyptian ports where Alexander's Ptolemaic successors were creating their own armies and desired to have war elephants as a central component, just as Alexander had done.

With a breeding population of captive elephants in Syria and Egypt it would seem that some of these Asiatic elephants were traded and shipped via boat to Carthage where they were to be further trained and to breed with the other elephants that had come, also via ship, from coastal areas of Morocco and Mauritania. The forests of Senegal are just below Mauritania and the African forest elephant could be found there.

It is likely that at least some Syrian elephants were traded abroad. As we have seen, the favorite, and perhaps last surviving elephant of Hannibal's 218 BC crossing of the Alps was an impressive animal named Surus ('the Syrian'), and may have been of Syrian-Iraqi stock, though the evidence remains ambiguous.

The Battle of Asculum

Before the Punic Wars between Carthage and Rome in which Hannibal famously took war elephants over the Alps, there was the Battle of Asculum in 279 BC between Rome and King Pyrrhus of Epirus, who was allied with Macedonia in northwestern Greece. The battle at Asculum was the second encounter between Pyrrhus' primarily Macedonian army and several Roman legions under the command of Consul Publius Decius Mus. According to several written accounts of the engagement, the two armies were of a similar size of about 40,000 men each. The Roman force was largely made up of infantry while the Macedonian army had about 20 war elephants.

In the previous Battle of Heraclea the presence of war

elephants on the Macedonian side had helped them win the battle, so now the Roman legions had equipped a portion of their force with anti-elephant devices: special chariots fitted with long spikes on the sides meant to wound the vulnerable legs of the elephants, clay pots filled with flammable materials meant to frighten the elephants into retreat, flares to frighten the animals, and support troops who were to hurl javelins at the legs of the elephants and the mahouts controlling them. Pyrrhus' Greek army had notable advantages in both cavalry numbers and in the unique presence of the war elephants.

The battle lasted for two days and as was customary in this period, both armies deployed their cavalry on the wings with their infantry in the center. Pyrrhus held his war elephants and personal cavalry in reserve behind the central infantry group. On the first day, the Greek cavalry and elephants went largely unused because they were blocked by woodland and hills in the vicinity of the battleground. Pyrrhus' Macedonians charged the Roman first legion while another Roman force on the flank attacked the Greek camp. Pyrrhus dispatched reserve cavalry to deal with a breakthrough along his lines and ordered his horse cavalry and several elephants to attack. When the Romans withdrew to an almost inaccessible position atop a steep hill, Pyrrhus ordered his war elephants to charge the third and fourth legions in the center of the battlefield. These legions also withdrew to heavily wooded areas on high ground. At dusk both sides withdrew to their main camps with neither having gained a significant advantage.

When dawn broke, King Pyrrhus sent some light infantry to occupy the wooded high ground that had been the cause of the stalemate the previous day, thereby forcing the Roman legions to either flee or fight in the open battleground. As is typical in such battles, the infantry and cavalry charged each other and then engaged in a massive line collision of fighters who could barely move forward or backward. Then the war elephants were ordered to charge, along with light infantry, which broke through the Roman line, stomping and goring men and horses as they charged through the panicked foe. At this point the special anti-elephant devices were deployed by the Roman commanders. This was briefly effective and the elephants began to panic and charge about the Greek forces, but Greek forces moved in during the chaos and forced the Romans to retreat. The Greeks had won the battle and the war elephants had been a major factor in their victory.

The Battle of Asculum is famous in military classes as it represents a victory that also decimated the victorious forces, even while it is estimated that the Roman casualties were about 8,000 and the Greek casualties about 3,000. King Pyrrhus was said to have famously commented: "One more such victory, and we are undone."

From this comment comes the phrase often heard in military circles, 'a Pyrrhic victory,' meaning a goal that is achieved at too great a cost.

War Elephants in India

So, we have established that the use of war elephants was extensive and that elephants were commonly transported on ships. After the Pyrrhic victory of the Greek king in his attempted invasion of Rome in 279 BC, the Carthaginian general Hannibal reached the Po Valley in 217 BC with his elephants, having taken them across the Alps from southern France. These elephants were also taken by ship across the Mediterranean, hanging from special harnesses inside the Carthaginian war ships. These elephants later succumbed to disease and Carthage ultimately lost its war with Rome.

Some historians think that the defeated Carthaginian fleet left Carthage and other North African ports and went west across the Atlantic to the Yucatan area of the Gulf of Mexico. Did they bring some war elephants with them? It is a fascinating thought.

Though war elephants were popular in the Mediterranean for a few hundred years up to 100 BC, it was in India, Sri Lanka, China and the mysterious land of Cham in Vietnam, Cambodia and elsewhere that they were used most extensively. War elephants have probably been used in India and Southeast Asia since 4000 BC or earlier. It is said that the earliest references to war elephants

The British Army Elephant Battery in Peshawar, India in the 1880s.

are in the Indian epic the *Mahabharata* which tells of events at least as old as 2000 BC. The *Mahabharata* speaks of war elephants, horse drawn chariots and flying vehicles.

The use of elephants in war and in such industries as logging and hauling heavy stones, is something that is deeply ingrained in the cultures of Sri Lanka, India, Myanmar, Thailand, Cambodia, Laos, Vietnam and Indonesia. The close relationship that mahouts have with their elephants is a trans-species relationship that is matched only by humans and canines. It is beyond the scope of this work to discuss the many amazing attributes of elephants, but suffice it to say that they are extremely smart and can be very good partners with humans if they are treated well.

Part of the problem with our knowledge of the Champa is that the extent of their trafficking with war elephants is not really known. Nor do we know much of the use of war elephants and warships in Southeast Asia, as the written records are lacking. We do know that war elephants were used extensively and that elephants as a whole were treated with reverence and even protected by law. A book called the *Arthashastra* advised the Mauryan government to reserve some forests for wild elephants for use in the army, and to execute anyone who killed them.

The *Arthashastra* is an ancient and influential Indian book on statecraft, economic policy and military strategy, written around 300 BC, slightly before the time of the famous Indian king known as Asoka. The *Arthashastra* was influential and copied by temple librarians until about 1300 AD after which copies were either destroyed or lost to gradual degradation from age and mold. Priests stopped copying the manuscript but it was rediscovered in 1904. A copy of the *Arthashastra* in old Sanskrit, written on palm leaves, was presented by a Tamil Brahmin from Tanjore in south India to the newly opened Mysore Oriental Library funded by the British Raj. The chief librarian R. Shamasastry recognized the arcane text as the *Arthashastra*.

Scholars were thrilled to have the text of this lost book again. The entire book has about 5,300 sentences on politics, governance, welfare, economics, protecting key officials and kings, gathering intelligence about hostile states and secret agents, forming strategic alliances, and the conduct of war. The book is attributed to a scholar named Chanakya, a philosopher, economist, jurist and royal advisor. He is considered the pioneer of the fields of political science and economics of modern India—writing at a time preceded by epic wars and alliances that are found in the *Mahabharata*, including stories of such famous warriors and saints as Krishna, Rama, Hanuman and others.

Chanakya assisted the first Mauryan emperor Chandragupta in his rise to power. He is widely credited for having played an important role in the establishment of the Maurya Empire. Chanakya served as the chief advisor to both emperor Chandragupta and his son Bindusara.

Says the *Arthashastra* about kings and rulership:

> The best king is the Raja-rishi, the sage king.
> The Raja-rishi has self-control and does not fall for the temptations of the senses, he learns continuously and cultivates his thoughts, he avoids false and flattering advisors and instead associates with the true and accomplished elders, he is genuinely promoting the security and welfare of his people, he enriches and empowers his people, he practices ahimsa (non-violence against all living beings), he lives a simple life and avoids harmful people or activities, he keeps away from another's wife nor craves for other people's property. The greatest enemies of a king are not others, but are these six: lust, anger, greed, conceit,

arrogance and foolhardiness. A just king gains the loyalty of his people not because he is king, but because he is just.

The *Arthashastra* offers protection for wildlife, particularly elephants:

> On the border of the forest, he should establish a forest for elephants guarded by foresters. The Office of the Chief Elephant Forester should with the help of guards protect the elephants in any terrain. The slaying of an elephant is punishable by death.

The Maurya Empire was founded in 322 BC by Chandragupta Maurya, who had overthrown the Nanda kingdom (5th and 4th centuries BC) and rapidly expanded his power westward across central and western India with the help of the sage Chanakya, taking advantage of the disruptions of kingdoms in western India caused by the attack and withdrawal back to Persia and Asia Minor of Alexander the Great's armies. The Maurya Empire was one of the largest empires of the world in its time. At its greatest extent, the empire stretched to the north along the natural boundaries of the Himalayas, and to the east into Assam, to the west into Balochistan and southern Afghanistan.

At one point Chandragupta won a battle against the Macedonian king Seleucus I Nicator, who was in the process of creating the Macedonian Seleucid Empire out of the easternmost territories of Alexander the Great beginning in 322 BC. In 305 BC he attempted to conquer the northwestern parts of India, but ultimately failed, in what is known as the Seleucid–Mauryan war. The two rulers finally concluded a complicated peace treaty in which the Greeks offered their princess plus ambassadors, while Chandragupta was able to move his lands farther west as the Seleucids retreated westward into Persia. Seleucus I in return received 500 war elephants including their mahouts and special archers. This huge contingent of fully armored war elephants would later have a decisive role in the Seleucid victory at the Battle of Ipsus in 301 BC against the western Hellenistic kings. Diplomatic relations were established and a number of Greek ambassadors and historians resided at the Mauryan court, while the Mauryans sent ambassadors to various Greek cities.

Chandragupta established his capital at Pataliputra, where the modern city of Patna in Bihar state is located. The Greek ambassador, Megasthenes, left a detailed account of its splendor referring to it as 'Palibothra,' and said the city was:

> ...surrounded by a wooden wall pierced by 64 gates and 570 towers—(and) rivaled the splendors of contemporaneous Persian sites such as Susa and Ecbatana.

During the reign of Emperor Asoka it was one of the largest cities in the world, with a population estimated at 150,000 to 300,000. It is estimated that there were at least 9,000 war elephants in the Mauryan army (400 to 200 BC) right through the reign of Asoka.

Pataliputra reached the pinnacle of prosperity when it was the capital of the great Mauryan emperors, Chandragupta Maurya and Asoka the Great.

The Empire was expanded into India's central and southern regions by Chandragupta's successor, Bindusara. Under the rulership of the famous king Asoka the empire grew even more, though the southern parts of India and Sri Lanka remained outside of the Maurya Empire. The Hindu-Buddhist empires to the east, including the mysterious Cham Empire, must have been heavily influenced by Asoka and the Mauryan Empire, including the amazing stonework and metalurgy that they were known to have.

At the end of his life Chandragupta became a Jain which increased social and

Two Thai war elephants fighting.

105

religious reform of traditional Hinduism across his society, and a few decades afterward the king Asoka became a Buddhist and, as we have seen, promoted non-violence and tolerance across all of India as well as Sri Lanka and Southeast Asia—including the lands of the Cham. Asoka sponsored other ambassadors to promote Buddhism to Asia Minor, Egypt and Mediterranean Europe.

Asoka's Mauryan Empire began to degrade in territory after his death and the final Mauryan king, Brihadratha, was assassinated in 185 BC, thus ending the dynasty. It is curious to note that his assassination was during a military parade—in which hundreds of war elephants were present—by a Hindu Brahmin general named Pushyamitra Shunga, who was commander-in-chief of the king's guard. Pushyamitra Shunga then took over the throne and established the Shunga dynasty. Buddhist records indicate that the rise of the Shunga empire led to a wave of religious persecution against Buddhists who had thrived during Asoka's reign.

So, the empire declined for about 50 years after Asoka's rule ended, and it dissolved in 185 BC with the foundation of the Shunga dynasty in Magadha. At the time of 185 BC and the Shunga Empire, we have a pretty good idea of how India and Sri Lanka looked as far as nation-states were concerned: south of the Sunga Empire centered on northern India was the Satavahana Empire and south of that was the Pandyan Kingdom and the island of Sri Lanka was ruled by the Tamraparni Dynasty.

But it is the mysterious eastern realms of the Cham that concern us here. They too were influenced by the Mauryan Asoka kingdom and like many people, including whole royal

An imaginative old print of a war elephant

106

families, they converted to Buddhism from their original religion of Hinduism. Entire royal families in northern India, all the way into the Hindu Kush and the Bamian Buddhas of Afghanistan, converted to Buddhism. Major Buddhist centers like Taxila were located in what is today northern Pakistan. Most of Afghanistan was Buddhist during this period.

Buddhism also spread into Champa and all of Southeast Asia. Buddhists continued to worship and adore Hindu gods, especially Rama, Garuda, Shiva and those mentioned in the Ramayana. Hindu areas and Buddhist areas were all part of the thalassocratic empire—a sea-based trading empire that had ports as major cities, linked to other city-ports that were hundreds and thousands of miles away from each other.

The Thalassocratic Rivalry Between the Cham and Srivijaya

As we said in the first chapter, the term thalassocracy comes from the Greek word, thalassa, meaning 'sea,' and kratein, meaning 'to rule.' This gives us thalassokratia, 'ruler of the sea,' and this is the description of an empire that is primarily a maritime realm—an empire of many port cities on islands and on the mainland of any area of the world. The opposite term would be tellurocracy—a land-based empire. A great empire could be both.

The Greeks first used the word thalassocracy to describe the government of the Minoan civilization, whose power depended on its navy. Herodotus also spoke of the need to counter the Phoenician thalassocracy by developing a Greek 'empire of the sea.' The term thalassocracy can also refer to naval supremacy, in a military or commercial sense, often both, as with the Phoenicians.

The Knights Templar and the powerful families of Venice created what we would call a thalassocracy during the middle ages. Also, the Republic of Ragusa can be seen as a 'thalassocracy.' The Republic of Ragusa was a competitor to Venice and was a Dalmatian maritime state centered on the city of Dubrovnik (Ragusa in Italian) located today in the very south of Croatia. The Republic of Ragusa existed from 1358 to 1808 and was known as a pirate republic with fortified forts; its motto was *'Non bene pro toto libertas venditur auro,'* which translated from Latin means 'Liberty is not well sold for all the gold.'

A good knowledge of thalassocracies is important here because transoceanic travel typically involves a thalassocracy of some sort, and, as I endeavor to show, the empire of the Cham was probably the greatest thalassocracy of the ancient era. This thalassocracy of the Cham was really only surpassed by the vast maritime empire of the British Crown with its many islands and colonial outposts around the entire globe. India was said to be the crown jewel in this vast empire. France had a similar thalassocracy with its many colonies including Tahiti and other islands.

At the time of 300 BC much of Southeast Asia, from Vietnam to Sumatra, Java and beyond was ruled by the thalassocratic empire of the Cham—a Buddhist-Hindu group of seafarers and traders who built megalithic cities with power tools and mined tons of iron ore, gold and other metals. They were the Cham, the

Champa!

Starting around the year 650 AD, other Buddhist thalassocracies sprung up in Southeast Asia, Srivijaya and Majapahit. From the 7th to the 15th century, Srivijaya (based on Sumatra) and Majapahit (from Java) controlled the sea lanes in Southeast Asia and exploited the spice trade of the Spice Islands, as well as maritime trade routes between India and China. These sea lanes were previously controlled by the Cham. Starting around this time Champa began to shrink back to Cambodia and Vietnam with Sumatra and Java becoming independent.

Srivijaya was centered somewhere in the eastern Sumatra area of Palembang starting sometime in the sixth or seventh century AD. Its capital has not been definitively located. It may be underwater. The Buddhist empire of Srivijaya interacted with the Cham of Vietnam and Cambodia but was now independent of this mother culture. Srivijaya became an important center for the expansion of Buddhism from the 7th to the 12th century. In Sanskrit, *sri* means "fortunate," "prosperous," or "happy" and *vijaya* means "victorious" or "excellence."

Says Wikipedia on Srivijaya:

The earliest evidence of its existence dates from the 7th century. A Tang Chinese monk, Yijing, wrote that he visited Srivijaya in 671 CE for 6 months. The earliest known inscription in which the name Srivijaya appears also dates from the 7th century in the Kedukan Bukit inscription found near Palembang, Sumatra, dated 16 June 682 CE. Between the late 7th and early 11th century, Srivijaya rose to become a hegemon in Southeast Asia. It was involved in close interactions—often rivalries—with the neighboring Medang Kingdom, Khmer Empire and Champa. Srivijaya's main foreign interest was nurturing lucrative trade agreements with China which lasted from the Tang dynasty to the Song dynasty. Srivijaya had religious, cultural and trade links with the Buddhist Pala Empire of Bengal, as well as with the Islamic Caliphate in the Middle East. The kingdom ceased to exist in the 13th century due to various factors, including the expansion of the Javanese, Singhasari, and Majapahit empires. After Srivijaya fell, it was largely forgotten. It was not until 1918 that French historian George Coedès of the École Française d'Extrême-Orient formally postulated its existence.

An inscription says that the first king came from a mysterious land called Minanga Tamwan. This place is somewhere else, either on Sumatra or in Malayasia, Thailand or Vietnam. Says Wikipedia on the mysterious land of Minanga Tamwan:

> Although, according to this inscription, Srivijaya was first established in the vicinity of today's Palembang, it mentions that Dapunta Hyang Sri Jayanasa came from Minanga Tamwan. The exact location of Minanga Tamwan is still a subject of discussion. The Palembang theory as the place where Srivijaya was first established was presented by Coedes and supported by Pierre-Yves Manguin. Soekmono, on the other hand, argues that Palembang was not the capital of Srivijaya and suggests that the Kampar River system in Riau where the Muara Takus temple is located is Minanga Tamwan.
>
> Another theory suggests that Dapunta Hyang came from the east coast of the Malay Peninsula, and that the Chaiya District in Surat Thani Province, Thailand, was the centre of Srivijaya. The city of Chaiya's name may be derived from the Malay name "Cahaya." However, some scholars believe that Chaiya probably comes from Sri Vijaya. It was a regional capital in the Srivijaya empire. Some Thai historians argue it was the capital of Srivijaya itself, but this is generally discounted.
>
> Around the year 500 CE, the roots of the Srivijayan empire began to develop around present-day Palembang, Sumatra. The empire was organised in three main zones: the estuarine capital region centred on Palembang, the

Musi River basin which served as hinterland and rival estuarine areas capable of forming rival power centers. The areas upstream of the Musi River were rich in various commodities valuable to Chinese traders. The capital was administered directly by the ruler while the hinterland remained under its own local datus or tribal chiefs, who were organised into a network of alliances with the Srivijaya maharaja or king. Force was the dominant element in the empire's relations with rival river systems such as the Batang Hari River, centred in Jambi.

From the Sanskrit inscriptions, it is notable that Dapunta Hyang Sri Jayanasa launched a maritime conquest in 684 CE with 20,000 men in the siddhayatra journey to acquire wealth, power, and 'magical powers.' Under the leadership of Dapunta Hyang Sri Jayanasa, the Melayu Kingdom became the first kingdom to be integrated into Srivijaya. This possibly occurred in the 680s CE. Melayu, also known as Jambi, was rich in gold and held in high esteem at the time. Srivijaya recognized that the submission of Melayu would increase its own prestige.

It seems that Minanga Tamwan was probably a Cham city in either Cambodia or Vietnam. It was the Cham who had ports in all these areas starting around 300 BC. The Cham were bringing war elephants to Sumatra and Java but also taking them across the Pacific. Later, as the core Cham base in Vietnam and Cambodia declined, some of their former strong ports began to conquer other areas and even attack the Cham themselves at their main northern base in central Vietnam at My Son and the Cham Islands. Says Wikipedia on the attack of Srivijaya on the Champa ports of Vietnam after taking over a port in Malaysia or southern Thailand:

> During the same century, Langkasuka on the Malay Peninsula became part of Srivijaya. Soon after this, Pan Pan and Trambralinga, which were located north of Langkasuka, came under Srivijayan influence. These

kingdoms on the peninsula were major trading nations that transported goods across the peninsula's isthmus. With the expansion into Java and the Malay Peninsula, Srivijaya controlled two major trade choke points in Southeast Asia. Some Srivijayan temple ruins are observable in Thailand and Cambodia.

At some point in the 7th century, Cham ports in eastern Indochina started to attract traders. This diverted the flow of trade from Srivijaya. In an effort to divert the flow, the Srivijayan king or maharaja, Dharmasetu, launched various raids against the coastal cities of Indochina. The city of Indrapura by the Mekong was temporarily controlled from Palembang in the early 8th century. The Srivijayans continued to dominate areas around present-day Cambodia until the Khmer King Jayavarman II, the founder of the Khmer Empire dynasty, severed the Srivijayan link later in the same century. After Dharmasetu, Samaratungga became the next Maharaja of Srivijaya. He reigned as ruler from 792 to 835 CE. Unlike the expansionist Dharmasetu, Samaratungga did not indulge in military expansion but preferred to strengthen the Srivijayan hold of Java.

All of this was the fighting between the various island nations that were left after the decline of the earlier Cham empire of My Son and the Cham Islands—with its connections to the Indian civilizations centered on the Bay of Bengal and the Ganges River. The Cham Islands and My Son were also ideally located for the important trade to ports in southern China. This trade would have included war elephants and it has been noted that war elephants were used at times by Chinese armies, though the origin of these beasts remains a mystery to many scholars. Most probably they came from the Cham and would certainly have stayed for a time at My Son before being transferred to ports in China where the locals would pay a handsome price for such powerful war machines. They were the Panzer tanks of ancient Persia, India and Southeast Asia. In Southeast Asia the evidence would suggest that it was the

Cham who controlled their trade.

The Trafficking in War Elephants

It seems clear that in ancient times an entire industry had built up around war elephants and all the trappings around them, including a private crew from India or Sri Lanka, and the specially-built howdah. Just like the military-industrial complex today can sell a tank or jet fighter complete with its own crew, the arms traffickers of 300 BC were selling war elephants and their operators at astronomical rates. Wars could be won or lost by them. Shipping was not included; it was an extra cost and required specially equipped ships which had to have stalls for the elephants, and these stalls would probably have had special harnesses of canvas and rope that were slung beneath the animal's belly and then tied to rails or posts above the beast. Horses were similarly slung this way, though smaller beasts such as goats and hogs were just kept in a pen. The slinging of a war elephant for transport, or the feeding, watering and general upkeep of an elephant (or horse) is not something that is discussed in most history books, but we know that it must have been carried out on a grand scale, one that made it a common occurrence at many ports. Elephants were used for a variety of work, but war elephants were specially trained and came with a crew of mahouts, often five or more, plus the elaborate howdah carriage that sat on top of the armored creature. These carriages were often several stories high, and the mahouts had a wide variety of weapons and poles as well.

As we have noted, the most popular of the war elephants in western India and Persia came from Sri Lanka. Any war elephant transported out of Sri Lanka would have to go by cargo ship, as it is an island. War elephants sent to Sumatra, Java, Borneo and the Cham areas of Vietnam and Cambodia would all have been sent by ship as well. It seems pretty clear that some Sri Lankan war elephants were transported by ship to ports in the Persian Gulf, a voyage of several weeks. We simply don't know how many elephants and mahout crews were put into a ship at one time. Perhaps it was only one elephant and crew per ship, or perhaps two or even four elephants were transported in one shipment. A small fleet of ships might transport as many as 14 to 20 war elephants at one time.

With many nations in India and Southeast Asia having thousands of war elephants each, we can see that this was a huge industry in 300 BC. Asoka was said to have 9,000 war elephants. Much like the military-industrial complex of today, the war elephant industry was something that fueled a large part of the economy with mahouts and archers joining the elephant corps and the iron, copper and bronze smiths making a wide assortment of weapons. Hindu and Buddhist soldiers were known to carry a clever push dagger that suddenly opened up into a triple dagger blade, known as a scissor katar. Iron works and other metal processing was a major industry in India as well as at My Son in Vietnam. Weapons and bronze statues were major exports for both of these areas.

We know that the trafficking of war elephants and all their accoutrements was a major industry and this continued right up to about 700 AD. War elephants were used in colonial times by the British in India and Burma, and the early army of modern Thailand had a regiment of war elephants.

As was mentioned earlier, war elephants were sometimes given as gifts from one ruler to another and they would transport them by ship. Wikipedia mentions one of the last such gifts around the year 1395 AD when the Raja of Java gave two elephants to the ruler Raja Baginda of Sulu. So, we know that war elephants were taken on relatively long ocean voyages. Is it possible that elephants were taken across the Pacific to North America? If so, what would be the evidence?

War Elephants Across the Pacific

Indeed, there is evidence of elephants being brought to North America. The Mayan city of Copán is situated in a valley among the hills of the mountainous border area of Honduras and Guatemala. It is closely connected by Rio Copán and Rio Motagua to Quirigua, the site of the tallest Mayan steles in the world.

Copán is known today as one of the great Mayan astronomical

observatories where calculations were made for the elaborate Mayan Calendar, the most accurate calendar ever devised. By heading down the Copán river one reaches the important Rio Motagua Valley in which the source of jade in the Americas was found. Jade was of mystical importance to both the Chinese and the ancient Mayas.

Copán was a temple city, perhaps a mining city, and an observatory. The area is famous even today for its clear nights that offer perfect oppertunities to view the stars. Copán has often been described as the Athens of the New World, and even though Mayan cities to the north are larger with grander pyramids and plazas, Copán has more carved monuments than any other city.

Copán may have been settled as early as 2000 BC, however the classic years of Copán are given by archaeologists as being from 465 to 800 AD. There is a certain air of mystery surrounding Copán, though some of the rulers are known: Smoking Rabbit lived to the ripe age of 82 and was succeeded by 18 Rabbit, who broke the tradition of destroying monuments with each change in ruler and using the rubble to fill in new structures. 18 Rabbit's successor, Squirrel, commemorated rulers of old whose monuments had been destroyed, and rebuilt the ball court. This custom of destroying the monuments of previous rulers is certainly one reason no hieroglyphs dating to earlier than 465 AD have been found at Copán—they have all been destroyed!

The city grew to perhaps 15,000 inhabitants and then suddenly, about 800 AD, the city was abandoned. Soon the great plazas and pyramids were covered with jungle growth. There is no archaeological evidence of any attack or violence, no hasty burials, lost weapons or valuables, no demolished houses or forgotten household goods. The ancient Maya seem simply to have moved away, leaving the city to the ravages of the jungle. For a thousand years the once magnificent city was lost to the world.

The city was brought to the attention of the archaeological world in 1835 when Colonel Jan Galindo, an officer of the Guatemalan army, published his *Description of the Ruins of Copán,* which contained many drawings of the site and its architecture. Intrigued

115

by Galindo's account, the American diplomat John Lloyd Stevens and the English artist Frederick Catherwood visited the ruins and spent several weeks there sketching the steles and buildings. Stevens liked the ruins so much that he bought them for fifty dollars!

Stevens and Catherwood produced the classic archaeology volume *Incidents of Travel in Central America, Chiapas and Yucatan* which was published in 1843. Said Stevens in the book when they came to Copán, "The sight of this unexpected sculpture once and for all dispelled from our minds all doubt on the character of American antiquities and confirmed us in our conviction that the objects we were looking for were worthy of interest not only as relics of an unknown people but also as works of art proving, as a newly discovered historical text might have done, that the peoples who once occupied the American continent were no savages."

Because of Stevens' book, the British archaeologist Alfred P. Maudslay traveled to Copán in 1881 and began the excavation of the city. Excavation continues to this day with the Government of Honduras and the University of Pennsylvania directing the work.

When I first visited in 1992, I walked around the Great Plaza and marveled at the magnificent statues, steles and altars, some as high as four meters (12-13 feet). They are some of the most beautiful statues carved by the Maya, and have a controversial archaeological history. Stele B commemorates the accession of the ruler 18 Rabbit. Yin-Yang symbols literally cover the stele and are especially prominent on the belt. Above the ruler's head on either side of the top of the stele are what appear to be the heads of elephants. When Maudslay first visited and drew the stele, a turbaned mahout was depicted leaning on the head of the left elephant, and it would seem there would have been a similar depiction on the right side,

The elephants at Copan.

116

but the stele was already damaged and that corner was missing. Curiously, the top left portion has now been destroyed, so that the man is no longer there. It is known that such a small figure was originally on the stele from Catherwood and Maudslay's early drawings, and others'. Some European archaeologists have even accused early American archaeologists of purposely defacing the stele.

Since elephants were no longer present in Central America in the year 800 AD, many archaeologists used this stele as evidence of contact between Southeast Asians and the Mayas. Since traditional archaeology does not accept this interpretation of cultural contact between Asia and the Americas, it was decided that these sculptures could not be elephant heads, but had to be something else.

Generally they are said to be stylized representations of the head of a macaw, with the beak curved backward in an exaggerated way. Why miniature turbaned men should be leaning on the stylized heads of these bizarre macaws has never been explained. But then, there are lots of things about the Mayas that remain unexplained, even to the traditionalists.

Archeologists, including myself, think that Chinese and Champa explorers, circa 500 to 300 BC, sailed down the coast of Central America in search of new lands and exotic products to take back to Southeast Asia and China. They probably used the Gulf of Fonseca as their base, founding a trading colony. According to historian Gunnar Thompson, this area was "located in a strategic position to dominate the coastal trade routes between Mexico and Panama; and it was at the center of abundant sources of trade goods that were suitable for Asian markets. These included exotic feathers, jadeite, gold, and hallucinogenic mushrooms."

Here Thompson alludes to the work of other anthropologists who suggests that Chinese voyages to Mexico, between 500 and 300 BC, may have been related to Taoist trade in magic mushrooms or "drugs of longevity."

Certainly, Chinese and Champa explorers would have been delighted to find their most precious of all stones, jade, as a commodity to trade for in Central America. At Copan and other Mayan sites there are many yin-yang type symbols and Chinese or oriental-looking men depicted in the many statues and ceramics.

The Strange Elephant Stones of New Mexico

The modern town of Aztec, New Mexico, was founded in 1880 on the opposite side of the Animas River from ancient stone ruins that early settlers believed had been built by the Aztecs of central Mexico. The first modern explorer to see the ruins was the geologist Dr. John S. Newberry, who visited them in 1859. He found walls 25 feet high and the remains of many-storied buildings gathered in clusters up and down the river. The anthropologist Lewis H. Morgan arrived in 1879, but by then nearly a quarter of the stones had been carted away by newly arrived settlers who needed building materials. The ruins became a national monument in 1923.

Self-guided trails wind through the lower story of the immense West Ruin. Here are precision-aligned rooms and doorways of shaped stone, a compelling testament to the engineering skills of the Anasazi, a mysterious group of people, probably related to the Hohokam people of central Arizona. In some rooms, original ceilings of pine and juniper logs, lashed together with yucca strands, are as solid as the day they were built 900 years ago.

Two dozen small kivas, probably used by individual clans, dot the ruins, while in the main courtyard is the Great Kiva, a community ceremonial chamber 43 feet in diameter. In 1934 an archaeological team carried out a two-year project to restore the kiva to appear as it did in the 12th century. It is the only fully restored kiva in the Southwest.

The fine walls and masonry are similar to that found at Chaco Canyon—alternating courses of large rectangular sandstone blocks with bands of smaller stones. The Great Kiva is especially impressive with its reconstructed huge pine poles to hold the roof, and three large stone disks as the base. The four large columns support a massive roof of latticed wooden beams, logs and earth weighing an estimated 90 tons. As noted, Aztec is on the Animas River, just north of the San Juan River into which the Animas flows.

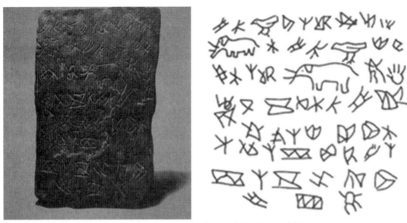

The Flora Vista elephant slab (front side).

The San Juan River then flows westward until it meets the Colorado River that then flows into the Grand Canyon. Chaco Canyon and the Zuni Indian Reservation are pretty much due south of Aztec. All of these places are essentially on the Continental Divide of the United States—the spot where rivers either flow east or west. Many rivers in New Mexico flow eastward to the Atlantic, such as the Rio Grande River which flows through Albuquerque. The rivers around Aztec, Chaco Canyon and Zuni flow westward.

In the Aztec ruins museum it was interesting to see boomerangs plus exotic trade and shamanic items like quartz crystals and feathers from Central America. Rubber balls for the ball courts have also been found. Archeologists believe that the early part of the extensive city was built between 1106 and 1124 AD. They think that it was abandoned shortly afterwards, in 1175 or 1200 AD; says the museum text: "perhaps because of drought or area-wide misfortune. There is no evidence the residents were driven away."

Curiously, archeologists think that the city was reoccupied in 1225 AD when people of the Mesa Verde culture arrived and took up residence with their distinct pottery, textiles and beadwork. They also abandoned the ruins by about 1290 AD. Who were these people and where did they go? Did they migrate to Mexico and become the Aztecs? Were they decimated in the Zuni-Apache wars of 1250 AD? Was Aztec the remains of a Toltec-Phoenician-Hohokam culture that farmed and mined in the rich river valleys of northern New Mexico

119

and the Four Corners region? Perhaps the mysterious Elephant Slabs found near Aztec are evidence of this lost civilization.

About 1910 a small boy playing in Flora Vista, New Mexico, a tiny settlement along the Animas River just north of the Aztec ruins, dug up two slabs of carved rock inscribed with what appeared to be some sort of ancient writing.

The young boy presented the slabs to local archeologists and a controversy raged. First of all, the slabs contained a number of symbols of an ancient language that no one could decipher, and secondly, the slabs contained petroglyphs (rock drawings) of easily recognizable local indigenous animals—and animals that were obviously elephants, drawn complete with trunks, floppy ears and tusks!

Figures on the Flora Vista elephant slab (front and back).

While at first no one suspected a hoax, the fact that elephants were carved on the slabs presented some serious problems. While mammoths had once roamed the area, they had become extinct, supposedly, over 10,000 years ago. Were these elephants brought by the Cham across the Pacific? Had they landed in the Sea of Cortez and then brought several elephants to the Hohokam lands of central Arizona, where Phoenix and the town of Casa Grande sit today, with their many canals and four-story mud brick houses? From there, were two of them marched to the area of Chaco Canyon, Zuni and the Continental Divide?

In his book *Ancient Man: A Handbook of Puzzling Artifacts*,[43] William Corliss has one brief page on the elephant slabs including an illustration of the inscriptions. They appear to be early Shang Chinese script, which was in use circa 1100 BC. Dating of the slabs by local archeologists, who thought they were authentic, was circa 1200 AD. They based this date on potsherds that were found at the site. However, the slabs may have been an ancient relic, kept in a safe place for hundreds of years at a time, while the potsherds could be of much more recent manufacture and come from the time of the destruction of Aztec, Flora Vista and the nearby Salmon Ruins, which occurred around 1200 AD.

Said the archeologist Charles Avery Amsden, who purchased the elephant slabs from the boy in 1910, "I can see no reason to doubt the authenticity of these specimens, but how to explain them I would not say. In all my experience I have seen nothing similar."

The smaller, principal slab measures six inches wide and six inches long with a deep groove on the left-hand side that shows where it was probably broken off from a larger stone. The unknown carver meticulously chiseled 55 signs and pictures into exceedingly hard stone and left no obvious traces of tool slippage or over-crossed lines.

The second slab is longer at six inches wide and 14 inches long. It bears only ten faintly incised signs including the outlines of an elephant as well as a bird and a mountain lion. So, three elephants were apparently carved on the elephant slabs, two on the smaller slab with more symbols, and one on the larger slab. Both were said

121

to be similar to stone hoes used throughout the Southwest, and may have been used as such for hundreds of years as important ritual objects.

In the book *Montezuma's Serpent,* Brad Steiger and his wife Sherry Hansen Steiger ask, "Is it possible for someone to draw a picture of an elephant without ever having seen one? And, more specifically, was it possible for an ancient Native American to have sat on a bank of the Animas and accidentally, by chance, have etched the image of an elephant on stone?"

Some historians have suggested that these were somehow mammoths that had survived until recently or that they were African elephants that found their way to ancient New Mexico via the trade ships of Phoenicians between 900 and 200 BC.

More likely is that an Asiatic potentate launched an invasion fleet, complete with war elephants, to colonize the New World. The best candidate for bringing elephants to North America is ancient Cham. These Egyptian-Asians were seafaring Hindus who later became Buddhists, and ranged far out into the Pacific, perhaps to areas that are now California and Mexico. Could these Buddhist Sea Kings have brought some war elephants with them to some port on the Colorado River and then brought them to the Colorado Plateau on an important visit to the Grand Canyon, Chaco Canyon and Aztec? It seems incredible! For the Champa, no task was beyond their reach.

Other authors support the idea of continual transpacific traffic from ancient India, Egypt and Southeast Asia, such as W. J. Perry (*Children of the Sun*[24]) and Igor Witkowski (*Axis of the World*[41]), both of whom present considerable evidence for ancient civilizations having crossed the Pacific and interacted with American cultures.

Perhaps the young boy in Flora Vista had somehow hoaxed the strange items he presented. But, other elephants have popped up in the Americas from time to time, including an elephant effigy mound in northeastern Iowa.

Even today, elephants are widely used for logging and other tasks in Southeast Asia, and any Chinese-Buddhist-Hindu expedition to the Americas would include people who certainly were familiar with

122

elephants. It is conceivable that such an expedition may have actually brought trained elephants with them, in a similar manner that horses and cattle were transported in ships. War elephants were popular in Southeast Asia and used up until relatively modern times. It seems likely that the elephants of New Mexico came from Southeast Asia during the time of the Cham, or perhaps even as late as the Srivijaya empire centered around Sumatra and Java. Not only were large fleets of ships crossing the Pacific, they were bringing elephants with them as well. Just as we are fascinated by the wonderful animal that is the elephant today, ancient peoples of the Americas were just as fascinated—and frightened—by elephants brought from Vietnam, Cambodia and Indonesia across the Pacific to North America.

A painting of a war elephant charge at the Battle of Hydaspes by Andre Casta (1899).

Chapter Three

THE CHAM & THE SEARCH FOR GOLD

The weapon of skepticism is dangerous—in the past many an over-skeptical scientist discredited himself by rash condemnation and lack of imagination.
—Andrew Tomas

When we look at the outstanding brickwork, stonework and metallurgical skill of the Cham the excellence of their work is pretty astonishing. As I pointed out in the first chapter, brick towers at My Son baffled early archeologists as to how they were built and fired. Similarly I pointed out the use keystone cuts on large basalt blocks at My Son. This use of keystone cuts and corresponding metal clamps or cramps shows that My Son and other Cham megalithic structures such as Angkor Wat and Preah Vihear were made by the same great architects who built Machu Picchu, Cuzco, Ollantaytambo and Tiwanaku.

These great architects were using a technique that had been used in Egypt as early as 1500 BC and they apparently continued their megalithic construction in Southeast Asia, Indonesia and across the Pacific in Central and South America. Along the way they built other megalithic structures on Pacific Islands such as Nan Madol and Kosrae, as well as Tonga, Fiji, Tahiti and the Marquesas. They are also responsible for the megalithic construction on Easter Island. As we shall see as we discuss all of this, the time frame is very agreeable to the dates that are assigned to these sites by modern archeologists.

The Egyptians, Sumerians, Hindus, Tibetans and the Champa were continually searching for gold and other metals in the territories that they occupied—and beyond. This search for gold, silver, copper, tin and other metals led to the discovery and exploitation of ancient mines, many of which are lost to us today. Ancient stories frequently feature quests for gold, gems, and magical elixirs such as psychedelic mushrooms or cactus.

The search for gems and other valuable stones was also a significant enterprise in ancient times and it was expected that royalty in ancient India, Egypt, Sumeria and Champa would carry various gems on them, either in a pocket or purse or encrusted in daggers, headbands, crowns and such. These gems had magical powers in almost all cases and diamonds were used in an industrial sense as they are today—as a diamond dust used with a drill or wire saw that can cut even the hardest rock.

In my recent book *Ark of God*,[18] I briefly discuss the use of diamonds in the building of King Solomon's temple in Jerusalem. In 1 Kings 6 we are told about Solomon building the great temple that was to house the Ark of the Covenant. The temple is furnished with much gold and special adornments and took seven years to build. In 1 Kings 6:7 we are told that no hammers or iron tools were used at the temple site:

> In building the temple, only blocks dressed at the quarry were used, and no hammer, chisel or any other iron tool was heard at the temple site while it was being built.

Because of this curious statement, a legend rose up that King Solomon possessed a magic substance—or "worm"—the size of a barleycorn, that could cut stone. This magical item was called the shamir and it could be used to cut any kind of metal or stone and was essentially harder than any other substance.

It is difficult to find a lot of information on the shamir but let us look at the Wikipedia entry under "Solomon's Shamir":

> In the Gemara [part of the Talmud], the shamir is a worm or a substance that had the power to cut through or disintegrate stone, iron and diamond. King Solomon is said to have used it in the building of the First Temple in

Jerusalem in the place of cutting tools. For the building of the Temple, which promoted peace, it was inappropriate to use tools that could also cause war and bloodshed.

Referenced throughout the Talmud and the Midrashim, the Shamir was reputed to have existed in the time of Moses. Moses reputedly used the Shamir to engrave the Hoshen (Priestly breastplate) stones that were inserted into the breastplate. King Solomon, aware of the existence of the Shamir, but unaware of its location, commissioned a search that turned up a "grain of Shamir the size of a barley-corn."

Solomon's artisans reputedly used the Shamir in the construction of Solomon's Temple. The material to be worked, whether stone, wood or metal, was affected by being "shown to the Shamir." Following this line of logic (anything that can be 'shown' something must have eyes to see), early Rabbinical scholars described the Shamir almost as a living being. Other early sources, however, describe it as a green stone. For storage, the Shamir was meant to have been always wrapped in wool and stored in a container made of lead; any other vessel would burst and disintegrate under the Shamir's gaze. The Shamir was said to have been either lost or had lost its potency (along with the "dripping of the honeycomb") by the time of the destruction of the First Temple at the hands of Nebuchadnezzar in 586 B.C.

According to the deutero-canonical Asmodeus legend, the shamir was given to Solomon as a gift from Asmodeus, the king of demons. Another version of the story holds that a captured Asmodeus told Solomon the Shamir was entrusted to the care of a woodcock. Solomon then sends his trusted aide Benaiah on a quest to retrieve it.

The shamir worm was also used by King Solomon to engrave gemstones. Apparently he also used the blood of the shamir worm to make carved jewels with a mystical seal or design. According to an interview with Dr. George Frederick Kunz, an expert in gemstone and jewelry lore, this led to the belief that gemstones so engraved would have

127

magical virtues, and they often also ended up with their own powers or guardian angel associated with either the gem, or the specifically engraved gemstones.

So what was the shamir? It is tempting to think it was some sort of laser technology, with the "eye" of the shamir being the focused beam of light emitted from the laser, which could easily burn through stone, metal or wood. The first modern laser, developed in 1960, used a synthetic ruby crystal to beam red light, and the shamir is associated with gems. Why did the shamir have to be kept in a lead box? Lead is usually used as a protective layer against excess radiation. "Laser" stands for Light Amplification by the Stimulated Emission of Radiation, and radiation injury is possible even from moderately powered beams. But having a laser device the size of a barleycorn seems far-fetched even by today's standards of miniaturization.

The general thought is that it is a diamond, the hardest substance in the mineral world. In fact, the shamir may have been some sort of diamond drill or saw that would cut other gems and saw and drill through such hard stones as granite or even basalt. To be "shown to the shamir" may have been akin to having an object placed on a diamond lathe or saw. Today it is necessary to use diamond saws and drills to cut modern granite blocks at quarries and we might imagine that ancient stonecutters—some of them at least—had similar such tools.

Again, was some highly developed civilization, or several of them, producing diamond saws, diamond drills, iron tools, electrical devices and even airships? Countries like ancient Egypt, Babylonia, India, China and Champa were all capable, in my mind, of producing such things in ancient times. Other countries, such as ancient Israel, Greece or Ethiopia had to import these items and they were therefore "magical" objects and only owned by kings and important princes.

A fascinating website called BibleSearchers.com has some interesting information on the shamir, which was most likely composed of small pieces of diamond, sapphire and/or ruby, probably from India:

128

In the Mishnah Avon 5:6, the Shamir was created on the sixth day of creation and was given to the hoopoe-bird (woodcock) who kept it in her custody throughout the ages in the Garden of Eden. This marvelous bird would on occasion take this worm and carry it across the earth, carrying it tightly in her beak, letting it down only to create a fissure on a desolate mountain peak so that the seeds of plants and trees could sprout and provide her food.

When the Israelites were camped near Mount Horeb/Sinai, the Lord brought the Shamir and gave it to Bezaleel to engrave the names of the twelve tribes on the twelve stones of the breastplate of the high priest, Aaron. Then the Lord gave it back to the custody of the hoopie-bird. Here she kept it in a leaden box, with fresh barley, wrapped in a woolen cloth. That is until Solomon needed it to build the Temple of the Lord in Jerusalem. Since that day, the Shamir has been lost.

As with all good rabbinic Talmudic debates, there was always a dissent. Judah R. Nehemiah claimed that the stones were quarried and then brought to the temple in a finished condition for the building of the temple. It appears that Rabbi Nehemiah's argument carried the debate as most scholars today believe this also to be true.

Of course, most Talmudic arguments were debated during the Roman imperial rule. In Latin, the Shamir was known as *smirks corundum*, the substance of sapphires and rubies and the hardest known gem next to the diamond. The substance of legends has a kernel of truth and now we know the 'rest of the story.'

These Bible scholars think that there was more than one shamir and they were none other than power tools, specifically diamond drills and such. Says BibleSearchers:

The whole passage in the Book of Kings suggests that

there was a certain dignity and quietness, a decorum that was to be maintained as the contractors and the artisans could feel the presence of the Lord in the House that they were constructing. There was to be a spirituality of the Presence. They were not to hear the pounding or banging of instruments of iron. Was the literalness of the message also to have a spiritual connection? Yet within the House of the Lord, there [were] no injunctions of the Lord against the humming of diamond drill bits as they cut, polished and finished off the massive limestone walls, or trimmed the edges of the cedars of Lebanon, or engraved the wood on the porticoes, or drill holes into the limestone to set beams and stabilize pillars, to embellish the trimming on the ceilings of the Holy Place, place engraved images on the Molten Sea or on the large doors that entered into the temple proper. Is it not time to consider that Solomon with all his wisdom and wealth also had access to technologies that we think are modern, only to someday know that the ancients were using them too?

...Maybe within the hoard of the treasures of Solomon's temple, we will find evidence of the technological sophistication, such as diamond drills, diamond and corundum bit saws that scholars have long felt did not exist in the 11th century BCE.

BibleSearchers gives us a good explanation for the shamir and the use of diamonds, rubies and other stones in the difficult cutting and drilling of very hard stone like basalt and granite. These same stones are used in lasers and other high-tech electrical devices that can also cut stone. It is conceivable that the technology in ancient India, Sumeria and Egypt—as well as Cham—might have been at the level of having such high power tools. Just as with ancient flight, the use of electricity must have been used for such high-power tools.

The Search for the Land of Gold
In my book *Ancient Technology in Peru and Bolivia*[38] I explain

that ancient man has always sought out materials from the earth. Rocks are typically abundant, but certain types of rocks are more desirable and valuable than others. Obsidian and flint can be easily found in certain areas, but can be quite rare in other areas and therefore more valuable. Jade is even more rare and difficult to find and therefore more valuable, particularly because jade is a very hard—yet workable—substance.

Very much like the search for spices in eastern Indonesia by the early Portuguese explorers, the search for good sources of obsidian, which can be made into super-sharp razors, spearheads, arrowheads and other objects, took ancient man to remote islands and volcanic outcroppings. The control of an obsidian source could mean tremendous power and wealth, as seen on the volcanic island group of Manu'a in Samoa, whose chief was supposedly the 'king' of all the Polynesian Islands. Hawai'i and Rapa Nui (Easter Island)—both extremely remote islands—also had valuable sources of obsidian. The area around Mexico City-Teotihuacan-Tenochtitlan is also rich in obsidian and the Aztecs, as did earlier cultures, centered their civilization in the vicinity of these important obsidian sources. Obsidian mines are also located in South America, and can be near volcanic areas in Ecuador, Peru, Bolivia and Chile among other places.

Metals were desired too, and many metals, such as gold and copper, can be easy to obtain. Both gold and copper can be found in large veins of pure ore and often nuggets can easily be hammered into flat sheets. Gold is too soft to be used for tools or weapons, though copper can be used to make such items. Alloys of metals are always harder than the original and once ancient man had figured out how to create intense heat with smelters and furnaces, the melting and refining of various ores into alloys such as bronze and electrum (plus other silver, gold or copper alloys of literally any mixture) was widely practiced. The ores could be turned into some molten metal product and then poured into a stone mold that cast it as an ingot, double axe head, spearhead or other metallic object.

The search for quartz crystal objects and the search for diamonds, emeralds, rubies and sapphires have their own fascination and lore.

131

Other valuable and rare commodities are the purple dyes derived from certain species of shellfish, sometimes known as murex, and certain spices like cloves and cinnamon. The search for and knowledge of the extraction of purple dyes around the world is discussed in *Myths of Pre-Columbian America*[14] by Donald Mackenzie, which was first published in 1923. Mackenzie discusses the curious royal purple dye that was deep in color, long-lasting and very expensive. Says Mackenzie:

> Murex purple, which had a religious value, was used in the New World as in the Old. It appears to have been first introduced in Crete as far back as 1600 BC. On Leuke, an island off the southeast coast and at the ancient seaport of Palaikastro, Professor Bosanquet discovered a bank of crushed murex shell associated with Kamares pottery. The Phoenicians of Tyre and Sidon adopted the industry and 'Tyrian purple' became famous. Other dyeing centers were established. The purple of Laconia in the Gulf of Corinth was greatly esteemed. Purple-yielding shells were searched for far and wide in the western Mediterranean. Tarentum, the modern Otranto, became an important dyeing town. Bede, 'the father of English history,' tells that on the British coasts were found, not only mussels which yielded pearls of all colors, including red, purple, violet, green and white, but also cockles, 'of which the scarlet dye is made: a most beautiful color which never fades with the heat of the sun or the washing of the rain, but the older it is the more beautiful it becomes.' 'Purpura mounds' have been discovered in Ireland... The Phoenicians are believed to have obtained from the British Isles a dark shade of shell purple called 'black purple.'
>
> Shells yielding purple were searched for and found and used, as far East as China and Japan. An interesting fact about the shells discovered in the mounds of Omori, Japan, is that many of them had a portion of the body-whorl broken away 'as if for the purpose of more conveniently extracting

the animal.' The Caithness broch shells [Scotland] were broken in like manner.

Traces of the purple industry have been found, as has been said, in the New World. Mrs. Zelia Nuttall has published a paper entitled 'A Curious Survival in Mexico of the use of the Purpura Shell-fish for Dyeing.'[14]

Mackenzie says that Nuttal and others point out that the purpura, or murex, shells have been taken from Inca graves in northern Chile as well as from middens in North America. The purple dye industry in both Europe and the Americas was closely associated with the search for pearls and the use of the conch-shell trumpet which needs a special hole cut into the back of it to work properly. It was strongly believed that the purple dye industry originally began in the Eastern Mediterranean—as well as the Red Sea—and Mackenzie says that "an intimate relationship existed between this art and skill in weaving, as well as the mining, working, and trafficking in metals, such as gold, silver and copper. In the New World the purple industry is associated with similar pursuits."

According to Mackenzie, these sailors and purple dye makers, the same people who went to remote islands and bays around the world "to work gold and copper, and incidentally to erect megalithic tombs and temples, were also searching for pearls and making use of shell trumpets." Mackenzie goes on to quote Professor G. Elliot Smith, a noted expert on the murex industry at the time:

> There are reasons for believing that all these special uses of shells were spread abroad along with the complex mixture of arts, customs and beliefs associated with the building of megalithic monuments.
>
> The earliest use of the conch-shell trumpet was in the Minoan worship in Crete. Thence it spread far and wide, until it came to play a part in the religious services, Christian and Jewish, Brahman and Buddhist, Shinto and Shamanistic, in widely different parts of the world—in the Mediterranean, in India, in Central Asia, in Indonesia and Japan, in Oceania

133

and America.[14]

So, evidence suggests that at various periods during ancient times there were some serious quests to remote locations around the globe in search of murex shells, pearls, gold, copper and other metals. We could add to that list the search for spices as well as hallucinogenic plants that contain active psychedelic ingredients. Many of these rare substances were thought to prolong life or even give immortality, much like ginseng might be seen today.

It would seem that the early purple dye industry could be much older than 1600 BC, and that it did not necessarily originate in Crete. It may have come originally from ancient India or Champa, or even from some now drowned land such as the legendary Atlantis. The first extraction of purple dye is lost to the mists of time although it was used by the Romans, Greeks and Phoenicians. In Greek myth, its discovery is credited to Hercules — or rather his dog, whose mouth turned purple after chewing on some snails or cockles. But we can suppose that some of the ancient seafarers who came to islands in the Pacific and Atlantic Oceans, as well as to the Americas, were wearing this regal purple cloth.

These ancient voyagers crossing the Atlantic and Pacific Oceans would have carried fishing gear with them as well as animals. One of the animals that was typically carried by ancient seafarers was the chicken, and because chickens have traceable DNA, their origins can be scientifically determined. Indeed, a study published in July of 2012 has done just that. The London *Telegraph* reported on August 12, 2012 that all chickens, including ones in Chile, the Pacific Islands and the Dominican Republic (in the Caribbean) were all descended from chickens in Southeast Asia.

Said the article, which quotes from the Australian Broadcasting Corporation (ABC):

> The team of researchers from the University of New England (Armidale, Australia) studied the ancient DNA– known as mitochondrial DNA–preserved within 48 archaeological chicken bones and found the same DNA

signature present in bones from Europe, Thailand, the Pacific, Chile, the Dominican Republic and Spanish colonial sites in Florida.

Project researcher Dr Alison Storey says chickens have been domesticated for at least 5400 years and it has been difficult to determine the ancient origin and dispersal of chickens because of the way successive civilizations carried the domesticated poultry with them wherever they went.

'What we found is that one of the sequences in the different chicken bones was very similar over a wide geographic area. This tells us that the chickens that we found in archaeological sites all over the world shared an ancient ancestor who was domesticated somewhere in southeast Asia a long time ago,' Dr Storey told the ABC.

'All of our domestic chickens are descended from a few hens that I like to think of as the 'great, great grandmothers' of the chicken world,' she says.

The report, published in the journal *PLos ONE,* has implications for the world of human movement as much as it does for the DNA of poultry. The report says: 'Understanding when chickens were transported out of domestication centers and the directions in which they were moved provides information about prehistoric migration, trade routes, and cross cultural diffusion.'

So, according to the researchers at the University of New England in Australia, chickens were transported across the Pacific from Southeast Asia to Chile (and other places) possibly as far back 3400 BC in a 'cultural diffusion' that provides information about 'prehistoric migration and trade routes.' That is, of ancient cultures coming out of Southeast Asia and probably crossing the Pacific, first to South America, leaving chickens on islands along the way. In other words, these chickens from Southeast Asia did not fly or walk to America on their own—they were brought by humans.

And, indeed, such a proclamation has far-reaching implications for the astonishing megalithic ruins in South America, Easter

Island, Tahiti and the Marquesas Islands, Tonga and many other places in the Pacific or along the Pacific Rim. The possibility that Easter Island remained an isolated dot in the ocean with no contact with South America would seem ever more remote—to the horror of isolationists—given that ancient chicken bones and their DNA in Chile have been scientifically traced to Southeast Asia.

What else was brought to South America from Southeast Asia besides chickens? Were iron tools, mining and refining technologies brought to South America from across the Pacific? Were ancient customs, such as tattooing and the elongation of the lower ear also brought across the ocean—even the odd custom of elongating the skulls of infants to create 'coneheads'? Canadian anthropologist Brien Foerster and I discuss this subject in our book *The Enigma of Cranial Deformation*.[61]

What would have brought Southeast Asians to cross the vast Pacific tot eh shores of America? The search for metals and other treasure? For now, let us look at the astonishing high technology that was used at the megalithic sites in the mineral-rich Andes Mountains—wherever it came from.

> *Speak to the earth, and*
> *It shall teach thee.*
> —Book of Job 12:8

The Ancient Mining Centers of Chavin and Tiwanaku

I first visited Chavin de Huantar (sometimes just called Chavin) in 1990, taking an overnight bus to Huaraz, the skiing capital of Peru. Huaraz is the capital of the Ancash Department and is about 420 kilometers north of Lima. Located at over 10,000 feet (3,000 meters), Huaraz is surrounded by the highest mountains in Peru known as the Cordillera Blanca, or White Range, because of their permanent glaciers and heavy snow covering.

I stayed for a couple of nights in this pleasant alpine town of skiers, mountain climbers and trekkers, and then took a local bus east over a high pass to the town of Chavin. I stayed there for two nights and investigated the archeological site during the day. I was

136

amazed by the complexity of the site at the time, and I returned for another visit in early 2011 with Jennifer.

Chavin de Huantar is thought by many Peruvian archeologists to be the genesis of South American civilization. They think that the early phases of Chavin began over 5,000 years ago, circa 3000 BC and the massive structures that can be seen today were in use before 900 BC. The building of Tiwanaku followed shortly after the building of Chavin, according to the mainstream view. Indeed, there are many similarities between Chavin and Tiwanaku and it would seem that the two are very much linked. Chavin is thought to have ceased to be a major center around 400 BC and became ruins in a remote and unpopulated mountain valley.

Today, the village of Chavin, hundreds, even thousands of years old, is largely built of stones salvaged from the old site of Chavin de Huantar. What remains of the archeological site is basically the largest megalithic blocks and the extensive underground structure. Portions have been reconstructed by modern archeologists.

The central feature of the underground temple is a monolith carved with a toothy monster said to be the object of worship at the temple. Legends speak of the complex going nine or 12 stories underground, where a huge gem can be found. Naturally, the complex has long since collapsed and is buried with rubble in the lower parts. Tourists today are allowed to go down to about the third level.

The site is massive and impressive. A good description can be found in the Time-Life book *The Search for El Dorado*:

> Much of Chavin de Huantar's drawing power stemmed from its awe-inspiring architecture and monumental sculptural details. In its early phases the temple consisted of three enormous platform mounds arranged in a U-shape atop a pedestal of cyclopean stone blocks. Gazing upon its massive walls, worshipers beheld a bas-relief frieze of anthropomorphic creatures, spotted jaguars, writhing serpents, and wild birds of prey, below which projected a row of monstrous human heads sculpted from stone blocks

weighing as much as half a ton each. Tenons at the back of the heads fit snuggly into mortise joints in the masonry, creating the illusion that the sculptures were floating some 30 feet above the ground. A frieze depicting similar figures—jaguars and exotically costumed humans—adorned the sunken, circular plaza that lay between the three mounds. A white granite staircase climbed from the plaza up to the temple's summit.

In time Chavin de Huantar's massive structures proved too small, and laborers doubled the size of the southern mound and added terraced platforms and sunken rectangular courtyards southeast of the circular plaza. A portico framed by black and white pillars graced the front of the southern wing, which is referred to as the New Temple, whose top now became the focal point of the public ceremonies.

Pilgrims gathering on the New Temple's main plaza would have had a commanding view of the ritual platform. No exterior staircase surmounted this new structure; the mound's apparently inaccessible summit was instead approached by a labyrinthine network of interior passages and stairways. Garbed in fine cotton, woolen, or feathered tunics and adorned with gold nose ornaments, earspools and headdresses, Chavin de Huantar's priests must have elicited considerable wonder when, as if by magic, they emerged on top.[44]

These pilgrims are then thought to have left with various mementos of their visit to the cyclopean complex, including clay objects, gold objects, painted textiles and other 'souvenirs.' These have been found in distant mountain and coastal areas of Peru. Renowned Peruvian archeologist Julio Tello discovered a gold gorget representing two intertwined snakes over 280 miles away from the site (at Chongoyape) that he identified as coming from Chavin de Huantar.[44] Was this gold artifact made at the megalithic site? Were other artifacts, such as the ceramics and fabrics made there as well? Was Chavin a manufacturing center? Archeologists

138

One of the massive walls at Chavin.

do not really address this issue.

Chavin de Huantar is usually described as a ceremonial center, located at the headwaters of the Maranon River. Two rivers converge at Chavin, the Mosna River and the Huanchecsa River. The builders of the complex actually diverted one of the rivers to enter the complex. Similar things were done at Tiwanaku. Chavin is at over 10,000 feet in the Andes and it is in a very steep valley. Why would such a complex, a huge engineering work, be placed in this rather remote and difficult spot?

Well, according to the major archeologists working at the site, it was a religious and ceremonial center 'centrally located' to the Andean people and the coastal areas as well. Here the people ingested psychedelic cactus extracts and generally attended religious ceremonies of some kind. While this may be partially true, and certainly such ceremonies with psychotropic substances must have occurred, it seems the builders were very sober geniuses who were designing very complicated facilities. They not only built a pre-designed underground complex with cut and dressed megalithic blocks, but they diverted a river into the complex as part of their design. Why did they do that?

139

Whenever gigantic blocks of granite, limestone or basalt are used in a building, it is obvious that a great deal of organized planning is involved. The quarrying of the blocks, dressing them, moving them to the site and then erecting them is a considerable task, not one that should be taken lightly. Whoever the minds behind this endeavor were, they were very smart, skilled in engineering and architecture—and had a forward-thinking mindset. In other words, they were putting a great deal of organizational effort and cost into something that would only pay off later.

Mainstream archeologists say that the goal of this extraordinary effort, especially for a presumably primitive society, was purely ceremonial. But, like at Tiwanaku, as we will shortly see, the building of these massive 'temples' is something that not only requires pre-planning, but also sophisticated stone working techniques—which involves metal chisels. It seems that other metal articles were worked at the site, too. Where were the ancient mines that produced these metals? Were they the real reason that Chavin de Huantar had been built in the first place, and a river diverted into the city?

Indeed, although Chavin may have been a cult destination as well, its original purpose may have been as a metallurgical processing plant with the diverted river used to wash ores brought down from nearby mines. Even today several mines operate in the vicinity of Chavin. The Andes Mountains contain a wealth of precious metals and other minerals, and mining occurs all over the place. The Chavin area is no exception.

In fact, the Spanish colonized Ancash and the surrounding Callejon area very quickly because of its mineral wealth. Soon there were silver, lead and tin mines being worked around Huaraz and Chavin, and by the 1570s hundreds or even thousands of Quechua-

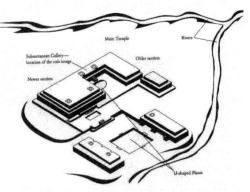

A map of Chavin showing the diverted river.

140

speaking workers were laboring in the mines. Mining has always been an important industry in the Andes, even before the Spanish.

In fact, one of the oldest metal objects ever found in South America allegedly came from Chavin de Huantar. It is a small snuff spoon dated to about 3000 BC fashioned 'out of sheets of gold and silver foil that had been hammered into form and soldered together.'[7] Therefore, we know that silver was being used at Chavin, as well as gold. Other metals may have been in use there as well, but they may have oxidized and vanished, as many metals do. Gold is virtually indestructible and items made of gold will last, unchanged, many thousands of years longer than other metal objects. Objects that are made of a mixture of gold and other metals, such as silver, will also outlast ordinary metal objects.

And what would this snuff spoon have been used for? The snuff would probably have been a hallucinogenic powder of some sort, snorted by the nose from the spoon. One of the figures carved into the upper register of the circular plaza at Chavin de Huantar shows winged beings with fangs holding a staff that resembles the hallucinogenic San Pedro cactus.[7] Other strange winged birdmen appear in other Chavin art.

Another mystery concerning Chavin de Huantar is that the pottery found there is said to be some of the earliest ever found in Peru, from around 2000 BC. Richard Burger in his book *Chavin and the*

A 1934 photo of the megalithic bridge at Chavin, now gone.

Origins of Andean Civilization[7] says pottery making was adopted in Peru over 1,000 years later than in Ecuador or Colombia and even probably the Amazonian lowlands. While the earliest pottery in South America is thought to come from Valdivia, Ecuador, circa 3500 BC, no pottery has been discovered or dated yet in Peru that is equally old. Valdivian pottery is often compared to identical Jomon pottery in Japan from the same time frame, circa 3500 BC.[7] Why did it take so long for pottery making to come to Peru? Maybe it didn't. Perhaps there was pottery in Peru from 3500 BC that has not been dated yet. Modern ceramic dating techniques are fairly recent and many tests simply haven't been done. Certain ceramic objects like the Fuente Magna Bowl now at the Precious Metals Museum in La Paz may well be from 3500 BC (as the Sumerian writing on it indicates), but no ceramic dating tests (like thermoluminescence) have been made on it yet, despite it being an important object in a major museum. We will discuss this curious object in more detail below.

So, was Chavin de Huantar an ancient mining center that later became a cult center over its hundreds of years of operation? As an early economic center, the source of copper, gold, silver, tin and bronze—and possibly even iron—Chavin would have attracted a lot of people and it must have had a very lively market during its heyday, much better then the one that can be seen there today. Indeed, when one visits Chavin in this day and time, one is struck by how lonely and isolated the spot is. This is certainly not the 'Center of the World' as Cuzco is often described. This seems like a remote valley in the Andes, and that is exactly what it is. What was the purpose of building such an elaborate complex in this location? A metallurgical processing center is the best answer, as far as I am concerned.

Another megalithic metallurgical center in South America is that of Tiwanaku-Puma Punku, which seems to have been completely misunderstood by modern archeologists. Not only do we find perfectly cut granite blocks with keystone cuts in them, like at My Son, but Bolivian archeologists have now in their possession two different objects with Sumerian writing on them: the bowl mentioned above and a statue called the Pokotia Monolith.

The important keystone cuts and the bronze clamps that were poured into the cuts are also found at Cuzco and Ollantaytambo in Peru. The Cham site of Preah Vihear on a mountaintop in northern Cambodia is very similar to the famous megalithic city of Machu Picchu near Ollantaytambo, and will be discussed shortly. All of these sites feature precision-cut-and-fitted megaliths and the use of keystone cuts and metal clamps. But the earliest of these megaliths seem to go back to the time of ancient Sumeria.

In 2009 when I visited the Precious Metals Museum on Calle Jaen in the old colonial section of La Paz, armed guards at the entrance took our tickets and warned us that no photography was permitted in the museum. [38] The Magna Fuente Bowl was in an unguarded room, and I was able to take a few photos of the bowl inside its glass case without being spotted. Cuneiform writing could clearly be seen on the inside rim of the bowl, as well as other writing. When I returned to the museum in November of 2011 with the crew of the History Channel's *Ancient Aliens* show, the Pokotia statue was being kept in a special vault out of the public's view. During our

The Fuente Magna Bowl at the Precious Metals Museum in La Paz.

A close-up of the Sumerian hieroglyphs on the Fuente Magna Bowl.

visit they brought the statue out of the special vault and allowed it to be filmed for the show. I encourage readers to look for this special episode of *Ancient Aliens* as it is the only television documentary that I know of which features the Pokotia Monolith and the Fuente Magna Bowl.

During the filming of that episode I had the opportunity to scrutinize at the Pokotia Monolith, which is made of red granite and is about three feet high. It is broken in two places and has inscriptions on its side and on its back. Incredibly, they are said to be Sumerian inscriptions thousands of years old.

According to Wikipedia, one of the few Internet sites with information on the two unusual objects:

> The Pokotia Monolith is a stone statue excavated from the pre-Incan site of Pokotia, six km from Tiwanaku in Bolivia. In December 2001 inscriptions and patterns on the front and back of the statue were photographed by a team led by the Bolivian archeologist Bernardo Biados. Photos of the statue show a worn male figure standing upright with

his arms at his sides. It appears to be partly clothed, with a loincloth-like garment, armbands and possibly a circlet or headdress. The face is almost entirely eroded away. There are rib-like lines on the chest. The statue is broken at the feet and at the neck. The symbols are found on the front of the legs, below the hands and on the right and left thighs. More are found back of the statue.

The Fuente Magna Bowl is made of earthen-brown fired ceramic which is beautifully engraved both inside and out with anthropomorphic characters, zoological motifs and several scripts, including what is obviously cuneiform. The script apparently comes from 3500 to 3000 BC, the Sumerian/Akkadian period. The Fuente Magna Bowl is now called the "Rosetta Stone of the Americas" because the two languages on the bowl are apparently Sumerian and the local Aymara language; the two appear to be related, with the local dialect apparently derived from Sumerian. The bowl is said to have been found in the 1950s by a worker doing digs in the vicinity of Tiwanaku.

Archeologists in Bolivia seemed to have no doubts as to the authenticity of both objects, and so the race was on to decipher the scripts. Dr. Alberto Marini analyzed the script on the Fuente Magna Bowl and reported that it was Sumerian. Then, ancient language expert Dr. Clyde A. Winters determined that the writing on the bowl was probably Proto-Sumerian,

The granite Pokotia Monolith.

145

which is a script found on many artifacts from Mesopotamia. Winters said that an identical script was used by the Elamites, and called Proto-Elamite.

Dr. Winters said he compared the writing to the Libyco-Berber writing used in the Sahara 5,000 years ago. He claimed that this writing was used by the Proto-Dravidians (of the Indus Valley), Proto-Mande, Proto-Elamites and Proto-Sumerians. As noted, he found that the Fuente Magna inscriptions are in the Proto-Sumerian script, and the symbols have several Proto-Sumerian signs joined together to represent words and sentences.[38]

Winter's work draws one more line connecting the "Old World" and the "New Worlds." One important book along these lines is *The God-Kings and the Titans* written by British historian James Bailey in 1973.[54] Bailey compares a great number of Old World and New World customs and artifacts such as pan pipes, gorgon heads, myths and construction techniques, and finds them to be identical. Bailey says that the Odyssey saga of Ulysses is a map-guide to the tin mines of Lake Titicaca. Bailey maintains that scholars still have no explanation as to where the huge amount of tin originated that enabled the Bronze Age to happen in the Middle East. He says that it came from Tiwanaku and the area around Lake Titicaca. Mythologists have tried to identify Ulysses' route by looking at sites around the Mediterranean, but on item after item, Bailey finds very interesting correspondences to what would have occurred on a boat trip from the Mediterranean to South America and concludes that the Odyssey was a transatlantic voyage to Brazil and then up the Rio La Plata to Bolivia, where the last part of the journey would have been conducted on foot.

Another archeologist who came to much the same conclusion as Bailey is the American history professor Hugh Fox of Michigan State University. In his book *The Home of the Gods*,[55] Fox maintains that a Sumerian-Phoenician-Indus Valley collection of sea-kings crossed both the Pacific and the Atlantic in order to reach the rich tin mines of South America, particularly around Lake Titicaca. In addition, Fox says that the area around Tiwanaku and Lake Titicaca corresponds to the landscape of the classical Hindu myth of Mount

146

An old print of the Gate of the Sun at Tiwanaku.

Meru, the "Home of the Gods" and that this "mythical" Hindu mountain is Tiwanaku. He also claims that the language of the Incas is related to Sanskrit, and that ancient Sumerian words are used around Lake Titicaca, including "Anaku" which he says is the Sumerian name for "Tin Lands."

Fox also discusses the Sumerian Gilgamesh story which he says describes a voyage across the ocean to Anaku, the Tin Lands, in search of a spiny thorn-apple that makes old men young again. This "apple" of eternal youth, Fox says, is representative of psychedelic drugs such as San Pedro cactus and ayahuascar.

Fox also highlights an episode in the *Argonautica* where Jason and the Argonauts, in pursuit of the Golden Fleece, arrive at the land of the Sun King and Jason is given a series of tasks to perform. One of them is to harness two fiery bulls and plow a field with them. These "bulls" are ovens or metal forges, with "feet of bronze and bronze mouths from which the breath came out in flame."[55]

Twins are part of the story of the land of Anaku, and Fox theorizes that the twins, including the two bulls breathing fire, are allegories for two different metals, tin and copper, which when mixed in the fire-breathing oven become the important final product, bronze. In Greek, he says, the twins are referred to as "anakes" which to him is a metaphor for this combining of the two metals. Gilgamesh was making his voyage to "Anaku" the land of tin—the "twins." Fox gives us this brief table:

Anakes—a Greek name for "The Twins."
Anaku—Sumerian name for the Tin Lands
Tiwanaku—The ancient House of the Sun in Bolivia right in the middle of tin country

Fox points out that the bronze twins (anakes) go to the ovens in the Tin Lands (Anaku) in order to be smelted. He says that metallurgy was "magic" and the metal worker himself was thought to be a magician who made chemical magic by marrying "the earth and the sky" or "twins," since an explanation of mineralogy and chemistry would have been impossible in the language of the time. The House of the Sun was an amazing complex for creating the bronze that would be the tears of sun. This same bronze was poured into the keystone cuts to create the clamps that held many of the giant blocks of granite together. Most of it, however, was exported, literally around the world!

Fox mentions that the land of Anaku is also spoken of as the home of the Annunaki, the elder gods. We see how part of Tiwanaku is found in the Anaku-Annunaki myths and that the Sumerian sky god, "An," is the King of the Annunaki. The area around Lake Titicaca was where the sky and earth met. Water was found here as well, a great inland sea. Also, Fox mentions the Sumerian words used in the local languages:

Titi-Tata: Father of Tin
Titi Wiyana: Altar of Tin to Adore the Sun Our King
Titi-Kaka/Thithi-Ccotta: Tin-Plated Cup that Contains All the Waters Reunited by the Four Winds of the Intis, Antillis, or Andes

Fox makes the point that the town of Oruru, south of Lake Titicaca, is another Bolivian mining center and derives its name from the Sumerian word "urruru" meaning "to smelt." Says Fox:

> So we have the tin at Tiwanaku/*anaku*, and the smelting at Oruru/*urruru*, although Arthur Posnansky, the great scholar who devoted much of his life to a study of Tiawanaku, was impressed by the size of the heaps of slag he saw at Tiawanaku when he first arrived there. The smelting wasn't all done at Oruru. The epithets connecting Lake Titicaca with charcoal and smelting intimately link the Sun King with intense metallurgical activity and again, the pre-Greek facts that are transformed into Greek myths link Helios [the Sun God] and Acetes, his son, with Hephaistos, the smith of the gods, and the chief architect for the Sun King's palace: Tiawanaku.[55]

Indeed, with the discovery of the Fuente Magna Bowl and the Pokotia Monolith with their Sumerian inscriptions, it becomes clear that there is indeed some Sumerian connection with Lake Titicaca and the megalithic ruins found there. But if that is the case, then

Huge sandstone blocks at Puma Punku.

the building of these complexes and their use as smelting/mining/ceremonial centers must have been thousands of years earlier than the present-day researchers have concluded. A storm is definitely brewing on the horizon of the Tiwanaku culture. The Great Lords, the En-Ka of the Sumerians, have yet to divulge all of their secrets to modern man.

With the discovery of the Fuente Magna Bowl and the Pokotia Monolith, we can now get a fairly accurate idea of who built Tiwanaku and when. We are also getting a better idea of what Tiwanaku was for. However, many enigmas remain, and the discovery of a Sumerian influence at Tiwanaku leads us to wonder: did the Sumerians have the kind of technology that was required to cut, shape, move and build with the gigantic blocks that are found at the site? Given the record-holding ashlars at Baalbek and the astonishing doors of Xerxes' Palace, it is clear that somebody in that area knew how to work megaliths.

What the evidence suggests is that that Tiwanaku is over 5,000 years old, dating to circa 3500-3000 BC. It was built as an ore processing plant, extracting metals from the ore that was brought to Tiwanaku from the surrounding mountains. At Tiwanaku, metal workers created molten metals of various types, from pure gold to alloys like bronze. At the site museum, a number of the bronze clamps from keystone cuts of the double-T shape can be seen, as well as gold and other metal artifacts. As noted above, even platinum, which requires a high melting point, has been found in South America, indicating some highly sophisticated metallurgical techniques. These same double-T shape keystone cuts are also found at the Cham cities of My Son, Angkor Wat and Preah Vihear. Were these cities also built prior to the time frame that modern historians typically give to these sites? It would seem so.

It is interesting to speculate that mercury may have been produced by the complex at Tiwanaku as well. Perhaps the "tears of the Sun" actually represented the liquid metal that was highly valued by the ancients, though we do not know why. Mercury has been found in sealed Mayan bowls at Lake Atitlan in Guatemala, and a lake of mercury is said to be in the tomb of the ancient Chinese

Excavations at Puma Punku revieal T-shaped keystone cuts on blocks.

emperor Chi Huang-Ti.

Mercury is derived from the mineral cinnabar, which is a Greek word that is thought to be derived ultimately from Persian and Sanskrit. Cinnabar is a red crystal associated with volcanic activity; it can be crushed and smelted to extract mercury, also known as quicksilver. Pure mercury separates from sulfur in a rotary kiln and easily evaporates. This creates a mercury vapor, and a "condensing column" is used to collect the liquid metal, which in Greek and Roman times was most often transported in iron flasks. Ceramic vessels can also be used to hold the liquid metal and this was

RECONSTRUCCION IDEAL DE AREA CIVICO CEREMONIAL DE TIWANAKU

Piramide de Puma Punku

7

8

Kerikala

6

Piramide de Akapana

Museo

Putuni 5

2

N.

1 Kantatallita

Templo de Kalasasaya

3 Templet Semisubterráneo

Javier Escalante M-88

common in China and the Americas.

The major cinnabar-mercury deposits of South America are near the town known as Huancavelica in Peru, northwest of Lake Titicaca. Huancavelica was known in pre-Inca times as the area of "Wankas." The Spanish took note of the area early in the conquest and founded the city of Huancavelica in 1572. The mines had been shown to the conquistador Jeronimo Luis de Cabrera in 1564 by the Indian Nahuincopa, who was his servant. Huancavelica became the main source for mercury in all of Spanish America, including all of Central America and Mexico. Mercury is often used to extract silver or gold from ores and the mercury from Huancavelica was used in the extraction of silver from the very important mines at Potosi, just south of Lake Titicaca.

This area was known as "Alto Peru" in colonial times. The Potosi mines and their silver were the single most important source of wealth for the Spanish in colonial America and it was the mercury from Huancavelica that made it possible. After the conquest, the entire world was flooded with Spanish "pieces of eight," the Spanish doubloon made of Potosi silver.

So, the question is: was the cinnabar and mercury from

Huancavelica exploited in ancient times by the early megalith builders at Tiwanaku and possibly Chavin? Activity is known to go back to at least 1400 BC. If not these mines of cinnabar, then perhaps some other mines now exhausted or undiscovered were the source?

As previously noted, mercury is mentioned in the ancient vimana texts in Sanskrit, texts that talk about ancient flying vehicles and other high tech devices, including weapons. Mercury was apparently a part of the vortex technology that powered the vimana aircraft. Mercury is also said to have been behind the Nazi "foo fighter" technology that produced glowing, pulsing globes that appeared to be some sort of flying gyro. Foo fighters were used in the final days of WWII by the Germans as a last ditch defense against the squadrons of Allied bombers that were flying over Germany at the time. The Germans had hoped that swarms of pulsing foo fighters emitting an electromagnetic field would interfere with the electrical systems of the bombers. Though it didn't work on a large scale, the foo fighters caused some RAF pilots to return home before dropping their ordnance. It is thought that modified versions of foo fighters were used as the plasma-gyro engines in the experimental designs of flying disks that the Germans were starting to develop.

At the famous Sun Gate at Tiwanaku the central figure is a "god" thought to be the Andean god-man Virachocha who wears a feathered headdress, holds a snake staff in each hand and his three tears going down each cheek. He is surrounded by winged-birdmen who are depicted running. Apparently they are very busy. Are these birdmen people who had the ability of flight? Might they be flying across the Pacific from Champa? Are the staffs of Viracocha surveying and mining tools? Are

Viracocha on the Gate of the Sun.

153

the drops or tears on the cheeks of Viracocha representative of the molten metals—the tears of the sun—that these busy flying men were producing? It would seem that the answer is yes to all of these questions.

While it would seem that Tiwanaku, Puma Punku, Cuzco and other sites may be 5,000 years old, mainstream archeology actually dates these sites as existing at the same time as the Cham Civilization. They date Tiwanaku to circa 200 AD and sites like Cuzco to circa 1200 AD, the almost exact dates that are given to Champa (I have also maintained that the dating of megalithic sites is tricky since the stone itself cannot be dated, only surrounding objects like bones or pottery). Still, no matter what the ultimate dating comes to with more precise studies in the future, the transpacific connection between the Cham and South America would appear very real.

So, if Champa was in contact with Tiwanaku, even if it was an older megalithic site, were the major sites in Southeast Asia also mining facilities, port facilities and, in some cases, airports? In fact, there is a megalithic city in Southeast Asia that is nearly identical to Machu Picchu! Let us examine Angkor Wat and the mountaintop city of Preah Vihear.

The Metal Clamps of the Cham at Angkor Wat

In 1999 I made my first trip the Cambodian town of Siem Reap by flying to the city from Bangkok. At that time Cambodia was just opening up to tourism after years of destructive wars. The area was just developing its now massive tourist trade. Like other tourists, I hired a motor scooter and driver as my taxi and visited the impressive ruins of Angkor Wat and Angkor Thom.

On this first trip I noticed the T-shaped keystone cuts on some of the blocks and this excited me. Japanese archeologists were doing work at Angkor Wat at the time and were also excited to find keystone cuts and even some of the metal alloy clamps that were used in the cuts. The Japanese, unlike most European or American archeologists, realized how important this unusual style of construction is. Hopefully they were also aware that this was found in Bolivia, Peru and other locations, like My Son. The Japanese even put posters of the metal clamp in various places around Angkor Wat and Angkor Thom.

In April of 2014 I visited Siem Reap again, this time with my wife, Jennifer. We were there to visit Angkor Wat and other ruins in the area. One of the impressive stone ruins is the mysterious temple of Preah Vihear, Cambodia's Machu Picchu. Indeed the construction at Preah Vihear is very similar to that at Machu Picchu, and keystone cuts are used there that are identical to those in Cuzco, Ollantaytambo and Tiwanaku!

Outside our hotel we met a young man with a motorized rickshaw who offered to take us around the extensive ruins of Angkor Wat and Angkor Thom. We negotiated a price and Jennifer and I jumped in the back. After negotiating the busy streets of Siem Reap for some blocks we were zooming northward on a perfectly straight tree-lined street that would take us to the ancient city of Angkor, the capital of the Khmer Empire. The founding of this city and the empire is traditionally dated to the year 802 AD when Jayavarman II had himself declared chakravartin ("king of the world," or "king of kings"). Tradition says that he had been a prince in Java (Indonesia) but was creating a new kingdom and capital at Angkor. This empire lasted about 600 years, collapsing sometime in the 15th century.

But, it would seem that civilization in this area and these cities go back many centuries more in time, and all of Cambodia, reached by the Mekong River of Vietnam, was part of Champa. Cham and Khmer are essentially the same word, and known Champa speaking people still live in northern Cambodia, a last remnant, aside from the megalithic ruins, of the Cham in Cambodia.

"Let's put the Cham back in Cambodia," I said to Jennifer as we got back into our rickshaw after looking at keystone cuts at Angkor Thom. "That would make a good bumper sticker. What do you think?"

"Well, I guess it seems that the Cham and the Khmer are all the same people," said Jennifer.

The Cham Empire, so vast that it spanned the Pacific Ocean, was breaking up starting around the time that Srivijaya began to assume power in southern Sumatra in 650 AD. From this time the

A pair of T-shaped keystone cuts missing the metal clamp at Angkor Wat.

Champa were unable to control Sumatra and Java and soon got into wars with these upstart states. In my estimation, what happened around 800 AD is that the Javan prince Jayavarman II invaded up the Mekong and took over Angkor Thom and Angkor Wat, which were already in existence. He is also said to have made a pilgrimage to the megalithic mountain city of Preah Vihear, a city already built by the Cham. Jayavarman II adopted and changed the Cham language to become the Khmer language of today, a mixture of Cham, Sanskrit and Javanese.

This was also Funan, the Chinese "Pacified South." Wikipedia says that one French archeologist proposed that use of the name Funan should be abandoned in favor of the names of some of its important cities, such as Bhavapura, Aninditapura, Shresthapura and Vyadhapura. This would imply that Funan was not one unified country but a number of city-states. This was the thalassocratic system of the Cham.

Did the prince, declaring himself "King of the World," mean that he was now the heir to the Cham Empire, one that spanned two oceans and several seas? In a seagoing empire like the Cham, the person who controlled the Indian Ocean, Bay of Siam, Java Sea and the Pacific Islands, would be the king of a seemingly endless empire.

The legend that Jayavarman II had been a prince in Java leads us in this direction, and if he were "king of the world" he may have been giving himself the traditional Cham title of sovereign over a vast area of the known world: Southeast Asia, Sumatra, Borneo, Sulawesi, Java, Bali and beyond! These ancient voyagers built great ships and knew navigation by the stars like experts. They were Hindu-Buddhists who built great temples, including huge artificial pyramid mountains like Borobadur in central Java. Many of their structures were megalithic, and blocks of granite and basalt were cut and articulated as if power tools had been used. And one other thing: they used the same keystone cuts and clamps that are found in Egypt, Greece, Peru and Bolivia as well as in Java, Vietnam and Cambodia.

I had visited Siem Reap and the Angkor ruins for a few days back in 1999, when it had only been open to tourists for a few years. I had seen some keystone cuts at the time, and on our recent visit, I

A T-shaped keystone cut at Angkor Thom.

158 A statue of the Hindu god Vishnu from Angkor Wat with an Egyptian-style hat.

wanted to find them again. I intended to look for more of the telltale T-shaped cuts in the rock that corresponded to matching cuts in adjacent rocks and held a metal clamp (or cramp) that spanned two blocks of hewn stone.

Our rickshaw driver let us off at Angkor Thom first, and we began exploring the impressive temples decorated with hundreds of faces of the bodhisattva Avilokitesvara. To behold the sightless faces of the saints staring off into the void is very moving, and, especially in places where the jungle has reclaimed some areas of the ruins, very atmospheric. There were some other tourists climbing through the many doorways and stairs, but we were fortunate that it wasn't too crowded. I soon found what I was looking for: some stone blocks with T-shaped keystone cuts in them, just like at Tiwanaku in Bolivia or Ollantaytambo in Peru. Was this proof of a transpacific connection between Southeast Asia and the Americas? I felt it was, but wanted to find more proof.

Preah Vihear Temple: Cambodia's Machu Picchu?

While we were in Siem Reap we discovered that there was a megalithic mountain temple in the very north of Cambodia called Preah Vihear. Until very recently it had been closed to tourists. It was perched on the edge of a high mountain cliff and had huge walls, windows and doors, though much of the site lay in ruins. We made arrangements through the hotel for a private taxi to drive us there and back; it was a several-hour drive north of Siem Reap so we would have to leave at six in the morning.

We left the next morning, stopping for some juice and breakfast buns along the way. We zoomed on the two-lane paved road north to the archeological site of Angkor, and then turned northeast for a distance to a large crossroads where the main north-south road joined this road from Siem Reap. We turned north and kept on driving, occasionally passing villages strung out along the paved highway. The nice road was a gift from various governments, and was continually improved upon by the Cambodian military because it was an important route to the mountainous Thai border where a number of skirmishes had occurred in the past 10 years—some of

An aeria view of Preah Vihear in northern Cambodia.

them focused around the Temple of Preah Vihear.

At one point, just after seeing a large snake in the road, the car began to shake like a tire had burst. Our driver stopped in a pleasant open stretch of the jungle road and we all got out to look at the problem. Sure enough, we had a flat back tire, but it turned out that the driver did not have a spanner that would undo the lug nuts on his tire. He did have a small spanner, but it was cracked and merely spun around the nuts. I looked up and down the road and there was no car in sight. We were in one of the loneliest spots in Cambodia, it seemed.

We knew that a car would come along at some point, and after about 10 minutes a man on a motorcycle came by going north. We flagged him down and our driver spoke with him. Suddenly he jumped on the back of the motorcycle and said he was coming back soon. "We'll wait here," I said, waving him off, knowing we had nowhere to go.

He sped off clutching the helmeted young man driving the steed of steel. The road was still paved in this part and we smiled as they disappeared into the distance.

I looked at Jennifer and started fishing in my backpack for some snacks and my water bottle. I looked cautiously around, and decided

160

to find a place to quickly relieve myself. There were probably all kinds of poisonous snakes just beyond the pavement in the dense green forest to the east and south of the road. I saw a muddy dirt track going off to the east and decided to follow it for a bit. It had been raining the night before and things were pretty messy. But soon I was back on the paved road by the car with Jennifer. There was still no sign of our driver.

After half an hour, our driver came back with all the right tools and soon we were back on the road heading north to the mountains of the Thai border. After a while we came to a small military control post with a number of police cars and military convoy transports parked around.

We were ushered into a small wooden cabin where we had to show our passports and then buy the special tickets for Preah Vihear. We also paid for special transport to the top of the mountain, as the road is too steep for regular cars and all visitors have to ascend on motorcycles or in special trucks. At the time of our visit, parts of the road were nearly washed out and it would be a difficult journey.

Clinging to the backs of our respective motorcycle drivers, we

The megalithic wall of three windows at Preah Vihear.

161

zoomed off up what began as a very nice paved road, but without any painted stripes or lines. It soon degraded in several places to a road that barely hung onto the cliff, with very steep grades up the mountain. The view was pretty spectacular, however. Suddenly we came to a halt at what was essentially a tea-stall camp and parking lot for tourists, but a Cambodian military base was located here as well.

A megalithic doorway at Preah Vihear.

A pile of highly articulated granite blocks at Preah Vihear.

Soldiers hung around the half dozen tea stalls with motorcycle drivers who were waiting for the visitors they had brought up to return from the ruins for the ride down the mountain. We bought more tickets to enter the archeological park and then proceeded along a trail to the partially destroyed temple on the northern slope of the mountain. Preah Vihear Temple is situated atop a 1,722-foot cliff along the Thai border in the Dangrek Mountains. A Thai military base could be seen across a steep mountain valley that was mostly covered in dark green jungle, though huge cliff faces of granite stuck out in the high mountain greenery. It was an exciting and spectacular vista, and around me I was just beginning to notice the stone steps and gutters that once formed a huge staircase to the top of the mountain and the megalithic temple buildings there.

Preah Vihear Temple is a megalithic Hindu temple that is said to have been built during the reigns of the Khmer kings Suryavarman I (1002–1050 AD) and Suryavarman II (1113–1150 AD). There is an inscription found at the temple giving a detailed account of Suryavarman II spending time at the temple doing sacred rituals, celebrating religious festivals and making gifts. These gifts were

163

A T-shaped keystone cut at Preah Vihear.

mainly golden bowls, white parasols and ceremonial elephants given to his guru, an aged Brahmin priest named Divakarapandita. According to the inscription the Brahmin donated a golden statue of a dancing Shiva known as "Nataraja" to the temple. Because of the sparseness of inscriptions at the site, some archeologists (such as myself) have suggested that the temple is many hundreds of years older and was already in existence during the reigns of Khmer kings Suryavarman I and Suryavarman II. The large lichen patches on parts of the temple that are already in ruins bear testament to the antiquity of the site. No matter who built it, the design and construction exhibit flawless megalithic engineering of the highest caliber.

The main stairway entrance to climb the mountain to the temple (which we avoided by taking the motorcycles up the newer road) is actually in Thailand, and Preah Vihear Temple has always been at the center of border disputes between the countries. The temple is so old and fantastic that Thailand would really like to see it inside of its own territory, where it would be an important tourist destination. However, in 1962 the lengthy dispute was settled in

Cambodia's favor by the International Court of Justice in The Hague, Netherlands.

This dispute flared up again in 2008 when some sort of military clash took place in the area, and the Thai military began shelling the vicinity of the ancient temple in April of 2009. Cambodia claims that parts of the temple along the extensive stairway were damaged. Both sides shelled the other's bunker positions every once in awhile in the ensuing years, which effectively closed the site to tourists. A photographer we met at the site told us that a shelling battle in 2011 left a Cambodian soldier dead. Finally in November of 2013 the International Court of Justice ruled again that the temple was part of Cambodia, though only a few hundred meters from the Thai border, and that all Thai military forces should leave the area. Tourism at the temple resumed shortly after this ruling, but the military still tightly controls the area.

According to the local guidebooks the temple complex runs 2,600 feet (800 meters) along a north-south axis facing the plains to the north (Thailand). A wide causeway and steps rise up the hill in a southerly direction toward the main temple sanctuary situated at the top. It is thought that the temple complex is meant to be a stylized representation of Mount Meru, the home of the gods, a mythical mountain that is traditionally thought to be in Tibet. The Chinese similarly believe that the Land of the Immortals is somewhere in the Kun Lun Mountains of Tibet. So, even remote temples like Preah Vihear are connected to Tibet within the Hindu-Buddhist universe. Curiously, certain Tibetan nomads (sometimes called bandits) are known as the Champa, the same name given to the Cham in Vietnam. Preah Vihear, like My Son in Vietnam, was essentially a Hindu temple, rather than a Buddhist temple. This also is an indication that Preah Vihear is a very ancient site.

According to the tourist guides the approach to the sanctuary is punctuated by five gopuras, or stone wall structures that shield the temple sanctuary beyond. The gopuras block a visitor's view of the next, higher part of the temple until (s)he passes through the gateway in the wall.

The path from the parking lot led us to the fifth (and lowest) gopura, where a group of soldiers invited us to climb past the security cordons onto a ruined platform where we could get a better view of the Thai valley below. Leaving this area and climbing some remnant stairs to the fourth gopura brought us to one of the temple's finest artistic relics, a depiction of the Churning of the Sea of Milk, a famous Hindu reference to the Milky Way and the cosmos. The third gopura is the largest, flanked by two large halls.

One of the gopura walls has three huge megalithic windows and I was reminded of Machu Picchu and its famous Temple of Three Windows. They were remarkably similar! Were the builders of Preah Vihear also the builders of Machu Picchu? It was an intriguing thought. The time frame was similar for both sites, at least within the timeline of traditional archeology.

Eventually, after walking past these several huge stone walls made with perfectly cut and fitted blocks of granite, we reached the final temple. Temporarily bypassing the main part of the temple, we walked outside to the back and, at the southernmost point of Preah Vihear, stood on the sheer cliff that dropped steeply into the jungle valleys below. The view over the vast plain going south to Angkor

A T-shaped keystone cut at Preah Vihear.

166

was very spectacular. It was an inspiring view and standing near the cliff edge was something of a thrill. No barrier wall had been built in ancient times or modern. At any time one could easily hurl himself off the cliff, or even possibly slip while looking over the edge. Being in remote Cambodia, the site was not carefully monitored nor were there any guides offering their services, at least at that time. There was the occasional soldier on the site but they did not bother or attempt to supervise any of the tourists who wandered about the ruins.

Khmer-Cham the builders of Preah Vihear and Machu Picchu?

Back in the main temple we found that many of the walls and ceilings had collapsed, so many parts were piled with huge stone blocks, dressed in many different ways. I found one pile that had blocks of granite that had keystone cuts on them and was thrilled. They were T-shaped keystone cuts chiseled into blocks that had once been part of an inner temple wall. Keystone cuts, of any kind, are not usually visible on the exterior of a building utilizing them. Rather, they are on blocks that are part of major structural walls. I took photos of several of these tumbled blocks with keystone cuts.

What struck me was the similarity to the T-shaped keystone cuts at Tiwanaku and Ollantaytambo, both in South America. As we have noted the Cham site at My Son in central Vietnam also has these same T-shaped keystone cuts. It would seem that the civilization that was constructing temples in northern Cambodia was the same civilization constructing buildings in Vietnam, Indonesia and South America. As I have stated, this same civilization would have constructed some of the megalithic remains that we see on Pacific Islands such as those in Fiji and Tonga and even the enigmatic basalt city of Nan Madol on Pohnpei in Micronesia.

Indeed, both Preah Vihear and Machu Picchu feature a well-constructed megalithic wall of three huge windows. The wall of three windows at Machu Picchu is probably the most photographed of all the walls in the central part of this mountaintop city. Both of these megalithic cities are perched on the edge of cliffs that offer spectacular views of the surrounding countryside. Let us note some of the important similarities between Preah Vihear and Machu Picchu:

1. Both are megalithic cities built out of perfectly cut and fitted granite blocks.
2. Both are built next to large cliffs on the top of a mountain.
3. Both feature a megalithic wall of three large windows.
4. Both had engineers who used the unusual T-shaped keystone cuts in which molten metals were poured (keystone cuts are not visible at Machu Picchu but are found at nearby Ollantaytambo, a temple acknowledged to have been built by the same culture).

Having been to Machu Picchu nearly 20 times over the decades, I am very familiar with this site and was astonished at how similar Preah Vihear was to the famous city in the Andes Mountains of South America. To me the builders of these and other similar megalithic cities in Southeast Asia and South America were the same—they used the same building techniques and styles.

While Machu Picchu, as well as Ollantaytambo and Cuzco, is said to have been built by the Incas around the period of 1200 AD, I have maintained in my book *Ancient Technology in Peru and Bolivia*[18] that these structures were already in existence when the Incas came into power and had been built by the same culture that had built Tiwanaku, Puma Punku and the megalithic towers at Sillustani and Cutimbo along the western side of Lake Titicaca.

What other civilization, aside from the Cham, could have made such similar structures on both sides of the Pacific Ocean?

What seems to be the big confusion among modern historians and archeologists is whether Southeast Asia and Indonesia were ever a unified, highly technological society. I say that there was a unified Cham-Kham civilization that stretched far into the many islands of the Pacific. Many of the island nations today may owe their patrimony to this early Cham-Kham civilization. It was one that encompassed all races of mankind: Orientals, Caucasians, Blacks, and even American Indians. They swept into the Pacific and built numerous monuments. Many of the islands were probably

Top: The wall of three windows at Preah Vihear. Below: The wall at Machu Picchu.

already inhabited from earlier ventures into the vast Pacific Ocean.

Are the Khmer and the Champa and the rulers of Java part of and the same Hindu-Buddhist Empire that once ruled the waves of the Pacific and even reached South America with its metal tools and amazing mastery of science, metallurgy and technology? I think they were all part of a mysterious Hindu-Buddhist civilization that seems lost to world history.

It would seem that the Egyptian-Buddhist-Hindu country that spanned Southeast Asia into Indonesia should simply be called Kham or Cham and recognized for what it was: a huge empire that, in fact, spanned the Pacific Ocean in the years 200 to 1200 AD, and probably long before. Many of the buildings, with their keystone cuts, may be from a time before 200 AD and hopefully further research will tell.

Clearly, the Cham civilization would have commanded thousands of large, ocean-going vessels. These vessels could carry war elephants, fully-armed troops of soldiers, and the stonecutting tools that were the hallmarks of this megalithic culture. While they may have used iron chisels, hammers and even diamond-ruby saws, we still do not know how they moved the largest of the blocks of granite or basalt, those weighing many tons, in some cases up to 500 tons.

The transpacific voyages may have started with the huge assembly of thousands of ships at the Cham Islands off of Da Nang in Central Vietnam, and then these ships set off for the southern Philippines and then out into the Pacific for the long crossing to the Americas. Along the way the sailors would have collected rainwater as well as caught fish in the lines that were continually dragging behind the ships. They would stop at various islands along the way to collect fresh water and food and some of these islands would have their own megalithic structures built, as we shall see.

Let's look at some of the enigmatic megalithic sites in Indonesia that may be associated with the Cham before we turn our attention to Pacific islands and sites in the Americas that were colonized by the Cham.

Chapter Four

THE ISLAND OF SULAWESI AND THE MYSTERY OF BADA VALLEY

The debt we owe to the play of imagination is incalculable.
—Carl Gustav Jung

In July of 2012 my wife and I had the opportunity to visit the remote Bada Valley on the Indonesian island of Sulawesi. We first learned about Bada Valley when photographer and Tiki art curator Douglas Nason of Los Angeles spoke at the conference we held in Sedona in 2003. He showed a few photos of the valley, and told us later that they were from the Tropenmuseum in Amsterdam. That stately museum, east of the city center, is part of the Royal Tropical Institute. According to its website:

> The Tropenmuseum …is one of Europe's leading ethno-graphic museums, renowned for its collection. The permanent and temporary exhibitions display art objects, photographs, music and film from non-western cultures. The permanent exhitions are Southeast Asia, Oceania, Western Asia and Africa.

After viewing more photos of the Bada Valley on the Tropenmuseum website, we realized that a megalithic mystery was hidden in this remote valley in Southeast Asia. On a visit to the museum, we were impressed with its extensive collection, and particularly interested in the birdman artifacts from diverse cultures worldwide.

Sulawesi and the Enigma of Bada Valley

After some years, we finally slotted a trip to Sulawesi. Even in the age of the Internet, details of the remote valley were hard to find, and many particulars had to be worked out on the road. One intrepid World Explorers Club member, John Feiertag of Cincinnati, Ohio decided to join us on our exploratory jaunt.

We flew via Japan to Singapore, where we stopped for a couple of days to de-jet lag. We stayed in the lively Chinatown neighborhood, and took a taxi over to the historic colonial Ruffles Hotel, where we had an obligatory Singapore Sling in its place of invention, the Long Bar. We continued on to Jakarta, on the island of Java, Indonesia and plotted our advance toward the Bada Valley. We had found out via the Internet that the best way to get there was from the town of Palu, on the island of Sulawesi. We went to a local travel agency booked our round trip plane tickets, which included stopovers on Borneo in each direction.

We found that Palu was a nice town located on the beautiful Palu Bay. We stayed at the upscale Swiss Belhotel, which had a good breakfast buffet and pool, and set about firming up our further plans. We had managed to make reservations at some cottages in the town closest to the Bada Valley, Tentena, via the Internet, but we weren't sure how to get there, or from there to the megaliths.

The first thing we did in Palu was go to the local museum. While we were taking pictures of a number of reconstructions of the region's megaliths that were displayed in the yard, a busload of young people training to be tour guides arrived. Seeing people who looked like actual foreign tourists, they formed a small swarm around us hoping to practice their language and hospitality skills. At first, we were not so thrilled with the attention, but it soon became obvious that a couple of the senior guides had a lot of valuable information and were happy to help facilitate our trip.

We learned that there were actually three main valleys that contained the strange megaliths, the Bada, Napu and Besoa; the latter two were even more remote than the former, but all were part of the Lore Lindu National Park. This cleared up some confusion we had experienced when trying to pinpoint the megaliths from afar. The senior guides confirmed that the valleys contained dozens of finely carved megaliths in the forms of statues and jars, and that the current residents were as mystified as to who built them as are archeologists. They also told us that the megaliths are thought by locals and Indonesian archeologists to be at least 6,000 years old.

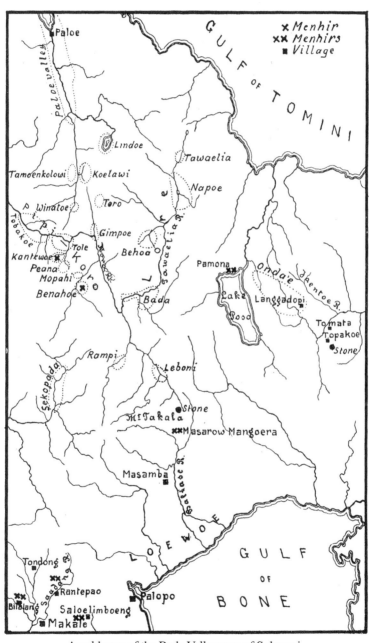

An old map of the Bada Valley area of Sulawesi.

Estimates we had read ranged from 5,000 to 1,500 years old. We also learned that irregular private buses ran the route from Palu to Tentena, and it was necessary to book seats in advance and let the drivers know where to pick you up and drop you off. Once near the Bada Valley, you need to either hike into the National Park (which would take days) or hire a jeep to drive you in and out. One of the guides gave us a contact name to help us make those arrangements, and we thanked them for getting us that much closer to the mysterious

An old photo of the largest statue in Bada Valley.

174

megaliths. We knew that they would be magnificent and enigmatic, and testify to a genius and high civilization that we know nothing about!

That night we phoned the contact to start making our travel arrangements. The next day, with plans underway, we decided to hire a taxi to take us to the Tanjung Karang beach area in the Donggala region, about an hour away from our hotel up the west side of Palu Bay. There are several scuba diving sites in Palu Bay, and we were told we could go snorkeling right off the beach in that area. Our driver took us to the Prince John Resort, where we hired fins and masks that cost a whopping $3 for the day. Entering the clear, warm water, we began to float over a spectacular coral reef teeming with life. The colorful corals and fish delighted us for hours, as did the cold beer at the thatch-roofed beach bar.

The next day we were ready to go, and boarded our slightly uncomfortable minibus for the seven-hour ride to Tentena. Although Bada Valley is relatively close to Palu as the crow flies, the bus had to take the road, which went around the east side of Palu Bay, over the mountains to the east, and down to the Gulf of Tomini (part of the Molucca Sea) on the other side. From there, we drove

One of the statues with tiki face in Bada Valley.

Two statues with tiki faces in Bada Valley.

southeast along the gulf to the town of Poso, where we headed inland toward Lake Poso.

The town of Tentena is on the north end of the scenic lake, which is the third deepest lake in Indonesia. Our cottages were located across a wooden pedestrian bridge from the center of town, and once we were settled in, we crossed the sometimes-rickety span to start exploring. We had to admit, there wasn't much excitement in town. A waterfall with ten drops was said to be a really nice attraction, but it was a serious hike away, and not on the agenda. We decided to have dinner at one of the restaurants on the lake, where we attracted the attention of a guy who worked at the local tourist information office, which was open very sporadically. He did not know more than anyone else about the strange megaliths nearby, but he did clear up one mystery for us. On the way to Tentena we had noticed quite a few Hindu-looking temples, especially along the Gulf of Tomini, but we knew that Hinduism had been displaced by Islam throughout most of Indonesia, except on certain islands such as Bali. We learned that the Indonesian government had continued until recent times to implement a transmigration program (actually begun in the early 20th century by the Dutch), wherein people from overpopulated islands like Java and Bali were relocated to the

176

more sparsely populated outer islands like Sumatra and Sulawesi. According to our friend from the tourism office, the Balinese implants on Sulawesi brought with them a keen work ethic, and their communities have really thrived.

When we returned to the Ue Datu Cottages, we found that a jeep and driver had been secured for our foray into the Bada Valley the next day. We would be picked up at 7 am, and Ellie from the Cottages would go along as our English-speaking guide. It was estimated that the 40-mile trip to the valley would take about four hours. This seemed excessive, and we held out hope that they were exaggerating the difficulty of the trip.

As it came to pass, they were not. The only road into the Bada Valley is unpaved and very rugged. Bridges were only built over the turbulent rivers five years ago, before which time the trip into the valley took several days. We held on to the sides of the jeep as we bumped and ground our way along. It did not help that the rainy season, normally lasting from November to April, did not seem to have come to an end, even by July. Many locals commented upon this situation. Finally (after, yes, four hours), we rounded a bend and

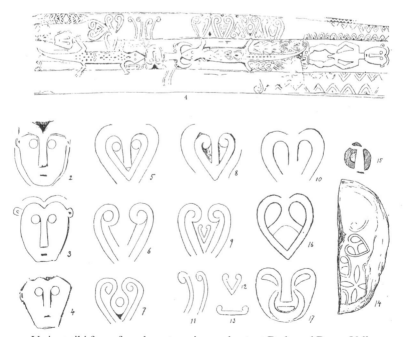

Various tiki faces found on stone jars and vats at Bada and Besoa Valley.

got a view of the beautiful green valley spread out below us.

The valley is part of the Lore Lindu National Park, which also includes the Napu and Besoa Valleys and is part of the UNESCO World Network of Biosphere Reserves. The area provides a habitat for many rare species, including 77 bird species endemic to Sulawesi. Wildlife ranges from the large mountain anoa (a kind of water buffalo) to thousands of species of insects. Of greater interest to us, there are over 400 worked granite objects in the area, most of which are megalithic; about 30 are in human form. There are also scores of giant stone urns, called kalamba, scattered around in a seemingly haphazard fashion. Large stone disks, called tutu'na, are also found; it is supposed these may be the lids of the kalamba. Other types of stones called batu dakon are flat or convex, and show channels and irregular pitting and other depressions. The local ethnic groups in the area are the Kaili, Kulavi and Lore, but they do not claim these megaliths, said to be the finest of their type in Indonesia, as their heritage. They do not even have stories built up around them, except for in a few isolated instances where a particular stone has played a part in the area's history. They say the statues were there when their ancestors entered the valley.

When we entered the valley, we were taken to the main

An old photo of some of the huge vats found in Besoa Valley.

Tiki face carved into a jar lid found in Bada Valley.

administrative center where we were joined by our local guide, Michael, who was in full military uniform complete with machete. Part of the arrangements made for us included getting a permit to enter the park, which entails being assigned such a guide. We assumed he was there more to protect the statues from us than to protect us from some danger. It seemed pretty calm amongst the villages in the valley and the ubiquitous rice fields. The people there are fairly well off by Indonesian standards, growing a strain of rice unique to the area as well as coffee to export. There is also gold in the rivers and streams, particularly the Sungai Malei that runs through the valley. The people were Christianized in the early 20th century by Dutch and other European missionaries.

We were taken to a wooden building next to a store, and Ellie told us it was time to eat. She brought out the box lunches she had brought along, and although we weren't really hungry yet, we were told that the stopping point was the only facility in the valley that could accommodate us for a meal. It was a hotel, although there

179

An old photo of a large jar and cover in Bada Valley.

appeared to be no guests at the moment, and they had a long table in a large room where we could spread out our fried chicken and vegetables. They also had a refrigerator so we could order Cokes or water. We had a leisurely meal, and provided great entertainment for the children of the hoteliers.

Finally, we got to the part we'd all been waiting for—we were let loose amongst the megaliths! First we went to some Tiki-looking statues that were a short drive out of the village to the north. The largest, standing about six feet high, had a long nose that was similar to Easter Island heads and Tiki statues.

We returned to the village and drove out of the southwest part into the lush green rice fields that stretched out through the large north-south valley. Soon we were shown various fields with large stone jars—or the remains of them—that seemed to dot the ancient fields. Michael told us that it was thought that the stone jars, statues and other monuments in Bada Valley were from around 4,000 BC, and that meant that these granite jars had been in these fields for

An old photo of some of the huge vats found in Besoa Valley.

quite a long time. The statues were probably treated as ancient gods, and farmers kept a certain safe distance from them, while the stone jars were safer to farm immediately in front of.

> A hard time we had of it,
> With an alien people
> Clutching their gods.
> —*Journey of the Magi*, T.S. Eliot

We marched through rice fields, carefully walking on the hard, raised walls that defined the different levels of the fields. We could see a large stone jar in the far side of the paddy and headed for it. We stopped to examine some exquisitely made objects, and to me it was evident that some sort of power tools were used to hollow out these large granite vessels.

The walls of the jars were, in many cases, extremely thin and finely made. A broken jar with the thin wall still imbedded into the rice paddy showed how strong and durable these things were. Who had made them? What were they for? Did the makers have power tools and gold mining equipment when they arrived at this remote

181

location? It would seem that they were looking for gold—and found it—at Bada Valley. Were they the Annunaki coming from Sumeria looking for gold? Perhaps they were the enigmatic Cham who, as we have seen, were megalith builders from central Vietnam who were allied with ancient China and India, as well as Egypt and the African continent.

We jumped back into the old Land Cruiser and with a grinding of gears we left these rice paddies and visited several other ancient statues near the top of a small hill south of the village. One looked very much like a small alien creature with large almond eyes, while another had a beard like the famous Kon-Tiki statue at Tiwanaku. The statues had a certain Easter Island/Tiki-air about them. Other statues at nearby Napu Valley had an Olmec-African look to them. This Egypto-African-Asian look is distinct and common to both the Olmecs of Mesoamerica and the Cham of Southeast Asia, including Indonesia.

Indeed, the old photos from the Tropenmuseum in Amsterdam underlined how much they looked like Olmec statues in central Mexico, on both the Pacific and Atlantic coasts of the Isthmus of Tehuantepec. An extensive treatment of the Olmecs and their connection to ancient China and Southeast Asia can be found in my book *The Mystery of the Olmecs*.[22] It provides as much proof as possible that the Olmecs were a transoceanic group that were connected with both the Egyptians across the Atlantic, and the Indo-

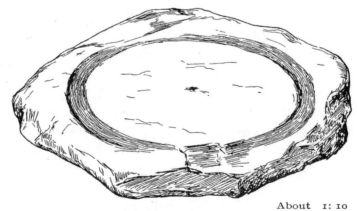

About 1: 10

A granite slab with a perfect circle cut into it found in Besoa Valley.

182

Chinese-Asians across the Pacific.

Our group continued south out of town and over a bridge that spanned the medium-sized stream that meandered through Bada Valley giving fresh water to everyone throughout the isolated mountain realm. The bigger, gold bearing river raged downhill on the eastern side of the valley and judging from the large boulders that one could see along the sides of the raging river, this riverbed was probably the quarry for the statues and jars.

We then came to a large cleared space where the largest of the statues was found looking south, leaning terribly to one side, like a drunken sailor who was about to crash into a table at any second. This statue is quite impressive and must weigh many tons. Made of fine-grained white granite and nearly 12 feet tall, it is an impressive Tiki statue by any standards.

We parked the jeep and filed out onto the grassy plaza. We all took some pictures and examined the imposing statue. It seemed to have been well cut and the sharp nose and eyes showed exact curves that only a power tool could possibly make. Even after many thousands of years the hard stone still held the perfectly cut sweep of the nose. The maker was a stonemason of the most excellent skill.

Were these the first Tiki statues, a style that was to spread across the Pacific to Fiji, Tonga, Samoa, Tahiti and the Marquesas and on to the Americas? Did the famous Tiki statues at Tiwanaku and Tahiti have their beginning in the remote highlands of Sulawesi in the Shangri-La world of Bada Valley? Indeed, Bada Valley is theorized by some anthropologists to be original home to the modern, genetically modified version of rice—a form of rice that is similar of modern rice but slightly more primitive, or wild, from which modern rice is derived. Is Bada Valley the home garden of the rice we eat now, created about 6,000 years ago? As we looked out around the valley in the mid-afternoon light on that cloudy day, it seemed mind-boggling.

Had an ancient civilization with large boats and power tools arrived at Sulawesi and come to Bada Valley in search of the golden metal? Ancient rice paddies, megalithic objects and gold are what are found in the area. Bada Valley seems to have been

A photo of the Plain of Jars in northern Laos.

some sort of mining center where the miners used their power tools to occasionally make statues and huge stone jars. But what were the large, nearly indestructible granite jars for? For that answer, we would be smart to look at another strange megalithic site in Southeast Asia: the Plain of Jars in Laos.

Companion to Bada Valley: The Plain of Jars, Laos

One cannot visit the Shangri-La of Bada Valley without noticing the profound similarities to the strange Plain of Jars in central Laos. "Plain of Jars" is the moniker given the Xieng Khouang Plateau located in a province of the same name at the northern end of the Annamese Cordillera, the principal mountain range of Indochina. Here, thousands of gigantic stone jars dot the landscape in groups ranging from a single jar to several hundred. Said Madeleine Colani, an early researcher, "They are disposed without regularity, some of them pressing one against another, others quite isolated. Each one is fashioned from a separate block of stone, and a small number of them are very well executed, as though turned on a lathe, bespeaking the hand of a true artist."

Unfortunately, the Plain of Jars was a target in the US carpet bombing of Laos during the Vietnam War. Laos is relatively sparsely populated for Southeast Asia, and during that conflict, it

184

became the most heavily bombed country per capita in the world. The US dumped more ordnance on Laos between 1964 and 1973 than it dropped during all of World War II. It is estimated that 80 million explosives failed to detonate, and the huge number of UXOs (unexploded ordnance) are a continuing problem for the people of Laos some 40 years later. In Xieng Khouang Province, 25% of the total land area is still contaminated with unexploded bombs and land mines. This situation has stood in the way of the Lao government's plan to develop the area for tourism and get UNESCO World Heritage status. The Lao-UNESCO Programme for Safeguarding the Plain of Jars was established in 1998 to promote cleanup endeavors and otherwise prepare the area for increased tourism. Laos has seen strong growth in tourism since 1990, and in Xieng Khouang visits include jar sites that have been cleared as well as colorful traditional ethnic villages and historic sites relating to the Indochina wars of the 20th century with Japan, France and the US.

A University of Iowa paper posted on its web site (uiowa.edu) says that the Plain of Jars became known in the West when it first drew the attention of a French customs agent named Vinet in 1909, when Laos was part of French Indochina, which also included the current states of Cambodia and Vietnam. A French archeologist named Henri Parmentier visited the site in 1923 and reported that the jars were being plundered by the local citizenry. Nevertheless, he was able to get an idea of what the jars originally contained: pots, hand axes, beads of glass or carnelian, earrings of stone or glass, bronze bells and, often, human bones. Also, something he enigmatically described as "a bizarre object which we call a lamp"—what might these have been? Some sort of electrical device? I haven't been able to come up with a further description as of the time of writing.

In the 1930s, Madeleine Colani entered the scene and documented the Plain of Jars in a 600-page thesis titled *The Megaliths of Upper Laos*. Colani was a French geologist, paleobotanist, archeologist and ethnographer who had decided to move to Indochina in 1899 at the age of 33. She earned her doctorate in Hanoi in 1920 at the age of 54. She was accompanied in her fieldwork by her sister Eleanor, and it was said that she would sometimes lower Eleanor into a cavern on a rope and not let her out until she found something. The sisters' contributions to uncovering the prehistory of Indochina are invaluable, including the discovery of a hunter-gatherer culture they termed the Hoabinhian (still called that by archeologists) in Veitnam that is now known to date back 18,000 years. Her work at the Plain of Jars convinced her that the giant urns were funereal.

Says the University of Iowa paper:

> Then who created the Plain of Jars? Colani, who was more willing to speculate than most modern archeologists, suggested that the sites in Laos were part of a far-ranging Bronze Age culture. She pointed out that some stone jars discovered in the North Cachar Hills of northeastern India, more than 600 miles to the northwest, had roughly the same design and dimensions as the urns in Laos. J.P. Mills and J.H. Hutton, the English scholars who discovered the Indian urns in 1928, found fragments of human bones in them, which they concluded were human remains. They noted that cremation was still being practiced by some of the Kuki, a people who had lived in the North Cachar Hills for centuries.

A close-up of the mouth of a jar at the Plain of Jars.

Colani also called attention to Sa Huynh, a site south of the city of Da Nang, Vietnam. There, urns of baked earth containing some human remains were found buried in the sand dunes along the shores of the South China Sea. Although these remains had not been cremated, the objects interred with them—including ceramic vases, small bronze bells, and beads—resembled those discovered on the Plain of Jars.

"If our interpretation is correct," Colani proposed, "we are in the presence of three links from the same chain: the ancient monoliths of Cachar, the stone jars of Tran Ninh [Xieng Khouang, Laos], and the necropolis of Sa Huynh." According to Colani, prehistoric salt traders had followed a caravan route from Sa Huynh to Luang Prabang, located near the northwest edge of the Plain of Jars. Perhaps, she concluded, that route once extended all the way to the North Cachar Hills, and the people who lived along it shared a similar culture, burying their dead (cremated or not, depending upon local custom) in megalithic jars. Colani even drew a map with a line connecting the three sites, and suggested that explorers venturing along this line would find yet more jar sites.

Apparently, well-traveled caravan routes passing through Xieng Khouang were in use until the early part of the 20th century, and salt is still an important local resource for producing the dietary staple of fermented fish paste. Salt from the Laotian highlands may have been the product traded for the cowrie shells and glass beads found among the jars. It is known that the original inhabitants of the Plain of Jars were Austro-Asiatic people who were skilled at river navigation using canoes, and that sailors would have been able to penetrate the hinterlands via the Mekong River and its tributaries to obtain trade goods.

Of the more than 90 jar sites known within the province, the most studied and visited is located just over a mile from the town of Phonsavan and is designated Site 1. Called "Ban Ang"

A photo of a very large vat at the Plain of Jars in northern Laos.

by Colani and "Thong Hai Hin" today, it is comprised of 60 acres of windswept land containing more than 250 stone jars. Fifty of them, including the largest ones known to exist (measuring over three meters high and one meter across, weighing several tons), are located on a ridge on the northeast edge of the site. There is also a limestone hill adjacent to the site that contains a natural cave. Colani had excavated the cave, the mouth of which was on the level of the plain, and found evidence that it was used as a central crematorium. The cave contains two natural chimneys formed by water erosion, and the blackened northeast wall signaled that it had been used to

188

cremate bodies, the remains of which may have been interred in the giant urns.

Because of the continuous conflict and turmoil in the region, further studies were not made until 1994, at which time a Japanese archeologist named Eiji Nitta dug four test trenches around a jar at Ban Ang (Site 1). The digging exposed an anthropomorphic carving on the side of the jar (the first found on the Plain of Jars) and also the existence of seven flat stones at a depth of eight to 12 inches below the surface that each covered a deeper pit. Six of the pits contained human bones, and the seventh had a two-foot-tall burial jar that contained small pieces of bone and teeth. None of these artifacts had been burned.

Nitta maintains that the burial pits are contemporary with the stone jars, as they are cut into the ancient surface on which the jars were placed. He suggests that the whole site is a place of "secondary burials," a practice prevalent in Southeast Asia. In this practice, a body is initially interred (perhaps in the large stone urns) so that the flesh and organs rot away, and the remains are subsequently dug up and then perhaps cremated and re-buried. It is thought that in this way, a person can gradually make his/her way from corporeal existence to the spiritual world. The placement of the stone jars indicates good feng shui, often important in the location of burial sites in the East—they are often at the foothills of mountains, giving a good view of the surrounding landscape.

Whatever the final determination regarding the jar sites might be, they are still a mystery at this point. Several quarry sites, or more precisely, boulder fields, have been recorded near the jar sites. The size and shape of the raw materials apparently dictated the resulting shape of the jars, which varies. Parmentier noted three different shapes in his early 1923 visit to the Plain. They are made of sandstone, granite and limestone. They have well-defined lips, but the stone disks found among them are not universally considered to be their caps—it is thought that they may have had caps made of wood or rattan, which have not survived. The "caps" have been found to be inscribed with designs ranging from concentric circles to a well-defined monkey.

189

Sulawesi and the Enigma of Bada Valley

One possible explanation, suggested to me by a mining engineer from Perth, Australia in 2015, is that the stone jars in Laos and Bada Valley are crucibles, used in the processing of metallic ores. The Encyclopedia Britannica defines a crucible as:

> ...a vessel of a very refractory material (as porcelain) used for melting and calcining a substance that requires a high degree of heat.

An old photo of a large stone jar from the Toba region of northern Sumatra.

An old photo of a Cham-looking carved boulder in Besoa Valley.

A crucible, particularly a large one, could be made of granite or basalt, such as the stone jars found at Bada Valley or the Plain of Jars. Similarly a crucible furnace is defined by the Encyclopedia Britannica as:

> Crucible furnace, metallurgical furnace consisting essentially of a pot of refractory material that can be sealed. Crucibles of graphite or of high-grade fire clay were formerly used in the steel industry, heated directly by fire; modern high-quality steel is produced by refining in air-evacuated crucibles heated by induction. Metals such as titanium, which must be protected from air while hot, are melted and annealed in hermetically sealed crucibles.

So, the granite jars of Bada Valley and the Plain of Jars may well have been large containers—crucibles—that could withstand high temperatures for the processing of metals. These stone jars, similar to ceramic crucibles, could have been used in the extensive mining operations in antiquity. Indeed, the use of crucibles must be as old as metallurgy itself. In his book *Early Metal Mining and Production*,[46] the mining engineer P. Craddock says that a crucible is a container that can withstand very high temperatures and is used for the melting of metal, glass, or pigment production, and a variety of other modern laboratory processes. While crucibles historically were usually made from clay, they can be made from any material that withstands temperatures high enough to melt or otherwise alter its contents. Therefore, granite stone would also be an acceptable material to make a crucible out of.

Indeed, once a suitable site of iron, gold or copper ore is found,

An old photo of a large statue discovered in southern Sumatra.

The Mayan-like Hindu temple of Candi Sukuh in the moutains of central Java.

Some of the impressive stone walls at Nan Madol.

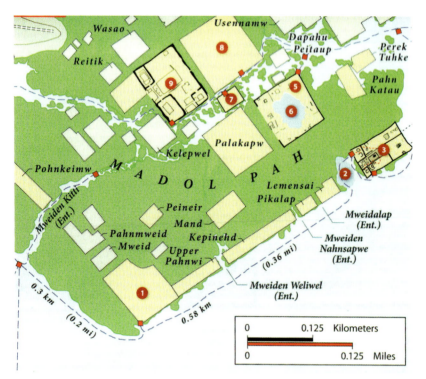

Wasao
Usennamw
Dapahu
Peitaup
Perek
Tuhke
Reitik
Pahn
Katau
8
9
5
7
6
Palakapw
Kelepwel
M A D O L P A H
Pohnkeimw
Lemensai
Pikalap
Peineir
Mweidalap
(Ent.)
Mand
Pahnmweid
Kepinehd
Mweid
Mweiden
Upper
Nahnsapwe
Pahnwi
(Ent.)
(0.36 mi)
Mweiden Kiti
(Ent.)
Mweiden Weliwel
(Ent.)
0.3 km
(0.2 mi)
0.58 km

0   0.125   Kilometers

0   0.125   Miles

Above: A map of a section of Nan
Madol. *Right*: An aerial photo of the
Nan Madol walls and canals. *Below*: A
photo from 1985 of one of the coral-
encrusted pillars in the Nan Madol
harbor.

The corner of the high walls of Nan Dowas, the largest structure at Nan Madol.

A section of the huge seawall at Nan Madol during high tide.

Some of the impressive stone walls at Nan Madol.

An underwater photo of some of the 250 million tons of basalt at Nan Madol.

Top: A dolmen with three carved statues for pillars at San Agustin. *Above*: A curious tiki-style statue at San Agustin. *Left*: A finely-dressed ceramic figure discovered at San Agustin. Is he one of the Cham?

Statues half buried at the quarry in the crater of Rano Raraku.

Statues on Anakena Beach with the red topknot. Does this represent the hairstyle of Shiva?

Above: Thor Heyerdahl and his team dug to the base of one statue to show how deep it was buried in the soil. *Right*: A satellite photo of Easter Island. *Below*: A painting of the statues at Anakena Beach from the artist Hodges in 1775.

Statues on Anakena Beach with the red topknot. Is this the work of the Cham?

then charcoal was to be made to get the high temperatures inside a kiln or crucible furnace in which to melt the ore. We see how these mysterious stone jars could easily have been part of the early metallurgical works in Southeast Asia. Areas like Bada Valley are known for the gold in the mountain

An old photo of a statue in Besoa Valley.

rivers, and it seems that the Plain of Jars in Laos is known as an area for mining iron ore. Later, after the early mining of these areas was finished, the granite jars—which are almost indestructible—were used (or not) by the locals as possible funeral jars. I should note, the stone jars in Bada Valley were not known to be used in any funerary rites and their use, other than as crucibles, is a complete mystery.

It would seem, at least in the case of Bada Valley, that a megalithic culture arrived in this remote mountain area in prehistory looking for gold and other metals. They brought with them the power tools and diamond-ruby saws with which to easily cut granite boulders into crucibles and to make the perfectly formed tiki-style statues that dot the valley. These mysterious people, forerunners of the Cham, mined gold and other metals in Bada Valley and then departed as mysteriously as they came. Did they have flying vehicles to help them survey the mountains and airlift the refined gold once it had been processed? It is a fantastic thought, but one in line with the evidence that we are being presented. Even today, Bada Valley is a remote, though idyllic spot.

There are also similarities between megaliths found on Sulawesi and the megaliths on the southeastern Indonesian islands of Sumba and Timor. Both of these islands have dozens of slab-dolmens where slabs of granite or basalt weighing many tons are placed on smaller stones. Thought to be ancient grave markers of some sort, exactly how these huge slabs of stone were created in antiquity is a complete mystery. They are often perfectly smooth and even, as

193

if they had been cut by a giant saw. This giant saw was essentially slicing rock as if it were a loaf of bread, making cookie-cutter slices of rock that would essentially be used as giant tables. And like a giant table, objects could be placed on top—or beneath—the slab, making it essentially a dolmen.

In his book *Megalithic Finds in Central Celebes*,[48] the Dutch ethnologist Walter Kaudern tells of his journeys around Sulawesi (formerly known as Celebes) from 1917 to 1920. He discusses Bada Valley but also other areas of Sulawesi like the Napu and Besoa valleys which contain slab dolmens as well as megalithic statues and even some stone jars.

Kaudern presents in his book a wealth of photos, drawings and maps of statues, jars, slabs and drilled-out rocks from Bada Valley and nearby Napu and Besoa. He has a photo of a large slab dolmen at a site that Kaudern calls Paloe Valley. He has photos of tiki-style statues and stone "vats" from Napu Valley. Other large stone vats are in Besoa Valley. These enigmatic stone jars are larger than the ones found in Bada Valley. Many have tiki faces engraved in the rims as a design.[48]

These tiki faces, with round eyes and a sweeping eyebrow that becomes the nose, are used in all the statues and vat designs. They

A drawing of the boulder carved into a tiki face in Besoa Valley.

seem to be an artistic style that encompasses the use of a power tool that easily cuts through the rock. Essentially, the artist has at his disposal a granite rock face and power tools that can make certain simple—but perfect—cuts into the hard rock. These simple cuts are circles, half-circles, sweeping arcs and straight cuts. With this basic ability to cut granite in these geometric shapes the artist is able to construct what is essentially a cartoon of a human face in stone. This simple, yet artistic, human face is the tiki face that is common from Sulawesi to Tonga and Tahiti. A beard is easily placed on the tiki face if need be, such as can be seen on the Kon-Tiki statue at the subterranean temple at Tiwanaku.

Whenever some extra embellishment is added, such as the tiki faces along the rims of some of giant stone vats, it is because the worker has the extra time and ability to do so. Putting perfectly-repeated designs onto a very difficult medium such as the very hard stone that is granite or basalt takes some effort. Why would someone accomplish the seemingly difficult task of creating a huge stone jar and then go to the extra effort to embellish it with art and pleasing designs if it were not something easily done? Indeed, with the right power tools, decorating a stone vat, slab or statue with extra embellishments would be something fairly easy to do and would give the person some satisfaction in the creation of a bit of enduring art while also making something functional. However, we are still at a loss as what the function of the stone jars—vats—was. Were they crucibles in the mining process, or merely almost indestructible vessels for storing rice, wine, or some other even more valuable substance such as a fermented psychedelic mushroom soup that was marketed as the mysterious longevity drink known to the ancients as Soma? We may never know the answer.

Exit from Bada Valley

As our jeep pulled out of the main village of Bada Valley, our guide Michael waving goodbye to us as we drove toward the east, we wondered about the mysteries we had just seen. The megaliths were said to be 6,000 years old, though no actual date has ever been as-cribed to them. They were well preserved by the people who were the custodians of the valley. They treated the ancient objects with respect.

As we came up the muddy hill where we had slid back and forth on the way into the valley, we approached a truck that had slipped and completely turned over on its side. We passed it carefully, our own tires slipping in the mud as we plowed forward by sheer force uphill to a safe distance from the truck. We stopped and the three of us conferred with the driver about helping them out of their muddy predicament with what little power the Land Cruiser could manage.

The truck driver produced a tow strap of 6-cm-wide webbing that we attached to both vehicles. The four of us passengers stood to the side of the road a safe distance away from all the action and made sure that none of the vehicles would come sliding suddenly toward us. It was a dangerous situation all around and the steep muddy road was on the edge of a virtual cliff. We looked over the edge of the road as we stood there, and it was a steep thousand-foot drop through a jungle-covered ravine to a raging river below. We wondered how many cars or buses had plunged over this cliff over the years? The dreaded bus plunge could happen any time.

Finally, with a sustained tugging from the Land Cruiser—to our great surprise—the truck was flipped over and suddenly driving itself uphill and past our jeep, the strap having been quickly detached from the vehicles. We all yelled and cheered as the truck spewed past us, great volleys of mud flying left and right and the oily diesel fumes stinging our noses. Bada Valley was hard to leave, you might say.

As we churned back to Tentena on Lake Poso, we passed a black passenger car making its way toward the valley through the mud and muck that comprised that part of the road for several long miles. We couldn't imagine this turning out well, but anything could happen on this road, we had all concluded. This remote valley in the middle of Sulawesi had a certain magic and mystery that made it into some sort of time-portal to another world—a world of the past and perhaps the distant future.

We then returned to Palu and our next journey would be a flight to Jakarta, the largest city on the island of Java and the capital of Indonesia.

Chapter Five

GUNUNG PADANG, BOROBUDUR AND THE BUDDHIST MASTERMINDS

On ancient so-called fables: Can we not read into them some justification for the belief that some former forgotten race of men attained not only to the knowledge that we have so recently won, but also to the power that is not yet ours?
—Dr. Frederick Soddy

In early November 2016 I flew into Jakarta with Jennifer and a small group of friends. We got several taxis at the airport and went to a hotel on the southwestern side of Indonesia's capital and largest city. Jakarta is sprawling mass of cars, trucks, motorcycles and street vendors that can take hours to drive through.

It was well over an hour to get to our hotel, but once there our check-in to our rooms went very swiftly. We were at a hotel on this side of Jakarta because in the morning we would be driving directly south to the town of Sukabumi and the strange ruins of Gunung Padang in the mountains outside the town.

We left early the next day and made it to Sukabumi, a small town in western Java, and checked into the Anugrah Hotel. The next day we hired vans from the hotel to take us to the strange basalt megaliths on a hillside that is known as Gunung Padang.

Wikipedia reports that the site was mentioned in *Rapporten van de Oudheidkundige Dienst* (ROD, 'Report of the Department of Antiquities') in 1914. A Dutch historian named N. J. Krom is also said to have mentioned the site in 1949. The site was also visited by employees of the National Archeology Research Centre at some

197

point in 1979.

Because the site is largely a vast stack of hexagonal basalt crystal "logs" these archeologists were not sure what to make of it. Plus, they were confused as whether this was some natural site or bizarre man-made site. What its purpose was, as there are no actual structures, was baffling to archeologists, but it does seem to be a man-made structure of some sort. It is basically a huge pile of basalt crystalline logs—naturally-forming basaltic pillars or columnar blocks. There may be many millions of tons in total material situated in this huge pile of basalt pillars. We do not know how deep this pile of rock goes. Indeed, Gunung Padang must have at least 100 million tons of basalt accumulated in the "pyramid" that the structure is said to be.

In the next chapter we will discuss a similar site, though much bigger, on a Pacific Island in Micronesia called Pohnpei. On that island is a huge city—40 times larger than Gunung Padang—called Nan Madol. It is built out of the very same basalt hexagonal "logs" and the material in that city is an estimated 250 million tons of basalt. The heaviest stone is estimated to weigh 80 tons. We will discuss Nan Madol at greater depth in the next chapter, a site seemingly connected to Gunung Padang.

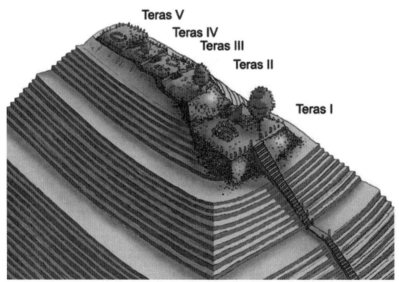

A drawing of the megalithic site of Gunung Padang.

The old staircase at Gunung Padang.

Gunung Padang (Gunung: mountain; Padang: pasture or field) is basically a hill in a series of terraces, bordered by retaining walls of volcanic stone. A visitor walks from the small visitor- center and car park up a series of about 400 successive basalt steps rising steadily for 100 meters. It is a short walk, but somewhat tiring. An ancient stairway of basalt steps is there to walk on, but the local government has built a secondary concrete path with a railing to walk up. The basalt steps can be slippery and they are narrow and irregular. There is also an ancient well and spring at the beginning of the steps with pure water surrounded by small basalt crystals.

At Gunung Padang these basalt crystals are five or six-sided and about six feet in length. Some are longer. They are heavy, but individually each piece of crystalline basalt might weigh up to 300 or 400 pounds. So, the site is a massive pile of basalt, though no blocks that can be seen on the surface weigh more than a ton.

The Legend of King Siliwangi

The local people are said to consider the site sacred and believe it was the result of legendary King Siliwangi's attempt to build a palace in one night. King Siliwangi was the popular name for a

199

The top of the last terrace at Gunung Padang.

king named Sri Baduga Maharaja who was a great Hindu king of the Sunda kingdom in West Java. He reigned from the relatively recent years of 1482 AD to 1521 AD from his capital called Pakuan Pajajaran. His reign is associated with greatness and prosperity and his exploits and life are the source of many legends and myths. Legends link Siliwangi as changing into a supernatural tiger that sometimes has a black and white leopard as his guard.

His reign coincided with the Islamic invasion of Java circa 1520 AD and at that time the Islamic sultanates of Cirebon and Banten were attacking Siliwangi's capital. But the Hindu king refused to fight against the Islamic forces because he was related to the Sultan of Cirebon. With his kingdom destroyed, Siliwangi wanted to avoid further bloodshed and was said to have retreated with a few followers to Mount Salak in western Java to become a monk. It was at this time legend says that he constructed Gunung Padang in his effort to build a city in one night with his magical powers. He failed, however, since instead of the city, there is really just a mysterious pile of rocks. Siliwangi then turned into a magical tiger—a hyang or spirit—considered a sacred beast, said to be seen occasionally by those in the deep mountain forests.

Gunung Padang has been dated by archeologists to 5000 BC and some think that it may go back to 20,000 BC. There are no stone structures at the site, although some of the stones have been placed in formation that suggests structures may have been present. It is hard to say at this point if the formations are original or made at later times. The main layout is a leveling off of the shoulder of the mountain into several terraces. These terraces are covered with prismatic basalt logs. The terraces face northeast and the jungle-covered slopes of Mount Gede are in the center of one's vision. This has caused some people to theorize that Gunung Padang is a megalithic viewing platform on the ridge of a mountain meant to facilitate the view or Mount Gede. Mount Gede was an active volcano thousands of years ago and researchers like Andrew Collins have suggested that the rock platform of Gunung Padang was built to view the volcano, which had some important significance to the ancient people. He also suggests that it was a viewing platform for the stars.

Collins says that the size of the blocks varies between 25 and 40 centimeters (10 to 16 inches) in width and height, and on average they are around 1.5 meters (five feet) in length, with a weight of approximately 250 kilograms (550 pounds). He says that the blocks which have either a roughly square or polygonal profile are the largest of the blocks, with weights exceeding 600 kilograms (1,300 pounds). This leaves the largest of the known blocks weighing less than a ton. By comparison, an obelisk might weigh more than 400 tons, as has been mentioned, and the heaviest stone at Nan Madol (to be discussed shortly) weighs an estimated 80 tons. So the stones at Gunung Padang are relatively small on the scale of megalithic building blocks, whether done by the Cham or other cultures.

Another explanation for Gunung Padang is that the site is a pyramid of sorts and there are chambers beneath the mass of rock that covers the terraces. Supposed chambers have been detected beneath the rock, though at the time we were there no tunnels or shafts to these chambers observable. It is possible that there is some kind of underground world beneath the mass of rock that is Gunung

Padang.

Of course, such claims draw a lot of criticism. The Indonesian vulcanologist Sutikno Bronto has said that the site is the neck of an ancient volcano and not a man-made pyramid. His explanation is that the crystalized blocks of basalt were an organ pipe formation in the neck of an ancient volcano which had collapsed, thereby creating a huge pile of rocks. These blocks, or stone logs, appear to be man-made because of the stone's smooth sides and uniform geometric shape. However, they are completely natural and no stone hammer or chisel has had anything to do with their creation.

Still, the mass of rocks at Gunung Padang is not haphazard at all, but clearly much of the rock has been carefully placed where it is. But for what purpose? The site is baffling: why would anyone build this site anyway? Obviously, it was a great deal of effort. Where had the basalt logs come from? Probably from very nearby if not from the site itself.

The basalt may have come from the site itself, but some construction has taken place. A few researchers have suggested that the stones were moved around during the Bronze Age, circa 2500-1500 BC. But, starting in 2011 an Indonesian geologist named Danny Hilman Natawidjaja of the Indonesian Centre for Geotechnical Research has said that his tests indicate that the monument has yielded dates from 22,000 BC to 12,700 BC to 9,600 BC, 4700 BC and 2800 BC, depending on the depth of the sample.

He did core drilling samples down into the many layers of rock and sent samples to the Beta Analysis labs of Miami, Florida. The Beta labs are the largest radiocarbon dating facility in the world. They dated the carbon component of a "glue" or cement the researchers say was found between slabs in the core drilling samples. The dates came back as between 13,000 and 23,000 years old. Chemical analysis of the "glue" does seem to indicate that it is not a natural material, but still I wonder if it might be a random organic compound that made it into the samples.

In March 2013 geoelectric surveys were performed that Hilman interpreted to show man-made stone structures, with horizontally placed columns seeming to defy how a natural formation would

A sidewall at Gunung Padang.

form. The surveys showed open chambers beneath the rock, which Hilman says are man-made rooms. Basic archeological excavations were carried out, during which Hilman says many man-made articles were discovered, and holes were dug down to the chambers.

Clearly there are many open spaces and tiny passages in the rock beneath the huge structure, but one would expect that from a giant pile of prismatic basalt logs that are heavy, durable and in geometric shapes.

Given the dates Danny Hilman Natawidjaja got from his samples, he concluded that the construction of the site spans four eras.

A survey conducted in 2012 dated a carbon based artifact to 6,500 BC and another to 12,500 years BP at 8 to 10 meters below the surface. He also pointed out that the wall-side construction of the terraces is similar to that of Machu Picchu in Peru.

Danny Hilman Natawidjaja has been criticized for his methods and conclusions, largely based on the dating techniques and assumptions he was making. In 2014, 34 Indonesian scientists signed a petition questioning the motives and methods of the studies. These detractors feel that it is the remains of an ancient volcano where convenient natural blocks can be moved and stacked into low walls.

We walked around the site and took photos. There is a steel and wood tower on the far corner of the site that allows tourists, the few that visit, to take some photos from a slight height above the highest terrace. In June 2014, the Education and Culture Ministry recognized the antiquity of the site and declared it a National Site Area with 29 hectares. Public bathrooms are maintained and there is a ticket office.

As we looked at the blocks and walls that had been made, wandering around the site, what struck me most was the sheer amount of material involved and the effort it would have taken to move all of this rock around. Even if the material was available at the immediate site, which it probably was, it was still a lot of material to shift. Did thousands of people spend years moving millions of tons of basalt around to make Gunung Padang? Maybe it was aliens moving the pile of rock with their levitation beams to create a convenient nest for their saucer—basalt prismatic boulders are naturally magnetic. Perhaps Gunung Padang is a place where

Some of the tons of prismatic basalt at Gunung Padang.

Our guide at Gunung Padang showing us one of the ringing stones.

builders, alien or not, wanted to test their ability to levitate rocks with their newly developed levitation guns!

Indeed, Gunung Padang is very similar, in a miniature way, to the equally mysterious basalt city of Nan Madol built into the ocean on the southeast corner of Pohnpei Island in Micronesia. The construction of Nan Madol is very similar to Gunung Padang and that island has a tradition that the stones were magically levitated and flown through the air.

As I walked down the stairs from the pile of rocks that is Gunung Padang I seriously contemplated if this site wasn't a place where prismatic basalt logs were practiced on for those who were developing the science of levitating rock. Here were hundreds of thousands of heavy, but manageable, basalt logs to play around with and move here and there. Perhaps in this way, there is no real purpose to Gunung Padang except for those who like to play with megaliths.

In the case of My Son, huge basalt slabs were cut by power tools and then had keystone cuts carved into the hard stone. Only the hardest iron chisels and diamond power tools can do this kind of work. However, we do not see any work by tools on the stones, at

205

Gunung Padang. No power tool has touched these stones and there are no decorations or inscriptions.

Still, that does not mean that Gunung Padang was not built and used by the Cham. Indeed, the Cham generally did not leave inscriptions, and many sites like Borobudur and Nan Madol lack inscriptions as well. Perhaps Gunung Padang had been a pile of rocks for the last 20,000 years and was used by the Cham and other early megalith builders as they explored the island of Java. Gunung Padang was very much a mystery—one of many mysteries on Java, where perhaps the greatest of all Cham monuments was built, the megalithic Buddhist stupa of Borobadur.

The Mystery of Borobadur

We checked out of the Anugrah Hotel the day after visiting Gunung Padang, and the hotel van drove us east through central Java to Bandung, a major city in the region. We discovered on this three-hour trip that the highways of western Java were essentially one long traffic jam. After much stop-and-go driving behind trucks and a sea of motorcycles, we eventually reached the large city of Bandung. Java today, as it must have been in ancient times, is a densely populated island.

We immediately went to the airport where we flew to Jogjakarta further east in central Java. Jogjakarta is considered one of the cultural capitals of Indonesia and is famous for its batiks and shadow puppet plays of the Hindu epic the *Ramayana*. We got to our hotel in the heart of the city and the next day we took a van to Borobudur to see the fine granite stonecutting including keystone cuts and metal clamps.

Borobudur is one of the great monuments of Southeast Asia. It is a colossal Buddhist stupa that rises out of the rice paddies and palm trees with the nearby volcano Gunung Merapi in the distance. This mysterious and beautifully constructed monument has survived volcanic eruptions, a 2006 earthquake and even terrorist bombs.

Even though Borobudur is the most important tourist site on Java, there is no written record of who built it or of its intended purpose. There are no inscriptions or dates on the monument—which

A view of the gigantic stone stupa mandala that is Borobudur.

was partially covered by a lava flow when it was rediscovered—and so historians must guess as to when it was probably built. Since it is a monument built on a grand scale, it would seem unusual that no ruler or dynasty takes credit for the structure. Borobudur is the world's largest Buddhist temple, and acknowledged as one of the greatest Buddhist monuments in the world. Yet, no one knows who built it!

The temple is actually a stupa that one is supposed to walk in a certain pattern, in a mandala fashion, to the summit. It consists of nine stacked platforms—six square and three circular—and is topped by a central dome which is not to be climbed. The stupa has many staircases and walkways. The temple is decorated with 2,672 relief panels and 504 Buddha statues. The central dome is surrounded by 72 Buddha statues, each seated inside a perforated stupa that is a stone screen. They look very much like life-size Buddhas inside a small flying saucer. A few of the Buddha statues inside the perforated stupas have had the outer stone stupa removed so that the Buddha statue can be clearly seen and photographed. The stonework is exceptional. Hourglass-style keystone cuts can be seen on some of the walls where stones have been removed.

It has been estimated that Borobudur was a building project

An old print of the early excavations at Borobudur.

on such a scale that it took many generations to complete the artificial stone mountain. Borobudur is built in the shape of a gigantic mandala-yantra that is meant to be walked by a pilgrim seeking enlightenment. One early suggestion by archeologists when they began to study Borobudur was that the huge stupa-hill was surrounded by an artificial lake. In this vision, Borobudur was to have been the symbol of a lotus flower coming out of the lake. This would have meant that pilgrimages to Borobudur would have begun by boat. However, modern Indonesian historians largely reject the idea of a lake being created.

Currently, historians prefer to ascribe Borobudur to the Sailendra (also spelled Shailendra) dynasty that is said to have begun circa 760 AD, some decades after the origin of the Srivijayan Empire in Sumatra. However, the Sailendra dynasty itself is shrouded in mystery, and like those of Srivijaya, its origins seem unclear to modern historians, who are unsure where these master seafarers came from. Says Wikipedia about Borobudur and the mysterious Sailendra dynasty and its connection with the building of Borobudur:

> The construction time has been estimated by comparison between carved reliefs on the temple's hidden foot and the inscriptions commonly used in royal charters during the 8th and 9th centuries. Borobudur was likely founded around 800 CE. This corresponds to the period between 760 and 830 CE, the peak of the Sailendra dynasty rule of [the] Mataram kingdom in central Java, when it was under the influence of the Srivijayan Empire. The construction has been estimated to have taken 75 years and was completed during the reign of Samaratungga in 825.
>
> The Shailendras are considered to be a thalassocracy and ruled maritime Southeast Asia, however they also relied on agriculture pursuits through intensive rice cultivation on the Kedu Plain of Central Java. The dynasty appeared to be the ruling family of both the Medang Kingdom of Central Java for some period and Srivijaya in Sumatra.
>
> The inscriptions created by Shailendras used three languages: Old Malay, Old Javanese and Sanskrit, written either in the Kawi alphabet or pre-Nāgarī script. The use of Old Malay has sparked the speculation of a Sumatran origin or Srivijayan connection of this family; on the other hand, the use of Old Javanese suggests their firm political establishment on Java. The use of Sanskrit usually signifies the official nature and religious significance of the event written on the inscription.

Suddenly, in 700 AD, Java has an organized thalassocracy that now spans eastward to New Guinea? Where did this network of Hindu seaports, rivers and rice paddies come from? Obviously from the Champa. Says Wikipedia on the subject of the mysterious origins of the Sailendras:

> Although the rise of the Shailendras occurred in Kedu Plain in the Javanese heartland, their origin has been the subject of discussion. Apart from Java itself, an earlier homeland in Sumatra, India or Cambodia has been suggested. The latest studies apparently favor a native origin of the dynasty. Despite their connections with Srivijaya in Sumatra and [the] Thai-Malay Peninsula, the Shailendras were more likely of Javanese origin.
>
> India: According to Ramesh Chandra Majumdar, an Indian scholar, the Shailendra dynasty that established itself in the Indonesian archipleago originated from Kalinga in Eastern India. This opinion is also shared by Nilakanta Sastri and J. L. Moens. Moens further describes that the Shailendras originated in India and established themselves in Palembang before the arrival of Srivijaya's Dapunta Hyang Sri Jayanasa. In 683, the Shailendras moved to Java because of the pressure exerted by Dapunta Hyang and his troops.
>
> Cambodia: In 1934, the French scholar Coedes proposed a relation with the Funan kingdom in Cambodia. Coedes believed that the Funanese rulers used similar-sounding 'mountainlord' titles, but several Cambodia specialists have discounted this. They hold there is no historical evidence for such titles in the Funan period.
>
> Sumatra: Other scholars hold that the expansion of [the] Buddhist kingdom of Srivijaya was involved in the rise of the dynasty in Java. Supporters of this connection emphasize the shared Mahayana patronage, the intermarriages and the Ligor inscription. Also the fact that some of Shailendra's inscriptions were written in old Malay, which suggested Srivijaya or Sumatran connections. The name 'Selendra'

was first mentioned in [the] Sojomerto inscription (725) as "Dapunta Selendra." Dapunta Selendra is suggested as the ancestor of [the] Shailendras. The title Dapunta is similar to those of Srivijayan King Dapunta Hyang Sri Jayanasa, and the inscription—although discovered in Central Java (north coast)—was written in old Malay, which suggested the Sumatran origin or Srivijayan connection to this family.

One of the Buddha statues inside a small stupa at Borobudur.

So this mysterious dynasty came from either India or Cambodia or Sumatra—these latter areas being clearly the land of the Cham. It may well be that the Cham originated at Kalinga in eastern India. The name of Funan is tossed in there as well. What is missing from this list is the thalassocracy of the Hindu Cham and the very same network from India that spawned the Hindu-Buddhist megalithic culture that existed in at least one way or another on every island, mainland bay and river port in the vast area that is Southeast Asia and Oceania. It is an endless island archipelago that stretches from Sumatra to Vietnam and Java and then out into the starry skies of the Pacific Ocean—a voyage to the middle of the world.

One has to start wondering: is there some sort of conspiracy to keep the sweeping nature of the empire of the Champa out of world history? Unfortunately, Vietnam went through a devastating civil war in our modern time, as well as Cambodia, but does their history have to be part of some cover-up of silence? As we shall see in upcoming chapters, the historical and archeological evidence for a megalithic culture crossing the Pacific Ocean starting circa 1000 BC is overwhelming. These voyages eastward across the Pacific started in Vietnam, Indonesia, and the land of Cham.

One of the questions that historians have, trying to figure out who built Borobudur and when, is why a gigantic Buddhist monument would be built by a largely Hindu dynasty? Did the Hindu and Buddhist rulers of Java circa 700 to 800 AD intermingle and allow a crossover of their faiths? Buddhism is merely a reform of Hinduism, largely doing away with the caste system and giving its faithful more freedom with less ritual. The same gods, such as Shiva and Brahma, plus historical characters such as Krishna and Rama from the *Mahabharata* and *Ramayana* are also important to Buddhists.

With the Cham, Buddhism and Hinduism were melded together and Hindu temples were built at the same time as Buddhist ones. This was apparently going on in Java as well, and in fact the Hindu Prambanan Temple is very near to Borobudur and is said to have been built in 9th century. Prambanan has been called the most

Some of the hourglass-shaped keystone cuts at Borobudur.

beautiful Hindu temple outside of India. The Sailendras may have built both Borobudur and Prambanan. Historians are confused as whether the Sailendras were Hindus or Buddhists. Says Wikipedia:

> There is confusion between Hindu and Buddhist rulers in Java around that time. The Sailendras were known as

213

ardent followers of Buddhism, though stone inscriptions found at Sojomerto suggest they may have been Hindus. It was during this time that many Hindu and Buddhist monuments were built on the plains and mountains around the Kedu Plain.

Without any formal record of any kind of the building of Borobudur—an astounding feat for any architect and builder—historians theorize that construction began sometime around 760 AD (but it may be earlier) and that the site was abandoned around 928 AD when volcanic eruptions covered much of the site with volcanic ash. It is thought that the Buddhist kings of the Sailendra dynasty of central Java were the builders, however they left no inscriptions. This dynasty may have been affiliated with the Buddhist Cham of central Vietnam as well as the Cham of Angkor Wat in today's Cambodia. I must personally conclude that Borobudur was built by the Cham before the Sailendra dynasty, and was probably already in existence by 400 AD if not earlier. The Sailendra dynasty, like Srivijaya in nearby Sumatra, was the result of the Cham Empire breaking up into smaller states. Later, in the various naval wars that went on starting around 700 AD, these warring Hindu-Buddhist kingdoms would even attack the Champa heartland in southern Vietnam. These wars, which included Angkor Wat and the Cambodians, were ultimately civil wars carried on by the large fleets that were based on Sumatra and Java as well as up the Mekong River in Cambodia. Essentially, the larger Cham Empire came to an end with these breakaway Hindu states starting in 650 AD, but it would seem that Borobudur was already in existence before this breakup. No one really seems to know the who and when of Borobudur—but they do know its purpose: it is a megalithic site for Buddhist pilgrimage.

Borobudur lay hidden for centuries under layers of volcanic ash and jungle growth. The facts behind its abandonment remain a mystery. It is not known when active use of the monument and Buddhist pilgrimage to it ceased. During a period sometime between 928 and 1006 AD, King Mpu Sindok moved the capital of the Medang Kingdom (part of the Sailendra dynasty) to the region of East Java after a series of volcanic eruptions. Historians tend to think that this influenced the abandonment, as portions of Borobudur were covered by a lava flow.

The whole period of the Sailendra dynasty and the building of Borobudur are shrouded in mystery. There are also reports that naval Javanese raiders, probably of the Sailendra dynasty, attacked the Cham outpost of Tran-Nam in 767 AD and then attacked the Champa in Vietnam in 774 AD. They reportedly attacked the

Some of the hourglass-shaped keystone cuts at Borobudur.

Vietnamese Champa again in 787 AD. It is likely that a huge Buddhist stupa like Borobudur was not built during these wars, but before them. Borobudur is likely to have been built during a time of regional peace, which was when the Cham ruled the entire area, prior to 650 AD.

Like the megalithic ruins of Tiwanaku, Ollantaytambo, Karnak, Angkor Wat and other Cham sites such as My Son in Vietnam, Borobudur was built of stone blocks that were sometimes linked with special hourglass-shaped or T-shaped cuts in two adjoining blocks and a molten metal that is then poured into the cavity creating a bronze or other alloy 'clamp' or 'cramp.' This method of fastening large blocks of stone together is unusual, but it is used by megalith builders on nearly all continents and is indicative of high technology—of cutting, moving and lifting gigantic blocks of stone with apparent ease. One would think that these metal clamps would not be needed by such large stone blocks, but they were used in nearly all the walls anyway. The architects were building structures with the goal of having them last for thousands of years. The buildings now seen in Egypt are a good example, and many of these elegant temples have stood for over 4,000 years!

Huge slab dolmens in the Anakalang district of central Sumba.

Huge slab dolmens in the Kampung district of Sumba.

So, we see at Borobudur the same keystone cuts to hold metal clamps that are found at Cham sites and other places. It would seem that these keystone cuts are further evidence of the Cham occupying Java and Sumatra and all of the Indonesian Islands, or at least their coastal areas and major cities.

The frescos at Borobudur show the life of Buddha plus scenes of typical life in Java such as farming and shipbuilding. One excellent fresco shows a large ship with several sails and lots of rigging on a sea voyage somewhere. Where is it going? It would appear to be one of the vessels of the Cham making one of their many journeys across the Java Sea to the Gulf of Siam, Vietnam and elsewhere.

Sumba Island: Gateway to the Pacific

It is said that the Sailendra dynasty controlled Java, Bali and other islands to the east. Bali is famous for keeping its Hindu culture—brought by the Cham—intact while other islands largely became Muslims.

Going east from Bali are the islands of Lombok, Sumbawa and Flores. To the south of Flores is the large, but little-visited island of Sumba and further east is the island of Timor. Going further east from Timor essentially puts a vessel in the Torres Straits between Australia and the island of New Guinea. Eastward from the Torres

217

Standing stones and perfectly round stone discs in the Anakalong district of Sumba.

Straits begin the Pacific Island archipelagos of the Solomon Islands, Vanuatu and Fiji. The archipelagos of Tonga, Tahiti and the Marquesas Islands lie even further east. Beyond these islands are the west coasts of North and South America.

In order to venture out into the Pacific with a fleet of ships, a navy needs to go either north or south of the island of New Guinea. In chapter one I discussed how important the Cham Islands were in the transpacific voyages of the Champa. A huge fleet would meet at the islands to take on provisions and then sail directly east to the Sulu Sea in the southern Philippines and then out into the Pacific, passing on the north side of the mini-continent of New Guinea.

This fleet could pass by Manus Island, off of northern New Guinea, and into Micronesia where the Cham naval bases on the islands of Pohnpei and Kosrae awaited them. The further passage east across the Pacific could take them to Hawaii or the Marquesas Islands before landing on the coast of Mexico or southern California.

There was apparently also a southern route into the Pacific for the Cham and their predecessors which took them from Lombok and Flores to the strange island of Sumba where they would pass on to Timor and the Torres Straits.

218

Sumba Island is one of the Lesser Sunda Islands, and has an area of 4,306 square miles (11,153 square kilometers). Despite its large size it is not very populated and is one of the poorer islands. Not much is known of the history of the island other than it exported sandalwood and was known to Indonesian sailors as Sandalwood Island. The inhabitants are related to Melanesian and Austronesian peoples. The island is also known for its strange megaliths and megalithic burials. Similar megaliths are found on Timor.

The first European explorers to arrive were the Portuguese in 1522 AD, and the island became part of the Dutch East Indies in 1866. The landscape consists of low, limestone hills, rather than the steep volcanic mountains of most Indonesian islands. The island is relatively dry, especially the eastern side.

What is quite strange on Sumba are the many megalithic stone slabs that seem to have been cut by giant saws, and the religion that has grown up around them. Though some of the coastal towns are about half Muslim, most of the population practices some form of the local religion known as Marapu, as well as being Dutch Calvinist Christians.

Despite contact with western cultures, Sumba is one of the few places in the world in which megalithic burials are used as a 'living tradition' to inter prominent individuals when they die. Almost all

Huge slab dolmens in the Bondokodi district of Sumba.

219

An unusual and perfectly-made slab monument in the Kampung district of Sumba.

of the Sumba artifacts consist of dolmen type burial structures. Their forms range from the simple to the advanced. These dolmens are still being used today (hence they are a living tradition), where the head of a family who owns the structure is buried beneath it. The megaliths are a source of prestige for the heads of clans, and a connection to their dead ancestors is made through the megalith. The slabs or cornerstones can be decorated with human figures, animals such as water buffalo or birds, flowers and geometric patterns. The largest dolmen is said to be 28 inches thick and nearly 17 feet in length. Many of these larger dolmens appear to be perfectly cut slabs of basalt or granite that must weigh many tons. They give every appearance of being made with power tools!

Indeed, who are these mysterious ancestors who created these massive slabs of sliced rock? No one knows who made them or how, but it is assumed that they are thousands of years old. There are no stories of great heroes or kings erecting the stone slabs, just a knowledge that the people are linked to their ancestors through these stones in some way. They believe that their lives are influenced by the spirits of their dead ancestors who protect the living from bad luck and bad spirits, giving them health and fertility.

What seems clear on Sumba is that some advanced maritime culture—such as the Cham—arrived at Sumba many thousands of years ago and created the megaliths. They used their advanced metal tools such as diamond saws and drills to slice rock and create the massive stone slabs. They also had the ability to lift and transport these heavy slabs of rock to the location of their choice. Was it the Cham on their way eastward to Timor and New Guinea?

At every location they would be looking for alluvial gold in the rivers, and if they found that they would look for the source of that gold. They were seeking gems and other metals as well. Not being volcanic, Sumba may not have been a good island for the mining of metals, and it would seem the megalith makers used Sumba as a base as the fleet headed east for Timor and the Torres Straits.

New Guinea was occupied by fierce tribes who lived upriver in thick jungle areas where they warred constantly with each other. Despite its mineral wealth, the island of New Guinea would not be a land that would be easy to colonize and exploit. Any upriver exploration trips would be met by dangerous warriors throwing spears.

The fleet preferred to voyage on to the east where volcanic islands might have gold, and ultimately across the Pacific to Central America and Peru. It is important to note in this regard that when Ferdinand Magellan crossed the Pacific in 1520-1521 AD, he

Several slab dolmens with decorations in the Kampung area of Sumba.

221

A huge slab dolmen and boulder cut into steps in the Kampung area of Sumba.

reached the Philippines without ever landing on one single Pacific island during his voyage. This is despite the fact that he would have passed much of Polynesia and Micronesia, and landing on just one of the hundreds of islands he would have come near to would have helped his voyage immensely as many would have had fresh water, coconuts and such.

An even more amazing crossing was reported by news agencies around the world in February of 2014, telling the story of a Mexican fisherman who spent 13 months as a castaway drifting across the Pacific. His name was Jose Salvador Alvarenga and he washed up on a remote coral atoll in the Marshall Islands of Micronesia in a heavily damaged boat. He said he had been living off fish and turtles he had caught, and relying on rainwater to drink. He left from a port called Paredon Viejo in Mexico's southern Chiapas state in December 2012 when the engine of his boat broke down. People around the world were amazed at such a long journey as a castaway but the story was not a hoax.

Both voyages show how it is quite possible to cross the Pacific Ocean without taking on extra water or food for the voyage—yet most transpacific voyages would involve stops in such places as Rotuma Island in the very north of Fiji, Tonga, Tahiti or the

Marquesas. Traces of a megalithic culture has been found on all of these islands and the similarity between the Tiki faces of Bada Valley, Sumatra and other places are clearly related to the Tiki faces and statues of Tonga, Samoa, Tahiti and New Zealand. But these megalith builders didn't voyage into the Pacific in single ships or a small group of ships. They voyaged into the Pacific in huge fleets of hundreds of ships. We know that Cham Islands were the assembly point for ships in the north. It would seem that Sumba and Timor were the islands where the southern fleet would assemble for the great voyages east.

A Strange Temple-Pyramid and the Road to Bali

After our all-day visit to Borobadur and the nearby Hindu temple of Prambanan we booked a van for the next day to take us to Candi Sukuh, several hours' drive from Jogjakarta. We drove to

The strange Hindu pyramid in central Java called Candi Sukuh.

223

Some of the strange carved stone reliefs at Candi Sukuh.

the town of Karanganyar in the mountains of eastern Java and then up steep paved roads among tea plantations to the strange pyramid temple of Candi Sukuh, or Sukuh Temple.

The temple looks very much like a small Mayan pyramid and has some curious Hindu statues that seem quite archaic. No one knows when the temple was built and the temple-pyramid was in great disrepair when first discovered. Not knowing how old the temple might be historians say it could be, as old as 400 AD, though they tend to attribute the structure to the Majapahit rulers who reigned from 1293 AD to 1468 AD in this part of eastern Java.

We paid for our admission and walked around the site which featured a gate to enter from the west. Walking up a stone pathway we came to a group of statues with the main pyramid in front of us. If the site were in Mexico or Guatemala one might think that it was a Mayan or Olmec pyramid, rather than a Hindu one.

Other archeologists have noted that the Baksai Chamkrogn pyramid at Angkor Wat is virtually identical to Temple I at Tikal in northern jungles of Guatemala. Both temples are steep pyramids with a steep staircase going to small room at the top of the structure. Mayan pyramids may have originated with the Cham.

The statues at Candi Sukuh were curious as well, with elephants and the winged god Garuda featured, plus people who looked distinctly like the Cham with wide noses and thick lips. The statues had a certain antiquity to them and were not at all like the fine statues and frescoes at Borobudur. It didn't really make sense: Borobudur with its fine statuary was supposedly built around 960 AD but Candi Sukuh was built much later circa 1293 AD? It would seem that Candi Sukuh was the older structure, perhaps dating to 400 BC

A statue at Candi Sukuh that appears to feature Garuda, the vehicle of Vishnu.

or earlier. The statues and people depicted also seemed to have a strong similarity to the Olmec statues in Mexico and to the statues found at Bada Valley and other nearby valleys.

It seemed like Candi Sukuh was some sort of bizarre mountain pilgrimage site, possibly a fertility temple for women who were not bearing children for their husbands. There are lingam and yoni symbols about the temple, and it may have had a sexual or tantric nature. No one is really sure about this mysterious pyramid temple.

To me it was more evidence of the long and complex relationship of the Cham with islands in Indonesia and the similarity of the statuary and construction styles that are also found with the Olmec in Mexico and certain sites in Peru.

The next morning we flew to the island of Bali, a prosperous island where the Hindu faith and sandy beaches have artists and tourists from all over the world coming to visit. We checked into our hotel for our last few days in Indonesia.

After a few days on the beach we took a van into the interior of the island to the town of Ubud. We had a pleasant lunch and then visited a strange cave outside of Ubud called Goa Gajah, or

This stone relief at Candi Sukuh seems to feature a giant from the *Mahabharata*.

226

The strange carved stone reliefs at Candi Sukuh. Note the tiki face and weird sword.

the Elephant Cave. Once there we bought our tickets and then descended a series of steps to the cave's relic-filled courtyard of bathing pools and fountains and the curious cave that was thought to have an elephant face around it. The cave is believed to have been created as a place for meditation, and a great deal of very fine rock cutting has taken place here. In fact, what is really remarkable here is the cutting of the granite rock to create the demon face (or is it an elephant?) and all of the embellishment around it. Someone with skill and iron tools—probably power tools—was cutting into solid granite and creating these chambers and designs. A lingam has been cut out of solid rock and can be seen at one end of the rectangular chamber that is inside Goa Gajah—the Elephant Cave.

The monster face—a gorgon or demon—is to scare off evil spirits and is ultimately for good luck, much like the Tiki face. Was Goa Gajah a temple cut out of solid rock by the Cham when the Hindu sea kings first arrived in Bali? It would seem so. And when did Hinduism first come to the island of Bali?

No one knows when Hinduism arrived in Bali, but according to most historians ancient Bali consisted of nine Hindu sects called

227

The Goa Gajah Elephant cave in Bali.

Pasupata, Bhairawa, Siwa Shidanta, Waisnawa, Bodha, Brahma, Resi, Sora and Ganapatya. Each sect revered a specific deity as its personal Godhead. There are inscriptions with dates of 896 and 911 AD, but no king is mentioned. Finally, in 914 AD the first king of Bali is mentioned, the king called Sri Kesarivarma. It is said that at this time Bali became an independent state, with a distinct dialect, where Buddhism and Shaivism were practiced simultaneously. Indeed, this is what was going on at Borobudur and elsewhere in Champa and Cambodia: both Buddha and the Hindu god Shiva were worshipped. A dual Hindu-Buddhist religion united the entire Cham area from Vietnam to Sumatra, Bali, Borneo and beyond.

Bali is a mysterious island, an idyllic land of mysticism and art, and the modern influx of tourists from around the world has stimulated this peaceful, spiritual and artistic culture to make it famous and the pride of modern Indonesia, a heavily populated nation with crowded cities, poverty and violent religious fanatics.

It would seem that Bali, like much of Indonesia and Southeast Asia, was a Hindu area by at least 1000 BC. Later, as ports and coastal areas became more familiar with Hinduism, the Buddhist

228

doctrine was introduced and the two similar religions existed side by side and intertwined for many centuries. This was the Cham way: Hindu Shiva worship was combined with Buddhism, and the activity of trade, fishing, farming and mining was combined with the love of the Cham for building great monuments.

As our jet lifted off from Bali's main airport a few days later I wondered about the amazing archeological sites of Bali, Sumba, Java and the rest of Indonesia. Indonesia was a vast land of headhunters in the highlands of Borneo and New Guinea, plus mysterious megaliths and temples that dotted the rivers and mountains of the islands. And we have the mysterious spread of Hinduism—and Buddhism—through a vast area from Sumatra, Java, Bali and the Champa states in Vietnam and Cambodia. No one is taking credit for these many monuments and the only civilization that can be identified at the time of 200 AD when all this must have been happening is the Champa of Vietnam.

It seems clear that the Hindu sailors voyaging from island to island in Indonesia and stopping at the Cham Islands from time to time were the great Cham and their wonderful and mysterious culture. The building techniques that they deployed can be traced to ancient Egypt and the keystone cuts and megalithic building found at the many ancient sites there. The high technology and Buddhist ideals had these advanced people occupying ports throughout Southeast Asia and Indonesia, yet these voyages in the Indian Ocean, Java Sea and Gulf of Siam were minor journeys compared to the greater journey to the east: to the land where the sun is born, the Americas.

This was the great journey, the one that started at the Cham Islands or at Sumba and Timor for the long journey across the Pacific. This voyage might take a year, or even a lifetime, depending the luck of the ship and the sailor. There would be stops along the voyage and these stops at various islands might last for weeks or more and involve all sorts of elaborate parties and ceremonies. Certain fertility festivals and sexual activity would be part of these festivals. Tantric sex was a subject that the Cham would have been familiar with, as most followers of Shiva are at least aware of the doctrine of Tantra and its practices.

A voyage by the Cham to Mexico and Peru would be a voyage that would take several years in total. Similarly, we are told in the Bible that the voyage to the land of Ophir where King Solomon got much of his treasure took three years. In general terms it is thought that a sea voyage of three years would be one year to go to the destination; one year at the destination (mining the gold, growing a crop of food); and one year for the return journey. It is not known where King Solomon's ships were going when they went to the land of Ophir, but it was likely at least as far as Sri Lanka, and more probably to Sumatra, Australia or even across the Pacific to Peru. Peru, indeed, was a land of gold. But other areas such as Sumatra or Western Australia could have been the source of the gold, and any volcanic island is potential source of gold.

It is a historical fact that seafarers, a mysterious group known as the Lapita culture, were voyaging from Indonesia to Fiji and Tonga before 1000 BC. Were they Hindus? Were they the Cham? Let us now look at the amazing Cham naval base on the Micronesian island of Pohnpei called Nan Madol. Built in a similar fashion as Gunung Padang in western Java, Nan Madol is the eighth wonder of the world and shows all the hallmarks of being built by the Cham.

Chapter Six

NAN MADOL: CHAM SEAPORT IN MICRONESIA?

Shall we go, you and I
While we can?
Through the transitive nightfall of diamonds?
—*Dark Star*, Grateful Dead

When I first discovered the keystone cuts in basalt slabs at My Son, I realized that the Cham must have had something to do with other megalithic cultures in Micronesia and Polynesia including megaliths on many Pacific islands. The unusual style of keystone cuts, clearly developed in Asia and Egypt, was also being used in South America. Whatever the equation was, the Cham were part of that equation. This was the conclusion that I came to, and I decided I needed to return to Pohnpei Island in Micronesia to refresh my memory.

The lost city of Nan Madol is one of today's great archaeological enigmas and is sometimes called "the eighth wonder of the world." *Smithsonian Magazine* recently called it "an engineering marvel." Known as the "Venice of the Pacific" since it was first discovered by Europeans in the early 1800s, the huge stone city is built out onto a coral reef and is intersected by artificial canals. According to island historian Gene Ashby, it was long known as the Reef of Heaven, or *Soun Nan-leng* in the local language.

In 2014 I visited the island with my wife Jennifer, flying there from Honolulu. It was my sixth trip to the island since 1985. I found that the island was as sleepy and quiet as ever, with several of the major hotels completely closed, including the iconic Village Hotel that hugged a narrow ridge along the north coast and was famous for its breezy tiki bar and great views.

I was excited to see Nan Madol again and we hired boats and a car to get us back to the ruins several days in a row. We visited the towering fortress of Nan Dowas several times and snorkeled the main seawall entrance that protects the main canals and harbor of the northeast part of the city. I had purchased a new underwater digital camera in Honolulu and was eager to use it. Indeed, I got a lot of great new digital photos of the ruins and you will see some of them here.

The megalithic city of Nan Madol is built on a shallow coral reef on the southeast corner of the Micronesian island of Pohnpei, today the capital of the Federated States of Micronesia. It is the only ancient city ever built on a coral reef and is comprised of 92 artificial islets intersected by canals. The islets and walls are constructed of basalt logs and boulders, weighing from several hundred pounds to up to 80 tons. The average weight of the basalt blocks is five tons, and some of the basalt logs weigh around 20 tons. A huge boulder on the southwest corner of the largest structure, Nan Dowas, is estimated to weigh 50 tons. The largest block is said to be a gigantic 80-ton basalt block that is part of a huge sea wall on the far southwest corner of Nan Madol, an area difficult to reach except by boat at high tide. At low tide, the area is shallow enough to walk through, the water being only a few feet deep.

Some of the walls are 50 feet high and 17 feet thick. Tunnels and "tombs" can be found on some of the islands, their construction as baffling as the construction of the high walls. An estimated 250 million tons of basalt were used in the construction of the megalithic city and no one knows where the massive amount of stone material came from, though there is some speculation. An entire mountain of basalt—or several—could have been dismantled to create the millions of tons of rock necessary to build the city. The basalt rocks are magnetic and at various places in the city, such as the entrance to Nan Dowas, a compass will spin if it is passed along the walls.

Estimates on the building of Nan Madol range from many

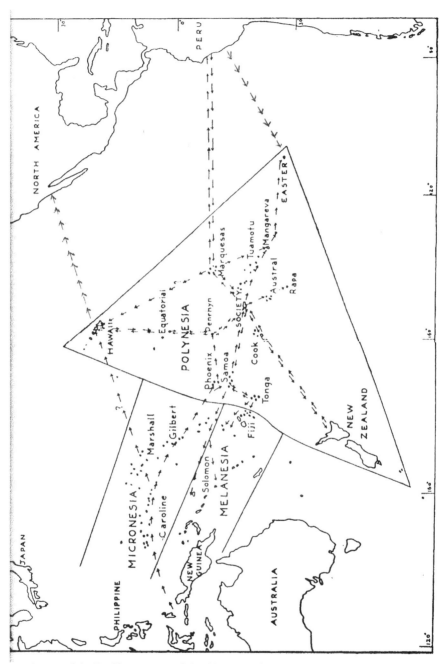

A map of the Pacific voyages of the Cham to Micronesia, Melanesia and Polynesia.

thousands of years ago to as recently as 1200 AD. Radio carbon dating of bone and shell material found at the ruins (they are in the ocean) has suggested that the ruins may be as old as 200 BC. There is no question that the city is entirely man-made and that each basalt block has been placed manually where it is located, rather than, say, accidently landing in its location due to a volcanic explosion or landslide.

The name Nan Madol means "the spaces in between," referring to the canals between the many islands. The city is located on the southeast corner of Pohnpei, adjacent to Temwen Island in the Madolenihmw district. The islands have no fresh water and life on the artificial islands would have meant importing all water and food (except for fish and other seafood). To add to the mystery, there are rumors of earlier sunken cities in the water off Nan Madol, and evidence to suggest the rumors are true.

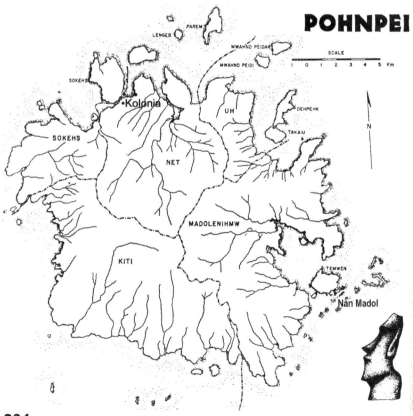

The city has baffled archeologists for the last 200 years. There is so much stone used at Nan Madol that modern engineers are at a loss to completely explain its construction. The locals insist that the stones were magically levitated and flown through the air. The similarity between the legends of Gunung Padang and Nan Madol should be noted. Both of these sites are built out of prismatic pillars of basalt and have legends that the stones were levitated into place. The main difference is that Nan Madol used these basalt logs in a far bigger way, with entire islands built up and walls of stacked basalt nearly 30 feet high. The islanders have long had a tradition that the ruins are haunted by spirits and to spend the night there may mean death (presumably by fright). There are also stories of lights that move about the ruins.

One modern story concerns the German governor of the islands, then called the Caroline Islands, named Victor Berg. He did early excavations at Nan Madol and in 1907 he is supposed to have found very large human bones that would have belonged to a person well over six feet tall, and possibly more than seven feet tall. On the evening of April 29, 1907, Berg was excavating at Nan Madol when a strong storm suddenly hit the island. The small

An aerial photo of a section of the megalithic canal city of Nan Madol.

235

town of Kolonia was hit by raging winds and lightning, and conch shells were heard blowing in the dark. That night Berg was struck by a mysterious illness that suddenly killed him. The next day the German doctor of Kolonia could find no reason for Berg's death, except perhaps sunstroke. The locals were convinced that the curse of Nan Madol had struck the governor.

The ruins of Nan Madol, and the similar ruins of Lelu on Kosrae, the next island to the east, intrigued early archaeologists a great deal — though few were able to visit these remote islands. One of the first

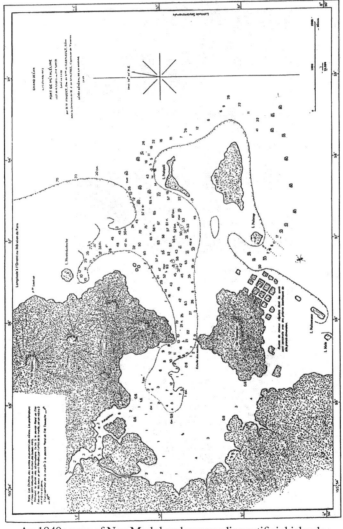

An 1840s map of Nan Madol and surrounding artificial islands.

236

archaeologists to collect data and artifacts at Nan Madol was the German-Pole, Johann Stanislaus Kubary. Kubary had four native wives, whom he kept on different islands in the Carolines. He loaded a ship with precious relics from Nan Madol that he had dug up in the 1870s, but the ship sank somewhere in the Marshall Islands. Kubary committed suicide a few years later on Pohnpei when one of his native wives left him for another man. Kubary wrote a valuable early manuscript on the history of Nan Madol that passed into the hands of a native Pohnpeian family (presumably his wife's), who kept it as an heirloom until it was accidentally burned in the 1930s.[66]

The German archaeologist Dr. Paul Hambruch of the Ethnological Museum in Hamburg accomplished some of the best work done at Nan Madol at the turn of the 20th century. Hambruch surveyed Nan Madol from 1908 to 1910, mapped the buildings and attempted to provide an explanation for each of the artificial islands in the complex. Much of what is known today comes from Hambruch's work, and he was the first person to take note of various tales of sunken cities, suggesting that a sunken city lay around Nakapw Island, near Nan Madol.

The great New Zealand scholar John Macmillan Brown was so fascinated by Nan Madol that after he visited, he wrote in his 1924 book *The Riddle of the Pacific*[33] that Pohnpei had been at the center of a now vanished empire. Says Brown:

> Four hundred miles to the northwest of Kosrae, on the southeast reef of Ponape [Pohnpei], there is a great cyclopean ruin that implies a vast subsidence of archipelagic land in the near or distant vicinity; there are eleven square miles of huge public buildings erected on square or rectangular islets artificially raised out of the water by a breastwork of great basalt crystals fencing in masses of coral debris. The walls of some of them, twelve feet thick, still rise thirty feet above the level of the surrounding water-streets; and to judge by the masses of cyclopean stones tumbled into their courtyards they must have vanished centuries ago. The rafting over the reef at high tide and the hauling up of these immense blocks,

most of them from five to twenty-five tons in weight, to such a height as sixty feet must have meant tens of thousands of organized labor; and it had to be housed and clothed and fed. Yet within a radius of fifteen hundred miles from this as a centre there are not more than fifty thousand people today. It is one of the miracles of the Pacific unless we assume a subsidence of twenty times as much land as now exists.[33]

Dating the Ancient City of Nan Madol

The Japanese administered the islands of Micronesia, except Guam, after World War I, taking them over from the Germans. They did extensive work on the ruins at Nan Madol, but most of their records were presumably lost or destroyed in World War II. However, an incredible account of the Japanese discovery of "platinum coffins" is given in the book *Der Masslose Ozean (The Measureless Ocean)* by Herbert Rittlinger, published in Germany in 1939. Rittlinger was a German writer and world traveler. Like many travelers before him, Rittlinger was very intrigued by Nan Madol.

In his 1973 book *Gold of the Gods*,[49] ancient astronaut theorist Erich von Daniken quotes Rittlinger's depiction of Pohnpei as:

… a brilliant and splendid centre of a celebrated kingdom that had existed there untold millennia ago. The reports of fabulous wealth had enticed pearl divers and Chinese merchants to investigate the seabed secretly and the divers had all risen from the depths with incredible tales. They had been able to walk on the bottom on well-preserved streets overgrown with mussels and coral. 'Down below' there were countless stone vaults, pillars and monoliths. Carved stone tablets hung on the remains of clearly recognizable houses.

What the pearl divers did not find was discovered by Japanese divers with modern equipment. They confirmed with their finds what the traditional legends of Ponape reported: the vast wealth in precious metals, pearls and bars of silver. The legend says that the corpses rest in the

'House of the Dead' (i.e., the main house in the complex). The Japanese divers reported that the dead were buried in watertight platinum coffins. And the divers actually brought bits of platinum to the surface day after day! In fact, the main exports of the island—copra, vanilla, sago and mother of pearl—were supplanted by platinum!

According to von Daniken, Rittlinger says that the Japanese carried on exploiting this platinum until, one day, two divers did not surface in spite of their modern equipment. Then WWII broke out and the Japanese had to withdraw. Von Daniken ends the story as follows: "The natives' stories, encrusted with century-old legends, are probably exaggerated. But the finds of platinum on an island where the rock contains no platinum, were and remain a very real fact."[49]

Separating fact from fiction on Pohnpei is not easy, and when it comes to this strange island, truth may indeed be stranger than fiction. The Japanese reportedly did discover very large human bones at Nan Madol, indicating that the previous inhabitants of the island were perhaps as tall as 2.1 meters (7 feet). An old Pohnpei native told me while I was there that he had found a human femur many years ago in the jungle that was "twice as big as a normal man's." This suggests a rather unbelievable height of 10 feet or so,

An old photo of one of the seawalls at Nan Madol.

making the early inhabitants giants.

One possible explanation has been postulated by authors such as David Hanlon in his book *Upon a Stone Altar: A History of the Island of Pohnpei to 1890*,[52] and Bill Ballinger in his *Lost City of Stone*[53]: Pohnpei may have been originally settled by Polynesians, although the population is now Micronesian. Polynesians are the largest (and heaviest) race of people in the world and central Polynesian islands such as Samoa and Tonga are still inhabited by unusually tall people, often well over the six-foot mark. The small island of Kapingamaringi, south of Pohnpei, has a Polynesian population, and this island is politically part of the Pohnpei state to this day. A population of Polynesians in Pohnpei may account for the unusually large human bones found at Nan Madol.

Hambruch, in his turn-of-the-century research, had early on rejected the theory that shipwrecked Spanish or Japanese sailors had built the ruins. However, Hambruch thought that the ruins had been built only 300 or 400 years before, an overly conservative estimate as the city had clearly been abandoned about that same time and the

A photo of one of the walls at Nan Dowas, the largest structure at Nan Madol.

locals now held it in superstitious awe.

After WWII, the sunken city was generally forgotten, and no other work was done on Nan Madol until the early 1960s when an American Smithsonian expedition came to the island to gather some hard scientific data on this strange city. The Smithsonian team carbon dated some ashes at the bottom of a fire pit on one of the artificial islands and discovered that they were 700 to 900 years old. Using this evidence, they ascribed a date of 1000 AD to the building of the city. The Smithsonian also suggested that the basalt rocks used to build the city came from a massif called Sokehs Rock near the main town of Kolonia.

The Smithsonian carbon dating at Nan Madol proved that the city must be at least twice as old as Hambruch had estimated. But this dating was also overly conservative because the dating of the charcoal was only an indication that the city was already inhabited 900 years ago, not that it was built then. The walls could have been built hundreds or thousands of years before the fire that produced that piece of charcoal was lit.

In fact, it must be remembered that the city is built into the ocean and isn't even on the dry land of Pohnpei at all. Hundreds of tropical storms, cyclones and tidal waves could have washed over the city during its many years of silent existence. The city may have been abandoned thousands of years ago, and then been occasionally inhabited by local fishermen or explorers who made large fires to cook their turtles. Local legend has survived about the city, but the time frame in which it was built has not come down to us.

In the 1970s, Steve Athens, an archaeologist for the Pacific Studies Institute in Honolulu, Hawaii, began the most extensive work on Nan Madol since the Japanese or possibly even the Germans. He discovered pottery shards that were dated by thermoluminescence as being at least 2,000 years old. This pushes back the date of Nan Madol by more than 1,000 years, and raises a lot more questions than it answers. Currently it is thought that the coral reef itself was occupied by 200 BC, but the ruins may still be thousands of years older than that. We simply do not know the age of this megalithic city built into a coral reef—the only one of its kind!

An photo of one of the walls at Nan Dowas, the largest structure at Nan Madol.

Built on a Coral Reef

From the air, Nan Madol looks like a gigantic mangrove swamp with big green squares in it. Over the thousands of years that it has lain there, unused for hundreds, mangrove trees and coconut palms have grown among the ruins, the roots tearing down walls, the canopies obscuring any view. Unfortunately, due to lack of funds and other resources, the destruction continues largely unabated to this day.

To gain access to the city, one must either go by boat or wade across the coral reef to the main complex of the 11-square-mile city, the "downtown" known as Greater Nan Madol. Today, a decently maintained path leads through the mangrove swamps to the canal at the largest structure, Nan Dowas, where one can wade across to the ruins. The walls are 30 feet high, constructed out of huge basalt stones. Some of the rocks are basalt logs five meters long in a hexagonal shape, formed naturally through crystallization. Other stones are not hexagonal but just huge boulders, roughly cut and dressed. These are the largest of the rocks, and the entire massive structure was built by stacking stones in the manner in which one might construct a log cabin.

All of the edifices are constructed out of such basalt blocks, and the islands, being man-made, naturally had to be constructed first. Basalt logs were placed on the coral reef, and then the center of the islet filled in with coral. The canals, too, were presumably hand cut into the coral, after which the megalithic walls and structures were built.

The whole project is of such huge scale that it easily compares with the building of the Great Wall of China and the Great Pyramid of Egypt in sheer amounts of stone and labor required, and the gigantic scope of the site.

Yet the actual source for the mountain of stone remains a mystery. Basalt rock formations do exist on the island, and there is no reason why the rock could not have come from Pohnpei. The main problem with finding the main quarry for the stones at Nan Madol is the incredible fact that 250 million tons of stone were quarried, such a huge amount of material that it could have totally consumed an entire basalt outcrop! And we don't know where it is—the stub of this mountain may even be submerged!

It is generally assumed that it came from two possible locations, both on the opposite side of the island from Nan Madol. One is at Sokehs Rock near the capital city of Kolonia, and the other is in the west of the island at an outcrop called "Chicken Shit Mountain." At neither location, however, has any evidence been found of the extensive quarrying that would have been necessary to gather the 250 million tons of stone used at Nan Madol.

As to how the stones reached Nan Madol, it has been suggested that they were moved from quarries by lashing bamboo to them, or placing them on coconut palm rafts, and then floating them to the site. However, two American engineers on Pohnpei told me that it was unlikely that such gigantic blocks could have been floated by raft or bamboo. The island is too mountainous for them to have been transported overland, and furthermore, these rocks are piled on top of each other to a height of ten meters or more. The largest movable crane on the island to this day can only lift about 35 tons.

Nan Madol: Cham Seaport in Micronesia?

In 1995 the Discovery Channel in the United States produced a documentary television show on Nan Madol. Crews attempted to float some of the smaller basalt columns on bamboo rafts. After many tries they remained unsuccessful in floating the columns, which weighed over one ton. They were eventually able to float a much smaller piece that weighed only a few hundred pounds. Realizing the tremendous effort that it would have taken to float and otherwise move the huge basalt columns found at Nan Dowas, the television crew was doubly impressed by the building skill of the ancient Pohnpeians.

The largest stone in the downtown complex is a massive basalt boulder on the southeast side of Nan Dowas, a cornerstone weighing possibly as much as 60 tons. Archaeologists have dug under the stone and found that there is a stone platform beneath it, deliberately placed where it is by the builders.

Local legend says that the blocks were "magically floated through the air from the other side of the island" to be placed where they are now. This legend either reflects the people's total ignorance of the city and how it was constructed, or, on the other hand, indicates that

A photo of a section of the massive seawall at Nan Madol.

244

the stones had genuinely "flown through the air" by magic or some other means. It may be the best explanation the people could muster for what they witnessed at the building of Nan Madol. As Arthur C. Clarke once said, "A technology sufficiently advanced from our own would seem to be magic." We will explore the possibility of floating stones in detail later.

University of Hawaii archaeologist Steve Athens, like Hambruch, made note of the extensive tunnel network throughout Nan Madol. Tunnel entrances can be found on many of the islets, and though now blocked, they are believed to connect major islands together. These tunnels are presumed by archaeologists to have been used for transportation between islets, yet why they were constructed is a mystery. Perhaps for defense? But if so, from whom?

The main fortress of Nan Dowas has a tunnel that was initially thought to be a tomb. When it was discovered in 1870 it was 40 feet deeper than it is today, and it was blocked by a giant boulder. It is believed that some of the tunnels at Nan Madol go beneath the reef and exit into underwater caves. Many such caves can be seen while diving along the sheer coral wall that cuts across Madolenihmw Harbor. How these tunnels could have been constructed through the coral reef on which Nan Madol lies is unknown. One tunnel was built between the islet of Darong and the outer reef. On the islet is a man-made lake lined with stone and used for ceremonial clam fishing. Fresh fish swim through the tunnel from the outer reef to the small lake. The pool was said to also contain a sacred eel with magical powers.

The entire city of Nan Madol is intersected by canals, and it is possible to boat through it at high tide. The canals are about nine meters wide and 1.5 meters deep at high tide, though they are largely filled with silt. Because of the continuing advance of the mangroves throughout the site, it is getting increasingly difficult to navigate the canals, and only the most major are kept clear. As one moves through the deserted city, fruit bats fly overhead, and the occasional call of a bird can be heard in the swamp. The ruins seem eerily deserted and silent, yet at one time this was a bustling, thriving canal city.

Island Magic and the Flying Stones

One of the greatest mysteries of Nan Madol is how the massive stones were moved and lifted into place, and several theories have been forwarded on the subject.

Donald Mackenzie, in his book *South Seas Myths and Legends*,[57] comments that, "Blocks had to be rafted, landing-stages constructed to receive them, and as we have seen, canals made in some cases so that these blocks might be transferred to a building site. A great deal of skilled labor had to be performed by men of experience before a wall or tomb of basaltic pillars could be constructed... The breakwater and artificial islets of the 'Micronesian Venice' were the work of men possessed of considerable engineering skill; withal they were experienced builders with a social organization which made it possible to provide immense gangs of workmen who had been well trained and disciplined."[57]

In his book, Mackenzie comments on W.J. Perry's 1923 book *The Children of the Sun*.[24] Perry refers to the founders of Nan Madol arriving from Yap "on stones that swam on the water." Perry says further:

> It is said on Ponape that certain spirits came from the sky and changed into stones; and the gods cannot be approached except through these stones, which are only found in certain places; if they are lacking in any place, so is the cult of gods. These stones are not only used in connection with offerings made to gods, but also possess magical powers and healing properties. When, for example, men wish to go fishing, they drop a holy stone into the sea.[24]

F.W. Christian, in his 1899 book *The Caroline Islands*,[35] also discusses some of the early theories of the building of Nan Madol. He mentions the theory of Kubary, the Polish archaeologist who said, "the stones were brought here by means of an inclined plane."

In the absence of cranes and other machinery, Christian considers this "very feasible," and writes:

In my mind's eye I viewed an even slope of felled tree trunks copiously sluiced with coco-nut oil, to avoid friction, up which the great blocks would be hauled, one relay of workmen above pulling upon long and thick cables of *coir* fibre or cinnet and supplementary ropes of green hibiscus bark, another relay below with solid staves and handspikes by turns pushing the huge mass upwards and resting with poles set against and below it to prevent it slipping back.[35]

Christian, like Perry, mentions the belief that the builders of Nan Madol and the people of Pohnpei had come from Yap, the most westerly island group in the Carolines. He says that the Yapese language "appears to be a crabbed form of some ancient tongue allied to the Dravidian (of India), colored with a tint of Malay and Japanese, crossed or chequered, in a very remarkable way, with unmistakable Polynesian words."[35]

F.W. Christian also relates in his book the traditional legend that Nan Madol was built by two brothers named Olo-chipa and Olo-chopa. By the magic spells of these men, "one by one the great masses of stone flew through the air like birds, settling down into their appointed place."[35]

The local claim that the stones were levitated through the air bears close attention. If the city had been built by brute force within the last few hundred years, as Hambruch thought, then it would seem logical that the local chiefs would still tell the tales of the mighty efforts of their forefathers in building the city.

Instead, the traditional history that has been handed down says that the movement of 250 million tons of prismatic basalt was no big effort at all. In fact, the stones were effortlessly moved through the air. Some stories relate that the great magicians even rode on the basalt logs as they came from the other side of Pohnpei.

Was there some sort of ancient science, possibly used by the ancient Hindus and Egyptians that could levitate stones? Basalt is not only a crystalline rock, but it is magnetic. It would be an ideal stone to try to levitate.

Levitation by sound is a technique that has been experimented with by NASA, and various authors have said that Tibetan lamas have been known to move stones by using sound.

Some physicists claim that gravity is really a frequency, part of Einstein's Unified Field. Crystallized blocks of basalt need only be resonating at the frequency of gravity (1012 hertz, or the

A photo of one of the walls at Nan Dowas, the largest structure at Nan Madol.

248

frequency between short radio waves and infrared radiation), and they will lose their weight. Crystals, even basalt crystals, are ideal for resonating in such a way. If that was the way that the stones 'magically' flew through the air, then they might have spun upward and to the east, just as the legend says, because of the spin of the earth. The centrifugal force of the earth's spin caused the stones to rise. It might be possible for people to ride on the logs as ballast, and help lower them into place at Nan Madol as the vibration lessened and the stones gained weight again.

The Canadian physicist T.B. Pawlicki said in his book *How to Build a Flying Saucer*,[13] "I believe the way the ancients transported megaliths for their monuments was to attach a small tuning fork to each stone, causing the module to levitate when the properly-tuned vibration was sounded. When a monolith is set to resounding, its vibrations keep it in the air most of the time. During the greater part of the wave cycle when the mass is floating, a light touch will move it in any direction. I believe the ancient engineers used this technology because the ancient myths describe it. This application of musical theory is far too sophisticated for a 'stone age' people to incorporate in their myths unless the authors actually witnessed the technology in operation." Perhaps, as Pawlicki suggests, this technology was used in moving the stones of Nan Madol.

In his scholarly study of Pohnpei for the University of Hawaii, *Upon a Stone Altar*,[52] David Hanlon curiously leaves out any reference to the islanders' beliefs that the stones were levitated and magically flown through the air. He refers only to the two brothers building Nan Madol. Despite the fact that details of this legend are known to just about everyone on Pohnpei, Hanlon apparently did not see fit to include this bit of history in his book, perhaps thinking that his superiors in Honolulu would think his book "unscholarly" should he mention this fantastic story.

Hanlon does mention another curious incident in the island's history, however. According to Hanlon, after the defeat of the Saudeleurs (who ruled Nan Madol and Pohnpei for centuries), a new political arrangement for the island was being made by the new paramount chief of the island, Isohkelekel. There came a report of a tree cut in the Eirke section Nansokele in the north that would not fall. The tree had been cut to make a canoe, but when the tree had been separated from its trunk, rather than fall to the ground, it rose up into the sky and vanished. Suspecting divine involvement, the men returned home mystified.

Then, after a considerable period of time there came word of a canoe, hewn from the tree that would not fall, descending from the sky. The flying canoe "came to hover over a spot called Pahn Akuwalap in the area known as Sounahleng on the north side of Temwen Island near Nan Madol. Failing to receive any response from the divine occupants of the canoe, the people of the area called for Soukise."[52] Soukise, an island chief, enlisted the help of a priest named Soulik en And, and the two went together to Pahn Akuwalap "where [the priest] immediately recognized the god Luhk sitting in the center of the canoe. The ruler-priest of Onohnleng stepped up onto the craft and beckoned to Soulik en And to follow. From the meeting between gods and priests in a canoe hovering over the land, there came about a new political organization on the island."[52]

This fascinating story has many curious elements in it: airships, levitating trees, and the local priest-kings having a conference with the "gods" aboard their airship. Even Nan Madol is part of the story, being the meeting place of the god Luhk and the ruler-priest Soukise of the district of Onohnleng on the other side of the island. Having recieved divine instruction aboard Luhk's airship, Soukise went back to his people and told them that Pohnpei was to be divided into sections that were self-ruling states, the eastern half of the island to be the largest state, Madolenihmw. This became the third of Pohnpei's ancient historical epochs, the *Mwehin Nahnmwarki* or 'Period of the Nahnmwarkis.'

Curiously, in ancient Egypt the districts were known as "nams" or "noms." Similarly, the word for "governor" in Egyptian was "marché" or "mwarki." A district governor in ancient Egypt had the title "Nam-mwarki." In Pohnpei we have the same words meaning the same thing; a Nahnmwarki is a district governor even today. Are elements of the Pohnpei language derived from ancient Egyptian? It would seem so.

Masao Hadley and Kahnihmweiso

I was fortunate enough on my first visit to the island in 1985 to have had the chance to interview Masao Hadley, a chief's son and the Nahnmwarki (governor) of Madolenihmw. I was also fortunate to accompany Masao Hadley to Nan Madol and the Madolenihmw Bay where he would show me where legend said several sunken cities, other than Nan Madol, lay.

Masao, now deceased, was considered during his lifetime to be the island authority on Nan Madol and the ancient history of Pohnpei. He spoke no English, and I interviewed him with the aid of an interpreter. Masao was a man of quiet power and knowledge, a true chief of the island.

It was explained to me earlier that on Pohnpei the natives believe if they tell you everything they know, they will die. Therefore locals, especially older people, are not likely to volunteer information. They will answer your questions, but will never say more than is required to answer any specific query.

The first thing that I asked Masao was who had built Nan Madol. Masao's answer was, "Nan Madol was built by men of Pohnpei. However, the architects of the city were two brothers who came from across the seas. They came from the southeast." He was apparently speaking about the land of Eir.

Eir is often said to be to the south, or as Masao was saying, the southeast. Other early reports talk about arrivals from the west, the area of Yap and Palau. Oceanic traffic would naturally move in both of these directions.

"Where do you suppose the builders came from?" I asked.

Masao shrugged his shoulders, "They came from the south and east. Maybe from South America. I don't know. When they first came to Pohnpei, they started to build their city at another place than where it is now, farther north along the east coast. However, they were not satisfied with the site of their new city. Then one day the brothers climbed a peak, the pyramidical peak near Nan Madol.

"The brothers climbed the mountain to get a view of the country to find a suitable site for their capital city. When they looked into Madolenihmw Bay, they saw the ancient city of the gods, Kahnihmweiso. Here was an important sign to the two brothers. A sunken city lay just offshore of Temwen Island, and to them it was a sign from the gods to build their great city on top of, or next to, the ancient city of the gods. We call this city Kahnihmweiso, and it is beneath the waters of Madolenihmw Bay."

By boat I accompanied Masao to the entrance of Madolenihmw Harbor. He pointed out toward the open ocean from our boat while our translator asked him if there were supposed to be ruins in the deep water beyond.

"Twice it has happened that a fisherman has speared a turtle with a harpoon in the bay," said Masao. "The turtle took the fisherman down to the bottom of the bay where the man saw the gates to the City of the Gods. The last time this happened was in the 1930s; the first time was hundreds of years ago.

"There is yet another sunken city outside the reef from Nan Madol and Kahnihmweiso. This city is called Kahnihmw Namkhet, and it is to the east near Nahkapw Island. In a deep and sandy place the gate to the city can be found. Some years ago a fisherman was dying. His spirit took a trip to the city outside the reef. After he had seen the city, which goes all the way to Kosrae, he returned to his body, told the people what he had seen, and then he died."

I asked Masao the important question of how he thought the great stones of Nan Madol were moved into place to form the islands, platforms and walls.

Looking directly at me with a serious expression Masao said, "The stones were made to fly through the air from the other side of the island and were put into place in this manner. The magic made the stones lighter than air and the men could even ride on top of them as they flew through the air and were placed on the islands among the canals in the ocean. According to legend, while the two brothers were building their city, a dragon came and dredged the canals. It was with this powerful magic that the men of Pohnpei built Nan Madol."

"Do some people on Pohnpei still know this magic today?" I asked Masao.

"Yes," he said.

Masao, being the guardian of Nan Madol, seemed like a good candidate for such secret knowledge, so I unabashedly asked him, "Do you know this magic?"

Masao looked at me with an expression of surprise. He raised his eyebrows and did not answer. I concluded that if such "magic" did exist, Masao was one of the few who still knew its secret.

Dive for a Sunken City

Back in 1985, I wanted to investigate the rumored sunken cities in the Madolenihmw Harbor area. I planned to dive with some others for both of the ancient cities mentioned by Masao. The sun was high and bright when we took our first dive in the open ocean just outside the reef where Masao said the second city of the gods, Namkhet, was located at a "deep and sandy place." The water was crystal clear and about 150 feet deep, dropping off quickly into the dark green oceanic depths below.

Our four teams fanned out, swimming at about 120 feet below the surface and scanning the ocean floor beneath us. We had floodlights, but they were unnecessary in such crystal clear water. We could easily see 200 feet or more.

The area was "deep and sandy" all right, but there was no trace of sunken structures, or even rocks or coral of any kind—just white sand and the occasional fish or shark. This was sort of unusual: elsewhere on the island coral is everywhere. Nonetheless, no gate

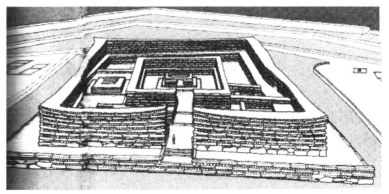

A diagram of Nan Dowas, the largest structure at Nan Madol.

253

of a city was to be seen in the vicinity.

Our diving team later concluded, as Masao had hinted, that Nahkapw Island near where we were diving was probably the location of the legendary second city. The German archaeologist Hambruch had concluded that portions of a sunken city lay around the island. Still, that is not to say that an isolated structure may not be out in the sand outside the reef. It is a vast area, and eight divers could not cover it.

We decided to concentrate our diving efforts inside the Madolenihmw Harbor, where sunken structures were known to exist, as documented by Dr. Arthur Saxe in his paper published in 1980.[5] Saxe had been asked to survey Nan Madol so as to clearly define the boundaries of the city. The Trust Territory of the Pacific was about to give Pohnpei and other Micronesian islands their independence. They wanted to create a national park of sorts, but for that they needed to know the boundaries of the ancient city.

Saxe confirmed what had already been reported but seemed incredible: that the city of Nan Madol did indeed cover 11 square miles. The "downtown" was about one square mile, and this is the area that tourists visit when coming out to the ruins for the day. Saxe noted the tunnels throughout the complex, and then began diving the waters of Madolenihmw Harbor to see what possible ruins might exist underwater.

In his report Saxe says (after explaining the logistics of their dive in the deep channel):

> A set of boulders was observed descending in a single line formation below the northwest edge of the channel. They were between depths of 85 and 95 feet, perpendicular to the drop-off. At 95 feet they disappeared into the oatmeal-like sand. The boulders were remarkable here because coral growth is sparse at these depths. The divers could not follow the line up the slope because it was obscured by more intense coral growth. Seven or eight boulders were observed in a line. They varied between two and six feet in diameter and were coral or coral-covered. There was not enough time

in this dive to determine whether the boulders had basaltic cores. After the dive was completed, the orientation of the line of boulders was estimated to be on a line between Pieniot and Nahkapw Islands.[65]

Saxe adds that they discovered two pillars covered with coral growth, one at a depth of 10 feet and one at 23 feet with the top reaching within 15 feet of the surface. Then he says:

> In a follow-up dive, our team confirmed this find by locating four additional pillars in this immediate area. We did not, however, relocate the column described as rising out of a flat pedestal.
>
> The first of the four was estimated (by surfacing) to be located about 75 feet to the east of Pahn Asang. It was 15 feet tall (depths: 40 ft. up to 25 ft.), three to four feet in diameter, and irregular in cross-section.
>
> The next two pillars (or more properly, pair of pillars) found by our team was located about 30 feet to the east or northeast. The larger of the pair had its base at a 60-foot depth, the top at 35 feet. The overall height was 25 feet. Height was measured by depth gauge readings. The diameter of this column was 4-5 feet, again irregular in cross-section.[65]

Saxe described more pillars and a "large boulder" at a 60-foot depth, saying that these finds were of extreme interest to many people on the island. Saxe says that they "were informed that the Ponapeans have legends about underwater cities in this area, and that these stories are sacred and close to the hearts of the people." Saxe continued:

> Legends tell of two such cities. One is to the east or under Nahkapw Island, with a gate or entrance outside the reef, at a 'deep and sandy place.' There is a sandy shelf outside Pwukeiso. The second city is in the deep channel between Nahkapw Island and Nanmwoluhei, the large rock in the

seawall east of Nan Dowas. This is where we located the columns. It was suggested that we may have seen the gate to this city. We were told the names of the guards stationed at the gates: Idengen Saralap and Idengen Saratik, both said to be women. [65]

And that is pretty much where Nan Madol and the mystery of the sunken ruins stood when we arrived at the city in 1985. A Japanese television crew had dived in the channel, and reportedly catalogued twelve columns standing in rows. An Australian television crew had also dived in the bay, discovering columns and filming a one-hour television show called *Ponape: Island of Mystery*. This is a very rare film, shown on Australian television only once. A copy of it can be seen at the Micronesian Community College in Kolonia.

After a picnic lunch on Nakapw Island, we anchored just off the fortress of Nan Dowas and began our second exploratory dive. We descended to 25 meters, keeping in sight of the steep edge of the shore. Coral grew down the edge, and there were quite a few fish. We had been warned of sharks and a giant "man-eating" grouper.

A photo of some of the millions of tons of basalt underwater at Nan Madol.

The water was very murky, and visibility only about five meters. We had to be careful not to lose our diving buddies. In general, it was rather spooky diving in Madolenihmw Harbor. One could not see very far into the green gloom, and therefore, things just suddenly loomed up in your facemask as you swam.

My diving buddy and I spotted a first column at a depth of 20 meters. It stood up perfectly straight from the bottom, was about 10 meters tall and was encrusted with coral. A shorter column, also coral-encrusted, stood just near it. We swam around this column, measured it and photographed it. We then continued our dive northward along the edge of the reef.

In the days to come, we made a total of nine dives with six to eight divers, each time fanning out in order to cover as much of the sandy, murky bottom as possible. We discovered a number of columns at various depths from 20 to 30 meters, often together in pairs. I personally saw five columns, diving down to about 35 meters toward the middle of the harbor. Fortunately, I never ran into any sharks or the "man-eating" grouper. But, our main goal of finding actual structures in the deep harbor and the so-called "platinum coffins" had still eluded us. Did they once exist?

Many of the stones we found underwater on the south side of Nakapw island (which is directly east of Nan Madol, across the Madolenihmw Harbor where the sunken city supposedly lies), easily weigh 10 tons; some are even exposed at low tide. Swimming along the coral reef, we also noticed straight lines in the coral, indicating that perhaps the coral had grown over walls of stone.

The German archaeologist Hambruch had suggested that Nakapw Island contained the remains of a sunken city. Masao Hadley also told us that there were two sunken cities, one in the Madolenihmw Harbor and one under Nakapw Island, or "beyond the reef."

The second city of the gods, Kahnihmw Namkhet, traditionally had its gate in a "deep and sandy place" to the east of Nakapw Island. We found no evidence for a city being beyond the reef; we did however, find a great deal of evidence that there are sunken structures to the south of the island, lending credence to the story of a sunken city beneath Nakapw.

On our recent trip, Jennifer and I and our companion Lee Sullivan were disappointed to find there were no longer any certified diving operations on Pohnpei, so we could not go diving. When we hired a boat for some recreational snorkeling on our last day, however, our guide told us that if we were not too finicky about the "certified operator" part we could have finagled a dive. Sadly, it seems that tourism is on the decline in Pohnpei—many people were happy and surprised to find that we were there as tourists as most foreigners are government-aide workers. The island is remote and expensive to get to. It is encircled by mangrove swamps and can't compete with the beaches of nearby Guam. Unless you know about Nan Madol, there does not seem to be very many reasons to visit the island.

Two Cities: One On Top of the Other

In my early efforts to find out more about the sunken ruins at Nan Madol, I contacted a diver named Isaiah Santos at the docks. I asked him about the "castle," or pillars, in the deep water.

"Yeah, I took some tourists to the bay and saw part of the castle," Isaiah said. "I dropped a 365-foot anchor chain down in the harbor and it got caught on something at 185 feet when I tried to pull it up. I put on tanks and was going to dive down to free the chain. I think it was caught on the castle. But as I started to follow the anchor chain down, I looked up, and there was a whole 'school' of rats swimming above me! I mean they were swimming under the water!" Isaiah's eyes were wide with fear as he told us of seeing hundreds of rats swimming through the murky green water. "I turned back and just cut the anchor," he said. "There is a legend that says that when you make a catch of fish in a net in the harbor, they will turn into rats."

I then contacted Pensile Lawrence, director of the Pohnpei Museum. He confirmed to me that Nan Madol was built on the reef next to Madolenihmw Harbor because it was the location of the sunken city of an earlier culture. He also said that there were 12 columns in a row, heading east underwater in the harbor, toward the gateway of the sunken city.

At the Registrar's Office I looked over aerial photos of

258

Madolenihmw Harbor and Nan Madol. I noticed several odd things. First, Joy Island, to the southeast of Nan Madol, was rectangular in shape with giant stones squaring it off. It was obviously man-made, and is generally considered part of Nan Madol.

Northeast of Joy Island, on the huge, flat reef on which Nan Madol is built, are what appear to be ruins in the water; square outlines in the coral reef and other large angular markings that could only be seen from the air.

A photo of one of the underwater columns at Nan Madol.

What is the answer to the mystery of Nan Madol and sunken Madolenihmw, the "Atlantis of the Pacific"? One theory is that part of Nan Madol was built on a gigantic limestone cavern that later collapsed, sending columns and structures down to the bottom of the harbor. Yet this does not explain how the columns would still be standing. Furthermore, nowhere else at Nan Madol are columns used in the construction of any buildings; they are only found underwater.

Another possible explanation is that the entire island has been sinking over thousands of years. This might explain how submerged and coral-encrusted square outlines of structures in the coral reef are still standing, yet it does not take into account the local legends.

One hypothesis that makes use of all the data is that there was once a former continent in the Pacific Ocean. Around 1980, coal deposits were found off Rapa Iti in French Polynesia, indicating that areas of the Pacific were once high and dry. In a cataclysmic upheaval in the remote past, this continent may have been submerged, and the sunken "City of the Gods" to be found off Pohnpei may have been a city of this now vanished culture.

Of course, this is a radical conclusion that would, in effect, rewrite current accounts of ancient history. Yet, perhaps ancient history needs to be rewritten. A major expedition should be sent to Pohnpei equipped with sonar, deep-diving and core-drilling equipment. The harbor needs to be mapped completely by sonar and all columns and other structures explored carefully with a miniature sub or diving bell. The coral reef needs to have a number of core samples taken, to ascertain what is beneath the mass of coral.

Did the Cham build Nan Madol?

A clue as to who might have built the structures of Nan Madol is found on the remote island of Kapingamarangi, a Polynesian atoll 415 miles to the southwest of Pohnpei. Located only one degree north of the equator, this atoll between New Ireland and Pohnpei is one of the lonely Polynesian outpost islands, such as Rotuma, which lead the way into Tonga, Fiji and Samoa in the heart of Polynesia. Kapingamarangi also has an artificial island on it, built in a manner similar to the construction of Nan Madol. This artificial island may be the important clue that archaeologists need in order to decipher the enigma of Nan Madol.

Kapingamarangi consists of 33 islets in a semi-circle around a lagoon. The largest islet is named Hale but it is virtually uninhabited. Rather, the entire population lives on the small man-made islet of Touhou near the natural islet of Veilua. Touhou, like the 92 or so islands of Nan Madol, is artificially made with coral fill piled up behind large stone blocks. In the local Polynesian dialect, *tou* means island and *hou* means new. Other islands, such as Hare Island, are suspected of being artificial as well.

Coral-faced walls exist on Touhou but foreign stones such as basalt occur as well in the building. The largest block of stone is a huge block of basalt known as the anchor stone for the island. This volcanic stone was brought from another island and does not occur naturally in the area. Incredibly, this may be a large stone from Pohnpei, probably from the same quarry from which the stones for Nan Madol came.[52]

Say Foss Leach and Graeme Ward in their 1981 monograph for the University of Otago entitled *Archaeology On Kapingamarangi Atoll*:

> It is most interesting that cultural material occurs right on the indurated coral basement of Touhou islet… this suggests that people were present on Kapingamarangi at a time when Touhou was virtually awash with the sea. Clearly, these people must have inhabited some other islet at this time, and only temporarily visited Touhou. …the lowest cultural layer occurs below sea level. [At one time] the islet existed as a low sandy flat, barely above the sea.

Were the builders of Nan Madol originally Polynesians? The people of this mysterious culture, centered in Tonga, Samoa and Tahiti in ancient times, are a mystery themselves. They built great monuments all over the Pacific and are presumed to have come from India by way of Indonesia, the same as the Cham. It is very possible these voyages by the Cham, including ships from India, were responsible for stones from Pohnpei appearing on Kapingamarangi. It would seem that it is the Cham that are behind the construction of the similar megalithic sites in Micronesia and Polynesia. There are other oddball islands with basalt megaliths, like Rotuma Island in the very north of Fiji.

Rotuma is a Polynesian island that is now part of the Melanesian island group of Fiji. Rotuma has huge slabs of basalt on the northeast corner of the island that weigh many tons. They are known to be man-made stone slabs that have been moved to several different spots around the nearby village. Rotuma would be a good stopping point on sea journeys between Micronesia and Polynesia, which lies further to the east.

It seems quite likely that the mythical land of Eir to the southeast of Pohnpei may have been the central Polynesian islands of Tonga and Samoa.

The Polynesians, like the Cham, apparently moved out into the Pacific from Southeast Asia by going both north and south of the great island of New Guinea. On the northern route into the Pacific were such islands as New Hanover, Kapingamarangi, Rennel Island, and finally Rotuma Island in the very north of Fiji. Kapingamarangi lay very near the equator, something that the early navigators must have appreciated.

Apparently the early Polynesians (Cham?) saw fit to create a small naval base, complete with an artificial island port, on this remote atoll. It is a perfect stopover island for a journey from Indonesia and New Guinea up into the many scattered islands of Micronesia (including Pohnpei). Rotuma is a similar, but larger, outpost-island, and did not have to be built up artificially like Kapingamarangi.

Were the first inhabitants of Pohnpei those brought by Champa priests who were able to use their arcane knowledge taken from India and Egypt to build the amazing seaport of Nan Madol? The ancient Indian epics such as the *Mahabharata* relate that a type of airship called a vimana was in use during these times as we discussed in chapter one. I have argued for the existence of ancient flight in

262

my book, *Vimana*.[67] Tales of early flight abound in all civilizations as well as in Polynesia. Was Pohnpei a remote Pacific base for an ancient navy, a navy that was occasionally visited by airships from a distant airfield? It boggles the imagination!

Curiously, a date of circa 200 AD would coincide with the time of the great Cham civilization that was conquering the Pacific in the name of Buddha and Shiva. I believe that the Cham journeyed to Tiwanaku in the South American Andes, and learned the building technique of the megalith builders there. Perhaps they brought this technique back to Champa where we see the same keystone cuts and metal clamps at My Son. Or perhaps the technique came from Egypt (Khem-Khemit) where some of the oldest keystone cuts can be found.

Did the ancient Cham, part Egyptian, part Southeast Asian Hindu-Buddhists, journey into the islands north of New Guinea, including Pohnpei and Kosrae, and then out to the Central Pacific islands of Hawaii, Tonga and Samoa? Did they bring some sacred and secret technology of levitation and anti-gravity that Hindu yogis and Tibetan priests are sometimes alleged to have? It is all as fantastic as the flying stones of Nan Madol!

One famous statue at My Son features the Hindu god Shiva with his third eye. Had the Hindu-Buddhist masters arrived at Pohnpei in 200 AD to work their special magic of stone levitation on a colossal scale? It seems incredible yet the evidence is leading us in this direction, back to a mystical empire of magicians and flying stones. Close your eyes and go there!

Stonecutting and building were two of the great skills of the ancient Egyptians, and some authors have claimed that the Egyptians used various forms of levitation and other "clever" building techniques. Could Nan Madol be connected to Egyptian explorations into the Pacific circa 1000 BC? The dating of Nan Madol is highly controversial. Ash found on one of the artificial islands was dated as 900 years old, yet pottery was dated as over 2,000 years old. Could the ruins of Nan Madol be even 1,000 years older than thought? So far there has been no evidence that would preclude this possibility.

Nan Madol: Cham Seaport in Micronesia?

In his book *Lost City of Stone*,[53] Bill Ballinger, posits that Nan Madol was built by Greek sailors circa 320 BC. The Greek sailors were remnants of Alexander the Great's army in Persia after Alexander was poisoned (323 BC) and his empire started to split up. These sailors, theorized Ballinger, left the Persian Gulf intent on making their own kingdom, and after sailing through Indonesia, settled on Pohnpei, where they built Nan Madol. However, as the

An old photo of one of the massive walls at Lelu, Kosrae.

reader knows, the Hindu-Cham had great fleets in the Gulf of Siam and the Java Sea at that time. Perhaps Alexander's lost fleet joined up with the Cham, as they were a mixture of people and sailors from around the region.

Harvard professor Barry Fell had a similar theory on the settlement of the Pacific, though he placed the voyages as earlier and ultimately traced them to Egypt. But would lost navies have the manpower and skill to have erected such massive architecture? Nan Madol would appear to be a well-planned megalithic ocean port built on a grand scale. One can't help but think that at one time, hopefully for hundreds of years, a great navy was based at Nan Madol—a prehistoric navy that conquered the Pacific and the lands beyond.

The combination of the Khemit from ancient Egypt and the Cham from Southeast Asia was a powerful force that was capable of sweeping into the Pacific with huge fleets of ships and of establishing ports-of-call for the long trading-exploration voyages. Somehow, the Cham-Hindu-Egyptian magicians were able to quarry the millions of tons of basalt from a still unknown location and then levitate them through the air to their spot. Indeed, an entire mountain of basalt could have been dismantled to create the huge city. Even vimanas may have used in the building of the port as reported in the legends.

The structures at Pohnpei and nearby Kosrae are very similar to the curious basalt structure at Gunung Padang in Java, plus the Olmecs in Mexico used prismatic basalt pillars in a similar way and carved their huge 20-ton colossal heads out of basalt. We will discuss the Olmecs at length in the next chapter.

Kosrae is about 560 kilometers southeast of Pohnpei and is part of the Federated States of Micronesia. The rugged interior of the island is virtually inaccessible and is crowned by the highest mountain on Kosrae, Mount Finkol, which is 2,069 feet high. A broad valley between Mt. Finkol in the south and Mt. Mutunte (1,951 feet) in the north divides the island in two.

Kosrae is called the "Island of the Sleeping Lady" because the profile of the island looks like the figure of a reclining woman.

265

Legend tells that Kosrae was shaped by the ancient gods. The view of the "sleeping lady" can best be seen from the small island of Lelu on the eastern side, which holds the megalithic walls and canals. Today it is connected to the main island by a causeway and paved road.

Little is known of the prehistory of the island, and modern history begins with the decimation of the island by diseases brought in by whaling boats in the early 1800s. But one can see the ruins of the ancient canal city of Insaru on Lelu Island. They are very similar to the basalt ruins of Nan Madol on Pohnpei. In ancient times Insaru was a giant stone city of huge basalt walls, canals and pyramids. Like Nan Madol, the islands and buildings of Insaru were intersected by a canal network that was connected with the open ocean. Large boats could enter at high tide into a stunning network of huge stone walls and docks at which to moor their ships.

Though the ruins of Insaru on Lelu are not as extensive as those at Nan Madol, they are only slightly less impressive. Some of the megalithic blocks of basalt used in the construction weigh up to 40 tons. The design and construction of Insaru would have taken a genius and even modern construction engineers would be very impressed to see these stones today. Today, the canals at Insaru are largely filled in, and the impression that archaeologists have is that the island of Lelu has risen slightly, since the canals are almost dry.

It was from Insaru that the legendary warrior Isokelekel and his 333 warriors left to conquer Nan Madol and end the Saudeleur dynasty. Today, Lelu is still the largest population center on Kosrae and many people actually live within the ruins and canals of the ancient city of Insaru.

Clearly, the ruins on both Pohnpei and Kosrae were built by the same megalith builders. What also seems pretty clear is that as the original empire broke down a small civil war broke out between the two islands. They had become isolated from the Gulf of Siam at this time and from Polynesia as well. What had once been a larger Cham-driven island empire was now breaking up into smaller island empires. Pohnpei itself was to become five different districts, each with its own chief.

The time frame for the dereliction of Nan Madol and Insaru also fits well into the Champa time frame. At the period of 200 AD or so the Cham were moving into the Pacific. They may have built Nan Madol at this time with their magical technology. Huge fleets of ships were also involved. As the Cham empire broke up starting around 650 AD the ships stopped massing on the Cham Islands every year, and the voyages out into the Pacific came to a stop. Once Sumatra and Java began to attack the Champa territories in Vietnam all voyages beyond the Sulu Sea by the Cham stopped. They were too busy fighting the civil wars back in the Gulf of Siam, with the Khmer in Cambodia also attacking My Son and the Cham Islands.

Our recent visit to Pohnpei was all too brief, but rewarding and fun since a sufficient number of sunset tiki bars and karaoke clubs still exist on the island. As I looked out the plane window at the mountainous, jungle island after our departure, I could see Nan Madol in the distance. It is one of the most mysterious places that I have ever been. Already I was thinking of things to do the next time I returned. Nan Madol is one of the great monuments of the world, erected by the megalith masterminds that were Buddhist-Shivites—the Cham. Or had some other great builders come with the magical machines?

Soon I would be back in Hawaii and then at my home in Arizona. My next journey would be to Mexico to examine the Olmecs and their connection to the Cham.

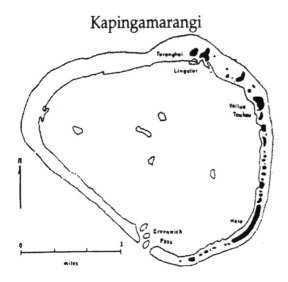

Above: A map of Kapingamaringi. Below: An aerial photo of Kapingamaringi showing the section around Touhou islet.

Chapter Seven

THE OLMECS AND THE CHAM

We can trace the progress of man in Mexico
without noting any definite Old World influence during
this period (1000-650 BC) except a strong Negroid substratum
connected with the Magicians (High Priests).
—Frederick Peterson, *Ancient Mexico (1959)*

When looking at Cham art, such as in the Museum of Cham Culture in Da Nang, the art of the Olmecs naturally comes to mind. The statuary of both cultures is very similar. Both the Cham and the Olmecs are little understood. But first, who are the Olmecs?

Until the 1930s it was largely held that the oldest civilization in the Americas was that of the Maya. The great number of Mayan monuments, steles, pottery, statues and other artifacts discovered throughout the Yucatan, Guatemala and the Gulf Coast of Mexico had convinced archeologists that the Maya were the mother civilization of Central America.

But some "Mayan" artifacts were different from the main bulk of the artifacts in subtle ways. One difference was that some carvings of large heads had faces with more African-looking features than many of the other Mayan works. Mayan paintings and sculpture can be quite varied but the African-looking features seemed distinctly un-Mayan. These African-looking heads often had a curious frown and often wore masks or appeared to be half-jaguar-half-man beasts. This recurring motif did not fit in with other Mayan finds.

In 1929, Marshall H. Saville, the Director of the Museum

of the American Indian in New York, classified these works as being from an entirely new culture not of Mayan heritage. Somewhat inappropriately, he called this culture Olmec (a name first assigned to it in 1927), which means "rubber people" in Nahuatl, the language of the Mexica (Aztec) people. Most of the early anomalous artifacts were found in the Tabasco and Veracruz regions of southern Mexico, a swampy region exploited for natural gas, but in ancient times a source point for rubber. Ancient Mesoamericans, spanning from the Olmecs to Aztecs, extracted latex from *Castilla elastica*, a type of rubber tree in the area. The juice of a local vine *Ipomoea alba*, was then mixed with this latex to create rubber as early as 1600 BC (and possibly earlier). "Olmec" was the Aztec name for the people who lived in this area at the much later time of Aztec dominance.

The ancient Olmecs are now credited with creating the ball game that played such a significant role in all Mesoamerican civilizations, and the rubber balls that were used in the game. This game may be even older than the Olmecs, in fact. Ball courts and the Olmec-Mayan ball game were popular as far north as Arizona and Utah and as far south as Costa Rica and Panama.

According to the famous Mexican archeologist Ignacio Bernal,[59] Olmec-type art was first noticed as early as 1869, but as noted above, the term "Olmec," or "Rubber People," was first used in 1927. Naturally, a number of prominent Mayan archeologists, including Eric Thompson who helped decipher the Mayan calendar, refused to believe that this new culture called the Olmecs could be earlier than the Mayas. Not until a special meeting in Mexico City in 1942 was the matter largely settled that the Olmecs predated the Mayas. The date for the beginning of the Olmec culture was to remain a matter of great debate, however.

Bernal sums up this curious archeological episode in his book *A History of Mexican Archaeology*:

> ...the whole Olmec culture is earlier than the Maya. This was anathema at the time because, as we have already seen, almost all the endeavors of the Carnegie and other

institutions, North American in particular, had been directed towards Maya research, the consensus of opinion then being not only that the Maya culture was the oldest, but that all the other Mesoamerican cultures had stemmed from it.

At the celebrated meeting held under the aegis of the Sociedad Mexicana de Antropología in 1942 to discuss the Olmec problem, archaeologists headed by Caso, Covarrubias and Noguera, along with Stirling, all maintained that the Olmecs belonged within the Archaic horizon. Caso claimed that the Olmec "is beyond doubt the parent of such other cultures as the Maya, the Teotihuacan and that of El Tajín" (1942:46).

…At the Mesa Redonda de Tuxtla in 1942 the Olmecs were given a provisional starting date around 300 BC. But somewhat later work at San Lorenzo, carried out with the aid of radiocarbon analysis—the use of which was spreading throughout the area—showed that 1200 BC was a more realistic date. This fitted in perfectly with what was being discovered all over Mesoamerica. It is a part of the general process that has already been discussed. Nineteenth-century scholars had often proposed fabulously early dates for the prehispanic peoples, and it produced in this century a vigorous counter-reaction which in its turn condensed them too drastically. But after 1950 this difficulty was to be overcome by the use of dating techniques that are not essentially archaeological.

The Olmecs had been discovered. However, this discovery created more questions than there were answers. The discovery of the Olmecs seemed to cast into doubt many of the old assumptions concerning the prehistory of the Americas. Suddenly, here was a diverse-looking people who built monumental sculptures with amazing skill, were the actual "inventors" of the number and writing system used by the Maya, the ball game with its rubber balls and even knew about the wheel (as evidenced by their

One of the 20-ton basalt colossal heads discovered at La Venta.

wheeled toys).

The greater enigma was upon the archeologists—who were the Olmecs?

What is the Origin the Olmecs?

Bernal continued to study the Olmecs and came out with the significant revelation of this early Central American culture in his 1969 book *The Olmec World*.[59] In that book, Bernal discussed the curious finds attributed to the Olmecs all over southern Mexico and Central America, as far south as the site of Guanacaste in Nicaragua. However, he could not figure out the origin of these strange and distinctive people whose art featured bearded men,

A jade Olmec mask showing oriental eyes and typical Olmec frown.

Negroid heads, and undecipherable hieroglyphs. Even such famous Mayan sites as Uaxactun and El Mirador were thought by Bernal to have been previously occupied by the Olmecs.

The idea that the these strange Negroid heads might be the result of early African or Asian exploration seems totally alien to the historians and archeologists who have taken over the archeology of the Americas. Despite depictions of various lords, kings, travelers, magicians and whatnot that look like Africans, Chinese, bearded Europeans, or some other strangers, most professors teaching at our major universities maintain that they are not evidence of ancient pre-Columbian explorers. They admit, though, that people might erroneously get this idea from a "superficial" view of these various statues and carvings.

So, even to mainstream historians, the origin of the Olmecs is a mystery. In the realm of alternative history, many theories exist on how Negroids arrived in Central America. One theory is that they are connected with Atlantis; as part of the warrior-class of that civilization they were tough and hard bitten. Or perhaps they were part of an Egyptian colony in Central America or from some unknown African empire. Others have suggested that they came across the Pacific from the lost continent of Mu, or as Shang Chinese mercenaries (culled from the ranks of the Cham?). Similarly, there is the curious association of "magicians" (or shamanic sorcerers using magic mushrooms and other psychedelics) with many of the Olmec statues—magicians from Africa, China, or even Atlantis?

Are the Olmecs Transoceanic Colonizers?

It is not known what name the ancient Olmec used for themselves; some later Mesoamerican accounts seem to refer to the ancient Olmec as "Tamoanchan." The classic period for the Olmecs is generally considered to be from 1200 BC ending around 400 BC. Early, formative Olmec artifacts are said to go back to 1500 BC, and probably earlier.

No one knows where the Olmecs came from, but the two predominant theories are the following:

1. They were Native Americans, derived from the same Siberian stock as most other Native Americans, and just happened to accentuate the Negroid genetic material that was latent in their genes.

2. They were outsiders who immigrated to the Olman area via boat, most likely as sailors or passengers on transoceanic voyages that went on for probably hundreds of years.

One of the colossal heads discovered at La Venta, this one with curious pock marks.

At the center of the debate about the origin of the Olmecs is the classic struggle between isolationists (who think that ancient man was incapable of transoceanic voyages, and therefore, nearly every ancient culture developed on its own) and diffusionists (who think that ancient man could span the oceans, which explains similarities in widely disparate cultures). There are a few proponents of diffusionism at the traditional academic level. Ivan Van Sertima of Rutgers University in New Jersey actively promotes the diffusionist theory that ancient man crossed both the Atlantic and the Pacific in prolonged transoceanic contact. His books, *African Presence in Early America*[16] and *African Presence in Early Asia*,[15] are filled with articles and photos that show without a doubt that Negroes have lived, literally, all over the world, including in the ancient Americas.

The Olmec seem to be connected to the Cham, yet mainstream historians would say the Olmec civilization started around 1000 BC while the Cham only originated circa 200 AD. Still, as we shall see, one of the cultures that influenced the Olmecs seems to the be the Shang Chinese, circa 1000 BC. However, how did the Shang reach Mexico? Did they assemble a fleet of ships at the Cham Islands and then go eastward to the Sulu Sea and into the Pacific in the same way that the Cham did?

Indeed, the strong connection that the Cham had with China—as well as ancient India—may have led to Shang Chinese expeditions to the Americas that included dark-skinned Negroid sailors who were part of Champa. This appears to be part of Van Sertima's reasoning as well. We know that Hinduism is one of the oldest religions in the world and probably goes back to 7000 BC or more. At Gobekli Tepe and nearby Nevali Cori the local limestone was carved into numerous statues and smaller sculptures, including a more-than-life-sized bare human head with a snake or sikha-like tuft. As we have seen, "sikha" is a tuft of hair on the back of an otherwise shaven head, often worn by Hindu priests. Many people recognize this tonsorial style because Hari Krishna devotees wear the sikha-tuft. Statues at Nevali Cori are dated to 8400 BC and are

276

evidence that Hinduism was being practiced in the Gobekli Tepe region of southern Turkey over 10,000 years ago. The sikha was one of the few symbols of Hindus that transcended caste, language or regional barriers. Although there were variations of the style of sikha amongst communities, in ancient times it was obligatory for all males to wear.

We just don't know how long Hindus have been sailing in the Gulf of Siam and the Java Sea but it would seem to be thousands of years. As I have said earlier in this book, it is likely Hindus were sailing in this area by at least 600 BC, at a time before the rise of Buddhism. While historians do not have a name for these early Hindu sailors, I believe that we can call them the Cham. And they seem to be tied in with the Olmecs and Mayas.

Unfortunately, most of the writers in the academic field prefer to champion the isolationist theory to the virtual exclusion of the diffusionist school of thought. In the scholarly book by Richard A. Diehl, *The Olmecs: America's First Civilization*,[58] Diehl has only one paragraph on the subject, saying:

> The origins of Olmec culture have intrigued scholars and lay people alike since Tres Zapotes Colossal Head I, a gigantic stone human head with vaguely Negroid features, was discovered in Veracruz 140 years ago. Since that time, Olmec culture and art have been attributed to seafaring Africans, Egyptians, Nubians, Phoenicians, Atlanteans, Japanese, Chinese, and other ancient wanderers. As often happens, the truth is infinitely more logical, if less romantic: the Olmecs were Native Americans who created a unique culture in southeastern Mexico's Isthmus of Tehuantepec. Archeologists now trace Olmec origins back to pre-Olmec cultures in the region and there is no credible evidence for major intrusions from the outside. Furthermore, not a single *bona fide* artifact of Old World origin has ever appeared in an Olmec archaeological site, or for that matter anywhere else in Mesoamerica.

With this paragraph Diehl summarily dismisses all theories and evidence of transoceanic contact. We don't really know what a *bona fide* artifact would be, since Old World and New World articles were often identical. Also, we are given no further information on the pre-Olmec cultures from which the Olmecs are presumably derived.

But for the Olmecs to actually be Africans—not just look like them—they would almost certainly have come to the Isthmus of Tehuantepec via ship. But since such voyages are dismissed immediately and there will be no further discussion of it, the Olmecs simply have to be local boys who have always pretty much been there. At some time in remote prehistory, their early genetic group walked into this Olmec heartland area.

According to Diehl, the Olmecs would have been an isolated group within their region as well, with little contact with other tribes in the Isthmus of Tehuantepec. Says Diehl:

> We do not know what these people called themselves, or if they even had a term that encompassed all the inhabitants of Olman. There is no evidence that they formed a single unified ethnic group, and almost certainly no Olmec considered people living more than a few hours' walk away as members of his or her own group. Nevertheless, the numerous independent local cultures were so similar to one another that modern scientists consider them a single generic culture.[58]

The Olmec settlements, according to Diehl, rose up independently in their corner of Mesoamerica without the influence of any other culture. They all suddenly began making monumental statues out of basalt (one of the hardest and most difficult stones to carve), and made large structures with sophisticated drainage systems. But they weren't really in contact with their early neighbors. The spread of Olmec-like artifacts was achieved only later when Olmec "styles" were used by other more widespread cultures.

Diehl was actually proved wrong on this account when it was announced in January 2007 that an Olmec-influenced city had been found near Cuernavaca, hundreds of miles from the Olmecs' Gulf Coast territory, at Zazacatla. Announcements at that time stated that a "2,500-year-old city influenced by the Olmecs, often referred to as the mother culture of Mesoamerica, has been discovered hundreds of miles away from the Olmecs' Gulf coast territory, archaeologists said." (*National Geographic News*, January 26, 2007) This discovery is not really surprising since the Olmec city of Chalcatzingo near Mexico City was excavated and written about in the 1970s.

So the preponderance of the evidence shows that the Olmecs were very aware of the villages near them, and aware of cities and peoples quite far from them. Were they aware of transoceanic civilizations as well?

Diehl's book, published in 2004, is an interesting but fairly dry read. Not only does he refuse to discuss Negroid features and transoceanic contact in his book, but, except for one brief mention (below) there is no discussion of cranial deformation at all, which is one of the more curious habits of the Olmecs and the Maya, and is found among many other cultures worldwide, including the Pacific island nation of Vanuatu.

The Olmecs had many unusual similarities with the Maya and other transoceanic cultures, such as: the reverence for jade and exotic feathers; the use of hallucinogenic mushrooms and other psychedelic drugs; the use of hieroglyphs on stone stelae as markers; and the practice of cranial deformation.

Even though cranial deformation is obviously a major feature of the Olmecs, Diehl only mentions it once, in passing, in his book. Says Diehl of artifacts and skeletons found at an Olmec burial at Tlatilco:

One high-status woman was laid to rest with 15 pots, 20 clay figurines, 2 pieces of red-painted bright green jadite that may have formed part of a bracelet, a crystalline hematite plaque, a bone fragment with traces of alfresco paint, and miscellaneous stones. Another burial held the remains of a male whose skull had been deliberately modified in infancy and whose teeth were trimmed into geometric patterns as an adult. He may have been a shaman since all the objects placed with him were likely part of a shaman's power bundle. They included small *metates* for grinding hallucinogenic mushrooms, clay effigies of mushrooms, quartz, graphite, pitch, and other exotic materials that could have been used in curing rituals. A magnificent ceramic bottle placed in his grave depicted a contortionist or acrobat who rests on his stomach with his hands supporting his chin while his legs bend completely around so that his feet touch the top of his head. Could this masterpiece be an effigy of the actual occupant of the grave?

Indeed, Diehl almost gets excited about the Olmecs. Could they actually be psychedelic jaguar shamans who like to make monumental heads to keep themselves busy?

The Olmecs, by any standard, are a fantastic, amazing, confusing, psychedelic, and in some cases, just plain weird people. We do not know where they came from. We don't know why they were there. We don't know what their "mission" was. In short we know very little about them. All we really know is that they are old, and they are strange.

While it is easy to see them as Proto-Mayans and Citizens of Olman (however large that country might have been), we should also consider them as the fantastic Proto-Mesoamericans they may have been: psychedelic aliens who used lasers to cut colossal basalt heads; Atlantean refugees who made a last stand in Tabasco; or Shang Chinese mercenaries taken from East Africa or Cham and specially trained to administer the Pacific (and later Atlantic) ports of the Isthmus of Tehuantepec; or perhaps a people originally from the Atlantic side all along, having come from Africa, possibly as a military force from Egypt or West Africa, circa 1500 BC. There are many possibilities.

So, with an open mind, let us look into the mysteries of the Olmecs, their fantastic art, their sophisticated technology, their unusual number system, writing system and other customs. What we find may surprise us. We are likely to find that the Olmecs were geniuses, but many other cultures had surprisingly similar ideas.

Olman: The Land of the Olmecs

The Olmecs are said to have occupied "The Land of Olman." This was a designation that the Aztecs used to describe the jungle areas of the nearby coast. The traditional definition of the Olmecs is that they were an ancient Pre-Columbian people living in the tropical lowlands of south-central Mexico, roughly in what are the modern-day states of Veracruz and Tabasco on the Isthmus of Tehuantepec. Their immediate cultural influence went much further though, as their artwork has been found as far away as El Salvador and Costa Rica, and possibly Panama.

The Olmec heartland is thought to be an area on the Gulf of Mexico coastal plain of southern Veracruz and Tabasco. This is because the area boasts the greatest concentration of Olmec monuments as well as the greatest number of Olmec sites. This area is thought to be the most northerly area of the Mayan realms, with such sites as Comacalco as the northernmost Mayan city along the Gulf Coast of the Ithmus of Tehuantepec.

The Olmec heartland is characterized by swampy lowlands punctuated by low hill ridges and volcanoes. The Tuxtla Mountains rise sharply in the north, along the Bay of Campeche. Here the Olmecs constructed permanent city-temple complexes at several locations: San Lorenzo Tenochtitlán (usually just referred to as just San Lorenzo), Laguna de los Cerros, Tres Zapotes, La Mojarra and La Venta.

The heartland of the Olmecs is also the narrowest land area in Mexico, an area extremely important if an ocean-to-ocean trade route were to be established. This narrow area of southern Mexico is known as the Isthmus of Tehuantepec and it represents the shortest distance between the Gulf of Mexico and the Pacific Ocean. The name comes from the town of Santo Domingo Tehuantepec in the state of Oaxaca, which in turn comes from the Nahuatl *tecuanitepec* ("jaguar hill").[6]

The Olmecs were able to link both the Atlantic and Pacific ports through the Isthmus of Tehuantepe. Ignacio Bernal has this to say in his book, *The Olmec World*:

> The Isthmus of Tehuantepec unites the Olmec area with the Chiapas depression and the Pacific watershed. It is a region which attracted the Olmecs, for no mountains cut across it and the climate was tropical. In the central depression, and generally speaking, in the entire state of Chiapas, Olmec remains or others related to it appear constantly, though—as in other regions of Central America—they do not constitute the basis or majority of archaeological finds. We are dealing with a culture related to the Olmec, though with its own peculiar features.
>
> Black ceramics with white rims or spots appear quite frequently. At other sites such as San Agustin and on the Pacific coast of Chiapas the same ware has been found in scientific explorations. At Santa Cruz it is clearly associated with other types belonging to the Olmec complex. At Mirador abundant Olmec figurines have been unearthed.[59]

What Bernal is trying to establish here is that Olmecs were not just on the Atlantic coast but also on the Pacific coast of Chiapas. Olmecs are now known to have been on the Pacific coasts of Guatemala and El Salvador, too.

The Olmecs are also known to have occupied, or at least influenced, large areas of lower Central America, from Guatemala and El Salvador to Nicaragua, Costa Rica and probably beyond. One of the most famous statues in the Nacional Museum in San Jose, Costa Rica is an Olmec hunchback figure with an elongated cranium and oriental-type Olmec eyes. Costa Rica is also the site of the enigmatic, perfectly formed granite balls that defy explanation. Were they made by the Olmecs in a similar manner as the colossal heads?

282

Given that sites like Tonalá and Izapa were early Olmec sites that were later occupied by the Maya, other sites such as Monte Alban further north toward the Valley of Mexico can be assumed to have been first inhabited by the Olmec and then by later cultures.

Once the Olmecs had been established as the oldest culture in Mesoamerica in the 1940s, by default they became the founders of many of the ancient cities. Essentially, if it could be proven that Olmec iconography was being used at an archeological site, then it must have been the Olmecs who founded that city, since the Olmecs are the oldest major culture.

Since the oldest Maya sites such as Uaxactun in the Peten jungles north of Tikal are thought to have been first built by the Olmecs, it is possible that other older Mayan sites were also founded by the Olmecs. This list of Mayan sites founded by the Olmecs could include Copan, El Mirador, Piedras Negras and many others.

La Venta and the Olmec Heartland

Perhaps the Olmec capital was at La Venta, one of the greatest and most famous of the Olmec sites, though now mostly destroyed. The site is typically dated to have been active between 1200 BC and 400 BC, which places the major development of the city in the so-called Middle Formative Period. Located on an island in a coastal swamp overlooking the then-active Río Palma river, the city of La Venta would have controlled a region between the Mezcalapa and Coatzacoalcos rivers. Today, the Rio Palma is an inactive river, the area having reverted into a mass of swamps. One wonders if the Olmecs, as part of a gigantic earthworks project, had created a river through the swamp in which they created their capital, if that is what it was.

Many of La Venta's fabulous monuments are now on display in the archaeological museum and park in the city of Villahermosa, Tabasco, the oil capital of Mexico. La Venta and nearby San Lorenzo have been the source of many of the colossal heads that the Olmecs are so famous for. The important basalt quarries for the colossal stone heads and prismatic basalt logs are found in the

Tuxtlas Mountains nearby.

Marking the southern end of La Venta's ceremonial precinct is an enormous pyramidal mound. Standing at the base of this pyramidal mound was Stela 25/26. This stela depicts a bundled zoomorphic creature with foliage at the top that is thought to represent a World Tree or axis mundi.

The northern end of Complex A is mainly an enclosed courtyard, with a massive underground serpentine deposit. This serpentine deposit is thought to represent the primordial waters of creation. Buried beneath the enclosed courtyard was Offering 4, a now famous funeral offering that is an arrangement of six jade celts (adzes) and 15 jade figures of Olmecs with elongated craniums and oriental-looking eyes. A single figure that faces the others is carved from granite. The entire group of figures stand together amongst the upright jade celts that are apparently representing in miniature the tall granite stelae that were commonly used by the Olmecs and Maya (as well as Egyptians, Hindus, and other cultures).

Although the significance of this miniature funeral arrangement is not known, it eloquently demonstrates the conceptual relationship between the forms of the celt-adze and granite stelae, by making the jade celts into miniature stelae with the jade figurines—each with an elongated skull—standing around the celt-stelae, as if at an important meeting. This exquisite arrangement can now be seen at the National Anthropology Museum in Mexico City and is one of the most famous displays in the Olmec section.

While it is thought that La Venta was the "capital" or most important city of the Olmecs, this may not actually be the case. We know so little about the Olmecs that it is impossible to say for sure how important La Venta was, or whether there were not more important cities and ceremonial sites.

For instance, some Olmec sites could be underwater in the Gulf of Mexico, or still buried in the swamps of Tabasco and Veracruz. Or, major Olmec sites might have been located in the interior of Mexico like Chalcatzingo or the recently discovered Zazacatla, nearby. These sites are are quite a distance from the so-called Olmec Heartland, and suggest that the Olmec lands—Olman—were quite extensive. As noted above, sites such as Monte Alban and Teotihuacan are thought by some archeologists to be associated with the Olmecs and it may be the case that these cities were originally important Olmec centers.

The more we find out about the Olmecs, the deeper the mystery surrounding them becomes. We find that the Olmecs seem to include nearly every racial type in the world. How is this possible? The Olmecs are credited with everything from inventing the wheel, the ball game and hieroglyphic writing, and it is now known they controlled most of southern Mexico from shore to shore. From a diffusionist point of view, the Land of Olman may well have been the "center of the world" as the Ithmus of Tehuantepec would indeed have been the center of the world if there was a strong transoceanic trade across both the Atlantic and Pacific Oceans. If such a trade and movement of ships had existed, the Olmecs may well have been a cosmopolitical center where worldwide cultures intermingled.

The Olmecs and Cranial Deformation

Among the many strange things about the Olmecs, cranial deformation is one of the most bizarre. It is a practice that was shared with the peoples of Peru, some Pacific islands, tribes in Africa, the Kurds of Iraq and the Egyptians—as well as many other cultures. It is an unusual custom that spans both the Atlantic and Pacific Oceans.

Anthropologists have long known that cranial deformation can be accomplished while humans are still infants. Infants would have their heads bound with pieces of wood and rope, or some sort of constrictive cloth, that forced their heads to grow in an elongated and unnatural way.

The skull is bound while the plates in a baby's skull have not yet fused together, and the materials are adjusted and tightened as time goes on. After two or three years of this skull binding, the child's head is permanently growing in an elongated fashion, and once the child becomes several years old the skull has formed in an elongated shape that no longer requires any binding.

It is known that the Olmecs and the Mayas of Central America had dolichocephalous crania in many cases. Though skeletal material is often difficult to find in tropical areas because of the fast rate of decomposition, jade figurines attributed to the Olmecs

A clay statuette of an Olmec showing an elongated cranium.

have been found that show persons with elongated heads, so we know that this curious "fashion" was widespread, found from the Andes to the jungles of Panama, Costa Rica and Nicaragua, to the coasts and mountains of Mexico. It even reached the Pacific Northwest of the United States.

Remember, University of Alabama archeologist Richard Diehl says that the Olmecs were an isolated group within their region with little contact even with other tribes in the Isthmus of Tehuantepec, and Diehl's book mentions a cranial deformation in an Olmec burial at Tlatilco. So, apparently, according to Diehl, the "numerous independent local cultures" only a few hours' walk from each other must have each decided, quite without the knowledge that anyone else was doing it, to bind up their babies' heads until they were grossly misshapen.

Perhaps Diehl's (and others') lack of discussion of cranial deformation is an actual avoidance of the topic. While little is really known about cranial deformation, except how it was done, it is a curious part of Olmec and Mayan culture, a custom that they are well known for, as are the ancient Peruvians along the desert coast, especially around Paracas, Ica and Nazca, south of Lima. As noted, it was practiced all around the world. One would think this strange practice would arouse curiosity and speculation, but since the Olmecs are said to be an isolated group, mentioning cranial deformation might just invite discussion of its widespread use, and prove counter-productive in a book promoting the isolationist point of view.

Cranial deformation, because it is so unusual and found worldwide, would seem to be clear evidence of transoceanic contact. The popularity of this rather bizarre cultural practice would seem to arise from cultural diffusion, not cultures isolated from each other.

Sticking Your Neck Out for Quizuo

The great debate within the archeological community concerning the Olmecs is whether there is any evidence of outside influence—transoceanic in nature—that can clearly be shown within the Olmecs' culture. One shred of evidence presented by some academics is the curious use of the unusual kneeling posture known as quizuo.

As we have mentioned, one of the proponents of diffusionism within the traditional university system is Dr. Ivan Van Sertima of Rutgers University in New Jersey. Ivan Van Sertima was born in Kitty Village, Guyana, South America on January 26, 1935. He was educated at the School of Oriental and African Studies at London University where he graduated with honors. According to his biography he served as a Press and Broadcasting Officer in the Guyana Information Services from 1957 to 1959. He came to the United States in 1970, where he completed his post graduate studies at Rutgers University. Dr. Van Sertima began his teaching career as an instructor at Rutgers in 1972, and he is now a Professor of African studies and the editor of *The Journal of African Studies*.

Van Sertima actively promotes the diffusionist theory that

An Olmec statue with a Mohawk haircut in the quizuo position.

ancient man crossed both the Atlantic and the Pacific in prolonged transoceanic contact. His books, *African Presence in Early America, African Presence in Early Asia,* and *They Came Before Columbus* are filled with articles and photos that show without a doubt that Negroes have lived, literally, all over the world.

Van Sertima draws many parallels between Olmec statues and those from ancient Egypt, India, China, and Pacific islands—parallels that he maintains could not be coincidental. One feature of statues from these many parts of the world is the curious quizuo posture. Van Sertima, primarily a linguist although accomplished in other fields, is a major proponent of fellow archeologist Wayne B. Chandler's fascinating treatise on the carving of statues in the quizuo position being a worldwide custom.

Figurines when they are in the quizuo position are kneeling with their hands to their sides, on their knees or folded in front of them. The face is generally looking directly ahead, but it can be looking down, or slightly up. These distinct and oddball-posture statues, apparently depicting some sort of subjugation to a king, priest, or other authority, have been found in such far-flung places as Easter Island, Bolivia, China, India, Egypt and the many Olmec sites of Central America.

In his 1986 monograph *Trait-Influences in Meso-America: The African-Asian Connection*, included in Van Sertima's book *African Presence in Early America*, Wayne B. Chandler asserts that the quizuo posture was in use in Shang China circa 1300-1100 BC as seen in statues dating to that period. He also shows a jade Olmec figure in a quizuo posture that is from the Lima Ulua Valley in Honduras and dated to circa 1150 BC.

Chandler goes on to show that certain figurines from the Shang Dynasty (1600-1028 BC) were kneeling in a quizuo posture and sporting the hairstyle we call a "mohawk." One famous statue from La Venta is identical, in a quizuo posture with a mohawk haircut. The similarity between these stones is quite astonishing.

Chandler says that this curious hairstyle, which was worn by the Olmecs, Columbians, Africans, Mohawk Indians of the St. Lawrence River as well as the Shang Chinese—and still seen in modern times—is associated with ancient Chinese magicians! Says Chandler:

> The presence of this hairstyle in Shang culture and then the Olmec denotes a strong and definite transmission of a trait characteristic. This style of cut was originally unique to the Shang and Olmec, but was later adopted by the Shang-influenced San Augustin culture of Columbia. This fact is evidenced in virtually all of their stone sculpture... The evidence indicates that this hairstyle was originally worn only by the shamen or magicians of the Shang and Olmec cultures, much in the way that dreadlocks were originally worn only by the high-priests or sadhu's of India.

This connection to the Shang Chinese magicians and the mohawk hairstyle lends further credence to the theory that the Olmecs were in part Shang Chinese admirals and ambassadors. These specially trained eunuchs, who would have understood the concept of quizuo are dealt with in a later chapter.

Quizuo statues around the world are variously wearing turbans or leather hats, have elongated crania, have some special hairstyle, or are bald. Sometimes in Olmec statues there are hieroglyphs on the leather hats that may signify the identity or rank of the person.

A man with both hands flat on his knees is in a very subservient position. In a gesture comparable to shaking hands or waving an open hand, the person is showing that he is not holding a weapon. It is this curious position of utter helplessness that is so fascinating about the quizuo kneeling posture. The person "committing quizuo" was engaging in an act of utter helplessness and subservience, literally sticking his neck out to be either rewarded or punished. Indeed, the position is quite reminiscent of someone about to be either beheaded or beknighted. In point of fact, when the Queen of England takes up a sword to knight a kneeling person, she could just as easily cut his head off!

It appears from the statuary that the quizuo position was not one for kings and emperors. It appears, rather, that it was a position for shamen, high-ranking dignitaries, ambassadors, generals, admirals and other servants of the realm. One possibility is that these figures represent an important servant or diplomat taking an oath of office. In that sense, it is both a posture of submission and of power!

Though statues in the quizuo posture have been found across the globe, they are mostly known because of the preponderance of them in Olmec settlements. Was the Land of Olman, spanning the Isthmus of Tehuantepec, like the Panama Canal of today, a land of international ambassadors, diplomats, admirals and sailors—a center for ports, markets, traders and wheeler-dealers? Was it in this way similar to Champa?

Olmec Connections to Africa and Asia

Van Sertima points out that the use by the Olmecs of jade nose plugs, tattoos and special facial adornment, odd hairstyles and special gestures are further proof that the culture was influenced by and shared with others.

One of the 20-ton basalt colossal heads discovered at La Venta.

The Olmecs and the Cham

Vis a vis African influence Van Sertima says in *They Came Before Columbus*:

> The destruction of African high-cultures after the massive and continuous invasions of Europe left many Africans surviving on the periphery or outer ring of what constituted the best in African civilizations. New facts that challenge this image create such consternation and incredulity that an extraordinarily emotional campaign is mounted by some of the most respected voices in the scientific establishment to explain away the new data.
>
> That drift of dynastic Egypt from Africa has now dramatically slowed. Recent archeological finds have caught up with the mythmakers. More and more the history of Africa is being reconstructed upon the basis of hard, objective data rather than upon the self-serving speculations and racist theories about the black barbarians.

Van Sertima is a respected member of the academic community, so the isolationists are forced to respond to his theories, but they essentially dismiss him in a few sentences, and never really counter his claims. The widespread use of quizuo, including by the Olmecs, is simply ignored. Van Sertima is called an "afrocentrist" by his critics, who assert that he wrongly believes that all culture, including that of Mexico, stems from Africa. While this is not his message, it serves to trivialize his careful research.

Modern archeology, dominated by the "isolationist" theories that say that oceans are barriers, not highways, has had a tough time dealing with Negroid and other features that obviously are different from our traditionalal image of the American Indian. One way that archeologists dealt with this was to simply suggest that these weren't really Negroid features at all, but merely stylized images of the Siberian hunters that created all the tribes of the Amazon, the Andes, Central and North America.

Another tack was to admit that these were Negroid features, but to assert that Negroes must also have migrated across the Bering

292

land bridge during the last ice age. This mainstream argument for Negroes having come across the Straits with other Siberian hunters circa 12,000 years ago is summed up in the book *The Ancient Kingdoms of Mexico,* by the British archeologist Nigel Davies, a critic of theories of ancient seafaring. Davies flatly rejects any theories of Phoenicians, Egyptians, Chinese, the Cham, Vikings, Africans or anyone else ever reaching Mexico by boat. Yet, unlike some historians, he readily admits that Olmecs are Negroes. His explanations of Negroid Olmecs in Mexico is interesting.

In the book (pages 26-27) Davies says:

Insofar as Negroid features are depicted in pre-Columbian art, a more logical explanation surely exists that does not depend upon flights of fancy involving African seafarers. Negroid peoples of many kinds are to be found in Asia as well as Africa, and there is no reason why at least a few of them should not have joined those migrant bands who came across the Bering land bridge that joined north-east Asia and north-west America for so many millennia.

Small men with Negroid features were the aboriginal inhabitants of many lands facing the Indian Ocean, including India itself, the Malay Peninsula and also the Philippines, where they still exist today. One need go no further than Manila International Airport to find proof of their existence. Nearby stands the Museum of Philippine Traditional Cultures; facing the entrance is a wall covered with photographs of 'unfamiliar faces'. In marked contrast to the typical Mongoloid Filipinos of today, many of these are dark-skinned aboriginals, known as 'Negritos', who now live scattered along the east side of the main island of Luzon; they mostly have thick lips and black skins. The Weddas of Ceylon are another of these Negroid aboriginal groups. It is therefore not in the least surprising that such elements should have joined the ranks of those early migrants who crossed the Bering bridge before it sank beneath the waves; their presence offers a more logical explanation of Negroid features than any other.

Therefore, even if one accepts the uncertain premise that Olmec art is based on the portrayal of true Negroids, this does not warrant the conclusion that such people were Africans. It is perfectly possible to find individuals in Tabasco today who have faces not unlike those of the colossal heads, whose features also somewhat recall the large stone carvings of the Cham culture of Cambodia, another country that still has a Negroid aboriginal population.

So, it is interesting that Davies says that the Negroid Olmecs might be connected to the Negroid Cham. However, he prefers that these Cham arrived in Mexico by walking, rather than by ship. Davies perhaps was unaware of the Champa naval abilities, including the massing of ships several times a year at the Cham Islands.

Davies' point that it is "perfectly possible to find individuals in Tabasco today who have faces not unlike those of the colossal heads..." is really neither here nor there. If Negroids had colonized Tabasco by land or by sea, then it would be only normal that they would have married and had children—children who of course looked like them, as did their ancestors.

Why does it seem impossible to mainstream archeologists that ancient people would have traveled anywhere by boat? How does Davies suppose that Negroes got to the Philippine Islands? How Negroes, who presumably all stem from Africa, are populating such remote western Pacific islands as New Guinea, the Solomons, Vanuatu, New Caledonia and Fiji is very much a mystery of history. Obviously much of this settlement occurred by ship, not just one ship, but fleets of ships. Might the Cham have had something to do with this great migration via fleets of ships?

Does Davies suppose that the myriad islands of the Pacific were populated by people walking across ancient land bridges? While these 'experts' are forced to admit that Polynesians and

Micronesians colonized remote islands in the Pacific, many of them tiny dots of land thousands of miles from anywhere, they cannot admit that seafarers in ancient times could similarly find such huge continents as North and South America! In the same vein, it is accepted that Madagascar was colonized by Malaysians traveling the entire length of the Indian Ocean to a remote corner of southeast Africa, yet it is denied that ancient seafarers with sophisticated navies such as the Chinese, Egyptians, Hindus or Phoenicians could have duplicated such a feat!

In order to sidestep such issues, a new tack has been taken by current isolationist archeologists: labeling anyone who suggests transoceanic traffic across the Atlantic or Pacific as a "racist" of one sort or another. This has been used successfully by the Mayan

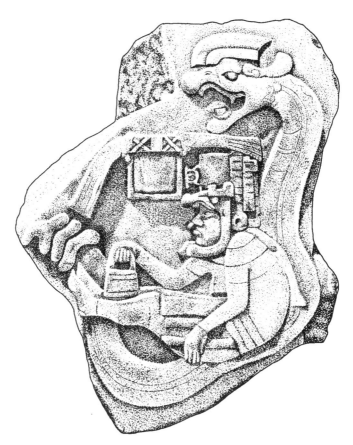

La Venta Monument 19 of a masked Olmec with satchel and serpent.

academics who maintain that it is a racist notion to suggest that Central Americans could not create their own culture and were influenced in various ways by other cultures.

Yet is it not racist to maintain that other cultures were not capable of building boats and crossing oceans just as Europeans were to do thousands of years later? Try telling an African-American history professor who believes in transoceanic traffic that he is a "racist" because he believes that Africans once traveled across the Atlantic and created an empire in Central America!

When one begins to accept that the Olmecs were part of some sort of sophisticated transoceanic naval empire, at a time when the world was being explored by great navies—when the ancient sea kings ruled the earth—one can begin to accept that the posture of quizuo was part of this ancient network. Also part of it was the strange custom of cranial deformation.

One Olmec port on the Atlantic, called Comalcalco, later became a major Mayan port city that flourished between 700 and 900 AD. Like Cham cities, Comacalco was made of fired bricks. Many of these bricks have inscriptions on them. In 1977 and 1978, the National Institute of Anthropology and History excavated the site and discovered that approximately three percent of the bricks which make up the site bore inscriptions.

In a study done by the archaeologist Neil Steede for the National Institute of Anthropology and History it was discovered that 3671 bricks had inscriptions on them. Of these bricks, 2129 or 58 percent had Maya hieroglyphs on them. Old World inscriptions appeared on 499 of the bricks (or 13.6 percent) in languages such as Arabic, Phoenician, Libyan, Egyptian, Ogam, Tifinag, Chinese, Burmese and Paliburmese. Other bricks had drawings on them (735 bricks or 20 percent) and 308 bricks were mixed or unknown (8.4 percent). Some of the bricks even had inscriptions of elephants on them. Were these war elephants of the Cham, brought to Mexico? The presence of Chinese, Burmese and Paliburmese would indicate transpacific voyages such as those of the Cham. Paliburmese is related to the Cham script.

296

Egyptians and the Transpacific Trade

In his 1923 book *The Children of the Sun*,[24] University of
Manchester archeologist W. J. Perry attempted to demonstrate how
a dual system of Egyptians and Hindu Indians ventured out into
the Pacific and colonized such places as Tonga, Tahiti, Hawaii and
Easter Island. Perry presented evidence that envoys of the ancient
Sun Kingdoms of Egypt and India traveled into Indonesia and
the Pacific circa 1500 BC, spreading their sophisticated culture.
Perry traces the expansion of megalithic building from its origin in
Egypt through Indonesia and across the Pacific all the way to the
Americas. These early mariners searched for gold, obsidian, and
pearls in their incredible explorations from island to island — Perry
says they were known as the Children of the Sun!

Lapita pottery that is found throughout the Solomons, New
Caledonia, Vanuatu and as far as Fiji, Tonga and Samoa, is only
dated to 4,000 years before present. Still, the obvious network of
trade, mining and commerce of 2,000 BC may well be connected
with Egyptian traders and their far-flung voyages to the distant
land they called Punt. It is believed by historians such as Harvard's
Barry Fell that the island of Sumatra played a major role in the
long sea voyages of antiquity. We noted in the first chapter how
Sumatra spoke a Cham dialect and was part of the Cham empire.

Fell has claimed that voyages beginning in the Red Sea and
the Horn of Africa went to Sri Lanka, Sumatra, Eastern Indonesia,
New Guinea and out into the Pacific. Manning these ships were
Caucasians and Negroes. Fell thinks that these voyagers, on a
one-year trip to the Isthmus of Tehuantepec (or alternately Peru),
would pass into the Pacific on either the north or south side of
New Guinea and then continue past such islands as New Britain,
New Ireland, the Solomons, Vanuatu and ultimately arrive at Fiji,
Tonga and Samoa. Indeed, Fell is talking about a culture very
much like the Cham.

Pyramids and other megalithic structures found on these
islands, like the Ha'amonga stone arch on Tonga, lend credence
to this idea. The traders brought Lapita pottery with them. Later,
Tahiti and Hawaii were settled and Rai'tea near Tahiti became the

eastern capital. From here such islands as the Marquesas, Rapa Iti and Easter Island (Rapa Nui) were settled. Fell surmises that the ancient seafarers voyaged to Mexico, Central America, Ecuador and Peru from these island bases. Throughout the Pacific, many of the islands' names include "Ra," the Egyptian name of the sun god.

Since there is a connection between the Egyptian sailors of Khem and the Hindu sailors of Cham, we might surmise that the Egyptian sailors ventured through the Red Sea to the Indian Ocean and crossed eastward to India and Sri Lanka. From southern India and Sri Lanka they proceeded further east to the Cham-held lands of Sumatra, Java and the coastal areas around the Gulf of Siam, including Cambodia and Vietnam.

Did these Egyptian sailors team up with the Cham fleets and cross the Pacific in conjunction with Cham sailors? Had some of the Blacks that are featured in Cham statuary originally come from Africa as sailors on the Egyptian boats? This is what Barry Fell and Ivan Van Sertima clearly believed.

As evidence of how far-flung Egyptian-led voyages into the Pacific was, consider this: the Egyptians built their ships without

A basalt Olmec statute at the Xalapa Museum with false beard.

nails, and a number of ancient ships, many without nails, have been found along the coasts of Australia. Two ships 40 feet long and 9 feet wide, built without nails, have been found near Perth, Western Australia. Another was found partially hidden underneath a sand dune at Wollongong, New South Wales.

There is a cave painting in the Prince Regent River Valley in the Kimberleys of Western Australia that includes a man with a beard and tall hat, looking very Middle Eastern or Egyptian in origin. Around him are three women with long hair that is tied at the end. These women have been identified as Egyptian dancers with weights at the end of their hair. Their long, weighted hair played an intricate part in their show.

While Australian aboriginals are famous for using boomerangs, it is not well known that Egyptians used them, too. The Egyptians frequently hunted ducks in the marshes of the Nile with boomerangs, and also played games with them. It is an archaeological fact (though not well publicized) that a trunk full of boomerangs was discovered in 1924 when King Tutankhamun's tomb was opened by the archaeologist Howard Carter. Many of these boomerangs, inlaid with gold and lapis lazuli, are on display in the Tutankhamun exhibit at the Egyptian Museum in Cairo. Next to them is an Australian boomerang for comparison.

Boomerangs were also used in southern Mexico, Texas, Arizona, and California. It is likely that the Olmecs used boomerangs as well, and boomerangs can be seen on display in Mexico City's Anthropology Museum. It is an interesting thought that the Australian Aboriginals, as well as tribes in the American Southwest, learned the use of the simple but ingenious boomerang from the Egyptians!

The French researchers Luis Pauwels and Jacques Bergier say in their book, *Eternal Man* (Souvenir Press, 1972):

> In 1963 a strange and disconcerting piece of information came to us from Australia. A pile of Egyptian coins that had been buried for about 4,000 years was found in terrain sheltered by rocks. The readers who gave us this

information referred to some rather obscure reviews for there was no mention of this find in any archaeological publication. However, the widely-read Soviet review *Tekhnika Molodezi* which devotes a regular column to unexplained facts with comments on them by experts took up this matter. It even published photographs of the excavated coins.

The anthropologist Elizabeth Gould Davis says in her book *The First Sex* (G.P. Putnam's Sons, 1971), "In Australia was found a pendant amulet of greenstone, carved in the shape of the Celtic cross, an exact duplicate of an amulet found in Egypt at Tel el Amarna, the site of the ancient city where Nefertiti and the Pharaoh Akhenaten held court thirty-five hundred years ago."

The time frame of Akhenaten and Nefertiti (circa 1200 BC) is also the time frame for Lapita pottery (circa 1100 BC) and of the Shang Dynasty of China (1600-1028 BC). This is also the time frame often given for the beginning of the Olmecs, and I believe it might have been the beginning of the Cham.

One clear link between Australia and Egypt is that the Torres Straits Islanders, between New Guinea and Northern Queensland, use the curious practice of mummification of the dead. The Macleay Museum at Sydney University has a mummified corpse of a Darnley islander (Torres Strait), prepared in a fashion that has been compared to that practiced in Egypt between 1090 and 945 BC.

In 1875 the Shevert Expedition found similarities between Darnley Island boats and ancient trans-Nile boats. The island boats were used to row corpses to sea and leave them on a coral reef. Egyptian practice was to ferry corpses across or down the Nile for desert burial.

Another similarity with the Torres Strait islanders (as well as people in the Solomon Islands, Fiji and Polynesia) is the use at nighttime of a wooden headrest. This carved headrest was used to slightly elevate the head, while the subject slept on his back. This custom is unusual to ancient Egypt and certain Pacific Islands around New Guinea.

As I have said, the Cham—and the Olmec—were a mixed group that included bearded and mustachioed Caucasians, and people with African, Oriental and classic "Chinaman" features. On top of this were dwarves and hunchbacks (both considered good luck), who often served as musicians and storytellers to amuse the crew on their long voyages and keep them entertained. No one was a slave on the ship, though there was a strict hierarchy. All were welcomed heartily in the festivities that were had at the many ports of call, and all shared in the booty. For the sailor who had made a few voyages, it would be a fulfilling and profitable life.

On board, beside the captain and his close mates, there would have been a priest of sorts, a shaman and magician. He would deal with the local plant experts and obtain the correct herbs and psychedelics. These priests apparently even wore pointed hats and otherwise acted as we might expect some ancient wizard to behave.

Chinese Circumnavigation

Not long ago, popular and well-reviewed books came out that champion the historical facts of early Chinese voyages, literally, around the world. In his best-selling book *1421: The Year China Discovered the World*, author Gavin Menzies maintains that a massive fleet of junks that were nearly 500 feet long was launched on March 8 of that year. This fleet was under the command of eunuch admirals loyal to the Emperor Zhu Di and they were to sail to the end of the earth to collect tribute from the barbarians. They were to go 'beyond the seas' and thereby unite the world in Confucian harmony. The journey of this fleet would take two years and circumnavigate the world, Menzies claims.

In another book about China's pre-Columbian explorations, *When China Ruled the Seas* by Louise Levathes, the author maintains that Shang Chinese were sailing to the Americas circa 1000 BC. I believe that they were accompanied by the Cham. Although she does not specifically maintain that Olmecs were part of the Shang Chinese contact with Mexico, other archeologists and historians have done so, including some linked to the prestigious Smithsonian Institution.

The Smithsonian Institution published a monograph in 1974 entitled "The Transpacific Origin of Mesoamerican Civilization" by Betty J. Meggers. Meggers was a career archeologist employed by the Smithsonian Institution until her death in 2012. In her monograph, Meggers says:

> Anthropologists generally assume that civilization developed independently in the eastern and western hemispheres. Review of the features that distinguish the Olmec culture of Mesoamerica from preceding village farming groups shows, however, that many are present in the earlier Shang civilization of China. If Olmec civilization

A wall painting from Oxotitlan of a dragon and a man with a jade mask and penis.

originated from a transpacific stimulus, this has important implications both for reconstruction of New World cultural development and for formulation of a valid theory of the evolution of civilization.

In her Smithsonian paper Meggers gives archaeological evidence of the Olmec as the earliest civilization in Mesoamerica, discussing their pyramids, monuments, art, calendars, trade, and religion. She then discusses the various characteristics of Shang civilization. Among the similarities between these two societies, she says, are their writing styles, the esteemed use of and long-distance trade in jade, the use of batons as symbols of rank, their settlement patterns as well as architectural styles, the long-range acquisition of luxury goods, worship of feline deities, and the use of cranial deformation.

While she admits the difficulty of the task, Meggers concludes that the Shang-Olmec similarities can be used to prove either independent development or cultural diffusion. The basic difficulty we face, she notes, is that a search for cultural origins is handicapped by both unrecognized biases and limitations of data.

Similarly, one of Meggers's students, Vincent H. Malmstrom, writes in his monograph "Izapa: Cultural Hearth of the Olmecs," published by Dartmouth College (available online at: www. dartmouth.edu/~izapa/M-6.pdf) that the ancient city of Izapa, near the Pacific Coast in the Isthmus of Tehuantepec was a major seaport with contacts with Ecuador, and probably Shang China. It also had knowledge of magnetism.

After showing that Izapa was probably the place the Olmec calendar was invented, Malmstrom says:

> ...Had Izapa served solely as the birthplace of Mesoamerican calendrics that would have been reason enough to regard it as a major cultural hearth amongst the Olmecs. However, in at least one other field of knowledge Izapa seems to have been in the vanguard of Olmec learning as well, namely terrestrial magnetism. For some

time, researchers have believed that the Mayas were aware of magnetism, apparently using it to align the structures in their major ceremonial centers (Fuson, 1969, 494).

Then, in 1973, Coe discovered a small bar of polished hematite at San Lorenzo that he assumed may have been used as part of a compass. Found in a layer dated to approximately 1000 B.C., this suggests that the Olmecs were aware of magnetism about a millenium before the Chinese (Carlson, 1975, 753). However, during field work at Izapa in January, 1975, the author discovered evidence that the inhabitants of this site not only knew about magnetism but that they also seem to have associated it with the homing instinct in the sea-turtle. Such a conclusion stems from the fact that a large sculpture of a turtle head, located about thirty meters to the southeast of the main pyramid, has been carved from a basaltic boulder rich in magnetic iron and executed with such precision that all the magnetic lines of force come to focus in the turtle's snout. Although no other magnetic stones have been found at Izapa, there are at least two other representations of the turtle present at the site.

One of these is a sculpture near the east wall of the main pyramid which has the shape of an upturned turtle shell and which, when filled with water during the rainy season, may have provided a frictionless surface on which to float a needle or sliver of lodestone. The other is a large altar in the form of a turtle at the west end of the ceremonial ball court, in whose north wall is embedded a carving of a bearded man standing in a boat moving across the waves. That the Izapans were a sea-faring people and maintained relatively regular contacts with places as far distant as Ecuador over a long period of time has been shown by the similarities in ceramics found in the two areas (Coe, 1966, 45; Badner, 1972, 24).

That they should have failed to observe the great migrations of east Pacific Ridleys moving between Baja

California and Ecuador or of the black turtle which migrates between the Guatemalan coast and the Galápagos Islands while on such voyages is quite inconceivable (Carr, 1967, 136, 216). And that they should have been impressed by the sureness of the turtle's navigational ability and compared this to the direction-finding property of the lodestone would have taken no great leap of imagination. Whether Izapa's maritime connections included trans-Pacific contacts cannot be demonstrated at this point, though Meggers, among others, has presented striking evidence of similarities between the Olmecs and the Shang-dynasty Chinese (Meggers, 1975, 17). In any event, it would appear that Izapa served as a major center of cultural innovation in Mesoamerica, whether as a trans-Pacific bridgehead or as a hearth in its own right.

Therefore, Izapa may have been a major Olmec-Shang port on the Pacific. As such, many of the overland roads from Oaxaca and other areas would have converged at Izapa or nearby. Goods from the Atlantic side of the isthmus would have been brought overland as well, and it may well be the case that tons of jade, gold, hallucinogenic mushrooms, chocolate and other valuable trade items were shipped out of Izapa back across the Pacific—some of it no doubt getting back to China and Champa. Later, Spain ran this lucrative trade through their ports in Manila and Acapulco.

In a *US News & World Report* story published November 4, 1996, it was reported that a Chinese language scholar named Han Ping Chen examined the famous Olmec figures and accompanying jade celts found at La Venta which are now at the National Museum of Anthropology. According to the news magazine he declared after examining some "writing" on the celts that, "Clearly, these are Chinese characters." Meggers became involved in this important discovery, as well. We will discuss the details of this subject later.

So, it is fairly obvious that the Olmecs were in contact with the Shang Chinese. I think that it is fairly likely that the Shang Chinese

*The Olmecs and the Cham*

were in contact with the Cham and that these dark-skinned master sailors went on Shang voyages to the Pacific and beyond. Maybe it was from the Shang that the Cham learned to navigate and build large seagoing vessels.

While the Olmec civilization is said to be older than the Cham, we can see how both may have started around 1000 BC. The Olmec may have been established by Shang Chinese at an

A granite Olmec statue of a woman with a curious hat at the Xalapa Museum.

306

early period and then the culture passed on to the Cham who were operating out of Vietnam and the Cham Islands.

It would seem that the Shang and other Chinese naval forces would meet up at the Cham Islands in central Vietnam. From the Cham Islands the fleet of ships would voyage eastward into the Pacific, stopping first at Nan Madol in Micronesia and then continuing on to North America. When they landed they continued south to the tropical bays of Acapulco and further south to Tehuantepec. Here the early Olmec-Maya civilization was founded by Chinese-Cham seafarers.

The Cham Islands are said to have been occupied by 1000 BC and only seafarers would have occupied this rocky granite island group. The beaches and bays of the Cham Islands were perfect for the gathering of large groups of ships and the trading of cargo. Being on an island that was far away enough from the mainland to keep large terrestrial armies at a good arm's length made it a safe place to harbor ships and to trade with others. Other ports were nearby on the mainland.

The Cham and the Maya

The Cham would appear to have had a great deal of influence in the development of the Mayan Civilization as well. The time frame for the Maya and the Cham are also about the same and fit pretty well. The collapse of the Maya and the collapse of the Cham occured at the same time, from about 700 to 900 AD.

As the Olmec lands of Soconusco and Guatemala became more culturally Mayan, the people became even more oriental in their appearance. As the British historian Graeme Kearsley documents in his book *Mayan Genesis*,[69] the art of the Mayan culture contains many Hindu elements, including hairstyles, decorative motifs, guardian demons, and the distinctive posture of arms, hands and fingers to communicate higher ideals. In Sanskrit such postures of the hands and fingers are known as mudras, and such postures have great meaning. We see these mudra postures in Mayan and Olmec statues and art. In a similar manner to the quizuo posture, the position of the arms, hands and fingers is universal and generally associated with Hinduism and Buddhism.

The areas that seem to be the earliest Pacific coast ports of the Cham or their predecessors are the sandy bays that start with the famous port of Acapulco and are found along the coast going south to the area known as Soconusco. These sandy bays were perfect for the Cham ships and the later the Spanish galleons. The Cham were used to the sandy bays of the Cham Islands where they assembled their fleets from time to time. The Spanish were essentially to repeat the Cham voyages with their Acapulco-Philippines trading that enriched the Spanish traders in Acapulco

An old photo of one of huge stelae at Quirigua.

and Mexico City, which was reached by mule train.

I mentioned earlier that elephants were believed to have been carved on Mayan statues at the temple city of Copan on the border of Honduras and Guatemala. Many of the statues at Copan, as well as at nearby Quirigua (in Guatemala), look very oriental in appearance. Both of these Mayan cities are located near the important jade mines in Motagua River Valley.

On my first visit to Copan in 1992, I was amazed at the oriental look to all the statues. Having lived and travelled in China for several years, I was immediately struck at how Chinese-looking everything was. Many of the men had thin mustaches and thin wispy beards that are the exact caricature of the Fu Manchu-type of Chinese. Had I not been completely aware that I was standing in the jungles of Central America, I would have thought that I was viewing a selection of statues from China or Vietnam!

Quiriguá and Copán share architectural and sculptural styles. Quiriguá is known for its wealth of sculpture, including the tallest stone monolith ever erected in the New World. These monolithic steles feature Mayan kings who are very oriental in appearance.

An old photo of horsemen at a huge stele at Quirigua.

An old photo of one of huge stelae at Quirigua.

They have whispy Chinese-style mustaches and beards and could easily be kings from China or Vietnam.

Quiriguá was ideally positioned on the Motagua River flowing down from the Guatemalan highlands to control the trade of uncut jade, the majority of which was found in the middle reaches of the Motagua Valley. Quiriguá also controlled the flow of cacao, maize and other important commodities up and down the river. Both cacao and maize were grown in the area and Quiriguá could be reached from the Atlantic Ocean by travelling up the Motagua River. Mayan ports like Tulum could be found along the Atlantic coast and the Maya were known to have oceangoing boats that went to such islands as Cozumel. To the west the Maya had ports along the Pacific coast as well, and therefore had cities on both oceans. With this site the Maya, who originated on the Pacific coast (as did the Olmecs), had access to the Atlantic Ocean and the Caribbean Sea. If the Cham were involved with these cities, which I think they were, then such river ports would have essentially given the Cham access to ports on the Atlantic Ocean—an astonishing acheivement.

The Shang-Cham-Olmec Connection

According to Chinese scholars the Chinese "invention" of writing goes back to the Shang Dynasty. The earliest Chinese characters are found on Shang Chinese oracle bones. These characters are similar to early Olmec characters.

As noted above, a *US News & World Report* story published on November 4, 1996, reported that a Chinese language scholar named Han Ping Chen examined the famous Olmec figures and accompanying jade celts found at La Venta that formed a display of celts and statuettes that is now at the National Museum of Anthropology in Mexico City.

Says the article:

> For diffusionists, Olmec art offers a tempting arena for speculation. Carbon-dating places the Olmec era between 1000 and 1200 BC, coinciding with the Shang dynasty's fall in China. American archaeologists unearthed the group sculpture in 1955. Looking at the sculpture displayed in the National Gallery, as well as other Olmec pieces, some Mexican and American scholars have been struck by the resemblances to Chinese artifacts. In fact, archaeologists initially labeled the first Olmec figures found at the turn of the [20th] century as Chinese.
>
> … There are only about a dozen experts worldwide in the Shang script, which is largely unrecognizable to readers of modern Chinese. When Prof. Mike Xu, a professor of Chinese history at the University of Central Oklahoma, traveled to Beijing to ask Chen to examine his index of 146 markings from pre-Columbian objects, Chen refused, saying he had no interest in anything outside China. He relented only after a colleague familiar with Xu's work insisted that Chen, as China's leading authority, take a

look. He did and found that all but three of Xu's markings could have come from China.

Xu was at Chen's side in the National Gallery when the Shang scholar read the text on the Olmec celt in Chinese and translated: "The ruler and his chieftains establish the foundation for a kingdom." Chen located each of the characters on the celt in three well-worn Chinese dictionaries he had with him. Two adjacent characters are usually read as "master and subjects," but Chen decided that in this context they might mean "ruler and his chieftains." The character on the line below he recognized as the symbol for "kingdom" or "country"—two peaks for hills, a curving line underneath for river. The next character, Chen said, suggests a bird but means "waterfall" completing the description. The bottom character he read as "foundation" or "establish," implying the act of founding something important. If Chen is right, the celts not only offer the earliest writing in the New World, but mark the birth of a Chinese settlement more than 3,000 years ago.

The article ends by saying that more than 5,000 Shang characters have survived even though the soldiers who defeated the Shang forces murdered the scholars and burned or buried any object with writing on it. In an excavation in the Shang capital of Anyang, archaeologists found a buried library of turtle shells covered with characters. And at the entrance lay the skeleton of the librarian, stabbed in the back and clutching some writings to his breast.

Since the Olmec figurines and celts were buried in a special arrangement under white sand topped with alternating layers of brown and reddish-brown sand, Chen thinks that perhaps it was hidden to save it from the kind of rage that sought to wipe out the Shang and their memory.

In the same article, Betty Meggers of the Smithsonian Institution is quoted as saying, "Writing systems are too arbitrary and complex. They cannot be independently reinvented."

The Olmec jade statuettes and celts from La Venta with Shang writing on them.

Is it possible that the Cham and the fleet at the Cham Islands were instrumental in bringing Shang Chinese priests and generals to Mexico? That would explain the strong Negroid presence in Olmec art and statuary. Indeed, the similarities between the Cham and the Olmecs are so strong that it is difficult to keep them from being connected in some way. And with the connection between Shang Chinese writing and culture with the Olmecs, and the proximity of China to the Cham Islands, we have a scenario where the Hindu Cham of 1000 BC might have been escorting Chinese dignitaries eastward across the Pacific.

It is curious to think that the rise of the Cham, Olmec and later Mayan civilizations may have had something to do with the collapse of the Shang capital back in China. The fortunes of many far-flung colonies would have been tied to events in the motherland. It would be an interesting course of study to review what we currently consider the "mysterious" rise and fall of certain civilizations to see if we can find correlations with the fortunes of cultures that have been heretofore considered unrelated. With the collapse of the Shang Dynasty in the year 1046 BC, the Chinese

313

were no longer making special journeys across the Pacific. The Cham then made these voyages themselves until about 400 BC when something happened that resulted in the destruction and elimination of the Olmecs.

The Maya now occupied the southern areas of the Olmec territories, while the central valleys of Mexico became Zapotec and Mixtec. Later the Aztec migrated from the north into this area. There is evidence to suggest that both Monte Alban and Teotihuacan were built by the Olmecs. The strange circular pyramid of Cuicuilco in the southern part of Mexico City, partially covered in a lava flow, was also probably built by the Olmecs.

So the Olmecs probably used the early Shang oracle script for a time, but with the collapse of the Shang civilization this evolved into its own script and later evolved into Zapotec and Mayan scripts. Areas like Comacalco, with its strange mix of Old World and other scripts inscribed on wet bricks, were literal university campuses where ancient seafarers and locals alike learned different languages. See my book *The Mystery of the Olmecs*[22] for further information on the fascinating evolution of Olmec script.

Mayan became the dominant language on the Atlantic coast, while Zapotec became the dominant language inland and along the Pacific Coast. The exception to this would be Izapa and certain other locations along the Pacific coast of Guatemala, which were under the Mayan sphere of influence.

The Hindu and Chinese influence on the Maya has been commented on by many historians and the use of the mudra hand and finger gestures suggests that the early Maya were Hindu-Buddhists, just like the Cham. In fact, it was in the Maya world where east literally met west. The Mayan lands on the Atlantic seaboard had ports, and Mayan trading ships went to Caribbean islands and around the Yucatan Peninsula to the Gulf of Mexico. The Mayan ships would certainly have crossed the Gulf of Mexico and gone up such rivers as the Mississippi and Alabama-Coosa Rivers. Mayan artifacts have reportedly been found at archeological digs in Georgia.

The Maya had ports that were visited by transatlantic traders as well, including Phoenicians, Romans, Vikings and Africans. In many ways the Atlantic was a much easier ocean to cross than the Pacific, and many cultures along the Atlantic seaboard of Europe and Africa (such as the Basque), may have been travelling across the Atlantic for thousands of years. With the Cham, and their patrons the Chinese and Hindus, we have an organized and sustained movement of fleets of ships across the Pacific that seems to begin about 1200 BC and continue until the collapse of the larger Cham Empire in Indonesia with the rise of Srivijaya in 650 AD.

Some approximate dates to take note of then:

2000 BC: Bada Valley, Sumatra, Sumba Island, etc. have tiki megaliths created.

1046 BC: The collapse of the Shang Dynasty in China. Olmecs rise in Mexico.

1000 BC: Cham seafaring empire begins?

905 BC: King Solomon sends ships to Ophir and builds the First Temple.

480 BC: The great Hindu reformer Buddha dies.

400 BC: Olmecs come to an end and the Mayas dominate Mesoamerica.

230 BC: End of the reign of Asoka in India, who became a Buddhist.

192 AD: First known Champa date at a temple in Vietnam.

200-700 AD: Megalithic culture at San Agustin in Colombia.

650 AD: Rise of Srivijaya and beginning of end for the Cham.

700 AD: Mayan civilization collapses.

1471 AD: The Dai Viet conquer last of Champa.

1500 AD: Remaining Cham peoples move to Vietnamese highlands.

The Cham were probably sailing their fleets from Sumatra and other Indonesian islands and Vietnam for a couple of thousand years. It was only with some official inscriptions at My Son that historians get the date of 192 AD for the rise of the Cham. They had apparently occupied the Cham Islands since 1000 BC or before. The Cham, or whatever we want to call them, were making constant voyages across the Pacific—stopping at various islands—with huge fleets of ships for over a thousand years, ending in 650 AD. The Olmecs, Zapotecs and early Maya seem to have been profoundly influenced by the Cham and their Chinese passengers.

But it would seem that the Cham and their Tiki-face predecessors would not stop in Central America in their search for gold, gems and psychedelic drugs. There is strong evidence that these same people were in the mountains near the Pacific Coast of Colombia. Let us now have a look at the Cham in Colombia.

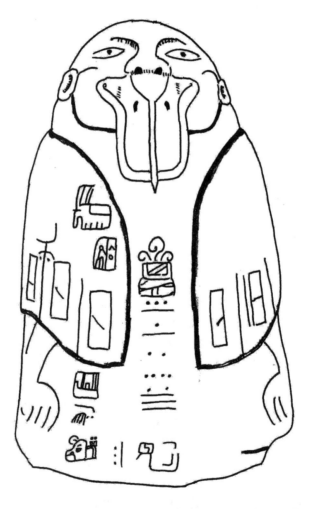

The Tuxtla statuette with early Olmec-Shang writing on it.

Chapter Eight

THE MEGALITHS OF COLOMBIA & THE CHAM

Who dares for nothing need hope for nothing.
—Friedric H. von Schiller

My quest for evidence of the Cham in the Americas led me to Colombia in February of 2015. It seemed likely that the Cham, or their predecessors, had reached the Pacific coasts of Colombia and Ecuador—but what was the evidence? Did El Dorado and the City of Gold have something to do with the Cham's search for gems, gold and other metals?

I flew into Bogota with Jennifer and a small group of World Explorers Club members and over the first few days visited the old city and various national museums, including the Gold Museum. I have travelled widely in South America, but had never been to Colombia. With the guerilla war going on for years, and the violent narco-terrorism, Colombia was something of a forbidden zone for decades. It seemed like the last guy to go adventuring in Colombia was Jack from the movie *Romancing the Stone*.

The famous drug kingpin Pablo Escobar, known as the richest criminal in the world, offered to pay off the Colombian national debt in 1989 in a bid for legitimacy, but was finally killed in a shootout with the Colombian army in Medellin in 1993. The Cali cartel took over his lucrative drug trade but it was largely quashed by 2005.

In the last few years, Colombia has settled down to become a prosperous—and largely peaceful—country, with a growing tourist industry. Colombia is a mountainous and ethnically diverse country. It was one of the earliest areas of Spanish exploration, with the Admiral Alonso de Ojeda (who had been one of the early explorers with Columbus) landing on the Atlantic coast in 1499.

By the year 1533 the important port of Cartagena was founded, and before that the ports of Santa Maria la Antiqua del Darien (1510) and Santa Marta (1525) were in use.

By April of 1536 the Spanish conquistador Gonzalo Jiménez de Quesada led an expedition to the interior and christened the districts through which he passed the "New Kingdom of Granada." Marching inland in August 1538, he founded the city of Santa Fé de Bogota as the capital. During this same period the conquistador Sebastián de Belalcázar, conqueror of Quito, an Inca capital, traveled into what is now Colombia and founded Cali (1536), and then Popayan (1537). The German conquistador Nikolaus Federmann crossed the mountains of the Llanos Orientales and went over the Cordillera Oriental during the years 1536 to 1539, spurred on by the persistent legend of El Dorado, the "city of gold."

This legend of a city of gold, and the many gold artifacts found in Colombia, continued to play a pivotal role in luring explorers from all over Europe to New Granada during the 16th and 17th centuries. Their goal was to find the fabled lost city of unimaginable wealth.

The Search for the City of Gold

Starting in 1535, the German conquistadors Georg von Speyer and Nikolaus Federmann searched the Venezuelan lowlands, then into the Colombian plateaus, and then the Orinoco Basin for the lost city of gold. Tradition had the gold city on an island, presumably in the jungles of the Amazon basin, which was yet to be explored — and remains today a vast area of little-known land. Federmann and von Speyer completely missed the megalithic sites of San Agustin and Tierradentro, which were high in the mountains and long lost to history. They would not be discovered until hundreds of years later.

Von Speyer was later accompanied by the German conquistador Philipp von Hutten on an expedition (1536-38) in which they journeyed through Colombia and reached the headwaters of the Rio Japura in southwest Colombia, near the current border with Ecuador. Hutten led an exploring party of about 150 men in 1541, mostly horsemen, from Coro on the coast of Venezuela into Colombia in search of El Dorado. This group wandered for several years, but

318

were continually harassed by the natives and finally returned to Santa Ana de Coro in Venezuela in 1546.

The stories of a golden city drew the Spanish conquistador Gonzalo Jimenez de Quesada and his army of 800 men away from their mission to find an overland route to Peru. From 1537 to 1538 Quesada's army moved into the Andean homeland of the Muisca people and essentially conquered them. His men noticed that the Muisca had a large number of small gold artifacts. In September of 1540 his brother, conquistador Hernan Perez de Quesada, set out with 270 Spaniards and thousands of Indian porters to explore the Orinoco Basin, but they found no golden city—mostly hostile jungle—and returned to Bogota.

News of the gold artifacts from the Muisca area of Colombia and stories told by the natives of the special rites that took place at Lake Guatavita convinced the Spanish that a kingdom of tremendous wealth existed somewhere in the area. The rites at Lake Guatavita included the gold dusting of a king who jumped into the crater lake, as well as throwing items made of gold into the waters.

A golden city, often called "Manoa," was thought to exist somewhere in the Amazon basin and began to appear on maps.

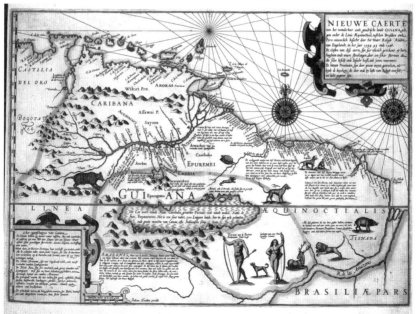

The 1599 Hondius map of Guyana showing Manoa as El Dorado.

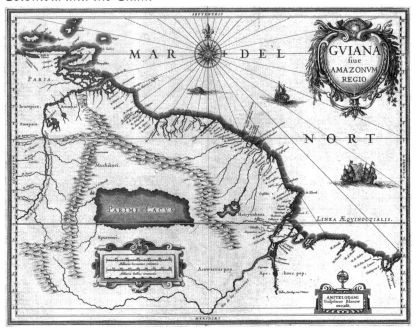

The 1635 Blaeu map of Guyana showing Manoa as El Dorado.

The Amazon basin got its first thorough search starting in 1560 when the notoriously violent conquistador Lope de Aguirre joined the expedition of Pedro de Ursua down the Maranon and Amazon Rivers in search of the golden city. This time the treasure might be some of the hidden Inca treasure that was reportedly sent to the legendary final Inca stronghold known as Paititi.

Aguirre and his daughter, Elvira, joined the 1560 Ursua expedition along with 300 other Spaniards and hundreds of natives at a time just after the civil war in Peru amongst the conquistadors who had conquered Cuzco, who were vying for control of the district. The Ursua expedition was meant at the time to get rid of some of the more troublesome conquistadors by sending them on something of a wild goose chase in search of the City of Gold.

Aguirre proved his troublesome nature when he assassinated Ursua while on the Amazon in 1561. He then assassinated Fernando de Guzman who took control of the group after Ursua's death. Aguirre now assumed command of the group and they continued in boats down the Amazon, battling natives and destroying villages as they went. At one point they battled long-haired natives, armed

320

with powerful bows and arrows, that Aguirre believed to be women. The river was then named the Amazon after the female warriors of Greek myth.

Aguirre and 186 men finally reached the Atlantic and then sailed northward to Venezuela and seized the island called Isla Margarita by killing the Spanish governor and his officers. Aguirre had himself proclaimed a prince of Peru and the lord of Tierra Firme and Chile. He famously said: "I am the Wrath of God, the Prince of Freedom, Lord of Tierra Firme and the Province of Chile."

Then, in the later part of 1561, Aguirre sent a letter to the Spanish monarch Philip II in which he declared Peru an independent state of which he was the ruler.

Using the Isla Margarita base and captured ships from the local government, Aguirre crossed to the mainland in an attempt to take Panama. Here he was defeated by the Spanish crown forces and withdrew. Eventually he was surrounded at Barquisimeto, Venezuela where he killed several followers who intended to capture him. He also shot and killed his daughter Elvira because he did not want her captured and defiled by the soldiers he was fighting. He was shot to death and his body was cut into quarters and sent as a warning to various cities across Venezuela.

A film was made in 1972 by the famous German director Werner Herzog called *Aguirre, Wrath of God* that starred Klaus Kinski as Aguirre and gave a realistic treatment of the incredible difficulties of the Ursua expedition and the explosive personality of Aguirre. While no city of gold was seen by Aguirre and his men, the vast nature of the Amazon basin was observed and recounted, confirming that much had yet to be discovered.

Furthermore, Aguirre and his men had been in Peru and had seen the gigantic and finely-built megalithic walls in Cuzco, Sacsayhuaman, Pisac and Ollantaytambo. These impressive structures, typically attributed to the Incas—but probably thousands of years older—and the vast gold treasures looted from Cuzco must have impressed the conquistadors a great deal. These megalithic structures probably led Aguirre and his men to believe that further megalithic cities of gold were to be discovered and conquered.

Indeed, the vanished explorer Colonel Percy Fawcett in the 1920s held a similar view.

More tales continued to come out of Colombia and the Amazon of a great country full of gold and wonderful buildings. In Wikipedia we learn that poet-priest-historian Juan de Castellanos, who had served under Jimenez de Quesada in his campaign against the Muiscas, wrote a poem titled "The Quest of El Dorado," circa 1574, but it was not published until 1850:

> An alien Indian, hailing from afar,
> Who in the town of Quito did abide.
> And neighbor claimed to be of Bogota,
> There having come, I know not by what way,
> Did with him speak and solemnly announce
> A country rich in emeralds and gold...
> A certain king he told of who, disrobed,
> Upon a lake was wont, aboard a raft,
> To make oblations, as himself had seen,
> His regal form overspread with fragrant oil
> On which was laid a coat of powdered gold...

Stories of the golden city continued to be told in South America and the city of Manoa continued to be featured on maps as a real place somewhere on a river in the Amazon Basin.

Manoa and Lake Parime

Around 1575 AD in Venezuela and Colombia a popular legend was told that one Juan Martinez, on his deathbed, claimed that he had visited the city of Manoa while exploring a river in the Amazon. The story went that he had been condemned to death because he had allowed a keg of gunpowder to catch fire. But friends of his allowed him to escape downriver in a canoe where friendly natives took him to a wonderful city, which was somewhere in "Guiana." Goes the text of the widely circulated legend (here from Wikipedia):

The canoe was carried down the stream, and certain of

the Guianians met it the same evening; and, having not at any time seen any Christian nor any man of that color, they carried Martinez into the land to be wondered at, and so from town to town, until he came to the great city of Manoa, the seat and residence of Inga [Inca] the emperor.

The emperor, after he had beheld him, knew him to be a Christian, and caused him to be lodged in his palace, and well entertained. He was brought thither all the way blindfold, led by the Indians, until he came to the entrance of Manoa itself, and was fourteen or fifteen days in the passage. He avowed at his death that he entered the city at noon, and then they uncovered his face; and that he traveled all that day till night through the city, and the next day from sun rising to sun setting, ere he came to the palace of Inga.

After that Martinez had lived seven months in Manoa, and began to understand the language of the country, Inga asked him whether he desired to return into his own country, or would willingly abide with him. But Martinez, not desirous to stay, obtained the favor of Inga to depart.

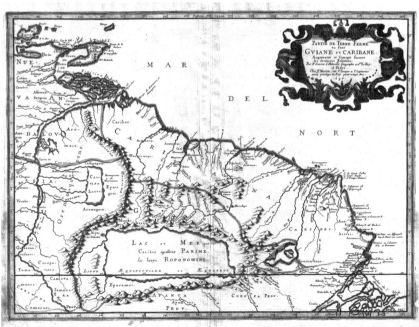

The 1656 Sanson map of Guyana showing Manoa as El Dorado. **323**

According to Wikipedia, the fable of Juan Martinez was founded on the adventures of Juan Martin de Albujar, well known to the Spanish historians of the Conquest and who, while with the conquistador Pedro de Silva in 1570, was captured and lived with the Caribe Indians of the Lower Orinoco. It seems doubtful that he visited a palace of the "Inga" and merely saw grass huts in small villages.

As noted above, the fabled City of Gold was featured on maps of South America in the 16th and 17th centuries, typically designated Manoa. Manoa was usually marked on maps on the shore of a large body of water in the Amazon jungle called Lake Parime. This only confirmed to many that the City of Gold's existence had been established and was a real location to which one could make a journey.

In 1595 and 1596 Sir Walter Raleigh made attempts to reach Manoa by following one of the many old maps to El Dorado, aiming to reach Lake Parime in the highlands of Guiana. He was familiar of the account of "Juan Martinez," recounted above. Raleigh apparently heard the story from Don Antonio de Berrio (an early governor of Venezuela who died in 1597). Raleigh's second-in-command, a sailor named Lawrence Keymis, had determined after discussions with natives in Guiana that Manoa could be reached by travelling up the Essequibo River, the largest river in Guiana and the largest river in South America between the Orinoco and the Amazon. The Essequibo River largely

An old print of Sir Walter Raleigh.

defines Guiana, which eventually became a Dutch colony and then a British colony and finally gained independence in the 1960s. It is the only country in South America where English is the official language.

However, Lake Parime did not exist in the interior of Guiana, nor did Manoa, the City of Gold—no matter what the maps of the time indicated. Raleigh searched for Lake Parime and Manoa and found only jungles, rivers and mountains. That he desired to establish an English outpost in Guiana was another factor in his explorations, and he was encouraged by finding some gold nuggets on a few riverbanks.

Raleigh went back to England but then returned to Guiana in 1617, this time with his son, Watt Raleigh. The father stayed at their main base of Trinidad while Watt went off to search for Manoa, but was unfortunately killed in a battle with the Spanish. Sir Walter returned to England in 1618 where King James had him executed for disobeying his orders not to come into conflict with the Spanish.

The mythical city of Manoa on Lake Parime continued to be marked on English and other maps for several hundred years. These maps usually included a link to the Essequibo River and Lake Parime. Typical of such maps were the Hondius map of 1599, the 1635 Blaeu map, the Jansson map of 1647, the 1656 Sanson map and others.

The existence of Lake Parime and the city of Manoa was finally disproven by the great German naturalist and explorer Alexander von Humboldt during his travels in South and North America from 1799 to 1804. Humboldt proposed that Lake Amucu in the North Rupununi, which had been described by a Dutch trader called Nicholas Horstmann in 1739, was the Lake Parime sought after by Raleigh. Later, German explorer Robert Hermann Schomburgk visited Lake Amucu in 1840 and noted that this area of the North Rupununi flooded at certain times of the year and linked the Amazon and Essequibo rivers as a huge swampy lake.

The Rio Negro region contains a tribe known as the Manoa and it is from these people that the major Amazon city of Manaus takes its name. British Guiana, along with Belize (British Honduras), became important Latin American colonies for the British during the 1800s and arguably Raleigh's search for El Dorado and Lake Parime helped Britain seal its claim on this territory.

Colombia: The Land of El Dorado

With Guiana being the focus of the quest for El Dorado for centuries, the original location of the City of Gold—Colombia—became lost to history. But the discoveries at San Agustin—starting in the late 1800s and continuing up to the 1970s—showed that a megalithic culture that mined gold and made astonishing monuments

existed in the mountains of western Colombia. This area, high in the Colombian Massif, was virtually unknown to the early Spanish colonizers of Colombia. Even today the extent of this amazing civilization is just beginning to be understood.

El Dorado was said to be a source of emeralds and gold. Colombia is today the largest producer of emeralds in the world. It also produces many other gems but it has a virtual corner on the emerald market, holding an estimated 95% of the world's emerald-bearing rock. It is interesting to consider that some of the world's emeralds in ancient treasuries may have come from old trading ports on the Atlantic and Pacific coasts of Colombia. Other sources of emeralds are India, Afghanistan, Canada, Australia and Madagascar, and Russia. Indonesia, Thailand, Cambodia and Vietnam are not significant emerald producers so for the Cham were likely to get their emeralds from India or Colombia.

Gold production in Colombia began by at least 400 BC, according to Wikipedia and other sources. Curiously, the gold trade was said to be centered on the Pacific Coast of Colombia, rather than the Atlantic. At any rate, one would think that gold work in

One of the many statues at San Agustin.

327

Colombia, and South America in general, would be much earlier than 400 BC. A date like 4000 BC would seem more correct, but since gold artifacts, such as those from Lake Guanavita or San Agustin, cannot be dated by carbon dating or other methods, we simply do not know how old many of these gold artifacts are.

Many of the artifacts are of a gold-copper alloy called tumbaga. Because of the plentiful amount of gold in Colombia and Peru, tumbaga was a common metal used to make artifacts; it was harder than copper by itself, plus other metals could be added to it. It had

A tiki-looking statue at the San Agustin site museum.

More tiki-looking statues at the San Agustin site museum.

a fairly low melting point, lower than copper or gold on their own, and furthermore, an acid mixture such as lime juice could eat away at the outer copper surface—leaving only the gold molecules which could then be polished into a shiny gold burnish, a process known as depletion gilding.

Says Wikipedia:

> The earliest examples of gold mining and goldwork have been attributed to the Tumaco people of the Pacific coast and date to around 325 BCE.
>
> Gold would play a pivotal role in luring the Spanish conquistadores to the area during the 16th century.
>
> Gold was considered sacred by most of the precolumbian civilizations of the area. In Muisca mythology, Gold (Chiminigagua) was considered itself a deity, and the force of creation. Copper mining was very important for the classic Quimbaya civilization, which developed the tumbaga alloy.

329

A display of statue heads at the San Agustin site museum.

Much of the gold in Bogota's famous gold museum probably came from San Agustin and Tierradentro, as it would seem that the entire purpose for building these sites was the mining of gold and other metals. Bogota's Gold Museum is one of the greatest collections in the world and probably Colombia's most important museum and tourist attraction. Gold was plentiful throughout the Andean countries, and museums in Ecuador, Peru and Bolivia also have substantial gold and tumbaga collections.

The Strange Megaliths of San Agustin

As mentioned, on our first day in Bogota our group visited the Gold Museum which has room after room of over 55,000 pieces of gold and other materials from all the major pre-Hispanic cultures in Colombia. Some of the gold objects were of some pretty interesting-looking people, wearing all sorts of strange headgear and clothes. Some literally looked like spacemen of some sort.

One of the rooms in the museum holds the famous display of gold "airplanes" that appear to be miniature models of winged craft, complete with a cockpit, wings and airplane-style tail. Mainstream archeologists insist that the objects must depict flying fish or birds. However, birds and fish do not have tails like these golden models—only airplanes have such tails. Could they actually depict flying craft from thousands of years ago? Are these what some vimanas from ancient India or Sumeria looked like? Ancient astronaut theorists would say yes, but mainstream archeologists cannot believe that such advanced technology existed in the past—only our own civilization has been capable of this technology, they insist. But in 1994, German enthusiasts Peter Belting and Conrad Lubbers fashioned radio-controlled scale models of some of the planes and proved that they could fly.

We left Bogota in a private minibus from our hotel for the long day's journey into the mountains of western Colombia. As dusk was falling on the small mountain hamlet of San Agustin our minibus pulled up to our hotel a few blocks from the main square of the small, but bustling, tourist town. The next morning we visited the main museum and megalithic site and after lunch we visited some of the other sites around San Agustin. San Agustin is a UNESCO World Heritage Site so let us get some official information from that organization.

The UNESCO website (http://whc.unesco.org/en/list/744) says that the San Agustin Archaeological Park is the:

…largest group of religious monuments and megalithic sculptures in South America [and] stands in a wild, spectacular landscape. Gods and mythical animals are skillfully represented in styles ranging from abstract to realist. These works of art display the creativity and imagination of a northern Andean culture that flourished from the 1st to the 8th century.

The San Agustin Archaeological Park includes four separate sites, with boundaries defined so as to include the main concentrations of burial mounds with megalithic statues of the Regional Classic (1-900 AD) period. A third of the 600 known San Agustin statues and half of 40 known monumental burial mounds that are dispersed throughout the Alto Magdalena region are located inside the boundaries of the archaeological park. These 20 burial mounds include the largest and also the most elaborate examples. The "Mesitas" site, 80 ha of the park, includes 8 mounds, more than a hundred statues, and the entire core of the largest demographic and ceremonial centers—containing not only the oldest and largest tombs—Mesita A and Mesita C—sites, but also the residential remains of the elite families that ruled over their society, constructed the monuments and used them as burials for their main leaders. Thus, the park includes not only a series of separate monuments but also the vestiges of the central communities that constructed and lived beside them. In spite of the impacts of natural phenomena on the material remains, conservation actions have preserved their material integrity. Challenges remain in maintaining the integrity of such a vast area in light of pressures for extended agricultural use and growth of local communities.

The UNESCO site goes on to say:

In the pre-agricultural period, from c 3300 to c 600 BC, San Agustin was occupied by a society with a rudimentary stone technology using unretouched basalt chips; their principal food was wild fruits, but hunting cannot be ruled out.

The UNESCO site mentions gold mining at the site and that the large statues date from approximately 100 AD:

Gold working is attested by radiocarbon dating from at least the 1st Century BC, and increased substantially in the following period. Around the 1st century AD there were profound cultural changes in the San Agustin area. This was the period of the great flowering of monumental lithic art, the so-called Augustinian Culture. Links with other regions

An old photo of one of the strange statues at San Agustin.

of the southwest increased, with the consequent evolution over the whole region of societies known as Regional Classic. Population density increased markedly, and earlier settlements were reoccupied. New house sites on hilltops were also settled and occupied over long periods. The

333

economy was still based on maize cultivation, and population pressures led to the opening up of new agricultural lands.

There was considerable social consolidation, and the concentration of substantial power in the hands of the chiefs made possible the production of gigantic works by the use of large bodies of men to carry out massive earth movements. Hundreds of elaborate stone statues were carved, some in complex relief and large in size. The huge monumental platforms, terraces, and mounds and the temple-like architecture reflect a complex system of religious and magical belief.

UNESCO defines the period from 3300 BC to 600 BC as "pre-agricultural," but it seems doubtful that this society did not have maize, beans or other cultivated crops until 600 BC. It would seem likely that they had corn (maize), squash, beans or other agricultural crops common to Peru and Mexico at the time. Probably they had all of this, plus bananas, sweet potatoes, cassava-yucca, and even quinoa and other grains common to Peru, Ecuador and Bolivia.

In fact, it is reported that in ancient times corn (maize) was grown from Argentina to the American Southwest to Kansas and

An old photo of one of the strange statues at San Agustin.

An old photo of one of a giant bird statue at San Agustin. Is it of Garudu?

Nebraska and probably at the mound sites at Cahokia in Illinois and other sites in Indiana, Kentucky, Tennessee and Ohio. That maize was not being grown at sites in Colombia seems almost impossible. Archeologists argue about the origin of corn, much like bananas, sweet potatoes, cotton and other crops. While archeologists in Peru claim that maize was first cultivated there, archeologists in Mexico claim that maize was first grown in the highlands of central Mexico by the mysterious Olmecs.

Corn grown in Peru can be very large, much larger than that in North America, and it seems likely that the highlands of Colombia and Ecuador were growing large crops of maize for many thousands of years. It may be that the Olmecs first domesticated maize in Mexico and spread it to South America, or perhaps it came to Mexico from South America—also with the Olmecs. The Fuente Magna Bowl at the Museum of Precious Metals in La Paz, Bolivia, indicates that the Sumerians were in Peru and Bolivia by 3000 BC. Possibly they brought maize from Mexico to Peru, or vice versa. Either way, it is likely that Colombia had maize cultivation by at least 4000 BC. Bio-archeologists currently put the cultivation of a domesticated maize—either in Peru or Mexico—at 9,000 BC. The banana was genetically engineered into a seedless fruit about the same time.

335

An old photo of a gigantic monolith and little girl at San Agustin.

UNESCO and mainstream archeologists maintain that the earlier megalithic mining culture of Colombia came to a sudden halt around 700 AD and that sophisticated terrace building and drainage projects, as seen at San Agustin, came to an end. Essentially, the culture underwent a slow decline until nothing was really left, some 800 years before the European explorations of rediscovery. The demise of the San Agustin culture was the same time as the decline of the Cham, circa 700 AD with the rise of Srivijaya and the Khmer.

The mystery of these imaginative and industrious people and where they came from persists today. San Agustin is similar to and of the same level of stonework and megalithic artistry as the work of the Olmecs in Mexico and Guatemala, the stone balls of Costa Rica and the statues at Tiwanaku.

Giant granite boulders from the mountain streams, some weighing many tons, were moved to artificial mound sites and then carved into grand monuments, some as tall as 21 feet (7 meters). It is estimated that more than 600 statues are scattered over a wide area in the green hills surrounding San Agustin. Many of the statues are of fang-toothed men holding clubs or babies, while others resemble masked monsters. Many have unusual hats or helmets on. Some hold their arms over their heart and stomach in the classic "tiki" pose. There are also sculptures depicting animals such as an eagle, frog and jaguar. There is a similarity of the San Agustin tiki statues to those at Bada Valley and Sumatra.

Nowhere are we told how these astonishing statues were

An old photo of the riverbed at San Agustin carved in perfect circles and other marks.

carved,or why. We are told that these statues had magical and protective qualities and some of them were "guardians" of the monumental tombs, complete with gigantic sarcophagi, that are scattered among the hills. The effort that all this must have taken, including the huge earthworks, is considerable. Archeologists portray these people as an isolated culture that suddenly decided to put their efforts into carving gigantic statues with an unmistakable artistic flair. Yet, the similarity with the Olmecs and the early tiki statuary in Indonesia is very much evident, and it would seem that there are links to the early Cham here.

The UNESCO site goes on to say that:

The Alto de los Idolos is on the right bank of the Magdalena River and the smaller Alto de las Piedras lies further north: both are in the municipality of San José de Isnos. Like the main San Agustin area, they are rich in monuments of all kinds. Much of the area is a rich archaeological landscape, with evidence of ancient tracks, field boundaries, drainage ditches and artificial platforms, as well as funerary monuments. This was a sacred land, a place of pilgrimage and ancestors worship. These hieratic guards, some more than 4 m high weighing several tonnes, are carved in blocks of tuff and volcanic rock. They protected the funeral rooms, the monolithic sarcophagus and the burial sites.

The main archaeological monuments are Las Mesitas, containing artificial mounds, terraces, funerary structures and stone statuary; the Fuente de Lavapatas, a religious monument carved in the stone bed of a stream; and the Bosque de Las Estatuas, where there are examples of stone statues from the whole region.

A new society appeared in the region in the 7th century BC: the people cultivated maize on the flat land or gentle slopes and lived in dispersed houses near the main rivers, possibly in simple groups headed by chiefs. The extended burials were in vertical shaft tombs, with simple grave-goods. The period probably lasted until the 3rd or even the

2nd century BC.

Around the 1st century AD there were profound cultural changes in the area: this was a time of a great flowering of monumental lithic art and the so-called Agustinian Culture. Links with other regions of the south-west grew, population density increased markedly, and earlier settlements were reoccupied. New house sites on the hilltops were also settled and occupied over long periods. There was considerable social consolidation and the concentration of substantial power in the hands of the chiefs made possible the production of gigantic works: hundreds of elaborate stone statues were carved, some in complex relief and large in size. The huge monumental platforms, terraces and mounds and the temple-like architecture reflect a complex system of religious and magical belief. Some 300 enormous sculptures (divinities with threatening faces, warriors armed with clubs, round eyes and jaguars' teeth of mythical heroes) stand in the region of Agustin in the heart of the Andes, El Huila Province.

Marveling at the many dolmens, statues and sarcophagi, I couldn't help noticing the similarity to Olmec statues and monumental works that can be found on the Gulf Coast of Mexico as well as on the Pacific Coast and in southern Mexico. The sharp features in the carving also made me think that these statues were not bashed out with a rock hammer. It would seem that metal chisels were being used, and possibly even power tools.

The similarity of San Agustin to places like the Bada Valley in Indonesia, the Plain of Jars in Laos and even the Cham statues of central Vietnam was evident to me. These stoneworkers cut and moved huge blocks of granite and basalt, like the Olmecs, and were known to have metals such as gold, bronze and iron. If the search for gold by the Cham and their predecessors had brought them to Colombia, they would have found it.

When the Spanish (and Portuguese) came to the Americas, explorers would carry various samples of metals, gems and

An old photo of a giant sarcophagus dug up at San Agustin.

minerals with them to show natives what they encountered. In this way helpful natives would show them gold and copper deposits plus the sites of other valuable minerals. Did the Cham and their Tiki-Sumerian predecessors come to Colombia with nuggets of gold and copper seeking the source of these metals for their technological devices, statuary and the glorification of Shiva and Buddha?

Was San Agustin part of a transoceanic trade network that included Asians, Olmecs, Africans and Phoenicians? Because of their practice of child sacrifice, the Phoenicians were known to have statuary of men holding babies—babies that were about to be consecrated to the gods.

The Road to Tierradentro

Our group left San Agustin early one morning and drove over the mountains to Popayan, the capital of Cauca Department. It was an all-day drive, passing through some beautiful and remote mountain country. As noted above, Popayan was founded by Spanish conquistador Sebastián de Belalcázar in 1537. It is also an area of gold mining that produced Escudo gold coins and silver Reales for the Spanish crown from 1760 through 1819.

We spent the night in Popayan's charming old town, and then our chartered bus took us back into the mountains to the curious archeological site of Tierradentro located about 40 miles (100 km) from the city.

Tierradentro ("Inner Earth") is the second most important archaeological site in Colombia, after San Agustin, but gets far fewer visitors. The rough mountain road, much of it very muddy from the frequent rains, was along steep mountain valleys and it was clear that parts of the road would wash out from time to time. A lot of road construction was taking place at the time of our journey!

There are some statues, like those at San Agustin, but Tierradentro is mainly known for its elaborate underground tombs. So far, archaeologists have discovered about 100 of these unusual funeral temples that are cut into solid rock and painted with geometric patterns. These underground funerary temples are known as hypogea (or a hypogeum in the singular).

These hypogea are scattered on various hills around the town with names such as Alto del Aguacate (Avocado Hill), Alto de Segovia, Alto de San Andrés, Alto del Duende and El Tablón. There are also two museums and an open-air granite statuary park.

The typical hypogeum has an entry, like a trap door, with a spiral hewn-stone staircase leading steeply down to the main chamber, usually 15 to 30 feet below the surface. Some of the tombs have several lesser chambers around the central chamber. Each would probably have contained a large ceramic pot in which the cremated remains of the deceased were kept. Some of these urns can be seen at the museums.

The walls of the tombs are painted with geometric, anthropomorphic and zoomorphic patterns in red, black and white. The domed ceilings of the largest hypogea are supported by pillars that are part of the solid rock. Most of the tombs have been looted, but the museums in town still have plenty of ceramic objects and fabrics on display. There are some monumental statues as well, which archeologists admit are very similar to those at San Agustin. Indeed, were they the same culture?

The time frame for Tierradentro is about the same as San

A boulder carved into a frog at Tierradentro. Was it done with power tools?

Agustin, approximately 300 AD to 600 AD, though it seems that no really good dating has been done at Tierradentro. The rock-cut tombs would probably have been used over and over again through the centuries, and one would think that the statues in Tierradentro were made at about the same time as those in San Agustin. Indeed, Tierradentro was apparently a gold mining area in ancient times, like San Agustin. Gold artifacts have been discovered at Tierradentro and some are now at the Gold Museum in Bogota.

We spent several days in Tierradentro, visiting the museums and hiking around the hills to the tombs that were generally kept under lock and key by guards. The steps of the cut-stone spiral staircases were often quite big, making me wonder if the people were literal giants who could walk down such staircases with ease.

Mainstream archeologists think that megalithic cultures like those at San Agustin and Tierradentro were isolated peoples who, for unknown reasons, independently began carving granite boulders into elaborate, beautiful and bizarre statues. They created artificial mounds and cut tombs into solid rock and must have had some pretty large houses, as well as kilns for firing the ceramic objects and even forges for working the metals.

Statues at Tierradentro were finely made of granite, a very hard rock, and in some cases the people depicted were as bizarre as the ones in San Agustin, with large eyes and strange hats. Mainstream archeologists would likely say that stone hammers and chisels were used in the making of the statues and the rock-cut tombs, but they are so well made that I would have to say that iron chisels and even power tools were used in their manufacture.

Indeed, what appears to have happened at Tierradentro and San Agustin is that a sophisticated group of foreigners arrived in Colombia and started two mining operations in the western mountains. With sophisticated mining tools, including possibly power tools, they began extracting tons of gold from the mountain streams and nearby gold mines. When not extracting gold or copper they built large homes with farms, and industries like ceramics. And, in their spare time, they used their mining tools to carve granite boulders into statuary. This statuary probably had some sort of magical or religious purpose though in some cases it may just represent some of the lords or ladies of this extended mining camp. One large boulder by the school in the center of town had a number of drill marks on it, seemingly made by a large power tool.

The way that the statues were dressed and the unusual ways that they held their hands and arms, often with a baby or club in their hands, made me think of the tiki statues in the Marquesas Islands and Tahiti, as well as the Kon Tiki statue at Tiwanaku in Bolivia. The Olmecs and Phoenicians also produced similar statues making unusual hand and arm gestures. As has been discussed, in Hindu sculptures such arm, hand and figure positions are known as "mudras" and every different position has a different meaning. The mysterious statues in Colombia seem to be also communicating in some way.

As we left Tierradentro after a few days I looked back at the steep mountain valleys that the road clung to. We stopped briefly at a spot where the road had collapsed and a bulldozer was pushing dirt and mud around to clear the road. Even today travel in this area is relatively difficult, and it must have been even more difficult in ancient times. Coming by helicopter or airship would be the easiest way to arrive in Tierradentro. Maybe the gold airplanes back in Bogota were souvenirs from the ancient airports that once existed at San Agustin and Tierradentro. The strange world of ancient Colombia was one in which it seemed anything could have happened.

The bizarre statuary and jewelry of Tierradentro, San Agustin and the Gold Museum speak for themselves. The mysterious ancient megaliths of Colombia and impressive gold artifacts were done by a sophisticated culture that was capable of exporting this gold to distant lands. In fact, the gold of ancient Colombia may have been taken as far away as Champa, helping to enrich their temples of stone, brick, gold and silver.

Still, in order to do the mining and the stonework, large machines and power tools would have to have been brought to the site. This would need to be done by air, with some sort of vimana airship to transport such expensive and necessary machinery. Other trips to the gold-bearing areas of Colombia and other parts of South America would be done by ship, utilizing the massive fleet of the Cham. Just as we have aircraft (and spacecraft) today, we still use ships—some of them gigantically huge—for the transfer of minerals, goods and machinery from continent to continent.

Contact between civilizations on both sides of the Pacific Ocean and Atlantic Oceans must have been going for at least 3,000 years, and probably earlier. Oceans are not barriers to travel but rather highways on which small or large groups of people are able to trade or migrate to distant lands. In fact, walking to some of these distant lands would either be very difficult or impossible—because they are islands—and ultimately traveling by boat is quicker and safer. You just have to know where you are going, and this is done by watching the stars.

The idea that ancient people could not have carried enough food and water to make a voyage across the Pacific or Atlantic Ocean is just simply wrong. Even small boats are capable of carrying enough food and water. Experienced seafarers are easily capable of catching fish, birds and sea turtles while at sea, as well as being capable of

344

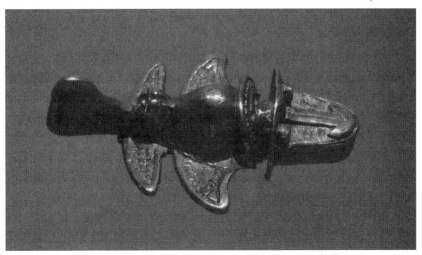

One of the small gold "airplanes" at the Gold Museum in Bogota.

catching rainwater when possible. Literally every ancient navy in the world was capable of crossing one of our oceans, and certain parts of the world were famous for having a lot of ships, large and small.

Historians around the world admit that Egypt, Sumeria, India and China had a significant number of ships—literal navies—by at least 3000 BC, and probably much before. But certain areas of the world are left out of this list of ancient navies—places such as South America, West Africa, or Southeast Asia—and seem to not have this history of shipbuilding and maritime navigation over large distances. But in the case of Southeast Asia, this is ridiculous. In no other area of the world, except Polynesia and the Caribbean, is there such a plethora of islands. Furthermore, Indonesia and Southeast Asia in general are extremely productive in terms of agricultural output and the exploitation of mineral wealth. Because of the volcanic nature of many Indonesian and Melanesian islands, those who search for gold and other valuable minerals are likely to be richly rewarded.

It is an interesting thought to think of Cham or Champa as Suvarnabhumi—the land of gold—while the Cham themselves exploited the gold of Indonesia and made the longer journeys to Mexico and South America. Colombia, like Peru and Bolivia, may have been key in this transoceanic quest for gold and larger and larger sources. The creation of newer and stronger (or, alternatively, longer lasting) alloys was probably also part of their quest. Mexico, although it has a number of gold mines, has never been a significant producer of gold. South America, on the other hand, has been.

The gold of Colombia seems to have been exploited by a number of ancient civilizations, including the Cham. Perhaps the ships of the Cham proceeded south to ports in Peru such as Chan Chan or Paracas and continued to take on cargo. From these ports, below the equator, they departed to the west, into the South Pacific. Perhaps their next stop, if they could find it, was Easter Island. For our next chapter, let us look at the evidence on this most mysterious of megalithic islands.

The rise of mysterious San Agustin culture circa 100 AD is a period in which the Cham ships were gathering at My Son and the Cham Islands. The demise of the San Agustin culture is also the time of the decline of the Cham. Once the wars with Srivijaya and the Khmer started in 650 AD the great fleets of ships stopped their transpacific voyages to Mexico, Colombia and Peru. Did the wars in Sumatra, Java, Cambodia and Vietnam with the collapse of the Cham cause the downfall of the San Agustin culture in Colombia? Certainly, both collapses came at the same time period in history.

Chapter Nine

EASTER ISLAND & THE CHAM

As we acquire knowledge,
things do not become more comprehensible,
but more mysterious.
—Will Durant

In chapter three I discussed the ancient mining operations at Lake Titicaca, Tiwanaku and Puma Punku. I have been to Peru and Bolivia many times over the last 30 years and it was on my earliest trips to this area that I noticed the keystone cuts at Puma Punku and Tiwanaku. Later I noticed the keystone cuts at the Qoricancha (Sun Temple) in Cuzco and the keystone cuts on massive andesite (granite) blocks at Ollantaytambo in the nearby Sacred Valley, where the trail to Machu Picchu begins. I write at length about these keystone cuts in my book *Ancient Technology in Peru & Bolivia*.[38]

I was aware of keystone cuts on blocks at certain temples in Egypt, like Karnak, and of keystone cuts at Delphi in Greece. But it was not until I saw the keystone cuts at My Son, Angkor Wat and Preah Vihear did I realize that the Cham were connected to the great sea kings who were navigating not just the Atlantic Ocean but the Pacific as well.

It is well known that Tiwanaku and Lake Titicaca were connected to the Pacific coast by a very good road system that went directly west out of the high Andean plateau—known as the altiplano—that holds the waters of the great Lake Titicaca, the highest navigable lake in the world. For thousands of years alpaca and llama pack animals would be loaded with freeze-dried potatoes and other highland produce and driven to the coast by herders. This was also done during the later times of the Incas, and the trip took about two weeks.

At Paracas and other ports along the dry coast of southern Peru, the thousands of alpacas and llamas would unload their cargo and then be loaded with dried fish and driven back into the Andes. Ships moved up and down the coasts of Peru and Ecuador, probably also to the Olmec and Mayan areas of Soconusco, Guatemala and Nicaragua.

The Sumerians were apparently mining tin and copper at Lake Titicaca circa 2000 BC (the Sumerians are largely thought to have come to an end by 1600 BC), as is evidenced by the Fuente Magna Bowl at the Precious Metals Museum in La Paz. At a time shortly after this the Shang Chinese (1766 to 1046 BC) were making the many curious Olmec statues that continue to baffle archeologists. Both of these civilizations were probably sailing across the Pacific Ocean to reach the Americas and both probably would have had to sail through the Philippines to reach the greater Pacific Ocean, although in the case of the Sumerians, they might have gone the southern route from Sumatra to Sumba and Timor and then to the Torres Strait on the southern coast of New Guinea.

The Shang Chinese—a very sophisticated culture with great maritime capability—apparently launched fleets to North America, and the Chinese writing in Olmec culture indicates that they did exactly that. These early Chinese fleets may have gone through Micronesia and Polynesia to California, or they might have gone a more northern route taking them to Alaska and the Pacific Northwest. The ships could continue south down the coast, past the barren coast of Baja California to the lush beaches and bays of southern Mexico.

Did the Cham accompany these early Chinese sailors on their transpacific junkets? One reason I suggest the Cham to go as far back as 1000 BC and may have had a hand in founding civilizations like the Olmec is that the occupation of the Cham Islands may go back to that date or earlier. Historians do not know exactly how long the Cham Islands have been inhabited, but they say that it has been for at least 2,500 years. Very little archeological work has been done on the Cham Islands and the Vietnamese government has admitted that it simply doesn't have the funds and resources to explore the many underwater shipwrecks that are known to be in the waters around the Cham Islands.

It may well be that an underwater archeological site around a shipwreck may yield evidence that the Cham Islands were being visited during periods around 800 to 1000 BC. But any such discoveries are in the future and all we can do is surmise that fleets of large ships were crossing the Gulf of Siam to Borneo and Sulawesi and virtually every island in Indonesia no matter how small or distant. These people were carving the tiki faces, tiki statues and stone vats still extant on these islands at an early time. Were they the early Cham?

It would seem that circa 1000 BC Hindu vessels—and, according to the Bible, the Phoenician ships of King Solomon—sailed to Sri Lanka and Sumatra and then entered the Gulf of Siam. They scattered ports and temples on the coasts or up navigable rivers on these islands. These hundreds of islands, big and small, were the Land of Gold—Suvarnabhumi—where volcanic landscapes held savage headhunters or giant man-eating lizards such as those still left on the island of Komodo. Even larger than these huge lizards are the many saltwater crocodiles that can overwhelm small boats and grow up to 30 feet in length.

An early print of the statues on Easter Island placed on a platform with a topknot.

349

Stone statues stand chest-deep in the soil of the slopes of Rano Raraku crater.

These early sailors would be mostly Hindus who turned to Buddhism starting around 300 BC, and though historians don't have a name for these ancient sailors and stonemasons I think they are the Cham. And it seems that this fraternal collection of sailors from Southeast Asia, India and Egypt met at the Cham Islands for the great voyage east into Micronesia and Polynesia, a voyage that would take six months or more. The fleet would likely stay for one

350

year and then take nearly a year to return. This return probably took the fleet westward into the South Pacific from ports in Peru and Ecuador. Was the first stop for this fleet the mysterious isolated island called Rapa Nui, or Easter Island?

Though I had been to Easter Island twice before, once in 1986 and once in 1999, I decided that I should go back and examine the many statues, platforms and quarries that dot the island. I returned on a windy day in the spring of 2013 with Jennifer and a small group of World Explorers Club members. We would spend the next four days on the small but mysterious island.

We hired a minibus to take us around and marveled at the giant statues and megalithic walls of basalt and granite. I was amazed at the fine carving and construction and wondered what the mainstream had to say about the local history. As I suspected, they maintained that the making of the statues was fairly recent and that most of the mysteries associated with the island had been solved. Had they?

I wondered about a few things that seemed to need explaining:

1. When and why did the islanders excavate and move such gigantic statues when smaller ones would have presumably served the same purpose? How were they moved?
2. Why are the statues buried with up to 30 feet of soil? Was this done on purpose or has thousands of years of soil buildup been created around the statues?
3. Why did the islanders think that putting statues facing inward around the island would keep it from sinking into the ocean like their lost land of Hiva?
4. How did they make fine drill holes and saw cuts on some of the stone walls?
5. Why would a small remote island population invent their own written language? Could such a script be related to other ancient forms of writing?
6. Could a remote island like Rapa Nui be related to thousands of years of transpacific contact that spanned Asia, Oceania and the Americas?

351

First, let us look at a brief, official history of this very enigmatic island. According to the UNESCO website, the official history of the remote island is as follows:

Rapa Nui contains one of the most remarkable cultural phenomena in the world. An artistic and architectural tradition of great power and imagination was developed by a society completely isolated from external cultural influences of any kind for over a millennium. The substantial remains of this culture blend with their natural surroundings to create an unparalleled cultural landscape.

The island was settled around AD 300 by Polynesians, probably from the Marquesas, who brought with them a wholly Stone Age society. All the cultural elements in Rapa Nui before the arrival of Europeans indicate that there were no other incoming groups. Between the 10th and 16th centuries the island community expanded steadily, settlements being set up along practically the entire coastline. The high cultural level of this society is best known for its monumental stone figures (*moai*) and ceremonial shrines (*ahu*); it is also noteworthy for a form of pictographic writing (*rongo rongo*), so far undeciphered.

However, there was an economic and social crisis in the community in the 16th century, attributable to overpopulation and environmental deterioration. This resulted in the population being divided into two separate groups of clans who were constantly involved in warfare. The warrior class that evolved from this situation gave rise to the so-called Birdman cult, based on the small islands offshore of Orongo, which superseded the statue-building religion and threw down most of the moai and ahu.

On Easter Sunday 1722 Jacob Roggeveen of the Dutch East India Company chanced upon the island and gave it its European name. It was annexed to Chile in 1888.

The most famous archaeological features of Rapa Nui are the moai, which are believed to represent sacred ancestors who watch over the villages and ceremonial areas. They range in height from 2 m to 20 m and are for the most part carved from the scoria, using simple picks (*toli*) made from hard basalt and then lowered down the slopes into previously dug holes.

A number of moai are still in an uncompleted condition in the quarries, providing valuable information about the method of manufacture. Some have large cylindrical pieces of red stone known as pukao, extracted from the small volcano Punapao, as headdresses: these are believed to denote special ritual status. There is a clear stylistic evolution in the form and size of the moai, from the earlier small, round-headed and round-eyed figures to the best-known large, elongated figures with carefully carved fingers, nostrils, long ears, and other features.

The shrines (ahu) vary considerably in size and form. There are certain constant features, notably a raised rectangular platform of large worked stones filled with rubble, a ramp often paved with rounded beach pebbles, and

Stone statues stand chest-deep in the soil of the slopes of Rano Raraku crater.

leveled area in front of the platform. Some have moai on them, and there are tombs in a number of them in which skeletal remains have been discovered. The ahu are generally located on the coast and oriented parallel to it.

Source: UNESCO/CLT/WHC

While Easter Island is thought to have been first discovered and inhabited by Polynesians (probably coming from the Marquesas Islands, north of Tahiti), around 300 AD, it is generally thought by mainstream archeologists that the time of the excavation and movement of the statues was 1100 to 1680 AD. This is based on radiocarbon dating of wood, bone and shell that has been found buried in and around the statues and the quarry of Rano Raraku. However, we do not know how deep these objects were buried, and they might have been placed there after the statues had been carved. (Wikipedia, *Encyclopedia Britannica*)

Currently, 887 statues of various sizes (some gigantically huge) have been inventoried on the island, and most are still around the quarry. Many of these are leaning over or fallen. Often they are buried under dozens of feet of "shifting soil." But where all this shifting soil came from is a big question since these statues are up against sheer cliff walls of the quarry that are virtually devoid of soil. Was this soil swept here by a tsunami? When one of the large moai statues was completely uncovered by archeologists in 2011 many people were astonished that the moai were not just heads, but have even larger bodies beneath the soil. This naturally got bloggers and others speculating on how old the statues seemed to be. Were they only built in 900 AD or were they thousands of years old — buried by the dust of time?

As I looked at my notes and thought about my first question concerning Easter Island, it seemed possible to me that these statues might have been carved by Sumerians who brought the Fuente Magna Bowl to Tiwanaku around 2000 BC—making them an astonishing 4,000 years old. While people may have been around these statues a thousand years ago, leaving all sorts of datable material for later analysis, they didn't necessarily make these statues. The moai may have been standing there then as enigmatically as they stand there today. Perhaps a fragment of a coke bottle from 2017 will be dug up by archeologists in the future who will similarly misinterpret their find.

Meanwhile, when gigantic stone walls and statues stand from the mists of time, many cultures and—in the case of Rapa Nui, beach parties—come and go. We will have lots of datable material to send to the laboratories, but it is the oldest datable material that matters. Was this material from the time that the statues were actually quarried from the living rock of the volcanic cliffs of Rano Raraku? Indeed, the date of the stonecutting has not been established yet by archeologists, and no such dating technique currently exists according to researchers.

Before we get any further into this, let us look at the discovery of Easter Island by Europeans. At the time, early explorers were out looking for a land in the South Pacific called Davis Land. A Dutch buccaneer named John Davis, who captained the English ship *The Bachelor's Delight*, was returning from raids in Panama and headed for Cape Horn when the ship's crew sighted land in 1687. The lieutenant of the ship, Mr. Wafer, described the sighting in a book published in 1688 in London entitled *Description of the Isthmus of Darien*:

> ...we came to latitude 27° 20' south when about two hours before day we fell in with a low sandy island and heard a great roaring noise like that of sea beating upon the shore ahead of the ship... so we plyed off till day then stood in again with the land, which proved to be a small flat island without the guard of any rocks... To the westward about twelve leagues by judgment we saw a range of high land which we took to be islands; for there were several partitions in the prospect. This land seemed to reach about fourteen or fifteen leagues in a range, and there came thence great flocks of fowls.

The *Bachelor's Delight* had actually been "pitchforked" out into the unexplored south Pacific by a gigantic tsunami wave generated by the great earthquake of Callao (Lima's port on the coast of Peru) in 1687. They kept steering south and headed back east to Chile. John Macmillan Brown in *The Riddle of the Pacific*[33] (from which

This finely-made basalt Rapa Nui statue is now in the British Museum.

Wafer is quoted) also quotes the navigator Dampier from his two volumes of voyages (London, 1699): "Captain Davis told me lately that... about five hundred leagues from Copaype on the coast of Chili in latitude 27° S. he saw a small sandy island just by him; and that they saw to the westward of it a long tract of pretty high land tending away to the north-west out of sight."

This mysterious land, "stretching to the north-west out of sight," was to be named "Davis Land" and it added to the popular belief that a great southern continent existed in the South Pacific. It was thirty-five years later that Easter Island was discovered on Easter Day, 1722, by the Dutch navigator Jacob Roggeveen. He was searching for Davis Land but all he could find was this tiny speck of an island. Davis Land, if it had ever existed, had disappeared! There is no large landmass near Easter Island, and it could not be the small sandy island described—there is hardly a bit of sandy beach on the entire island.

Suddenly we have the elements of a lost continent in the Pacific that is not thousands of years old, but was submerged only recently! Says Brown in *Riddle of the Pacific*:

> And yet no one who has visited Easter Island but must deny its identity with either of the lands that Davis saw, either the low, flat, sandy island or the long, partitioned range of land stretching away to the north-west over the horizon. If we have any respect for a sailor's evidence on a sailor's question, we must accept the existence of both lands in 1687 and their non-existence in 1722 when Roggewein [sic, usually spelled Roggeveen] sailed along the latitude in search of them. In other words, land of considerable extent, probably archipelagic, has gone down in the southeast Pacific away to the east of Easter Island. ...we cannot entirely reject his evidence that considerable tracts of land in the southeast Pacific have gone down. [33]

Whatever the truth may be about the existence of Davis Land, it is clear that the Easter Islanders had felt that they were alone in the world for quite some time by the time the first European explorers landed on the island. Yes, the islanders were very, very glad to see them! While large ships had come to the island in the past—from Tahiti, the Marquesas Islands or even South America—these ships had long ago stopped coming and the islanders felt abandoned. Had these voyages stopped only a few hundred years before the year 1722?

At the time of Captain Cook (c.1770) only Tonga had large oceangoing ships big enough to make the long journeys necessary to reach Hawaii or Easter Island. Other Polynesians such as those in Tahiti or the Marquesas had only smaller ships for inter-island navigation.

Roggeveen landed on an island inhabited by Polynesians, some of whom had light skin, red hair and looked like Europeans. He assessed the total population at about 5,000; they wore the simplest of clothes and lived in reed huts. Were some of the Easter Islanders natural redheads? Many of the statues had a red topknot on them to symbolize the tying of very long hair on the top of the head in a knot. This hairstyle is still used today by women around the world, and by male wandering holy men in India called sadhus. Vikings were also said to wear their long hair in this manner as well.

The first contact with the newcomers was unfortunately marked by a bloody incident. Roggeveen, at the head of 150 of his men, was alarmed at the excessive curiosity and outright thievery of the islanders. As they closed in on his men—apparently out of curiosity, rather than meaning harm—Roggeveen ordered his men to fire on the crowd, which they did, killing some of the natives. They dispersed, chiefly frightened by the noise, and later came back with gifts from the bounty of the island. They also offered their wives and daughters for sex. Easter Islanders certainly knew the value of fresh blood, and it became common in early contacts for women to swim out to arriving ships and board them, and then dance and have sex with the sailors. The men would wait on shore to steal what they could when the strangers arrived on the island to visit.

After this first meeting, the Dutch were allowed to roam freely throughout the island and saw for the first time the gigantic statues, which were apparently already toppled and lying on the ground. Some of the statues at the quarry of Rano Raraku were still standing, however. Roggeveen was unable to believe that the great figures could have been carved from rock, and thought they were made of clay and filled with stones. The islanders he found inhabited thatched huts and eked out a meager living from the windy land. They had bananas, fish and South American plants like yucca and sweet potato. Roggeveen described them as being heavily tattooed, with their earlobes pierced and hanging down to their shoulders.

An old print of long-eared man from Easter Island.

Easter Island had no further contact until almost fifty years later; in 1770 it was visited by two Spanish ships and then three years later by Captain Cook who wrote compassionately about the island—which he saw as arid and windswept—and the people, as poor as the earth on which they lived. Yet, he was amazed at the enormous statues, and awed by the implications for the civilization that had made them.

In 1786, a French expedition under the Comte de La Perouse stopped for a short time on the island and was quick to note the thieving propensities of the islanders. However, the Comte generously informed his crew that any clothing stolen would be replaced, and he even distributed presents among the eager population. After a short stay, the expedition sailed away, leaving the people of this strange, solitary region with pleasant memories.

More incidents followed, including the abduction of nearly a quarter of the population to work as slaves on the Peruvian guano islands of Chincho in 1862. The Chilean Navy arrived in 1870 for a geographical survey and then officially claimed the island for Chile in 1888.

The Strange Rongorongo Script

Little is known of this strange script which includes pictographic and geometric shapes; often the figures are of a birdman with his arms and legs in various positions. The script was written in the unusual boustrophedon pattern of writing where the successive lines are read ("as the ox plows") alternately left to right and then right to left. According to the *Encyclopedia Britannica* and Wikipedia, certain older forms of Greek, such as Doric Greek, were written in the boustrophedon pattern, as were Etruscan, Sabaean, Safaitic, Hittite and possibly Indus Valley writing such as that from Harrapa or Mohenjo Daro.

The writing was first reported by Eugene Eyraud, a French missionary on the island, in 1864. Eyraud sent some specimens to the Archbishop of Tahiti, since he recognized the significance of a written language being developed on a tiny, remote island in the South Pacific—it was against all accepted theories of the time. It

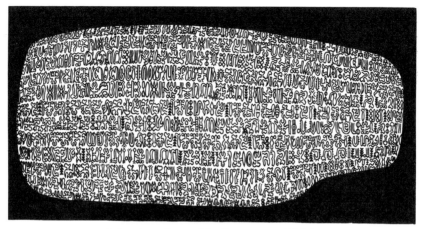

A drawing of one of the Rongorongo tablets.

was generally thought that only peoples with contact with different cultures could rise to a high level of civilization that included written communication. But here at Easter Island, it was then surmised, was a culture that had independently of the rest of the world developed writing, art, megalithic construction and more. The notion that a few hundred people should create all that without the aid of the outside world was astounding, and still is. This is still the accepted anthropological theory on the island's development.

At the time of Eyraud, a few of the island "royalty" were known to still be able to read the rongorongo tablets. These few people were quickly dying out, and some had been taken to the guano islands in Peru. The French author and archeologist Franis Maziere claimed in his book *The Mysteries of Easter Island*[32] that the last initiate of the rongorongo tablets died of leprosy and had once told him: "The first race invented the rongorongo writing. They wrote it in stone. Of the four parts of the world that were inhabited by the first race it is only in Asia that the writing still exists." The native was apparently speaking of the Indus Valley culture and the writing at Mohenjo Daro and other cities.

Said the native of the four places that the first race came from, "The island's first race was once to be found on two Polynesian Islands, in one part of Asia and one part of Africa where there are live volcanoes." Today, the only active volcanoes in Africa exist along the Great Rift Valley at the borders of Zaire, Rwanda and Burundi. There are two volcanoes, Nyiragongo and Nyamulgira.

The Polish researcher and author Igor Witkowski examines rongorongo writing in his book *Axis of the World*.[41] Witkowksi notes how Easter Island is one of the most remote and isolated places in the world and is "a very small island, the size of a not-too-large city district, almost devoid of resources, the very symbol of isolation, the inhabitants of which nonetheless 'created' a sophisticated system of writing. This is an unquestionable milestone in human development that, for instance, did not evolve in all of North America, despite a far longer period of time at the disposal of the people of that continent. Isn't something wrong with this picture?"

Witkowski says that according to legend:

> ...the first king, Hotu Matua, "brought with him 67 most precious tablets from their land of origin in the west. We can only suppose that they contained the "core" of their religious, and perhaps historical texts. It is also known that he brought the religion tied with the "bird-man" and with Make Make. It has generally nothing in common with the different variants of purely Polynesian beliefs, based on the cult of the Tane and Kon Tiki gods. All in all, presently we know of 26 various genuine artifacts covered with the Rongo Rongo hieroglyphs. They contain around 16,000 signs in all. Thus, contrary to appearances, there is quite a lot of material to study.
>
> ... This writing has a certain unique feature (characteristic exclusively to it, the Indus Valley script mentioned above, and to certain evolved variations used on a small scale on the Andean altiplano) which is namely a variation on a method of writing known as "bustrophedon," from the Greek meaning "like a plowing ox," i.e., alternately from left to right and from right to left. Although ancient writing from several cultures follows this pattern (where the first line is written from left to right, and the second line is written from

right to left, etc.) the scripts we have just mentioned have every other line inverted. After recording one line, the writer turned the tablet *upside down* and kept writing.

This similarity in writing gives us something that resembles a chain of traces from the Indus Valley (the capital of which was the city of Mohenjo Daro located in today's Pakistan), to Easter Island itself, and on to Tiahuanaco on the Andean altiplano—over 2,300 miles farther to the east. However, this presents a certain problem, namely that Mohenjo Daro and its Indus Valley civilization literally vanished from the archaeological scene around 1000 - 1200 years BC. This means that at the moment when Easter Island was inhabited, Mohenjo Daro's unique system of writing, its religion, etc., lived only in human memory. It had been gone for over two millennia (at least according to officially accepted theories)! It was simply one of the three oldest civilizations on our planet, along with the Sumerians and the empire of the pharaohs. Could Easter Island's culture reach that deep into the prehistory of mankind? Incidentally, these circumstances make the rongorongo script the oldest system of writing in use in historical times, for no less than four thousand years (although nobody can be sure if it was used continuously). In the case of this chain of traces, the truth seems so obscure, and so strange at the same time, that one has to ask himself a question: what really happened there, in the Pacific and the Indian Ocean, all those thousands of years ago? And last but not least: who were these people?[41]

Rongorongo has eluded translation, as have many ancient languages, but similarities have been noted, starting in the 1960s, between it and the undeciphered Indus Valley script. A Hungarian scholar named de Hevseg made a comparison of the writing on Easter Island and that found at the Indus Valley civilization cities of Mohenjo Daro and Harappa. These cities existed at about 1500 BC if not earlier, and the culture literally vanished about 1300 BC. That rongorongo writing is very similar, if not identical, to this ancient,

Indus Valley	Easter Island	Indus Valley	Easter Island	Indus Valley	Easter Island	Indus Valley	Easter Island
I	II	III	IV	V	VI	VII	VIII

A comparison of similar Indus Valley symbols with those on the Rongorongo tablets.

undeciphered language, is extraordinary. They are precisely on opposite sides of the earth: Mohenjo Daro is located at 27°23' North and about 69° East; Easter Island is at 27°08' South and 109°23' West. No other land area could be farther away from the Indus Valley cities as Easter Island.

The script at Mohenjo Daro is now believed to be related to ancient Dravidian; the fragments of this language still exist in southern India in the language of Tamil. An article in *Scientific American* (vol. 248, No. 3, March 1983) by Walter Fairservis, Jr. entitled *The Script of the Indus Valley Civilization* describes the author's attempts to decipher the writing. A fairly dry article, it makes no reference to the similarity with rongorongo script, but does say the author believes that a form of Dravidian was the spoken language of the valley. Significantly, Fairservis does say that there are 419 "signs" and that the script is neither alphabetic (as in Sanskrit or English) or logographic (as in Chinese) but rather logo-syllabic, meaning that some signs represent words and others serve purely for their symbolic value or sounds. The author says that other examples of such writing are Egyptian hieroglyphs, early Sumerian ideographs and modern Japanese. It has also been noted that some early Shang Dynasty symbols found in "oracle bone script" are also similar to rongorongo.

Were Sumerians and Indus Valley seafarers making transpacific voyages starting sometime around 3000 BC? As I have already stated, I believe so. Did they bring with them a complicated form of writing that came down through history on a small island on wooden tablets with rongorongo writing on them? What sort of cataclysm stopped the ancient seafarers from returning to tiny Easter Island in the middle of the South Pacific?

The islanders patiently waited year after year for the big ships to come back, but they never did. Or maybe some did. Polynesians on great epic voyages, such as the ones to Hawaii, must have managed to arrive at Easter Island. Pitcairn Island, the nearest island to the north, was uninhabited when the *Bounty* mutineers settled there, but there was evidence of statues on that island as well. Pitcairn may have been a stopover island between Tahiti and Easter Island.

365

Easter Island and the Cham

Easter Island is also associated with the Marquesas Islands, which are not the closest Polynesian Islands to it—and the big question is whether there was contact with South America. The mainstream says no, but scholars such as Thor Heyerdahl say yes!

The Lost Land of Hiva

Easter Island may have been first discovered over 5,000 years ago, though the oldest carbon dating is from about 300 AD. Most sites are near the ocean and would have been washed and destroyed by waves over the many hundreds and thousands of years that man may have been on the island. Did a cataclysmic tidal wave bury the statues in mud and muck around 300 AD? It is known that Polynesia was settled thousands of years before this—humans have been on Tonga since before 1000 BC according to the dating of Lapita pottery found there.

In his fascinating book *Mysteries of Easter Island*,[34] Francis Mazier explores the legends of the statues and the lost land of Hiva. Mazier was able to talk with a dying leper named Gabriel Veriveri who was allegedly the last initiate of the secrets of Easter Island. Said Veriveri to Maziere, "King Hotu-Matua came to Easter Island in two canoes. He landed at Hangaroa, but he gave the bay the name of Anakena, because it was the month of July." He notes that the winds from Polynesia to Easter Island blow in July and August.

"King Hotu-Matua's country was called Maori [in the Maori dialect of New Zealand, the word maori means "ordinary people"], and it was *on the continent of Hiva*. The place where he lived was called Marae-Rena... the king saw that the land was slowly sinking in the sea. The king therefore called all his people together, men, women, children and the aged, and he put them into two great canoes. The king saw that the disaster was at hand, and when the two canoes had reached the horizon he observed that the whole of the land had sunk, except for a small part called Maori."

Says Maziere:

The tradition is clear: there was a cataclysm; and it appears that this continent lay in the vast hinterland that

366

reaches to the Tuamotu archipelago (what is largely today French Polynesia) to the north-west of Easter Island.

Another legend, handed on by Aure Auviri Porotu, the last of the island's learned men, says this: 'Easter Island was a much larger country, but because of the sins of its people Uoke tipped it up and broke it with a crowbar...' Here too we have a cataclysm.

A more important point is that according to tradition Sala-y-Gomez, an islet some hundred miles from Easter Island, was formerly part of it, and its name, Motu Motiro Hiva, means 'small island near Hiva'.

We have three signs pointing to this cataclysm. Yet generally accepted geology does not acknowledge any vast upheaval in this part of the world, at least not within the period of human existence. However, there are two recently discovered facts that make the possibility of a sunken continent seem reasonable. When the American submarine *Nautilus* made her voyage round the world she called attention to the presence of an exceedingly lofty and still unidentified underwater peak close to Easter Island. And secondly, during his recent studies carried out for the Institute of Marine Resources and the University of California, Professor H.W. Menard not only speaks of an exceedingly important fracture-zone in the neighborhood of Easter Island, a zone parallel to that of the Marquesas archipelago, but also of the discovery of an immense bank or ridge of sediment.[34]

Maziere's book came out in 1965 in France, four years before the revolutionary geological theory of tectonic plates changed geology forever. It was certainly true then, and seemingly so today, that geologists generally do not acknowledge a cataclysmic upheaval (or downheaval as the case may be!) in this part of the world. Yet, Maziere sought to make sense out of the legends of the Easter Islanders. Were they just talk? Traditional anthropologists typically ignored the natives' own legends, and said that they came by way of Tahiti, possibly after some war, a few hundred years before Europeans first visited them. Such mysteries as rongorongo writing and the incredible stone platform at Vinapu are ignored.

Maziere favored the existence of an archipelago and even a long, thin "continent" extending south and north of Easter Island between the Marquesas Islands and the Galapagos Islands. Easter Island was the last peak (along with Sala-y-Gomez) of this former continent not "wrent beneath the sea by Uoke's crowbar."

> Apart from preserving the memory of these upheavals, tradition also states that King Hotu-Matua came from the west. Now in Easter Island on the Ahu A'Tiu there are seven statues and they are the only ones on the island that look towards the sea, and more exactly, the western sea. Their precise placing might well fix the area of the cataclysm, which would thus lie between the Marquesas and the Gambier islands. It seems probable that during one of those sub-oceanic upheavals still so frequent in the zone between the Cordillera of the Andes and the New Hebrides, an archipelago—I do not presume to say a continent—may have sunk or been altered. Moreover, according to Professor Metraux's findings, it seems possible that King Hotu-Matua's men emigrated from this area of the Marquesas; the reasons for believing this are based on linguistics—the use of Hiva is an example—and many points of ethnological agreement. The date of this migration, according to the genealogies that we collected, would be towards the end of the twelfth century.
>
> This settlement in no way excludes the possibility of other contacts at far earlier periods—contacts that we shall speak of later. [34]

Maziere then goes on to discuss the legend of seven explorers sent out to find "the navel of the world" who were expected to return and guide the two giant canoes to safety on Rapa Nui. He finds it odd that in the Marquesas, where some of the islands actually have the name of Hiva in them, there is really no legend of a sunken continent. He then says that the footless, handless old leper Veriveri told him of a legend he had learned that the island was inhabited already when Hotu-Matua came by "very big men, but not giants, who lived on the island well before the coming of Hotu-Matua."

It seems very clear to me that this is a legend based on a great deal of analogy and mythos. It also seems to have some basis in fact. There is one level of Hiva being an allegory for a spirit world where one goes upon transition, much as that of Hawaiki. On the other hand, the legend seems to be of a physical place, an ancient homeland that went down in a catastrophe. Is this event then the actual sinking of some island mass many thousands of years ago? Or, rather, is it the final subsidence, perhaps only a few thousand years ago, of the last large area that remained above the surface? Maziere seems to think that the last remnants of this land, called Davis Land, sank as late as the 1600s. In his book he proposed a long landmass that stretched from Easter Island to the Baja California Peninsula in Mexico.

Statues Walking

The theory that the statues had been moved to their places by the use of wooden rollers or sleds has some problems: one is that the island is so rocky, it would have been impossible to roll any logs across it, with or without statues on them.

Jean-Michel Schwartz says in his 1975 book *The Mysteries of Easter Island* that he believes the statues were not moved by wooden rollers or sleds but rather by using ropes around the statues which "walked" the statues in the same way as one might walk a refrigerator: by tilting it first to one side, shifting the airborne portion forward, and setting it down again. By this method, the statues would truly walk in a waddle fashion around the island.

Later, a Czech mechanical engineer named Pavel recreated this method along with Thor Heyerdahl. With twenty other men, they tied ropes around a statue and leaned it from side to side while pulling it forward with the rope, a slight variation on Schwartz's method. The method worked, but was excruciatingly slow. It is an ingenious theory which takes into account the legends of the walking statues, but was it the actual method used?

National Geographic featured the "walk-like-a-refrigerator" theory as a major story in their July 2012 issue. The article, with the headline "Easter Island, The Riddle of the Moving Statues" mentioned the various mundane theories, although they omit any reference to Schwartz, who first wrote about his theory in French in 1971, with his book published in English by Avon Paperbacks in 1975.

National Geographic gives the following timeline of "theories" on how the statues were moved: 1) Thor Heyerdahl and crew move a statue on a crude wooden sled pulled by a rope (1955); 2) the William Mulloy theory of rocking a statue forward on its belly in a basic cradle and frame above it with ropes (1970); 3) Pavel's standing up with rope twist and turn theory (1986); 4) the theory of Charles Love of wooden rollers and sled (1987); 5) Jo Anne Van Tilburg's sled pulled over a wooden ladder matrix (1998); and finally, 6) the 2011 demonstration by Terry Hunt and Carl Lippo of a newer version of the "walk-like-a-refrigerator" theory which incorporates their unique "D-shaped" patterns that the tall moai made as they walked it with ropes.

In 2011, the team of 18 moved a ten-foot-high statue weighing about five tons several hundred yards during their test of their method. Hunt and Lippo theorized that only three teams of rope managers were needed to move the statues: two up front to twist and manipulate the statues from side to side in the "D-shape" and one group in the back to keep the statue stable. The

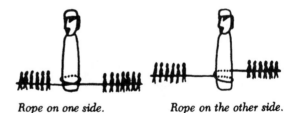

Rope on one side.   *Rope on the other side.*

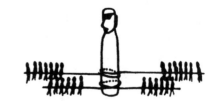

Double system of ropes.

The system of "walking" a statue with ropes.

National Geographic issue featured a team of islanders maneuvering a statue in this manner.

Essentially, we can put modern archeologists' explanations of the moving of the statues into two categories: 1) moving the statues on their backs or stomachs on sleds or 2) moving them while they are standing up like a refrigerator. All the proposals are clearly based on these two schools of thought and Thor Heyerdahl is a leader in both, having jumped ship to the Schwartz-Pavel theory in the early 1980s.

But clearly, all the early investigators, when confronted with the problem of moving five-ton statues all over the island (not just a few hundred yards) saw that moving them on some sort of sled on their backs and bellies would have been the easiest way to do it when you consider the crude methods that we would suppose they had to use. So, dragging them downhill and across fields on a slick rainy day on sleds seemed like something that could have been achieved on a good day with a bunch of geniuses in control and lots of manpower to put energy into the project. The island is very rocky so roads and cleared pathways would have to have been made.

But, this theory didn't really jibe with what the Rapa Nui folk said about their history. They said that the "statues walked." They weren't saying the statues slid into place and then got stood up... they were saying that they walked. It is worth noting that mainstream archeologists say this was occurring only a few hundred years before contact, so the memory should be fresh in their minds, historically speaking.

The "walk-like-a-refrigerator" theory is really the theory to go for, and it explains the walking part. Also, the Mulloy theory of rocking the statues did not work for the taller statues which were very tall and thin. Such 30-foot-tall statues being walked slowly around the island with ropes is certainly possible, but it would be slow going. It would be faster to drag them on sleds. Evidence indicates that they were completely finished, with all decorations, including ankh-like designs on their backs, before they left the quarry.

The questions that naturally come up when the moon is rising and the snow is falling off the pine trees are: Why are these people even trying to move gigantic statues that weigh at least five tons and are more typically 20 to 40 tons? Were they such superb engineers and architects that after building all sorts of other moments (maybe on other islands?) they just thought they would carve up a volcanic crater into hundreds of giant statues—and then move about a third of them around the island to "protect" it from some further cataclysms that had already devastated the island earlier?

On our 2013 visit, our group stood on a trail on a slope of the volcano where a dozen moai stood twenty feet tall around us, buried up to their waists or chests. One moai that Heyerdahl excavated in 1956 has a masted ship on its stomach. Heyerdahl believed that this was an ancient sailing ship used by explorers who came from Peru. Others say that the ship is an early carving of a European ship that visited the island. The only problem with this explanation is that the carving was only discovered after Heyerdahl had dug the soil around it away. It seems likely that the several feet of soil that had amassed over the drawing would have taken hundreds of years to accumulate.

The statues seem originally to have been standing on the slope just as they are found today and were typically forty to fifty feet tall. Indeed, some stood as tall as a seven-story building, and the largest, still in the quarry, was more than seventy feet tall. Therefore, it would seem that the carving of the ship on the belly of one of the statues would be far older than the discovery of the island in 1722. The statue itself must be centuries older than that.

I was immediately struck by the fact that the crater and the statues around it were quite different from the moais and ruins around the rest of the island. While the moais that were erected on platforms around the edge of the island were put there to protect the island, the purpose of these statues around the crater was something else. Many researchers believe that these statues around the crater were just waiting to be moved out, to "walk" as it were, to their ahu-platform somewhere on the island. Looking around, I thought not.

Something else that immediately came to my attention as I wondered at the gigantic statues around me, were the large lichen spots on all of them. Lichen eats living rock and grows very slowly—fractions of an inch over hundreds of years. Ages of rocks are sometimes estimated by how large the lichen patches on them are. A large lichen patch would suggest that these statues were thousands of years old. In an effort to check this out, I measured lichen patches on uncut rock. They were only slightly larger than those on the statues themselves.

While at the ancient ceremonial center of Orongo I scanned the cliffs to the south along the Rano Kau volcano for the elusive ahu and statues of Rikiriki ("very small, very little" in Rapa Nuian). In 1889, William Judah Thomson visited Easter Island for the Smithsonian Institution and wrote in the paper published by the institute in 1891 (called *Te Pito Te Henua, or Easter Island*) that Ahu Rikiriki was a statue at the extreme southwest end of the island which was placed midway between the sea and the top—on the face of a perpendicular cliff nearly 1,000 feet high. Thomson stated that 16 small statues were lying on this platform and seemed to be in excellent condition. "We could find no way of reaching the narrow ledge upon which this platform stands. No roads lead down from the top; it cannot be approached from either side, and from below it is a straight up and down wall against which the sea dashes continually. It is hardly probable that the images were lowered from the top by ropes, and the natural conclusion is, that a roadway once existed…"

That statues had "walked" or even rolled to such a position seems incredible. Yet, more mysteriously, no trace of this platform or the statues has been found since, although the British traveler Katherine Routledge reported in 1919 that the statues were then lying at the floor of the cliff, presumably in the water. However, many researchers now question whether this remarkable ahu ever existed.

The Shaivites and the Bird Men

One thing that archeologists have grappled with is the purpose of the red topknots that were separately quarried and then placed on top of some of the statues. Not all of the statues had these topknots, made from a red volcanic tuff that is lighter and easier to carve than the granite that makes up most of the statues. The statues that are found on the slopes of Rano Raraku never had a red topknot on their heads, only statues that had been moved from the quarries and walked to their spots on the coast where they would sit on a stone platform and face inland. These statues had the red topknots on them, as well as inlaid eyes of obsidian and ivory from which the powerful mana (magical force) could emanate and keep the island from

A Khmer statue of Shiva with his hair in a topknot.

sinking like the homeland of Hiva. It was these statues that got this special topknot. What was the importance of the red topknot? Was it the hairstyle that the men in ancient ships had worn? Was the red color of importance? We do not really see this with other statues in Polynesia or South America. However, with the Olmecs we do have statues that show men, sometimes in a quizuo position, that have very long hair tied in a big bun on the top of their heads.

No, they are not women who have tied their hair in a bun; these are men who chose to wear their hair long, probably for a religious-spiritual reason. In many ancient cultures it was common for men to have long hair, though in more advanced cultures this hair was cut into various styles and lengths and often worn beneath a turban or other elaborate head gear.

It was not that common in the Hindu world for men to have long hair and tie that it into a big bundle on the very top of their heads. As has been noted, most male Hindus in ancient times wore a tuft of hair on the back of their head called a sikha, and the rest of their head was shaved. But there is one sect of Hinduism whose followers wear their hair up, and that form of Hinduism is called Shaivism. And it is associated with the Cham.

Says Wikipedia:

> Shaivism or Shivaism is one of the major branches of Sanathan Dharma (Hinduism), revering Shiva as the Supreme Being. Shiva is sometimes depicted as the fierce god Bhairava. Followers of Shaivism are called "Shaivas," "Saivas," "Shaivites," or "Saivarkal." They believe that Shiva is All and in all, the creator, preserver, destroyer, revealer and concealer of all that is. Shaivism, like some of the other forms of Hinduism, spread to other parts of Southeast Asia, including Java, Bali, and parts of the Southeast Asian continent, including Cambodia.
>
> Saivists are more attracted to asceticism than adherents of other Hindu sects and may be found wandering in Nepal and India with ashen faces performing self-purification rituals. They worship in the temple and practice yoga, striving to be one with Shiva within. Within Hinduism an estimated 252 million or 26.6% followers are Shaivites.

The Shaivites often feature the third eye as part of their imagery and the depiction of Shiva with his long hair in a topknot and a third eye in his forehead is very common. This is a common theme in Champa art and essentially any Shaivite who is wearing his hair in this manner is imitating the god Shiva. Shaivites are allowed to engage in sex with very little restriction. There is no call for celibacy as there is for Buddhist monks or nuns, for instance.

The god Shiva also carries a trident. He smokes marijuana and has tantric sex with goddesses. In a similar way Shaivites also practice yoga, wear their long hair in a topknot, sometimes put ash on their faces and carry a trident with them—even on the remote mountainsides of the Himalayas. At some Shaivite shrines in the Himalayas, such as the one near the sacred mountain Gauri Shankar

375

Statues on a platform with topknots at Anakena Beach.

in Nepal, hundreds of tridents are left in enclosed shrines as they complete their Shaivite pilgrimage. Don't we view the trident as a symbol of gods like Neptune and the sea?

So is Shiva also a god of the sea, the patron of sailors who wear long hair in topknots and carry a trident for fishing? It would seem so. As the Wikipedia entry notes, Shaivites were notable in the area that I am calling the Cham Empire: Java, Bali and Cambodia. We can add Vietnam and Sumatra to that list, and probably such islands as Borneo, Sulawesi and the Sulu Islands of the southern Philippines.

The question now is: are the statues at Easter Island meant to be statues of longhaired Shaivites who wear their hair in a topknot? It would also be interesting to speculate that the red topknot that was to be placed on the head of the grey granite statues symbolized red hair. If this was the case we can imagine red-haired Vikings with their hair tied up on top of their heads. As noted above, when Roggeveen landed on Easter Island in 1722, he found that some of the population looked European with red hair and light skin.

It may just be a coincidence that the stone topknots for the Easter

Island statues was made of a red volcanic tuff, as most of the Cham sailors were likely to have dark black hair. Still, it was and still is popular for Egyptians and some Hindus (and Muslims) to die their hair red with the common herb known as henna. Muslims, for some unknown reason, are supposed to die their beards red after they have made the pilgrimage to Mecca. It is quite common to see older men in Pakistan, Afghanistan and India (which has a significant Islamic population) who have dyed their beards red.

Also, a high percentage of the Melanesian population of New Ireland, a large island just east of New Guinea which I visited in 1997, has sandy red hair. Anthropologists tend to say that this red hair is a result of malnutrition but when I was on New Ireland I noticed many children with this sandy red and kinky hair and they did not seem to be undernourished to me. Another explanation for the redheads of New Ireland that I was given was the theory that during WWII a number of red-haired British and Australian soldiers were stationed on the island. Is the real explanation that red-haired Cham Shaivites were stopping at the island?

Red-haired mummies have been found along the coast of Peru and are prevalent in the necropolises around Paracas and Nazca. Many of these red-haired skeletons also have elongated crania, that is, they are coneheads. Many of the statues at Easter Island also seem to depict men with elongated heads. When fully completed, an Easter Island statue was a man with an elongated head with a red topknot placed in the top of the head. Inlaid eyes were made for the statue and some statues have what appears to be a girdle for the penis and testicles that is tied in the form of an Egyptian ankh on the

An Indus Valley seal of Shiva in a yoga position.

lower back.

It would seem that the statues that were moved from the quarry and placed along the coast of the island were effigies of Shaivite-Egyptian-Cham sailors who were making the round-trip voyage from India and Southeast Asia to Mexico and Peru and then returning via Easter Island, Tahiti and Tonga.

Certainly, someone was coming to Easter Island via ship and possibly by air as well. They had with them their power tools, diamond saws and iron chisels. They could create the great statues and make the fine cuts at the wall of Vinapu, which we will discuss next. At some point contact between Easter Island and Peru—and even with Tahiti—stopped circa 900 AD. Was it because of the collapse of the Cham Empire in Southeast Asia starting in 650 AD?

The Megallithic Wall of Vinapu

When Jacques Cousteau came to Easter Island, he performed several important investigations. One was diving around the island searching for statues and other possible artifacts in the ocean. The presence of statues in the ocean, he believed, would prove the theory that the statues had been moved around the island using rafts. He found none. The only unusual feature he discovered were underwater tunnels, which he theorized to be volcanic in origin.

He mentioned that the oldest carbon date on the island is 690 AD at a "well developed site" indicating actual habitation must be older. He also noted the songs of the island were "reminiscent of the Epic songs of India and China," and that the islanders practiced cremation of the dead until wood became too scarce. Other ancient cultures that cremated the dead were Hindus, Buddhists, Atonists of Egypt, and Nestorian Christians. Shaivites also practiced cremation like most Hindus.

On one morning of our 2013 trip, our group took the hotel van to the famous stone ruins of Vinapu, at the end of the airport's huge airstrip, built long enough to land the space shuttle in case of an emergency. The Vinapu site to me is a key clue in unraveling the mystery of Easter Island.

Vinapu consists of a partially-destroyed wall with megalithic

378

construction that is basically unique on the island, but not unique in the world. The main wall consists of enormous slabs very skillfully laid. I stood in front of the wall and was genuinely amazed at the construction which was not just similar, but identical, to that at Cuzco, Machu Picchu, Sacsayhuaman, Pisac and Ollantaytambo in the high Andes of Peru.

Like those constructions, the wall at Vinapu is perfectly fitted together with irregularly-shaped stones, and has rounded edges, and small triangular stones filling in gaps. One would describe the construction in the Andes the same way: polygonal blocks that were smoothed and rounded, perfectly cut and fitted together, with small keystones placed in the wall to help make it earthquake proof. It is the most sophisticated construction technique in the world, essentially unduplicated today.

It is important to note that no keystone cuts are to be observed at Vinapu. But this is not surprising because this technique of securing the construction requires molten metal to be poured into the cuts. Since Easter Island is not a mining site (except for obsidian) the building of Vinapu was done with precision tools but did not use

The finely-worked megalithic wall Vinapu on the southeast coast of Rapa Nui.

metal clamps.

It is often said that the construction at Vinapu is identical to that at Tiwanaku, although Tiwanaku lacks the pillowed walls, which are mainly found around Cuzco. However, pillowed or rounded walls can be found at the ruins of Sillustani and Cutimbo, both on mesas—flat-topped mountains—near Lake Titicaca, which are usually said to be of Tiwanaku origin.

Probably the confusion arises from the general consensus that Tiwanaku is of pre-Incan construction and is thousands of years old. The massive ruins found in Peru, many in the vicinity of Cuzco, a still-vibrant city, are usually said by academics to have been built by the Incas a few hundred years ago. That the ruins at Vinapu on Easter Island are identical in construction then raises the unlikely notion that the Incas built the platform.

The answer is simpler than might be thought. While the Incas did indeed construct large cities and were excellent stonemasons, their construction is with small rectangular blocks that are perfectly fitted together. This construction can be seen in Cuzco and elsewhere on top of the earlier and larger polygonal construction. The construction that I am speaking about, found at Easter Island and the Peruvian Andes around Cuzco—both places called "the navel of the world" (coincidentally?)—are apparently built by the same mysterious people, and are pre-Incan. Considering the lichen growth on the wall at Vinapu, I would venture to say they lived thousands of years ago.

The Incas undoubtedly inhabited those ancient structures high in the Andes. They are still inhabited today, but not by the Incas. Construction of this type is so solid it will easily outlast most empires and civilizations. When a wandering culture happens to discover the gigantic walls of an uninhabited city still standing, it seems only natural to move in, put a roof over the structures, and call them home. This, say many archaeologists, especially Peruvian ones, is what happened with the Incas. The many phases of construction are obvious, and the most superior is identical to the wall at Vinapu and is the oldest.

I walked around the wall and examined the construction. It

380

was not until I had looked at each block carefully that I noticed something that confirmed my suspicions about the builders of this wonderful, ancient structure. At Ollantaytambo, Sillustani, Cuzco and other sites in the Andes, many of the large polygonal blocks have strange knobs on them, the function of which has never been understood. Here, on the southeast corner of the wall was a knob, just like the ones in the Andes! The corner, too, was rounded, and in fact, so was the entire face of the wall, again just like in the Andes.

The upper levels of the platform and a portion of the center had been torn down. It was obvious that it had been used as a moai platform at one time, and one moai was toppled over on the top. The stones around the statue were of cruder construction, identical to that on the rest of the island. I concluded, as I sat in the grass and looked at the wall, that it was much older than the rest of the platforms on the island, and was not originally constructed to be an ahu-platform for a moai. What then was its purpose?

I surmised that Vinapu was part of the original purpose of Easter Island, along with the gigantic statues in Rano Raraku and the ceremonial site there. The other moais and platforms were built later, possibly in an effort to call back the ancients who had abandoned the island, or just to protect the island as legend said.

I thought back to the legends of the Rama Empire. Rongorongo writing has been shown to be extremely similar to Indus Valley writing found at the ancient Rama Empire cities of Mohenjo Daro, Harappa, and Lothal. The ancient city of Dwarka—where Krishna is said to be from—is under water off the coast of Gujarat.

Shaivism is thought to go back to the Harappan culture, circa 2500 BC, which is famous for its finely made brick cities and ceramic seals which often feature its mysterious script. The Champa in Vietnam were also known for their excellent brickwork (as I discussed in chapter one). One of the ceramic seals apparently depicts Shiva in a yoga posture with an elephant, a tiger, a long-horned bull and a rhinoceros. Archeologists believe that this seal is evidence that Shaivism is at least 4,500 years old.

The Rapa Nui legends share with Sanskrit the same word for supernatural mental powers: "mana." Meanwhile we have the *Ramayana* tales of fantastic battles, flying machines and a technology and culture that in some ways surpasses our own. Just as we do today, these cultures had the ability to travel all over the world, by air and by sea. It seems likely, therefore, that they did so. Were the last visitors to Easter Island the Hindu Shaivites that we call the Cham?

Vimanas were said to take off and land vertically, as a hovercraft, zeppelin or "flying saucer" might. Whether this is true, I do not know. However, I thought of a worldwide network of vimana landing pads stretching from ancient India to the massive platform of Baalbek in Lebanon (here are found the largest cut blocks of stone in the world, estimated to weigh 1,000 tons or more) to Abydos in Egypt to Sacsayhuaman in Peru, to, (dare I say?) Easter Island! Could the platform at Vinapu be what is left of an ancient vimana landing pad? The idea seemed incredible! The wall even faces Peru...

The Museum in Hanga Roa

Our last stop was the archeological museum in the main town of Hanga Roa. Our group made a walk to the museum at the far end of town. We bought our tickets trailed in to look at the various exhibits in the two-room, one-floor museum.

I noted on a geological map of the island that the area of the strong magnetic disturbance at the Rano Aroi volcano was a basalt formation. This made sense since basalt becomes permanently magnetized by the earth's magnetic field as it cools. I also saw a perfectly round stone ball, about the size of softball, in a glass display case with some other stone artifacts. The sign said that they did not know what it was for. Was it a stone hammer?

I also noted a very Negroid head found in 1973 at Rano Raraku titled a "Moai Maea" head. It was much smaller than most moai, and its features were indeed very different and African looking, similar to the Olmec heads found in Mexico. There was also an unusual statue of a woman with breasts and an extremely long head. Was she some sort of female conehead? Were the big statues in the quarry also figures of coneheads? It would seem so. There was also an alien-looking head with round eyes and only two holes for a nose that was excavated somewhere on the island in 1960 but not put on display at the museum until about 2006.

Also interesting were the *kava kava* statues. These are small wooden carvings, hundreds of years old, and traditionally depict what appears to be an emaciated man, a virtual living skeleton. In island legend, the king was walking one night on the island and saw

The strange long-headed female statue at the museum in Hanga Roa.

two kava kava men lying on the ground in a vision. They appeared to the king just as they are drawn today. A kava kava is generally said to be a kind of spirit. They appeared to me to be starving sailors or even islanders. Crossing the Pacific can be a difficult ordeal, and living on Easter Island was probably difficult as well. With a sustained annual arrival of a fleet of ships, coming from Peru, or from Tahiti for that matter, the island could survive and continue its statue carving and other activities such as those that involve the birdmen and the annual race to retrieve a bird's egg at Orongo.

But when the wide movement of ships across the Pacific—especially those returning to Southeast Asia from Peru—stopped,

the economy and culture of Easter Island became isolated and crashed. A war between the "short ears" and "long ears" took place and then eventually the age of European discovery came about that eventually brought Easter Island back onto the maps of the world.

Looking at the shrunken, almost mutated figures, I could not help but think that they bore a striking resemblance to someone dying of radiation sickness. I was then reminded of the startling tales of nuclear war in the *Mahabharata*, the ancient Dravidian text of pre-Aryan India. With the possible link to the Rama Empire through rongorongo writing, the platform at Vinapu and even Indo-Dravidian words like "mana," was it possible that this was some sort of bizarre memory of radiation victims from that global war of pre-history? Or, more in line with Thor Heyerdahl's

A kava kava statue.

more mainstream theory of transoceanic cultures making frequent yet dangerous trading trips across the Pacific and Indian Oceans, was this some starved sailor coming from Peru or Tahiti who had not seen an island for some months?

As a group, we watched the sunset at Ahu Tahai, a slow orange glow fading into the starry night. The four moai on their ahu platform were silhouetted against the golden glow. Later, I sat on the steps of the hotel and looked up at the constellations.

To the south was the Southern Cross, pointing the way to Antarctica, the next stop directly south. Had ancient voyagers stopped at Easter Island on their way to the lands of the pole? Someone had apparently mapped that continent in prehistory, as evidenced by the Piri Reis map now in the Topkapi Museum in Istanbul.

Easter Island undeniably was a culture in decline at the time of European discovery. When the first explorers reached the island the natives were living in reed huts. Yet, someone had constructed megalithic stone blocks of incredible perfection as witnessed at Vinapu. Was the precision stonework at Vinapu the result of power tools as some surmise were used at Tiwanaku and Puma Punku? Was the written language of the Rama Empire the same written language called rongorongo? It seemed fantastic!

What of the great cataclysm that had affected Rapa Nui? Had some tsunami hit the island, burying the statues in many meters of mud and muck? Had it struck thousands of years ago, or only a few hundred years ago?

It seems that Easter Island had two cataclysms. One was a natural disaster that halted the quarrying of the statues at Rano Raraku. The other was a cultural disaster marked by the sudden halt of large ships arriving on the island and going elsewhere, either to Tahiti or Southeast Asia. When large ships arrived on the island there would have been festivals that included sex with the sailors to bring new blood into the island gene pool plus there would have been opportunities for men and women to leave the island and go elsewhere. Similarly, sometimes one or more of the ship's crew might stay on the island to serve as a priest, architect or physician.

Once the islanders became isolated they tried to preserve their history by the continual copying of the Rongorongo tablets, yet most of their history was irretrievably lost. All that we get today are confusing tales of Hiva and a world that is gone, or the strange tale of the war of the long ears and the short ears. It should be pointed out here that Buddha and Shiva are typically depicted as having very long ear lobes, particularly in the case of Buddha. The Inca royalty were also depicted as having very long ear lobes. This was also the style of the Cham.

Had Easter Island first been colonized by Sumerians returning from South America? Did the Shang, along with the Cham, arrive at Easter Island by 1000 BC? As long as the Cham were returning from South America via Easter Island and Polynesia, Easter Island would have visitors. Did Easter Island become isolated around 700 AD when the Cham empire began to collapse in Southeast Asia?

As waves washed onto the shore near the small port of Hanga Roa, I wondered how long the island had been isolated. When one is on Rapa Nui, there is a feeling that things are incredibly ancient. Easter Island must have been hit by a number of typhoons and tsunamis in its thousands of years, plus perhaps earthquakes that made the island much smaller than it had originally been. Rapa Nui was an island of enduring mysteries, but I felt that the connection with Shaivites and the Cham was strong.

Chapter Ten

THE CHAM AND
THE GRAND CANYON

In Xanadu did Kubla Khan
A stately pleasure dome decree
Where Alph, the sacred river, ran
Through caverns measureless to man
Down to a sunless sea.
—Samuel Taylor Coleridge, *Kubla Khan*

Back at my home in Arizona I thought about my recent journeys in search of the Cham. As I reflected on the multitude of evidence for the Cham to have visited the Americas, I realized that Arizona and New Mexico held evidence of the Cham as well.

As I write in my book *Lost Cities & Ancient Mysteries of the Southwest*[73] there is a ghost town in western New Mexico called Mogollon. The ghost town is along the west side of Mogollon Mountain, a broad peak over 10,000 feet high. Mogollon Mountain is named after the governor of the Spanish colony of Nuevo Mexico in the early 1700s, Don-Juan Ignacio Flores Mogollon. The proper Spanish pronunciation of Mogollon is "moh-goh-YOHN" but in local usage it is often said "muggy-YON."

In 1870, when the New Mexico and Arizona Territories were part of the United States, a US Army sergeant named James Cooney scouted in the area and discovered a rich vein of silver near Mogollon Mountain. Cooney kept his find a secret until he finished his military service and then returned to stake his claim and open his silver mine.

His efforts eventually made him rich and created a small mining town named Mogollon deep in the canyons of this remote part of New Mexico, literally straddling the Continental Divide.

EXPLORATIONS IN GRAND CANYON

Mysteries of Immense Rich Cavern Being Brought to Light.

JORDAN IS ENTHUSED

Remarkable Finds Indicate Ancient People Migrated From Orient.

The latest news of the progress of the explorations of what is now regarded by scientists as not only the oldest archaeological discovery in the United States, but one of the most valuable in the world, which was mentioned some time ago in the Gazette, was brought to the city yesterday by G. E. Kinkaid, the explorer who found the great underground citadel of the Grand Canyon during a trip from Green river, Wyoming, down the Colorado, in a wooden boat, to Yuma, several months ago. According to the story related yesterday to the Gazette by Mr. Kinkaid, the archaeologists of the Smithsonian Institute, which is financing the explorations, have made discoveries which almost conclusively prove that the race which inhabited this mysterious cavern, hewn in solid rock by human hands, was of oriental origin, possibly from Egypt, tracing back to Ramses. If their theories are borne out by the translation of the tablets engraved with hieroglyphics, the mystery of the prehistoric peoples of North America, their ancient arts, who they were and whence they came, will be solved. Egypt and the Nile, and Arizona and the Colorado will be linked by a historical chain running back to ages which staggers the wildest fancy of the fictionist.

A Thorough Investigation.

Under the direction of Prof. S. A. Jordan, the Smithsonian Institute is now prosecuting the most thorough explorations, which will be continued until the last link in the chain is forged. Nearly a mile underground, about 1480 feet below the surface, the long main

fect ventilation of the cavern, the steady draught that blows through, indicates that it has another outlet to the surface.

Mr. Kinkaid's Report.

Mr. Kinkaid was the first white child born in Idaho and has been an explorer and hunter all his life, thirty years having been in the service of the Smithsonian Institute. Even briefly recounted, his history sounds fabulous, almost grotesque.

"First, I would impress that the cavern is nearly inaccessible. The entrance is 1486 feet down the sheer canyon wall. It is located on government land and no visitor will be allowed there under penalty of trespass. The scientists wish to work unmolested, without fear of the archaeological discoveries being disturbed by curio or relic hunters. A trip there would be fruitless, and the visitor would be sent on his way. The story of how I found the cavern has been related, but in a paragraph: I was journeying down the Colorado river in a boat, alone, looking for mineral. Some forty-two miles up the river from the El Tovar Crystal canyon I saw on the east wall, stains in the sedimentary formation about 2000 feet above the river bed. There was no trail to this point, but I finally reached it with great difficulty. Above a shelf which hid it from view from the river, was the mouth of the cave. There are steps leading from this entrance some thirty yards to what was, at the time the cavern was inhabited, the level of the river. When I saw the chisel marks on the wall inside the entrance, I became interested, secured my gun and went in. During that trip I went back several hundred feet along the main passage, till I came to the crypt in which I discovered the mummies. One of these I stood up and photographed by flashlight. I gathered a number of relics, which I carried down the Colorado to Yuma, from whence I shipped them to Washington with details of the discovery. Following this, the explorations were undertaken.

The Passages.

"The main passageway is about 12 feet wide, narrowing to 9 feet toward the farther end. About 57 feet from the entrance, the first side-passages branch off to the right and left, along which, on both sides, are a number of rooms about the size of ordinary living rooms of today, though some are 30 or 40 feet square. These are entered by oval-shaped doors and are ventilated by round air spaces through the walls into the passages. The walls are about 3 feet 6 inches in thickness. The passages are chiseled or hewn as straight as could be laid out by an engineer. The ceilings of many of the passages converge to a center. The side passages near the entrance run at a sharp angle from the main hall, but toward the rear they gradually reach a right angle in direction.

The Shrine.

"Over a hundred feet from the entrance is the cross-hall, several hundred feet long, in which was found the idol, or image, of the people's god, sitting cross-legged, with a lotus flower or lily in each hand. The cast of the

The original story as it appeared in the Phoenix Gazette.

Mogollon is now basically a ghost town, though some signs of genuine human life can be seen around the few scattered cabins. There are still a few residents, and the town supposedly hosts an art fair on weekends.

Spreading out from Mogollon Mountain is the famous Mogollon Rim. This precipitous ridge of cliffs, canyons, craggy granite mountains and plentiful water is in many ways the defining landmark of the state of Arizona, running from southeast Arizona past Flagstaff. It was my intention to drive from Mogollon Mountain northwest along the Mogollon Rim to the Hopi Mesas and on to the Grand Canyon. As Jennifer and I headed out back in 2008, my quest was to research a story about Egyptians in the Grand Canyon—a story of a legendary vault of treasures and mummies that had been revealed in a newspaper article in 1909, and, I had begun to suspect, a story that had long been known but kept secret by the ancient and mysterious Hopis. This secret repository in the Grand Canyon seems to me now to be a place where Cham treasures were stored after the Cham had come to the Grand Canyon, Chaco Canyon and the Four Corners Area of Arizona and New Mexico.

Why was this treasure never heard of again? It is a mystery that strikes deep into the golden heart of the lost cities of the Southwest: treasure found in man-made caves at a secret location in the Grand Canyon, a secret society that protects this treasure, and the ultimate cover-up of an astounding archeological find. Even today, no clear answers have emerged. Was the newspaper story an elaborate hoax? Was it a confused tale of a more mundane discovery? The article, as you will see, mentions that the statues did not look so much like Egyptian statues as statues from Tibet! Is it that the artifacts that were discovered were actually Cham artifacts that displayed a mixture of Hindu, Buddhist and Egyptian cultures and iconography? Indeed, the statuary and weaponry of the Cham would have a certain Tibetan look to them.

The Egyptian City of the Grand Canyon Newspaper Story

Was it the Cham who brought these "Egyptian" artifacts to Arizona? Could they have left an Egyptian-type tomb in the Grand

Canyon, something similar to those found cut into the rock in the Valley of Kings near Luxor, Egypt? An article published on the front page of the *Phoenix Gazette* on April 5,1909 claimed that just such an Egyptian-like rock-cut cave was found!

While many mummies have been found in Egypt, very few were in pyramids—and those that were dated from the later historical periods. The older pyramids dating from the early dynasties (or before!) show no signs of funerary use. Mummies in Egypt are most often found in rock-cut tombs in desert canyons. The tombs often feature tunnels going deep underground with various rooms and passageways along the way. Multiple mummies are often found in one tomb, and the crypts of the wealthy and royalty were filled with precious items and everyday necessities to ease the dead person's continued existence in the afterlife.

According to the article in the 1909 *Phoenix Gazette*, a necropolis of mummies and artifacts similar to an Egyptian tomb was found in the Grand Canyon! An explorer named G. E. Kinkaid apparently discovered a series of catacombs complete with statues, swords, vessels and mummies in 1908 (the exact date of the discovery is not given). As we shall see, Kinkaid may not have been the first explorer to have seen this "cave." The account of Kinkaid's adventure was reproduced as a chapter entitled "Citadel of the Grand Canyon" in Joseph Miller's 1962 book *Arizona Cavalcade*.

The *Phoenix Gazette* article, dated April 5, 1909, starts with four headlines, and then continues through a most amazing account. The story is quoted below in full:

EXPLORATIONS IN GRAND CANYON
Mysteries of Immense Rich
Cavern Being Brought to Light
JORDAN IS ENTHUSED
Remarkable Finds Indicate
Ancient People Migrated from Orient

The latest news of the progress of the explorations of what is now regarded by scientists as not only the oldest archaeological discovery in the United States, but one of the most valuable in the world, which was mentioned some time ago in the *Gazette,* was brought to the city by G. E. Kinkaid, the explorer who found this great underground citadel of the Grand Canyon during a trip from Green River, Wyoming, down the Colorado river, in a wooden boat, to Yuma, several months ago.

According to the story related to the *Gazette,* the archaeologists of the Smithsonian Institute [sic], which is financing the explorations, have made discoveries which almost conclusively prove that the race which inhabited this mysterious cavern, hewn in solid rock by human hands, was of oriental origin, possibly from Egypt, tracing back to Rameses. If their theories are borne out by the translation of the tablets engraved with hieroglyphics, the mystery of the prehistoric peoples of North America, their ancient arts, who they were and whence they came, will be solved. Egypt and the Nile, and Arizona and the Colorado will be linked by a historical chain running back to ages which stagger the wildest fancy of the fictionist.

Under the direction of Professor S.A. Jordan, the Smithsonian is now pursuing the most thorough explorations, which will be continued until the last link in the chain is forged. Nearly a mile underground, about 1,480 feet below the surface, the long main passage has been delved into, to find another mammoth chamber from which radiates scores of passageways, like the spokes of a wheel. Several hundred rooms have been discovered, reached by passageways running from the main passage, one of them having been explored for 854 feet and another 634 feet. The recent finds include articles which have never been known as native to this country, and doubtless they had their origin in the orient. War weapons, copper instruments, sharp-edged and hard as steel, indicate the high state of civilization reached by these strange people. So interested have the scientists become that preparations are being made to equip the camp for extensive studies, and the force will be increased to thirty or forty persons.

Before going further into the cavern, better facilities for lighting will have to be installed, for the darkness is dense and quite impenetrable for the average flashlight. In order to avoid being lost, wires are being strung from the entrance to all passageways leading directly to large chambers. How far this cavern extends no one can guess, but it is now the belief of many that what has already been explored is merely the "barracks", to use an American term, for the soldiers, and that far into the underworld will be found the main communal dwellings of the families. The perfect ventilation of the cavern, the steady draught that blows through, indicates that it has another outlet to the surface.

Kinkaid was the first white man born in Idaho and has been an explorer and hunter all his life, thirty years having been in the service of the Smithsonian. Even briefly recounted, his history sounds fabulous, almost grotesque:

First, I would impress that the cavern is nearly inaccessible. The entrance is 1,486 feet down the sheer canyon wall. It is located on government land and no visitor will be allowed there under penalty of trespass. The scientists wish to work unmolested, without fear of the archaeological discoveries being disturbed by curio or relic hunters. A trip there would be fruitless, and the visitor would be sent on his way. The story of how I found the cavern has been related, but in a paragraph: I was journeying down the Colorado River in a boat, alone, looking for mineral. Some forty-two miles up the river from the El Tovar Crystal canyon, I saw on the east wall, stains in the sedimentary formation about 2,000 feet above the river bed. There was no trail to this point, but I finally reached it with great difficulty. Above a shelf which hid it from view from the river, was the mouth of the cave. There are steps leading from this entrance some thirty yards to what was, at the time the cavern was inhabited, the level of the river. When I saw the chisel marks on the wall inside the entrance, I became interested, securing my gun and went in. During that trip I went back several hundred feet along the main passage, till I came to the crypt in which I discovered the mummies. One of these I stood up and photographed by flashlight. I gathered a number of relics, which I carried down the Colorado to Yuma, from whence I shipped them to Washington with details of the discovery. Following this, the explorations were undertaken.

The main passageway is about 12 feet wide, narrowing to nine feet toward the farther end. About 57 feet from the entrance, the first side-passages branch off to the right and left, along which, on both sides, are a number of rooms about the size of ordinary living rooms of today, though some are 30 by 40 feet square. These are entered by oval-shaped doors and are ventilated by round air spaces through the walls into the passages. The walls are about three feet six inches in thickness. The passages are chiseled or hewn as straight as could be laid out by an engineer. The ceilings of many of the rooms converge to a center. The side-passages near the entrance run at a sharp angle from the main hall, but toward the rear they gradually reach a right angle in direction.

Over a hundred feet from the entrance is the cross-hall, several hundred feet long, in which are found the idol, or image, of the people's god, sitting cross-legged, with a lotus flower or lily in each hand. The cast of the face is oriental, and the carving shows a skillful hand, and the entire is remarkably well preserved, as is everything in this cavern. The idol most resembles Buddha, though the scientists are not certain as to what religious worship it represents. Taking into consideration everything found thus far, it is possible that this worship most resembles the ancient people of Thibet. Surrounding this idol are smaller images, some very beautiful in form; others crooked-necked and distorted shapes, symbolical, probably, of good and evil. There are two large cactus with protruding arms, one on each side of the dais on which the god squats. All this is carved out of hard rock resembling marble. In the opposite corner of this cross-hall were found tools of all descriptions, made of copper. These people undoubtedly knew the lost art of hardening this metal, which has been sought by chemists for centuries without result. On a bench running around the workroom was some charcoal and other material probably used in the process. There is also slag and stuff similar to matte, showing that these ancients smelted ores, but so far no trace of where or how this was done has been discovered, nor the origin of the ore.

Among the other finds are vases or urns and cups of copper and gold, made very artistic in design. The pottery work includes enameled ware and glazed vessels. Another passageway leads to granaries such as are found in the oriental temples. They contain seeds of various kinds. One very large storehouse has not yet been entered, as it is twelve feet high and can be reached only from above. Two copper hooks extend on the edge, which indicates that some sort of ladder was attached. These granaries are rounded, as the materials of which they are constructed, I think, is a very hard cement. A gray metal is also found in this cavern, which puzzles the scientists, for its identity has not been established. It resembles platinum. Strewn promiscuously over the floor everywhere are what people call 'cats eyes,' a yellow stone of no great value. Each one is engraved with the head of the Malay type.

On all the urns, or walls over doorways, and tablets of stone which were found by the image are the mysterious hieroglyphics, the key to which the Smithsonian Institute hopes yet to discover. The engraving on the tablets probably has something to do with the religion of the people. Similar hieroglyphics have been found in southern Arizona. Among the pictorial writings, only two animals are found. One is of prehistoric type.

The tomb or crypt in which the mummies were found is one of the largest of the chambers, the walls slanting back at an angle of about 35 degrees. On these are tiers of mummies, each one occupying a separate hewn shelf. At the head of each is a small bench, on which is found copper cups and pieces of broken swords. Some of the mummies are covered with clay, and all are wrapped in a bark fabric. The urns or cups on the lower tiers are crude, while as the higher shelves are reached the urns are finer in design, showing a later stage of civilization. It is worthy of note that all the mummies examined so far have proved to be male, no children or females being buried here. This leads to the belief that this exterior section was the warriors' barracks.

Among the discoveries no bones of animals have been found, no skins, no clothing no bedding. Many of the rooms are bare but for water vessels. One room, about 40 by 700 feet, was probably the main dining hall, for cooking utensils are found here. What these people lived on is a problem, though it is presumed that they came south in the winter and farmed in the valleys, going back north in the summer. Upwards of 50,000 people could have lived in the caverns comfortably. One theory is that the present Indian tribes found in Arizona are descendants of the serfs or slaves of the people which inhabited the cave. Undoubtedly a good many thousands of years before the Christian era a people lived here which reached a high stage of civilization. The chronology of human history is full of gaps. Professor Jordan is much enthused over the discoveries and believes that the find will prove of incalculable value in archaeological work.

One thing I have not spoken of, may be of interest. There is one chamber the passageway to which is not ventilated, and when we approached it a deadly, snaky smell struck us. Our lights would not penetrate the gloom, and until stronger ones are available we will not know what the chamber contains. Some say snakes, but others boo-hoo this idea and think it may contain a deadly gas or chemicals used by the ancients. No sounds are heard, but it smells snaky just the same. The whole underground installation gives one of shaky nerves the creeps. The gloom is like a weight on one's shoulders, and our flashlights and candles only make the darkness blacker. Imagination can revel in conjectures and ungodly day-dreams back through the ages that have elapsed till the mind reels dizzily in space.

In connection with this story, it is notable that among the Hopi Indians the tradition is told that their ancestors once lived in an underworld in the Grand Canyon till dissension arose between the good and the bad, the people of one heart and the people of two hearts. Machetto, who was their chief, counseled them to leave the underworld, but there was no way out. The chief then caused a tree to grow up and pierce the roof of the underworld, and then the people of one heart climbed out. They tarried by Paisisvai (Red River), which is the Colorado, and grew grain and corn. They sent out a message to the Temple of the Sun, asking the blessing of peace, good will and rain for the people of one heart. That messenger never returned, but today at the Hopi villages at sundown can be seen the old men of the tribe out on the housetops gazing toward the sun, looking for the messenger. When he returns, their lands and ancient dwelling place will be restored to them. That is the tradition. Among the engravings of animals in the cave is seen the image of a heart over the spot where it is located. The legend was learned by W. E. Rollins, the artist, during a year spent with the Hopi Indians. There are two theories of the origin of the Egyptians. One is that they came from Asia; another that the racial cradle was in the upper Nile region. Heeren, an Egyptologist, believed in the Indian origin of the Egyptians. The discoveries in the Grand Canyon may throw further light on human evolution and prehistoric ages.

And so ends the *Phoenix Gazette* tale of underground chambers, crypts, granaries, copper urns, broken swords plus mummies, poisonous gasses and assorted snakes. What became of these amazing artifacts? Since the find did not become the history-altering event it should have been, one has to wonder what exactly happened. Notice that he author used phrases like "Malay type" and "Thibet" when describing some of the artifacts. What we seem to have here is the description of a secret cave that contains a trove of Cham artifacts. These Hindu-Buddhist-Tibetan-Egyptian statues, plates, swords, vessels and spears would be confusing to the viewer. They recognized the oriental-look to the statues, but realized that they were not really Chinese. They also noticed an Egyptian element to the statues which is a characteristic of Cham statuary—and Olmec. Indeed, some of the statues in Cambodia and Vietnam seem to show oriental men wearing what is an Egyptian crown.

The Cham treasure in the Grand Canyon continues to be a controversial topic today and is often featured on television shows and late night radio. However, the Smithsonian denies any connection with a G.E. Kinkaid or S.A. Jordan during this time period. The State of Idaho denies that Kinkaid was the first white baby born there, although Kinkaid and Kincaid are common family names in the state. On the other hand, the *Phoenix Gazette* did run a previous story on Kinkaid's journey down the Colorado, a brief account published March 12, 1909 that ends with the sentence, "Some interesting archeological discoveries were unearthed and altogether the trip was of such interest that he will repeat it next winter, in the company of friends."

In addition, John Wesley Powell, who famously navigated the Colorado River in the years around 1870, reported some things that are very interesting in light of Kinkaid's story. In his 1875 book *Exploration of the Colorado River and its Canyons*, he mentions that while passing through the Marble Canyon area of the Grand Canyon he saw up in the cliffs a lot of large, hollowed-out caves, and suggestions of massive "architectural forms." At a later point, he reports:

> I walk down the gorge to the left at the foot of the cliff, climb to a bench, and discover a trail deeply worn into the rock. Where it crosses the side gulches in some places steps

have been cut. I can see no evidence of its having been traveled for a long time. It was doubtless a path used by the people who inhabited this country anterior to the present Indian races—the people who built the communal houses of which mention has been made. I return to camp about three o'clock and find that some of the men have discovered ruins and many fragments of pottery; also etchings and hieroglyphics on the rocks.

So it would seem that the great explorer Powell's accounts corroborate the existence in the Grand Canyon of stone-carved steps that climb the walls, hollowed-out caves in the cliffs and hieroglyphics left by some ancient race!

Did the Smithsonian actually perform the explorations described by Kinkaid, and then engineer some kind of archeological cover-up reminiscent of the last scene in the movie *Raiders of the Lost Ark* (where the Ark of the Covenant is placed inside a crate in one of the Institution's giant warehouses never to be seen again)?

One interesting suggestion is that, while the discovery was real, the archeologists might not have been. These men may not have been working for the Smithsonian out of Washington D.C. at all, but merely claiming to be doing so. This may have been a cover-up for an illegal archeological dig that was raiding the ancient site and claiming legitimacy from a very distant, venerated institution. It may have proved difficult, in 1909, to check on the credentials of the archeologists, and there is no hint that anyone was actually trying to do this. These men may well have disappeared shortly after the article appeared, but not to Washington D.C. as we might suppose, but rather to San Francisco, Los Angeles or Denver.

Seth Tanner and the Secret Hopi Cave

A film with similarities to the *Phoenix Gazette* story was *Mackenna's Gold* (1969) starring Gregory Peck, Omar Sharif, Telly Savalas, Edward G. Robinson, Julie Newmar and others. *Mackenna's Gold* takes place around the Grand Canyon and the area north of Flagstaff and west of the Hopi Mesas. The film combines

398

elements familiar to aficionados of lost treasure lore including: the story of an Egyptian cavern system, a secret canyon, the lost John D. Lee gold mine, and a man named Seth Tanner among others. The film, in the introduction, says it is based on the treasure story of the Lost Adams Diggings, a fabulous vein of gold in a box canyon that "ran for miles." Apaches kept the canyon a secret and killed any prospectors who might ever enter.

A poster for Mackenna's Gold.

The Adams Gold, or Adams Diggings, was a famous "lost" (some wondered if it had ever been found) bend in a stream rich with gold nuggets, plus a vein of pure gold on the canyon wall. This famous lost treasure was generally thought to be in New Mexico, somewhere near the Arizona border. It has generally been placed in the area north of Silver City and Reserve, and south of the Gallup area. However, in *Mackenna's Gold*, partially based on the Adams story, they are clearly in the area around present-day Cameron, Arizona, which is at the mouth of the Little Colorado River Gorge.

In *Mackenna's Gold*, Omar Sharif plays the villain, a bandit named, in fact, Colorado. Early in the movie, Colorado has captured Sheriff Mackenna (Gregory Peck), who has seen a map of the route to the secret canyon. With his hands tied, Mackenna and the bandit gang cross a precarious rope-bridge across a narrow, but very deep canyon. With Ray Harryhausen-type special effects in this brief sequence, the group makes its way across the rickety bridge and ends up on the north side of what I believe to be the Little Colorado River Gorge. Today, this area is a largely off-limits and roadless part of the Kaibab National Forest, and part of it lies in the Navaho Reservation.

It is somewhere beyond this crossing that Mackenna and

399

Colorado find a secret canyon with a rich vein of gold along one of its walls, and ruins high up on a cliff which must have been part of an ancient mining operation. It is an exciting and imaginative western that claims to be based on fact—but perhaps the facts in this case are even more bizarre than the fictional movie itself.

One of the most important books (in fact, one of the *only* books) on the Grand Canyon and secret mines and tunnels is the book *Quest for the Pillar of Gold*.[74] This compilation of scholarly papers on ancient mines, mineral wealth, and modern-historical mining ventures in the Grand Canyon gives us the tantalizing reality behind all the fantastic stories. One would think that a geological wonderland such as the Grand Canyon would offer a wealth of minerals, including gold. There is definitely an ancient salt mine and other sites that are sacred to the Hopi. And tales of gold, such as the John Lee gold mine, were well-known stories that circulated around the Grand Canyon. Was one of the ancient mines in the Grand Canyon a Cham empire gold mine?

Indeed, with ancient mining, by definition, there would be ancient tunneling! Placer gold could be found on the surface in riverbends, but following a vein of gold—even in ancient times— would mean tunneling into a canyon wall. A number of early pioneer mines in the Grand Canyon were created in this way, sometimes necessitating ladders and walkways on sheer cliffs.

Prospectors were expecting to find veins of gold in the Grand Canyon, but astonishingly, to date no substantiated gold claims have been recorded. Part of the reason for this is that the canyon was difficult to explore on the best day, and deadly during flash floods or chance meetings with Navaho or Hopi warriors. Among the prospectors was a man who apparently discovered a secret cave in the Grand Canyon or Little Colorado Canyon and was then captured by Hopi warriors. His name was Seth Tanner.

Seth Tanner (1828-1918) was a Mormon miner and trader who had gone west with Brigham Young in 1847 when the Mormons settled Salt Lake City. From Salt Lake City he was sent out to set up a small Mormon colony in San Bernardino, California and it was rumored that he and his brother Myron had some luck in the

California gold fields. Tanner also spent some time in San Diego, investing in a coal business that reportedly did not do too well. He returned to Utah and was married; later, he was sent on a scouting expedition to northern Arizona. In 1876, he moved his family to an isolated cabin on the Little Colorado River near Tuba City. The cabin was strategically located on old trade routes, and Tanner, who got along well with both the Hopi and Navajo and spoke their languages, set up a trading post. Because of his burly countenance and extraordinary strength, the Navajos called him "Hosteen Shush" (Mr. Bear).

Tanner became a well-known Grand Canyon character and *Quest for the Pillar of Gold* gives some of his early mining history. He at one time had a mine in an area of heavy quartzite in Seventyfive Mile Creek. He first filed claims in 1890, and worked several claims in the following years. He improved ancient Hopi trails into the Canyon, and one main access point is called Tanner Trail even today. At some time during his explorations, he discovered a hidden Hopi cave (or mine?) of treasure. Tanner was captured by Hopi warriors at the secret cave in the Grand Canyon sometime around 1896.

His final fate is told in *Grand Canyon Stories: Then and Now*,[75] a book published by the famous magazine *Arizona Highways*. The brief story includes a photo that tantalizes us: Seth Tanner—a grizzly old man who is blind! According to the book, the Hopi blinded Tanner by throwing a potion in his eyes because he was "the discoverer of a cave containing sacred religious treasures of the Hopi tribe, which no white man was allowed to see." The book maintains that it would normally have meant death to see the secret cave, but Tanner was spared because his mother was Hopi. This is highly

A photo of the blinded Seth Tanner.

unlikely, since he was born in New York; it is much more likely he had taken a Hopi wife or had some other significant relationship to cause the tribe to debate his fate. He remained a prisoner of the Hopi, however, and was put in a cave and supplied with daily

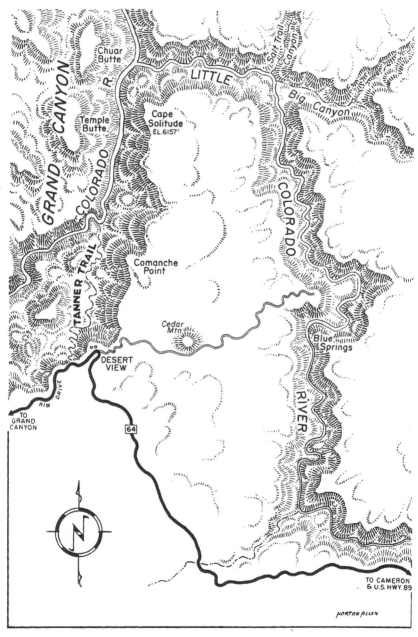

A map of the Little Colorado River and Tanner Trail.

provisions for years. Supposedly, Tanner became accustomed to his blindness and began to venture out. But because of his alarming appearance, he frightened villagers around Cameron and Tuba City. To scare him off, they would throw water on him. Thinking it was more of the dreaded Hopi potion that had blinded him, he would run back to his cave.

At some point, he must have been released. The photo of him as a blind man is known to have been taken some time shortly after the year 1900. He died near Tuba City in 1918. He is still a famous character in the area, and visitors to the Grand Canyon can see Tanner Springs, Tanner Wash and Tanner Crossing in addition to Tanner Trail. His children and grandchildren became wealthy trading post owners in the Tuba City and Gallup areas. But part of Seth Tanner remains a mystery and he never divulged the terrible secret or incredible treasure he had seen.

What did he see in the Grand Canyon or Little Colorado Canyon that meant death? Did Tanner discover in the early 1890s the caves full of statues and mummies that were to be reported years later in 1909 by the *Phoenix Gazette*—ancient caves filled with forgotten Cham artifacts, now sacred to the Hopi?

The similarities between the real-life Seth Tanner and the fictional Ed Adams in the film *Mackenna's Gold* are striking. As we have seen, Ed Adams was a real historical figure, but the fact that he was not blind and the description and location of the Adams Diggings make it seem unlikely that he was the real person upon which the film character was based. That person is actually Seth Tanner—a man who had seen the "Canyon of Gold" and had his eyes burned out for it.

As Jennifer and I headed up into the Hopi Mesas I caught a glimpse of Holbrook in the rearview mirror. We were headed for Walpi and then Cameron. As we passed through Jeddito and Keams Canyon I looked at the ancient pueblos on the Hopi Mesas and wondered if the Hopi were the descendants of these special visitors from the Egyptian-Cham empire. The word Djed, or Jedd, is a common word in ancient Egyptian and was associated with the god Osiris. Was the Hopi language possibly derived from ancient

Egyptian? Perhaps the ancient Hohokam language as well? It is said that the Zuni language contains elements of Sumerian!

As we have previously discussed, prior to the European expansion into New Mexico and the American Southwest, the Hopi and other Pueblo Indians hunted with boomerangs, as did the ancient Egyptians. Prior to the Spanish introducing sheep, cattle, and horses, the Hopi hunted jackrabbits and birds with their boomerangs. Jackrabbits are still a popular food in parts of Arizona and New Mexico, and a boomerang can be seen at the museum at the Aztec Ruins in Aztec, New Mexico.

If the Cham had sought out the Grand Canyon as some sacred spot where the River Styx disappeared into the underworld of Set, they may have built small outposts and forts for journeys to the Grand Canyon. Exactly such places exist, such as Wupatki and Tusayan, both ancient cities near the Grand Canyon. Wupatki and other nearby ruins are close to the Little Colorado River, and are thought to have been built by the ancestors of the Hopi, though some archeologists dispute this. Signs at the Wupatki Ruins Museum run by the National Park Service are ambiguous as to who the builders of this remarkable little town—complete with a ball court—really were.

But, if there was at one time a Cham presence down deep inside the Grand Canyon, one would expect to find some sort of town or outpost down on the canyon floor. And in fact, there is such a place, though to date it has not been tied to any specific culture. Excavations started in 1967 at an archeological site known as Unkar, where the Unkar stream meets the Colorado River creating the Unkar Delta. Unkar Delta is just downstream (west) of where the Little Colorado meets the main Colorado River, deep inside the canyon.

After years of research and digging, the discoveries were published in a scholarly book called *Unkar Delta: Archeology of the Grand Canyon*[76] by Douglas Schwartz of the School of American Research out of Santa Fe, New Mexico. His team cataloged building foundations, cut stone blocks and broken pieces of pottery. Because of occasional superfloods in the Grand Canyon, much of the Unkar Delta would have been periodically washed away. Schwartz concludes in his book that the Unkar Delta was inhabited circa 900 AD.

One would think that if Unkar had originally been built by the Cham, it would have been built around 500 AD, if not before. Perhaps earlier dates will eventually come from Unkar, or perhaps this earlier city, if it ever existed, was washed away thousands of years ago, and is not lying beneath the current Unkar.

And what of the curious name Unkar? It could be an Egyptian word, perhaps a corruption of Ankh-Ka or Ankh-Ra. Is this a reference to the sun god Ra? Recall that many islands in the Pacific (the playground of the Cham navies) have names containing the syllable Ra. One of the ancient Southwest legends held that the sun rose and set inside the Grand Canyon, and indeed, one could see the sun set into the canyon if one stood on the eastern rim looking west. Modern maps of the Grand Canyon indicate a Cham influence from somewhere—just look at all of the many Hindu names given to the distinctive geological features of the Grand Canyon: Shiva Temple, Vishnu Temple, Brahma Schist, Buddha Temple and even Rama Temple. Is it just a coincidence that the Grand Canyon has been given so many Hindu names?

Quicksand, the Sipapu and the Hopi Salt Mines

Jennifer and I drove to the Hopi Mesas northeast of Flagstaff and stopped for a short time to visit the Hopi Villages at Walpi and Oraibi. Old Oraibi is thought to be the oldest inhabited town in the United States, going back to at least 1150 AD. When the early archeologist Victor Mindeleff visited Oraibi in 1882-83, he found that it was the largest of the Hopi pueblos and contained nearly half of the entire Hopi population. In 1968, there were only 167 people living in the ancient town, most Hopis having moved to Hotevilla or to Kiakochomovi, also called New Oraibi, or other small towns closer to schools.[98]

Oraibi is probably much older than originally thought, and it may have been much larger in ancient times. Archeologist Harry James says that wherever a hole is dug, evidence of an ancient city beneath Oraibi is found. He said that some years ago a road was being cut through the edge of the village, and it exposed a huge trash mound at the bottom of which were found "buried remains of even older and better built houses."[78]

So, the very ancient, pre-1100 AD buildings were larger and better built? Perhaps they were as well made as the Hohokam structures, or even the mysterious buildings at Wupatki and Tuzigoot.

Among the many curious customs of the Hopi is the wearing of an unwed woman's hair in circular coils on either side of her head. This unusual hairstyle is also found on the ancient statue found in Elche, Spain known as "Our Lady of Elche." E.M. Whishaw gives a drawing of what the full statue looked like in her book *Atlantis in Spain*.[77] The woman depicted in the statue, who is associated with Atlantis and Tartessos according to Whishaw, wears her hair in wheels on either side of her head. Is there some relationship between this statue and the Hopis and their ancient customs? This is also the way that Princess Leia of the *Star Wars* films wears her hair, perhaps a nod from George Lucas to the Hopis and "Our Lady of Elche."

We continued our drive on Highway 264 to Tuba City and then

Unmarried Hopi women wear their hair in circular coils on the side of the head.

headed west on Highway 160 and then south on Highway 89 to Cameron. As we came into Cameron, I got a good look at the green valley that the Little Colorado was creating. Soon after Cameron, the valley becomes a narrow gorge that the Little Colorado runs through on its way to meeting the Colorado River in the Grand Canyon. We crossed the river on a big steel bridge, the last bridge over the Little Colorado before it sinks into the gorge. We were now in Seth Tanner country. As noted above, because Tanner spent a lot of time in the area, a number of important features are named after him. On the Little Colorado, near Cameron, a rock crossing used in the 1800s was named after Tanner. The Little Colorado is famous for quicksand when water is flowing, and the important crossing was located a mile upstream from the present highway bridge.

Looking west up the canyon of the Little Colorado, I thought of how Seth Tanner must have struggled through quicksand as he scoured this canyon for gold—and had instead found a wondrous cave of treasure (mummies, artifacts and swords?) so hallowed, he was blinded for what he saw. A canyon in the Little Colorado Gorge is named after him; Tanner Canyon is a secret box canyon somewhere deep inside the towering cliffs.

As we drove west along the Little Colorado Gorge I wondered about the Hopi and their creation stories, which you may remember were mentioned in the 1909 *Gazette* article. The Hopi believe the world has been destroyed several times, but each time certain good people were saved. Twice they were given harbor underground while the earth above was destroyed, and were supported by the Ant People. The Hopis believe that they emerged from the underground world of the Ant People at the end of the Third World from a hole in the Grand Canyon known as the "Sipapu."

The Sipapu is near the Hopi Salt Mines and both areas are off-limits to hikers, generally. The Forest Service has issued a few, rare photos of these places, with little explanation. They are reprinted here. The Sipapu is said to be a lava dome from a hot spot in a volcanic hot spring area, a bit like a dry geyser at Yellowstone National Park. It is a hole in the ground (sometimes smoking) and could easily help foster creation myths.

407

The Hopi Salt Mines comprise another ancient area that maintains significance today. Salt was an important trade item within ancient cultures and salt mines, like obsidian mines, were considered highly important. The famous salt mines near Cuzco in Peru were used by the Incas, and the Romans paid their soldiers with a ration of salt (hence the word "salary"). Throughout northern Mexico and the American Southwest, "payment" could be made with turquoise, gold dust (often inside a goose quill), salt, gourds, jade, crystals, fossils and other small trade items. Tanner would have been familiar with the Hopi Salt Mines, and this knowledge may have led him to the secret caves that ultimately became his doom.

Jennifer and I pulled up to the parking lot at Desert View on the southern rim of the Grand Canyon, inside Grand Canyon National Park. The spectacular view of the meeting of the Grand Canyon and the Little Colorado spread out in front of us.

Nearby were the cliffs where the Tanner Trail begins to descend down the steep canyon walls, switchbacking its way to the bottom. The Tanner Trail starts at Lipan Point on the Desert View Drive. If a hiker were to hike down Tanner Trail to the bottom of the canyon, he would then be in the general vicinity of the Hopi Salt Mines, the Sipapu and the Unkar Delta.

Archeologists largely agree that many sections of the Tanner Trail were originally part of old Anasazi and Hopi Indian routes into the Canyon. As Seth Tanner worked and improved the path, it became known by his name, as did the part of the Grand Canyon first entered by the trail. It is

A Hopi boomerang.

408

somewhere in the vicinity of Tanner Canyon that Europeans first "discovered" the Grand Canyon. The first of the known European explorers to visit the area was Garcia Lopez de Cardenas, who was shown the canyon by his Hopi guides in 1535, while in search of the fabled Seven Cities of Gold. Today, hikers can visit Cardenas Butte, accessible via the Tanner Trail, named in his honor.

Tanner's mine was just off the trail at a spot near Palisades Creek, upriver from Tanner Delta. The trail was used by other prospectors as well, and a number of small copper mines existed inside the Grand Canyon in the late 1800s.

In the early days prospectors and others also used the trail to cross the Canyon. Most notoriously, horse thieves used the trail to drive horses into the Canyon—so many, in fact, that Tanner Canyon was also called Horsethief Canyon. It is reported that this side canyon was used by horse thieves to hide stolen horses on their way into Utah. While in this secret canyon, the brands on the horses would be changed; the horse thieves got out of the canyon by taking the Nankoweap Trail up to the northern side of the Little Colorado. Was this Tanner Canyon-Horsethief Canyon part of the puzzle leading to the location of the Cham catacombs?

We stood on the rim of the Canyon at Tanner Trail. Somewhere out there was a cave entrance, perhaps now with a locked iron door over it, that would lead into an underground world of marvelous treasures—so the story goes. Did this legendary treasure trove belong to Cham explorers who saw the Grand Canyon as the awesome work of Shiva—the destroyer and creator of everything? Were the Hopi and Zuni religions vestiges of the Shaivism and Buddhism of the Cham?

The Cham and the American Southwest

In chapter two I discussed the elephant slabs that were discovered in 1910 at Flora Vista, New Mexico, near the stone ruins called the Salmon Ruins. Nearby is the town of Aztec, New Mexico which also has sizable stone ruins.

In his book *Ancient Man: A Handbook of Puzzling Artifacts*,[43] William Corliss has one brief page on the elephant slabs including an illustration of the inscriptions. They appear to be early Shang Chinese script, which was in use circa 1100 BC. Dating of the slabs by local archeologists, who thought they were authentic, was circa 1200 AD. They based this date on potsherds that were found at the site. However, the slabs may have been an ancient relic, kept in a safe place for hundreds of years at a time, while the potsherds could be of much more recent manufacture and come from the time of the destruction of Aztec, Flora Vista and the nearby Salmon Ruins, which occurred around 1200 AD. This slab was probably much older than the Salmon Ruins, coming perhaps from Chaco Canyon or the Anasazi Ruins near the Grand Canyon.

I speculated in chapter two that the elephants depicted on the slabs were war elephants that had been brought by the Cham across the Pacific. Had they landed in the Sea of Cortez and then brought several elephants to the Hohokam lands of central Arizona, where Phoenix and the town of Casa Grande sit today, with their many canals and four-story mud brick houses? From there, were two of the elephants marched to the area of the Grand Canyon or to Chaco Canyon, Zuni and the Continental Divide?

Now we can link these elephant slabs, and the live elephants themselves, to the mysterious passageways in the Grand Canyon that hold what is likely a Cham treasure. The statues from "Thibet" must certainly be statues of Buddha and Shiva. Are elephants also depicted on vessels and statues that were once in the secret passageways of the Grand Canyon? We will probably never know.

It was amazing that the 1909 story said that the tunnel-vault system goes for "nearly a mile underground... Several hundred rooms have been discovered... The recent finds include articles that have never been known as native to this country... War weapons, copper instruments, sharp-edged and hard as steel, indicate the high state of civilization reached by these strange people."

And what of Kinkaid mentioned in the article? In a letter that I received in 2005, signed by a "Colin," I was told that there is a mention of an E.K. Kincaid in correspondence archives for the Smithsonian Institution, Record Unit 189, Box 68 of 151, Folder 8. Said Colin, "These are records dating from 1860-1908, which is

410

in the correct time frame for the Kinkaid mentioned in the *Phoenix Gazette*. It is a possibility that different first initials were used and that this is the folder that may contain the valuable information needed to locate the site." Perhaps Kinkaid had gone to Washington D.C. after all.

The Mystery of the Zuni

Jennifer and I spent the night in Flagstaff and then drove into Zuni the next day, stopping at one of the local craft shops. This one had a huge selection of Zuni fetishes plus many raw stones for the local craftsmen themselves to buy.

Zuni is said to be the largest inhabited Pueblo in the United States. It was built upon the ruins of the ancient site of Halona, thought to be one of the fabled Seven Cities of Cibola sought by the Spanish conquistador Francisco Coronado in 1540 AD, as well as other adventurers. Ruins of other "cities" may be found along the Zuni River watershed.

Archaeological evidence from the nearby site of Hawikuh demonstrates that the Zuni people (who call themselves *A:shiwi* in their language) have lived in the area since at least 1300 AD. Although the Zunis were forced to move around, and did not always occupy the same "cities," there is an unbroken continuity of settlement in the area from at least 650 AD. This is coincidently also the date of the rise of Srivijaya in Sumatra and start of the decline of the Cham Empire.

The Zunis themselves say they have lived there for thousands of years. Their traditional history states that they emerged from the underworld somewhere west of their present location (the Grand Canyon and the Mojave Desert have been suggested) and wandered until they found Itawanna (the "Center Place," the center of the world), which is their present home.

Like the Hopi, the Zuni believe that they came from inside the earth. Legends say that there "were four caves, one over the other. Men first lived in the lowest cave. It was dark. There was no light, and the cave was crowded. All men were full of sorrow." Similar stories are told in the creation legends of the Maya, Zapotec and presumably, the Olmecs.

The search for the "gold" cities of Cibola had brought the early explorers into the area. The Spanish had heard tales of seven cities that were paved with gold far to the north. Arriving in the area, Coronado found, not streets paved with gold, but a community rich in tradition and living a highly adjusted, organized existence. The Zunis were an agrarian people with irrigated farms of corn, beans, squash and cotton. Strict religious beliefs of maintaining high moral standards and peace toward peoples, combined with their daily routines, made their society an exceptional one.

The Spanish had little trouble in conquering the peaceful Zuni people. But, in spite of Spanish occupation and a decree from the King of Spain to force Zuni acceptance of Roman Catholicism, the people continued to perform their ceremonies in hidden kivas or ceremonial rooms.

The Zuni people first encountered Europeans in 1539 when Fray Marcos de Niza set out from Mexico with the former Black slave Esteban hoping to discover the fabled Seven Cities of Cibola, which Esteban had been repeatedly told about as he wandered in the area now known as Texas. Esteban had been shipwrecked with the Narváez expedition on the Gulf Coast in 1528 and had, with Alvar Nuñez Cabeza de Vaca, wandered for seven years across Texas and the Southwest (possibly as far as southern Arizona) before returning to Mexico City. Their tales of the fabled Cibola excited everyone in Mexico City as well as in Spain, and this led to the Niza expedition.

Marcos de Niza was a Franciscan friar who led Spain's first big expedition across the northern deserts. In northern Mexico, Niza sent Esteban ahead, but when Esteban reached Zuni, he was regarded with suspicion and is said to have been imprisoned and ultimately executed when he demanded women and loot. When Niza returned to Mexico City, he claimed that Esteban was killed and that he had come within sight of large towns rich in precious stones, gold and silver.

The legend of Cibola was thus further promoted by Niza, which led to the 1540 expedition of Francisco Vásquez de Coronado. Coronado found the Zunis living in six villages, including Hawikuh and Halona. The Zunis attempted to stop Coronado, but after a brief battle they retreated due to the military superiority of the Spaniards who had rifles, armor and horses. Coronado was disappointed to find that Zuni was not the fabled Cibola; no riches were to be found. What had made Zuni wealthy were the salt mines that they controlled.

We have seen that certain cultures were accomplished jewelers and metalworkers in ancient times, and that they were working with gold, silver, copper and other metals that were coming from ancient mines in northern Mexico and the whole Four Corners region. But, at the time of the Conquest, the Zuni were not working metals too much, although they had copper beads that they used with turquoise and other material in jewelry making. Silversmithing was introduced to the Zuni in the 1870s, and since that time, the tribe has made the craft its own. Most of the turquoise used by the excellent Zuni jewelers comes from around the mountains just east of Sante Fe, on the "Turquoise Trail."

Zunis share many Pueblo traits with other Southwestern people, including strong beliefs about witchcraft, but their language is unique and cannot be linked to any other Native American language. The language of the Zuni is called by linguists a "language isolate" because no connections with other languages have been found. Attempts to connect it with some California Indian languages have not been convincing. The uniqueness of the Zuni language adds support to the idea that they have lived in the present location for millennia.

Nancy Yaw Davis, in her book *The Zuni Enigma*,[83] says that she has found evidence for the Zunis speaking a form of ancient Japanese. Davis thinks that the Zunis are connected to ancient Japanese Buddhists who were searching for the "Middle of the World." Asks Davis on the back cover of her book: "Did a group of thirteenth-century Japanese journey to the American Southwest, there to merge with the people, language, and religion of the Zuni tribe?"

Davis acknowledges that for many years, anthropologists have understood that the Zuni in the American Southwest occupy a special place in Native American culture and ethnography. Their language, religion, and blood type are startlingly different from all other tribes. Most puzzling, she says, is tlhat the Zuni appear to have much in common with the people of Japan. She goes on to describe the circumstances that may have led Japanese seekers on a religious quest—searching for the legendary "middle world" of Buddhism—across the Pacific and to the American Southwest more than seven hundred years ago. I think the group may have come much earlier than that.

Davis also mentions the curious peach grove at Zuni. The peach grove is sacred to the Zuni who hold an annual ceremony at this special spot. Peaches are from China and are difficult to grow. Davis wonders if the sacred peaches at Zuni came from China or Japan. Perhaps they came from China by way of the Cham? Did Chinese, Japanese and Cham Buddhists bring peaches and elephants to Arizona and northern New Mexico? It would seem so. A Zuni friend of mine, a tribal elder, has the last name of Mahooty. This is an ancient Zuni family name and it is also the Sanskrit word for an elephant driver: a mahout. Are the Mahooty clan of Zuni the descendents of the Cham elephant drivers? It is a fascinating thought!

The Sphinx of the Grand Canyon

In 2009 I was sent a color photocopy of an old postcard of the Grand Canyon from the early 1900s. It showed what seems like a northern bluff in the Grand Canyon with a series of steadily rising rock cliffs that came to a rounded but sharp point. In the middle of the very top is a face, and it has a canopy on either side of the head in the manner of an ancient Egyptian headdress. On the right side of the photograph were the stereograph instructions, which ironically tell the reader to hold the *face* of the photograph to the glass of the stereograph viewer.

I scanned the photo at 1200 dpi and made the best blowup of the old photo (circa 1910) that I could. I looked at a printed version of my high-resolution scan and pondered the photo. The peak did have a face at the top, and at least viewed at this angle at this time of the day, it could serve as a landmark of sorts. It looked very

414

similar to the famous Face on Mars. Was it just a trick of the light? Had ancient man actually carved this mesa to look like a man—or a sphinx?

The carving of a mountain had certainly been done before, notably by the ancient Egyptians, whose most famous example of

The mysterious Sphinx of the Grand Canyon.

such work are the four gigantic statues of a seated Ramses II hewn into the rock face at Aswan. The Chinese, Hindus and Buddhists also produced such monuments—witness the giant statues at Bamiyan in central Afghanistan that were destroyed by the Taliban in the 1990s. They were giant depictions of Buddha standing hundreds of feet high, chiseled into the massive cliff faces. I was glad I had seen them years ago, before they were lost forever in the name of Muslim fundamentalism.

I wondered if features like this played a part in the decision to give many of the features of the Grand Canyon Egyptian and Hindu-Buddhist names. Many of the rock formations have names such as Tower of Set, Tower of Ra, Osiris Temple, Shiva Temple and Buddha Cloister. These are exactly the type of names that we would expect from the Cham. Was it just a coincidence? Was it a man-made attempt to make a sphinx or other signal for mankind's pilgrims—or just a natural formation that was a simulacra (something that is natural but has a resemblance to something else). Was it still there? I looked at it for some time, and then contemplated it some more. It was odd, but considering the other strange stories concerning the Grand Canyon, seemed like it somehow fit in the whole milieu.

At around the same time, I received a different photo from a man in Albuquerque named Robert, who sent me a picture of Canyon de Chelly taken by the famous photographer of the old Southwest, Edward S. Curtis. Robert told me that it showed a very faint statue of a standing or sitting Buddha that was colossal in size. I could faintly see the outline of what he was talking about, and if it is an artificially carved image, it would have to be absolutely monumental in scope. It was a fascinating idea that huge Buddhist figures rivaling those in Asia might have been carved in the American Southwest!

The sun was setting in the west as Jennifer and I drove back to Flagstaff. I thought of the elephants depicted on the slabs in New Mexico and the "Tibetan" artifacts that were supposedly discovered in the Grand Canyon. Was this land around the Grand Canyon and the Colorado Rivers once the land of the Cham?

416

Those who came before, searching for the Middle Land of Buddhist-Taoist lore—did they arrive from the Pacific to the Hohokam lands of southern Arizona and then journey to the Grand Canyon area and on to the area around Aztec, New Mexico? Here we have a large kiva and the elephant slabs from the Salmon Ruins nearby. That the Cham had brought some of their war elephants all the way to northern New Mexico seemed fantastic, but no more fantastic than Hannibal taking war elephants across the Italian Alps to attack Rome.

A Curious Incident in the Old West

Like the Cham themselves, we have covered a lot of ground in this book. We have discussed transpacific journeys, airships and ancient flight, megalith building, power tools, and the levitation of stones weighing many tons. Certain things about the Cham and Shaivite-Buddhists remain unknown. Were vimanas used in the Cham Empire as discussed in Hindu epics? How did they levitate stones? What sort of power tools did they use to perfectly cut and fit granite blocks? Where did they get the building technique of using keystone cuts and metal alloy clamps? Did it come from Egypt?

I will conclude this book with a curious story about an oddball airship incident in 1880 in New Mexico that may somehow involve the Cham. Like some episode of the 60s television show *The Wild West,* it is a futuristic western-sci-fi story. The incident near Galisteo, New Mexico makes us wonder if truth is stranger than fiction. Throughout the 1880s and 1890s there were a number of mysterious newspaper reports of airships cruising the American West, including an early report from the March 29, 1880, issue of the *Weekly New Mexican* headlined: "A Mysterious Aerial Phantom."

The newspaper article said that several men had been walking near the railroad tracks at Galisteo Junction the evening of March 26, when they heard voices that seemed to come from the sky. At first, they thought it was an echo from someone talking in the nearby hills, but looking up, they saw a large airship approach from the west. Though not mentioned in the story, the object may have been following the railroad tracks, apparently going east.

417

As the airship approached, they were able to make out what they said was a gigantic balloon, shaped like a fish. It swooped low enough that the amazed observers could see distinct writing, or characters, on the side of the gondola that carried the passengers. The article mentioned that, "The air machine appeared to be entirely under the control of the occupants, and guided by a large sailing apparatus." They described it as "monstrous in size," and speculated that it could carry eight or ten persons. The unnamed men were amazed by the speed and maneuverability of the "air machine."

Inside the airship, the people were apparently having a great time, as the men could hear music, laughter, and voices speaking a language they could not understand coming from the vessel. Several objects were suddenly dropped from the balloon. In the darkness, however, the men found only "a magnificent flower, with a slip of exceedingly fine silk like paper," on which there appeared to be some sort of writing that they thought resembled Japanese. Then the vessel "assumed a great height and moved off very rapidly towards the east."

On the very next morning the men returned in search of the other objects dropped from the balloon. They uncovered a cup "of very peculiar workmanship," and very different from anything the men had ever seen. Both the cup and the flower they had found the night before were reported to be on display at Galisteo Junction, where they could be examined "by anyone who desire[d] to see them."

Then, according to the bizarre article, the following day, a "collector of curiosities" had gone to see the flower and cup. The unnamed collector was quite taken by the objects dropped from the balloon and he offered the men "such a sum of money for them that it could not be refused." The new owner of the airship artifacts then proceeded to express his opinion that the balloon was undoubtedly from Asia, most probably, he said, "from Jedde."[73]

Like many newspaper stories of the old frontier, this one seems quite farfetched. That some mysterious airship had indeed been seen, or even landed, along the tracks at Galisteo Junction seems possible. That the airship was of Chinese or Japanese manufacture, or from "Jedde," is a fascinating assumption, perhaps made because (in those days) all things strange and fantastic must come from the Orient or exotic Arabia where Mecca and Jeddah were at the time the major cities.

Perhaps they were ancient masters flying in their vimanas, those who followed the teachings of Osiris; they were the Djedi, named after the Djed column of Egyptian iconography. Many Arabian names originally come from ancient India, like Jeddah, Oman, Mohamed, Socorro, and others. Had the craft just visited the Grand Canyon?

In the first chapter I discussed Asoka and the legend of the Nine Unknown Men. Is there some secret base or bases of the Cham with their flying machines and levitation technology still being used by some ancient organization—like the Nine Unknown Men—that has airships that still occasionally go on missions across various areas like South America, Mexico and the American Southwest? Does some secret society keep a small fleet of vimanas inside hollowed-out mountains in Peru, Mexico, Tibet or some Pacific Island? Indeed, there could be secret vimana bases in many countries around the world.

These secret bases, which I discuss at length in my book *Vimana*, are said to be mountain fortresses similar to the NORAD military command center at Cheyenne Mountain in Colorado Springs. They are also similar to legends that surround Mount Shasta in northern California. Those legends suggest that some oriental secret society—perhaps the Nine Unknown Men—have a secret city inside the mountain as well as UFO-type flying vehicles. According to a strange book published in the late 1890s, *A Dweller on Two Planets*, the leader of this secret brotherhood inside of Mount Shasta is a mysterious oriental man named Quong.

It is an astonishing thought that a portion of the UFO enigma might possibly have to do with the Cham. But it seems that when it comes to the amazing Cham—nothing is impossible!

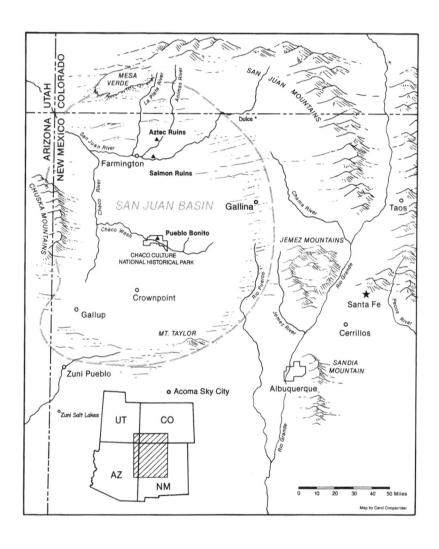

BIBLIOGRAPHY

1. *Champa: Ancient Towers, Reality & Legend*, Ngo Van Doanh, 2002, Gioi Publishers, Hanoi.
2. *My Son Sanctuary*, Thanh Dia, 2005, Hanoi.
3. *Cu Lao Cham: An Introduction to the Islands*, Di Tich and Danh Thang, 2005, Da Nang.
4. *Cham Sculpture and Indian Mythology*, Huynh Thi Duoc, 2007, Hanoi.
5. *Minorities of Central Vietnam*, by Jacques Dournes, 1980, Minorities Rights Group, London.
6. *Ancient Angkor,* M, Freeman and C. Jacques, 2003, River Books, Bangkok.
7. *Chavin and the Origins of Andean Civilization*, Richard L. Burger, 1992, Thames and Hudson, London.
8. *Jade: A Study in Chinese Archaeology and Religion*, Berthold Laufer, 1912, Dover Books, New York (reprinted 1974).
9. *1421: The Year China Discovered the World*, Gavin Menzies, 2002, Random House, New York.
10. *When China Ruled the Seas*, Louise Levathes, 1994, Simon & Schuster, New York.
11. *The Morning of the Magicians*, Louis Pauwels and Jacques Bergier, 1960, Dorset Books, New York.
12. *The Lost Continent of Mu*, James Churchward, 1926. Reprinted by Adventures Unlimited Press, Kempton, IL.
13. *Atlantis in America*, Ivar Zapp and George Erickson, 1998, Adventures Unlimited Press, Kempton, IL.
14. *Myths of Pre-Columbian America*, Donald Mackenzie, 1923, Dover Books, New York.
15. *The African Presence in Early Asia*, edited by Runoko Rashidi and Ivan Van Sertima, 1988, Transaction Publishers, New Brunswick, NJ.
16. *The African Presence in Early America*, edited by Ivan Van Sertima, 1987, Transaction Publishers, New Brunswick, NJ.
17. *Borobudur and Temples of Java*, 2008, Ariswara Publishers, Magelong, Indonesia.
18. *Ark of God*, David Hatcher Childress, 2015, Adventures Unlimited Press, Kempton, IL.
19. *Gods and Spacemen in the Ancient East*, W. Raymond Drake, 1968, Sphere Books, London.
20. *Harscha Charita of Bana*, Translated by E.B. Cowell and F.H. Thomas, 1897, Oriental Translation Fund, London.

Bibliography

21. *War in Ancient India*, Ramachandra Dikshitar, 1944, Oxford Press, UK.
22. *The Mystery of the Olmecs*, David Hatcher Childress, 2003, Adventures Unlimited Press, Kempton, IL.
23. *They Came Before Columbus: The African Presence in Ancient America*, Ivan Van Sertima, 1977, Random House, New York.
24. *The Children of the Sun*, W. J. Perry, 1923, Hutchinson, London. Reprinted by Adventures Unlimited Press, Kempton, IL.
25. *Esoteric Egypt: the Sacred Science of the Land of Khem*, J.S. Gordon, 2015, Inner Traditions, Rochester, VT.
26. *Midget Ninja & Tactical Laxatives: Bizarre Warfare Through the Ages*, Philip Sidnell, 2012, Pen & Sword Military, Barnsley, UK.
27. *Saga America*, Barry Fell, 1980, New York Times Books, New York.
28. *Maps of the Ancient Sea Kings*, Charles Hapgood, 1966, Chilton Books. Reprinted by Adventures Unlimited Press, Kempton, IL.
29. *The Megalithic Culture in Indonesia,* W.J. Perry, 1918, University of Manchester Press, Manchester, UK.
30. *The Land of Osiris*, Stephen Mehler, 1999, Adventures Unlimited Press, Kempton, IL.
31. *Hindu America?,* Chaman Lal, 1960, Bharatiya Vidya Bhavan, Bombay (Mumbai).
32. *The Mystery of Easter Island*, Katherine Routledge, 1919, London. Reprinted by AUP, Kempton.
33. *The Riddle of the Pacific*, John MacMillan Brown, 1924, reprinted by AUP, Kempton, IL.
34. *Mysteries of Easter Island*, Francis Maziere, 1968, W.W. Norton, New York.
35. *The Caroline Islands*, F.W. Christian, 1899, London.
36. *Aku-Aku*, Thor Heyerdahl, 1958, Rand McNally Co., Chicago, IL.
37. *Kon Tiki*, Thor Heyerdahl, 1950, Rand McNally Co., Chicago, IL.
38. *Ancient Technology in Peru and Bolivia*, David Hatcher Childress, 2012, AUP, Kempton, IL.
39. *The Civilization of Angkor*, C. Higham, 2001, Weidenfeld & Nicolson, London.
40. *Eden in the East,* Stephen Oppenheimer, 1998, Weidenfield & Nicolson, London.
41. *Axis of the World,* Igor Witkowski, 2008, Adventures Unlimited Press, Kempton, IL.
42. *In Search of Quetzalcoatl*, Pierre Honoré, 1963, Hutchinson & Co. London. Reprinted by AUP, Kempton, IL. (Original title: *In Quest of the White God*)

43. *Ancient Man: A Handbook of Puzzling Artifacts*, William Corliss, 1974, The Sourcebook Project, Glen Arm, MD.

44. *The Search for El Dorado*, 1994, Time-Life Books, Alexandria, VA.

45. *Notes on Inka Architecture*, Luis Oscar Chara Zereceda, 2006, Cuzco.

46. *Early Metal Mining and Production*, P. Craddock, 1995, Edinburgh University Press Ltd, Edinburgh.

47. *We Are Not the First*, Andrew Tomas, 1971, Souvenir Press, London.

48. *Megalithic Finds in Central Celebes*, Walter Kaudern, 1938, Goteborg Ethnographical Museum, Goteborg, Sweden.

49. *The Gold of the Gods*, Erich von Daniken, 1973, Putnam, New York.

50. *Inca Architecture and Construction at Ollantaytambo*, Jean-Pierre Protzen, 1993, Oxford University Press, Oxford.

51. *Arquitectura Y Construccion Incas en Ollantaytambo*, Jean-Pierre Protzen, 2005, Fondo Editorial de la Pontificia Universidad Catolica del Peru, Lima (Spanish language edition of the Oxford Press book).

52. *Upon a Stone Altar*, David Hanlon, 1988, University of Hawaii Press, Honolulu.

53. *Lost City of Stone*, Bill S. Ballinger, 1978, Simon & Schuster, New York.

54. *The God-Kings and the Titans*, James Bailey, 1973, St. Martin's Press, New York.

55. *Home of the Gods*, Hugh Fox, 2005, Galde Press, Minneapolis.

56. *Lost Cities of Ancient Lemuria & the Pacific*, David Hatcher Childress, 1988, AUP, Kempton, IL.

57. *South Seas Myths and Legends*, Donald Mackenzie, 1930, Senate Books, London.

58. *The Olmecs: America's First Civilization,* Richard A. Diehl, 2004, Thames & Hudson, New York.

59. *The Olmec World*, Ignacio Bernal, 1999, University of California Press, Berkeley.

60. *Xalapa Museum of Anthropology: A Guided Tour*, 2004, Governors of the Museum, Xalapa. Mexico.

61. *The Enigma of Cranial Deformation*, David Hatcher Childress and Brien Foerster, 2012, AUP, Kempton, IL.

62. *The Ra Expeditions,* Thor Heyerdahl, 1965, Hutchinson, London.

63. *The Zuni Enigma*, Nancy Yaw Davis, 2001, Norton & Co., New York.

Bibliography

64. *Man's Conquest of the Pacific,* Peter Bellwood, 1978, William Collins, London.

65. *The Nan Madol Area of Ponape*: Researches Into Bounding and Stabilizing an Ancient Administrative Center, Dr. Arthur Saxe, 1980, Office of the High Commissioner, Trust Territory of the Pacific, Saipan, Marianas Islands.

66. *Citadels of Mystery*, L. Sprague de Camp, 1964, Ballantine Books, New York.

67. *Vimana*, David Hatcher Childress, 2015, AUP, Kempton, IL.

68. *A Guide to Ponape*, Gene Ashby, 1983, Rainy Day Press, Eugene, Oregon.

69. *Mayan Genesis: South Asian Myths, Migrtions and Icoography in Mesoamerica*, Graeme Kearsley, 2001, Yelsraek Publishers, London.

70. *Incidents of Travel in Central America, Chiapas and Yucatan,* Stevens and Catherwood, 1843, Harper and Sons, New York.

71. *The Mysteries of Easter Island,* Jean-Michel Schwartz, 1975, Avon Books, New York.

72. *Argonauts of the Western Pacific*, Bronislaw Malinowski, 1961, E.P. Dutton & Co., New York.

73. *Lost Cities & Ancient Mysteries of the Southwest*, David Hatcher Childress, 2009, AUP, Kempton, IL.

74. *Quest for the Pillar of Gold*, Billingsley, Spamer and Menkes, 1997, Grand Canyon Association, Grand Canyon.

75. *Grand Canyon Stories: Then and Now*, Leo Banks and Craig Childs, 1999, Arizona Highways, Phoenix.

76. *Unkar Delta*, Douglas Swartz, with Chapman and Kepp, 1980, School of American Research Press, Santa Fe.

77. *Atlantis in Spain*, E.M. Whishaw, 1928, Rider & Co., London (reissued by AUP).

78. *Pages From Hopi History*, Harry James, 1974, University of Arizona Press, Tucson.

Get these fascinating books from your nearest bookstore or directly from: Adventures Unlimited Press

ANCIENT ALIENS & SECRET SOCIETIES
By Mike Bara

Did ancient "visitors"—of extraterrestrial origin—come to Earth long, long ago and fashion man in their own image? Were the science and secrets that they taught the ancients intended to be a guide for all humanity to the present era? Bara establishes the reality of the catastrophe that jolted the human race, and traces the history of secret societies from the priesthood of Amun in Egypt to the Templars in Jerusalem and the Scottish Rite Freemasons. Bara also reveals the true origins of NASA and exposes the bizarre triad of secret societies in control of that agency since its inception. Chapters include: Out of the Ashes; From the Sky Down; Ancient Aliens?; The Dawn of the Secret Societies; The Fractures of Time; Into the 20th Century; The Wink of an Eye; more.

288 Pages. 6x9 Paperback. Illustrated. $19.95. Code: AASS

THE CRYSTAL SKULLS
Astonishing Portals to Man's Past
by David Hatcher Childress and Stephen S. Mehler

Childress introduces the technology and lore of crystals, and then plunges into the turbulent times of the Mexican Revolution form the backdrop for the rollicking adventures of Ambrose Bierce, the renowned journalist who went missing in the jungles in 1913, and F.A. Mitchell-Hedges, the notorious adventurer who emerged from the jungles with the most famous of the crystal skulls. Mehler shares his extensive knowledge of and experience with crystal skulls. Having been involved in the field since the 1980s, he has personally examined many of the most influential skulls, and has worked with the leaders in crystal skull research, including the inimitable Nick Nocerino, who developed a meticulous methodology for the purpose of examining the skulls.

294 pages. 6x9 Paperback. Illustrated. Bibliography. $18.95. Code: CRSK

AXIS OF THE WORLD
The Search for the Oldest American Civilization
by Igor Witkowski

Polish author Witkowski's research reveals remnants of a high civilization that was able to exert its influence on almost the entire planet, and did so with full consciousness. Sites around South America show that this was not just one of the places influenced by this culture, but a place where they built their crowning achievements. Easter Island, in the southeastern Pacific, constitutes one of them. The Rongo-Rongo language that developed there points westward to the Indus Valley. Taken together, the facts presented by Witkowski provide a fresh, new proof that an antediluvian, great civilization flourished several millennia ago.

220 pages. 6x9 Paperback. Illustrated. References. $18.95. Code: AXOW

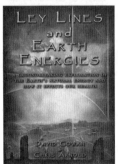

LEY LINE & EARTH ENERGIES
An Extraordinary Journey into the Earth's Natural Energy System
by David Cowan & Chris Arnold

The mysterious standing stones, burial grounds and stone circles that lace Europe, the British Isles and other areas have intrigued scientists, writers, artists and travellers through the centuries. How do ley lines work? How did our ancestors use Earth energy to map their sacred sites and burial grounds? How do ghosts and poltergeists interact with Earth energy? How can Earth spirals and black spots affect our health? This exploration shows how natural forces affect our behavior, how they can be used to enhance our health and well being.

368 PAGES. 6x9 PAPERBACK. ILLUSTRATED. $18.95. CODE: LLEE

ANCIENT ALIENS ON THE MOON
By Mike Bara
What did NASA find in their explorations of the solar system that they may have kept from the general public? How ancient really are these ruins on the Moon? Using official NASA and Russian photos of the Moon, Bara looks at vast cityscapes and domes in the Sinus Medii region as well as glass domes in the Crisium region. Bara also takes a detailed look at the mission of Apollo 17 and the case that this was a salvage mission, primarily concerned with investigating an opening into a massive hexagonal ruin near the landing site. Chapters include: The History of Lunar Anomalies; The Early 20th Century; Sinus Medii; To the Moon Alice!; Mare Crisium; Yes, Virginia, We Really Went to the Moon; Apollo 17; more. Tons of photos of the Moon examined for possible structures and other anomalies.
248 Pages. 6x9 Paperback. Illustrated.. $19.95. Code: AAOM

ANCIENT ALIENS ON MARS
By Mike Bara
Bara brings us this lavishly illustrated volume on alien structures on Mars. Was there once a vast, technologically advanced civilization on Mars, and did it leave evidence of its existence behind for humans to find eons later? Did these advanced extraterrestrial visitors vanish in a solar system wide cataclysm of their own making, only to make their way to Earth and start anew? Was Mars once as lush and green as the Earth, and teeming with life? Chapters include: War of the Worlds; The Mars Tidal Model; The Death of Mars; Cydonia and the Face on Mars; The Monuments of Mars; The Search for Life on Mars; The True Colors of Mars and The Pathfinder Sphinx; more. Color section.
252 Pages. 6x9 Paperback. Illustrated. $19.95. Code: AMAR

ANCIENT ALIENS ON MARS II
By Mike Bara
Using data acquired from sophisticated new scientific instruments like the Mars Odyssey THEMIS infrared imager, Bara shows that the region of Cydonia overlays a vast underground city full of enormous structures and devices that may still be operating. He peels back the layers of mystery to show images of tunnel systems, temples and ruins, and exposes the sophisticated NASA conspiracy designed to hide them. Bara also tackles the enigma of Mars' hollowed out moon Phobos, and exposes evidence that it is artificial. Long-held myths about Mars, including claims that it is protected by a sophisticated UFO defense system, are examined. Data from the Mars rovers Spirit, Opportunity and Curiosity are examined; everything from fossilized plants to mechanical debris is exposed in images taken directly from NASA's own archives.
294 Pages. 6x9 Paperback. Illustrated. $19.95. Code: AAM2

ANCIENT TECHNOLOGY IN PERU & BOLIVIA
By David Hatcher Childress
Childress speculates on the existence of a sunken city in Lake Titicaca and reveals new evidence that the Sumerians may have arrived in South America 4,000 years ago. He demonstrates that the use of "keystone cuts" with metal clamps poured into them to secure megalithic construction was an advanced technology used all over the world, from the Andes to Egypt, Greece and Southeast Asia. He maintains that only power tools could have made the intricate articulation and drill holes found in extremely hard granite and basalt blocks in Bolivia and Peru, and that the megalith builders had to have had advanced methods for moving and stacking gigantic blocks of stone, some weighing over 100 tons.
340 Pages. 6x9 Paperback. Illustrated.. $19.95 Code: ATP

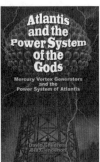

ATLANTIS & THE POWER SYSTEM OF THE GODS
by David Hatcher Childress and Bill Clendenon
Childress' fascinating analysis of Nikola Tesla's broadcast system in light of Edgar Cayce's "Terrible Crystal" and the obelisks of ancient Egypt and Ethiopia. Includes: Atlantis and its crystal power towers that broadcast energy; how these incredible power stations may still exist today; inventor Nikola Tesla's nearly identical system of power transmission; Mercury Proton Gyros and mercury vortex propulsion; more. Richly illustrated, and packed with evidence that Atlantis not only existed—it had a world-wide energy system more sophisticated than ours today.
246 PAGES. 6x9 PAPERBACK. ILLUSTRATED. $15.95. CODE: APSG

THE ANTI-GRAVITY HANDBOOK
edited by David Hatcher Childress

The new expanded compilation of material on Anti-Gravity, Free Energy, Flying Saucer Propulsion, UFOs, Suppressed Technology, NASA Cover-ups and more. Highly illustrated with patents, technical illustrations and photos. This revised and expanded edition has more material, including photos of Area 51, Nevada, the government's secret testing facility. This classic on weird science is back in a new format!
230 PAGES. 7x10 PAPERBACK. ILLUSTRATED. $16.95. CODE: AGH

ANTI–GRAVITY & THE WORLD GRID
Is the earth surrounded by an intricate electromagnetic grid network offering free energy? This compilation of material on ley lines and world power points contains chapters on the geography, mathematics, and light harmonics of the earth grid. Learn the purpose of ley lines and ancient megalithic structures located on the grid. Discover how the grid made the Philadelphia Experiment possible. Explore the Coral Castle and many other mysteries, including acoustic levitation, Tesla Shields and scalar wave weaponry. Browse through the section on anti-gravity patents, and research resources.
274 PAGES. 7x10 PAPERBACK. ILLUSTRATED. $14.95. CODE: AGW

ANTI–GRAVITY & THE UNIFIED FIELD
edited by David Hatcher Childress
Is Einstein's Unified Field Theory the answer to all of our energy problems? Explored in this compilation of material is how gravity, electricity and magnetism manifest from a unified field all around us. Why artificial gravity is possible; secrets of UFO propulsion; free energy; Nikola Tesla and anti-gravity airships of the 20s and 30s; flying saucers as superconducting whirls of plasma; anti-mass generators; vortex propulsion; suppressed technology; government cover-ups; gravitational pulse drive; spacecraft & more.
240 PAGES. 7x10 PAPERBACK. ILLUSTRATED. $14.95. CODE: AGU

THE TIME TRAVEL HANDBOOK
A Manual of Practical Teleportation & Time Travel
edited by David Hatcher Childress
The Time Travel Handbook takes the reader beyond the government experiments and deep into the uncharted territory of early time travellers such as Nikola Tesla and Guglielmo Marconi and their alleged time travel experiments, as well as the Wilson Brothers of EMI and their connection to the Philadelphia Experiment—the U.S. Navy's forays into invisibility, time travel, and teleportation. Childress looks into the claims of time travelling individuals, and investigates the unusual claim that the pyramids on Mars were built in the future and sent back in time. A highly visual, large format book, with patents, photos and schematics. Be the first on your block to build your own time travel device!
316 PAGES. 7x10 PAPERBACK. ILLUSTRATED. $16.95. CODE: TTH

TECHNOLOGY OF THE GODS
The Incredible Sciences of the Ancients
by David Hatcher Childress

Childress looks at the technology that was allegedly used in Atlantis and the theory that the Great Pyramid of Egypt was originally a gigantic power station. He examines tales of ancient flight and the technology that it involved; how the ancients used electricity; megalithic building techniques; the use of crystal lenses and the fire from the gods; evidence of various high tech weapons in the past, including atomic weapons; ancient metallurgy and heavy machinery; the role of modern inventors such as Nikola Tesla in bringing ancient technology back into modern use; impossible artifacts; and more.

356 PAGES. 6x9 PAPERBACK. ILLUSTRATED. $16.95. CODE: TGOD

COVERT WARS AND BREAKAWAY CIVILIZATIONS
By Joseph P. Farrell

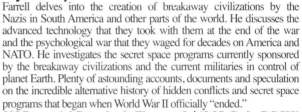

Farrell delves into the creation of breakaway civilizations by the Nazis in South America and other parts of the world. He discusses the advanced technology that they took with them at the end of the war and the psychological war that they waged for decades on America and NATO. He investigates the secret space programs currently sponsored by the breakaway civilizations and the current militaries in control of planet Earth. Plenty of astounding accounts, documents and speculation on the incredible alternative history of hidden conflicts and secret space programs that began when World War II officially "ended."

292 Pages. 6x9 Paperback. Illustrated. $19.95. Code: BCCW

THE ENIGMA OF CRANIAL DEFORMATION
Elongated Skulls of the Ancients
By David Hatcher Childress and Brien Foerster

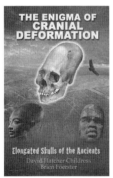

In a book filled with over a hundred astonishing photos and a color photo section, Childress and Foerster take us to Peru, Bolivia, Egypt, Malta, China, Mexico and other places in search of strange elongated skulls and other cranial deformation. The puzzle of why diverse ancient people—even on remote Pacific Islands—would use head-binding to create elongated heads is mystifying. Where did they even get this idea? Did some people naturally look this way—with long narrow heads? Were they some alien race? Were they an elite race that roamed the entire planet? Why do anthropologists rarely talk about cranial deformation and know so little about it? Color Section.

250 Pages. 6x9 Paperback. Illustrated. $19.95. Code: ECD

ARK OF GOD
The Incredible Power of the Ark of the Covenant
By David Hatcher Childress

Childress takes us on an incredible journey in search of the truth about (and science behind) the fantastic biblical artifact known as the Ark of the Covenant. This object made by Moses at Mount Sinai—part wooden-metal box and part golden statue—had the power to create "lightning" to kill people, and also to fly and lead people through the wilderness. The Ark of the Covenant suddenly disappears from the Bible record and what happened to it is not mentioned. Was it hidden in the underground passages of King Solomon's temple and later discovered by the Knights Templar? Was it taken through Egypt to Ethiopia as many Coptic Christians believe? Childress looks into hidden history, astonishing ancient technology, and a 3,000-year-old mystery that continues to fascinate millions of people today. Color section.

420 Pages. 6x9 Paperback. Illustrated. $22.00 Code: AOG

REICH OF THE BLACK SUN
Nazi Secret Weapons & the Cold War Allied Legend
by Joseph P. Farrell

Why were the Allies worried about an atom bomb attack by the Germans in 1944? Why did the Soviets threaten to use poison gas against the Germans? Why did Hitler in 1945 insist that holding Prague could win the war for the Third Reich? Why did US General George Patton's Third Army race for the Skoda works at Pilsen in Czechoslovakia instead of Berlin? Why did the US Army not test the uranium atom bomb it dropped on Hiroshima? Why did the Luftwaffe fly a non-stop round trip mission to within twenty miles of New York City in 1944? *Reich of the Black Sun* takes the reader on a scientific-historical journey in order to answer these questions. Arguing that Nazi Germany actually won the race for the atom bomb in late 1944, 352 PAGES. 6x9 PAPERBACK. ILLUSTRATED. BIBLIOGRAPHY. $16.95.
CODE: **ROBS**

THE GIZA DEATH STAR
The Paleophysics of the Great Pyramid & the Military Complex at Giza
by Joseph P. Farrell

Was the Giza complex part of a military installation over 10,000 years ago? Chapters include: An Archaeology of Mass Destruction, Thoth and Theories; The Machine Hypothesis; Pythagoras, Plato, Planck, and the Pyramid; The Weapon Hypothesis; Encoded Harmonics of the Planck Units in the Great Pyramid; High Fregquency Direct Current "Impulse" Technology; The Grand Gallery and its Crystals: Gravito-acoustic Resonators; The Other Two Large Pyramids; the "Causeways," and the "Temples"; A Phase Conjugate Howitzer; Evidence of the Use of Weapons of Mass Destruction in Ancient Times; more.
290 PAGES. 6x9 PAPERBACK. ILLUSTRATED. $16.95. CODE: **GDS**

THE GIZA DEATH STAR DEPLOYED
The Physics & Engineering of the Great Pyramid
by Joseph P. Farrell

Farrell expands on his thesis that the Great Pyramid was a maser, designed as a weapon and eventually deployed—with disastrous results to the solar system. Includes: Exploding Planets: A Brief History of the Exoteric and Esoteric Investigations of the Great Pyramid; No Machines, Please!; The Stargate Conspiracy; The Scalar Weapons; Message or Machine?; A Tesla Analysis of the Putative Physics and Engineering of the Giza Death Star; Cohering the Zero Point, Vacuum Energy, Flux: Feedback Loops and Tetrahedral Physics; and more.
290 PAGES. 6x9 PAPERBACK. ILLUSTRATED. $16.95. CODE: **GDSD**

THE GIZA DEATH STAR DESTROYED
The Ancient War For Future Science
by Joseph P. Farrell

Farrell moves on to events of the final days of the Giza Death Star and its awesome power. These final events, eventually leading up to the destruction of this giant machine, are dissected one by one, leading us to the eventual abandonment of the Giza Military Complex—an event that hurled civilization back into the Stone Age. Chapters include: The Mars-Earth Connection; The Lost "Root Races" and the Moral Reasons for the Flood; The Destruction of Krypton: The Electrodynamic Solar System, Exploding Planets and Ancient Wars; Turning the Stream of the Flood: the Origin of Secret Societies and Esoteric Traditions; The Quest to Recover Ancient Mega-Technology; Non-Equilibrium Paleophysics; Monatomic Paleophysics; Frequencies, Vortices and Mass Particles; "Acoustic" Intensity of Fields; The Pyramid of Crystals; tons more.
292 pages. 6x9 paperback. Illustrated. $16.95. Code: GDES

HIDDEN FINANCE, ROGUE NETWORKS & SECRET SORCERY
The Fascist International, 9/11, & Penetrated Operations
By Joseph P. Farrell

Pursuing his investigations of high financial fraud, international banking, hidden systems of finance, black budgets and breakaway civilizations, Farrell investigates the theory that there were not *two* levels to the 9/11 event, but *three*. He says that the twin towers were downed by the force of an exotic energy weapon, one similar to the Tesla energy weapon suggested by Dr. Judy Wood, and ties together the tangled web of missing money, secret technology and involvement of portions of the Saudi royal family. Farrell unravels the many layers behind the 9-11 attack, layers that include the Deutschebank, the Bush family, the German industrialist Carl Duisberg, Saudi Arabian princes and the energy weapons developed by Tesla before WWII.
296 Pages. 6x9 Paperback. Illustrated. $19.95. Code: HFRN

THRICE GREAT HERMETICA AND THE JANUS AGE
By Joseph P. Farrell

What do the Fourth Crusade, the exploration of the New World, secret excavations of the Holy Land, and the pontificate of Innocent the Third all have in common? Answer: Venice and the Templars. What do they have in common with Jesus, Gottfried Leibniz, Sir Isaac Newton, Rene Descartes, and the Earl of Oxford? Answer: Egypt and a body of doctrine known as Hermeticism. The hidden role of Venice and Hermeticism reached far and wide, into the plays of Shakespeare (a.k.a. Edward DeVere, Earl of Oxford), into the quest of the three great mathematicians of the Early Enlightenment for a lost form of analysis, and back into the end of the classical era, to little known Egyptian influences at work during the time of Jesus.
354 Pages. 6x9 Paperback. Illustrated. $19.95. Code: TGHJ

THE FREE-ENERGY DEVICE HANDBOOK
A Compilation of Patents and Reports
by David Hatcher Childress

A large-format compilation of various patents, papers, descriptions and diagrams concerning free-energy devices and systems. *The Free-Energy Device Handbook* is a visual tool for experimenters and researchers into magnetic motors and other "over-unity" devices. With chapters on the Adams Motor, the Hans Coler Generator, cold fusion, superconductors, "N" machines, space-energy generators, Nikola Tesla, T. Townsend Brown, and the latest in free-energy devices. Packed with photos, technical diagrams, patents and fascinating information, this book belongs on every science shelf.
292 PAGES. 8x10 PAPERBACK. ILLUSTRATED. $16.95. CODE: FEH

LOST CITIES & ANCIENT MYSTERIES OF THE SOUTHWEST
By David Hatcher Childress

Join David as he starts in northern Mexico and then to west Texas amd into New Mexico where he stumbles upon a hollow mountain with a billion dollars of gold bars hidden deep inside it! In Arizona he investigates tales of Egyptian catacombs in the Grand Canyon, cruises along the Devil's Highway, and tackles the century-old mystery of the Lost Dutchman mine. In California Childress checks out the rumors of mummified giants and weird tunnels in Death Valley—It's a full-tilt blast down the back roads of the Southwest in search of the weird and wondrous mysteries of the past!
486 Pages. 6x9 Paperback. Illustrated. $19.95. Code: LCSW

ORDER FORM

10% Discount When You Order 3 or More Items!

One Adventure Place
P.O. Box 74
Kempton, Illinois 60946
United States of America
Tel.: 815-253-6390 • Fax: 815-253-6300
Email: auphq@frontiernet.net
http://www.adventuresunlimitedpress.com

ORDERING INSTRUCTIONS

✓ Remit by USD$ Check, Money Order or Credit Card

✓ Visa, Master Card, Discover & AmEx Accepted

✓ Paypal Payments Can Be Made To:

　　info@wexclub.com

✓ Prices May Change Without Notice

✓ 10% Discount for 3 or More Items

SHIPPING CHARGES

United States

✓ Postal Book Rate { $4.50 First Item / 50¢ Each Additional Item

✓ POSTAL BOOK RATE Cannot Be Tracked!
　Not responsible for non-delivery.

✓ Priority Mail { $6.00 First Item / $2.00 Each Additional Item

✓ UPS { $7.00 First Item / $1.50 Each Additional Item

　NOTE: UPS Delivery Available to Mainland USA Only

Canada

✓ Postal Air Mail { $15.00 First Item / $3.00 Each Additional Item

✓ Personal Checks or Bank Drafts MUST BE

　US$ and Drawn on a US Bank

✓ Canadian Postal Money Orders OK

✓ Payment MUST BE US$

All Other Countries

✓ Sorry, No Surface Delivery!

✓ Postal Air Mail { $19.00 First Item / $7.00 Each Additional Item

✓ Checks and Money Orders MUST BE US$
　and Drawn on a US Bank or branch.

✓ Paypal Payments Can Be Made in US$ To:
　info@wexclub.com

SPECIAL NOTES

✓ RETAILERS: Standard Discounts Available

✓ BACKORDERS: We Backorder all Out-of-
　Stock Items Unless Otherwise Requested

✓ PRO FORMA INVOICES: Available on Request

✓ DVD Return Policy: Replace defective DVDs only

ORDER ONLINE AT: www.adventuresunlimitedpress.com

10% Discount When You Order 3 or More Items!

Please check: ☑

☐ This is my first order　　☐ I have ordered before

Name				
Address				
City				
State/Province			Postal Code	
Country				
Phone: Day		Evening		
Fax		Email		

Item Code	Item Description	Qty	Total

Please check: ☑

☐ Postal-Surface
☐ Postal-Air Mail (Priority in USA)
☐ UPS (Mainland USA only)

Subtotal ▶	
Less Discount-10% for 3 or more items ▶	
Balance ▶	
Illinois Residents 6.25% Sales Tax ▶	
Previous Credit ▶	
Shipping ▶	
Total (check/MO in USD$ only) ▶	

☐ Visa/MasterCard/Discover/American Express

Card Number:

Expiration Date:　　　　　　Security Code:

✓ SEND A CATALOG TO A FRIEND: